DATE DUE

DEMCO 38-296

LEO: The Incredible Story of the World's First Business Computer

LEO: The Incredible Story of the World's First Business Computer

David Caminer
John Aris
Peter Hermon
Frank Land

McGraw-Hill

New York San Francisco Washington, D.C. Auckland Bogotá
Caracas Lisbon London Madrid Mexico City Milan
Montreal New Delhi San Juan Singapore
Sydney Tokyo Toronto

Library of Congress Cataloging-in-Publication Data

LEO : the incredible story of the world's first business computer
David Caminer . . . [et al.].
     p.   cm.
   ISBN 0-07-009501-9 (alk. paper)
   1. LEO computer. 2. Business—Data processing—History.
   3. Computers—Great Britain—History. I. Caminer, David.
   QA76.8.L46L46   1997
   338.7'61004'0941—dc21   97-37095
                                                            CIP

McGraw-Hill

A Division of The **McGraw·Hill** Companies

1 2 3 4 5 6 7 8 9 0   DOC/DOC   9 0 2 1 0 9 8 7

ISBN 0-07-009501-9

Editor: David Tresman Caminer
Editorial Board: John B. Aris
                  Peter M. Hermon
                  Frank F. Land
Associate Editor: John A. Gosden
Sponsoring Editor: Susan Barry
Editing Supervisor: Barry Brown
Production Supervisor: Tina Cameron

Printed and bound by R. R. Donnelley & Sons Company.

Contents

Contributors   ix
Foreword   xv
Preface to the American Edition   xvii
Preface   xix

Chronology   1

Part 1. The Story of an Innovation   5
DAVID TRESMAN CAMINER

1. The World's First Office Computer Job   7
   1951
2. The Background at Lyons   9
   1894–1947
3. LEO: Idea and Realization   16
   1947–1951
4. Loading LEO I   33
   1951–1954
5. The Second LEO and LEO Computers Ltd.   43
   1954–1957
6. LEO II in the Field   59
   1957–1958

7. End of the First Generation   73
   1958–1960
8. Arrival of LEO III   86
   1960–1963
9. The Merger with English Electric   97
   1963
10. The Range Revolution   110
    1964
11. The 1965 Paradox   123
    1965
12. LEO Winds Down   130
    1966–1968
13. Postlude   141
    Notes   146

Part 2. Pioneers   **155**

14. The Early Days   157
    LEO FANTL
15. The Widening Field   168
    FRANK LAND
16. Toward System Software   185
    JOHN GOSDEN
17. A Reminiscence   207
    PETER HERMON

Part 3. Innovators   **221**

18. Lyons Teashops   223
    RALPH LAND
19. Glyn Mills Bank and Army and Air Force Officers Payroll   229
    JOHN LEWIS
20. Stewarts and Lloyds Steelworks   243
    HAMISH ARCHIBALD
21. The General Post Office (I)   249
    NINIAN EADIE
22. The General Post Office (II)   257
    MURRAY LAVER

23. Freemans Mail Order 261
    MIKE JACKSON
24. The Royal Dockyards 274
    REG CANN

Part 4. Innovating Abroad and an Evaluation 287

25. Into South Africa 289
    LEO FANTL
26. Behind the Iron Curtain 306
    RALPH LAND
27. The LEO Approach—An Evaluation 321
    JOHN ARIS

Appendices

A. Extracts from the Report of T. R. Thompson and
   O. W. Standingford on their visit to the United States:
   May/June 1947 337
B. Interview between J. R. M. Simmons, Director and
   Chief Comptroller of J. Lyons & Co. and the Science Museum,
   London, circa 1970s 360
C. Demonstration Script (1955) for the Teashops
   Distribution Job (L2) 375

Index 385

Contributors

David Tresman Caminer OBE* carried out the systems analysis for the world's first routine business computer job. He joined J. Lyons & Co. as a management trainee in 1936, and, after war service in North Africa with the Green Howards, became Manager of the Lyons Systems Research Office before concentrating on the computer innovation. He became a Director of LEO Computers Ltd. in 1959 and was subsequently General Sales Manager of English Electric LEO Marconi, while retaining his responsibility for consultancy and systems implementation. After the merger to form ICL his positions included the delineation of the systems software requirements for the New Range and Director of New Range Market Introduction. He chose to complete his formal career as Project Director for the implementation of the computer and communications network for the European Economic Community. Caminer was decorated in 1980 with the OBE "for services to British commercial interests in Luxembourg."

John Aris TD* joined LEO Computers as a trainee programmer in 1958 after graduating with a degree in Classics from Magdalen College, Oxford. He became a Senior Consultant to particularly innovative users of LEO Computers and then occupied senior positions with ICL in London and in European Division headquarters in Paris. Later, as Head of Computing at the Imperial Group, he was a pioneer in the replacement of a mainframe by small local computers. Aris was Director of the National Computer Centre from 1985 to 1990, where he won 75 percent of the world market in conformance testing software for open systems. He chaired the Alvey Program's User Panel, led the European Commission's 1989 panel of experts on technology transfer, and delivered the IEE Mountbatten Memorial Lecture on the Information Revolution in that year. In 1990 he became a Director of IMPACT, the club sponsored by KPMG in which the top management of large IS users pool experience. He served as a Royal Artillery officer in Korea, continuing his service in the Territorial Army and commanding a Para Unit.

Peter Hermon graduated with a degree in Mathematics from St. John's College, Oxford, where he was awarded the University prize in mathematics. He joined LEO Computers as a trainee programmer in 1955 and became a Senior Consultant, guiding leading enterprises with their entry into computing. He continued in the LEO environment with Dunlop, where he became responsible for Group computer developments worldwide. His next 18 years were spent with BOAC and British Airways, where he pioneered and masterminded the celebrated BOADICEA and BABS systems (global networks of real-time computers), which won Queen's Awards both for technological innovation and export achievement. During this period served as advisor on Computer development to the Civil Service. He eventually became Managing Director of the airline's European Division and served on the boards of both BOAC and British Airways. Hermon is the author of the definitive two-volume work *Hill Walking in Wales*.

After graduating with a degree in Economics from the London School of Economics, **Frank Land** joined the Statistical Office of J. Lyons & Co. in 1951 and became a trainee programmer in 1952. With innovative studies in many application areas, he rose to become Chief Consultant, leading a distinguished team in LEO Computers and its successors. In 1967 he returned to the LSE to establish teaching and research in systems analysis, and in 1982 became Professor of Systems Analysis. Later, at the London Business School, he became Professor of Information Management. He has been Visiting Professor at the Wharton School, University of Pennsylvania, at Sydney University, Australia, and in Egypt and India. He currently is Visiting Professor of Information Management at LSE. The author of many books and papers on information management, Land served as Technical Advisor to the House of Commons Select Committee on Trade and Industry during their 1988 investigation of the British computer industry.

Hamish Archibald, following National Service with the Black Watch, the famous Scottish infantry regiment, and his graduation in Economics from Queen's College, Dundee, joined Stewarts and Lloyds at their Corby, Northants, steelworks in 1956. After practical training with LEO Computers he became programmer, then Chief Programmer, during the company's implementation of business, production, and engineering applications on the first LEO computer to be delivered to the field. Later he became Senior Project Manager of Organization and Methods. Subsequent to nationalization of the steel industry, he held a number of senior management positions in British Steel, including Manager of Management Services, Teesside Division, and Manager of Computer and Communications Services, General Steels Group. He was awarded the Williams Prize of the

Iron and Steel Institute for his paper on the use of LEO for planning the extraction of iron ore and its supply to the Corby ironworks.

Reg Cann DFC* joined Civil Service, Admiralty, at Portsmouth Dockyard in 1939, and enlisted in the RAF in 1942. He trained as a navigator and completed two tours of operations in the Bomber Command Pathfinder Force that guided the main waves of bombers to their strategic targets and was awarded DFC. On return to Civil Service in 1946, Cann served at Portsmouth, Devonport and Lee-on-Solent on the Flag Officer Air's Staff and in Singapore in an accounting capacity. As Manager of the large Punched Card Installation at Portsmouth, he introduced PCCs (ICT's Program Controlled Computer) in 1960. Cann led the team that recommended the adoption of LEO Computers with innovative "turn-round" mark-sensed document input and then managed the programming, installation, and operation of the systems at the Royal Navy Dockyards at Portsmouth, Devonport, Rosyth, and Chatham. Cann served in the Royal Navy at Bath, until his premature retirement in 1978.

Ninian Eadie graduated with a degree in Philosophy, Politics, and Economics from Balliol College, Oxford. After National Service in the Royal Navy, he joined LEO Computers in 1960 as a trainee programmer, and following experience in programming, systems analysis, and consultancy was appointed Sales Manager of LEO Computers Services Pty, in South Africa. On return to Britain in 1965 he became Senior Consultant to the "flagship" Post Office account. He spent thirty six years in ICL and its progenitors, including thirteen years on the Board, during which time he was responsible, at one time or another, for most of ICL's activities including sales, marketing, development, and manufacturing. His final appointment was as Group Executive Director responsible for the technology businesses. In his leisure interest of sailing he has gained his Transvaal colors in the Finn dinghy class. He also represented the UK in two European championships and was runner-up in two national championships.

After war service in the Royal Air Force, where he continued his interrupted mathematics studies by correspondence course, **Leo Fantl** joined the Lyons Labour Planning Office in 1948, becoming a trainee programmer two years later. Among the earliest group of LEO programmers, he did much to develop the techniques that enabled correct and timely results to be produced despite the inevitable vagaries of the early technology. Many programmers, both from LEO and outside users, received their formative on-the-job training under Fantl's direction. In 1960 he was appointed General Manager of the joint LEO venture in South Africa with Rand Mines. He returned to the UK to become Manager of Product

Planning for English Electric LEO Marconi in 1965. He ultimately settled in South Africa after his appointment as Chairman of LEO, SA, and later as Managing Director of Sage Computers.

After graduating with a degree in Mathematics from Sidney Sussex College, Cambridge, **John Gosden** joined J. Lyons & Co. as a trainee programmer in 1953. Following early scientific and actuarial programming, he took successful charge of the definition of the system software and related logical design for LEO III. In 1960 he joined the Auerbach Corporation in the United States, where he developed the Standard EDP Reports and managed the production of a multi-computer operating system for the US Navy. At the MITRE Corporation, he was responsible for planning the database needs of the Joint Chiefs of Staff. Later, at the Equitable Life Assurance Society of New York, he was VP responsible for major projects and policy. Retired in 1986, Gosden has since advised the Museum of Modern Art and the Cornell Medical Center on database systems. Among many other activities, he has chaired a review of White House Support systems.

Mike Jackson graduated with a degree in Mathematics from Queen Mary's College, London. He joined LEO as a trainee programmer in 1957 and became a Senior Consultant with responsibility for installations in insurance, engineering, and the Government service and Post Office. In 1964 he joined Freemans Mail Order, initially as Data Processing Manager for their new large LEO system, and was subsequently promoted to Board Director for Agency Administration with full line responsibility. Later, he served as Group Director of Management Services at Perkins Engines. In 1980, he became Director of Compustar Ltd., designing bespoke systems and retired from business in 1995. As a sailor he has three times won the National Championships in the National Twelve class, and has been equally successful as a designer. He has held many administrative posts in the sport and, since 1990, has served as British Delegate to the Council of the International Sailing Federation. He has been heavily involved in the planning for the 1996 and 2000 Olympic Games.

Ralph Land CBE* graduated with a degree in Economics from the London School of Economics together with his twin brother, Frank. He joined J. Lyons & Co. in 1959, where he initially worked as a Management Accountant in the Teashops Division. He transferred to LEO Computers in 1959, and, after a period in computer bureau management and London area sales, was appointed General Manager of Eastern Europe for English Electric Computers and then ICL. Subsequently, he served as Marketing Director of ICL Western Europe and Managing Director of ICL Deutschland, and later General Manager of Eastern Europe Export Operations, Rank-Xerox Ltd., and Director of Eastern Europe Affairs, Rolls Royce Ltd. In retirement he remained an Advisor to the Rolls Royce Board and is a member of the ICL European Strategy Board, and either chairs or is a member of many committees guiding British business relationships with countries of the former Soviet bloc. Land was awarded the OBE "for services to exports" in 1985 and raised to CBE in 1996.

Murray Laver CBE* entered the Post Office Engineering Department in 1935, gaining first place in open competition. After an eventful career at the PO Research Station and at HQ he was appointed Assistant Secretary of HM Treasury, with responsibility for approval and advice for all British Government computer proposals. In 1965, Laver became Director of the Computer Division of the Ministry of Technology, where he set up the National Computing Centre and the Cambridge Computer Aided Design Centre. He sat on the Flowers Committee on Universities' computer needs and was "midwife" of the mergers leading to the formation of ICL. In 1965 he became Director of the National Data Processing Service and a member of the Post Office Board. Laver graduated by private study in 1951 and in his retirement has been awarded an honorary Doctorate by the University of Exeter, where he has served as Chairman of Council and Pro-Chancellor.

John Lewis graduated with a degree in Mathematics from Worcester College, Oxford, after National Service in which he was commissioned in the Royal Engineers serving in the Middle East. He joined LEO Computers as a trainee programmer in 1956, and in 1958, after programming and consultancy experience in many business applications, was given responsibility for the implementation of the challenging Army and Air Force Officers Payroll application in which LEO used Master Routine controlled magnetic tape and backing store for the first time. He was appointed Service Bureau Manager in 1962 to run the first LEO III system and its new software. In 1965 he moved from English Electric LEO Marconi to BOAC, where he joined other ex-LEO consultants and programmers working on the BOADICEA airline system. In a management role he took part in systems development, computer operation, and marketing applications abroad.

*Notes: CBE and OBE are British decorations for distinguished service to the Nation. TD is the "Territorial Decoration" for distinguished service in the Volunteer Reserve Army. DFC is the Distinguished Flying Cross, a wartime decoration for gallantry.

Foreword

RICHARD L. NOLAN
The Class of 1942 MBA Professor of Business Administration
Harvard University
Graduate School of Business Administration

As an American professor, I am honored to be asked to write a foreword to what is such a great British story of innovation and vision about a company, and its management, who saw the future of computers before most and acted to make it "happen." In 1949, John Simmons, Chief Comptroller of J. Lyons and Company, envisaged "Lyons Electronic Office (LEO). In two short years after the Lyons Board approved the project, LEO was designed, built, and brought into regular, time-critical use in J. Lyons and Company. The reader must experience this wonderful story through the words of the people who were there to fully appreciate what was accomplished, and how. So rather than say much on the story in this foreword, I would like to make some personal observations about the story.

First and foremost, it is a story about extraordinary people. People such as John Simmons, as a senior executive of a great company, had a vision of how to make the company even better. As confident executives, they looked outside their company, in other countries, at universities, to discover new ways to do things and fresh ideas. In their bold actions, trust shows through as a foundation in implementing their vision. Young people are given free rein, and do not disappoint. A resulting exciting, challenging, "can do" culture is heard in the words of the people who were there.

It is exciting to see the commentaries from the people on how they approached their new tasks in designing and applying the new LEO computer. These commentaries reflect a great deal of the body of knowledge that we have today on implementation of information technology (IT). Indeed, it is impressive to see the number of innovations in systems analysis, programming, and implementation that had to be invented then, and are still around today. These innovations came from such a small group of people with limited hardware and software resources compared with what we have today.

The group of people that was associated with J. Lyons and Company and LEO went on to play an important role in the emerging IT industry. I had the good fortune to cross paths with several of them. I got to know the quality of mind of Frank Land as an academic colleague and through his daunting list of scholarly publications in the field. I had the privilege of working with John Gosden at the Equitable and Peter Hermon at Dunlop when I was a consultant to Nolan, Norton & Company. These two professionals made major contributions to the leadership of their companies in the use of IT to extract shareholder value. Then, upon the acquisition of Nolan, Norton & Company by KPMG Peat Marwick, I had the opportunity to work with John Aris as a professional colleague. John has demonstrated continued leadership in bringing important ideas about IT management to the professional field of IT practitioners. I never had the opportunity to meet David Caminer, principal author of the book, but I have been told of his immense contribution to the whole project.

This story has the best qualities of a Harvard Business School case study. The situation is real; it is an important event in the study of business. And the story is told through the words of the people who were there. I have already mentioned the value of the stories of the people who were the "doers" and managers. There are also other accounts that provide the reader with insights. The original trip memo of T. R. Thompson and O. W. Standingford, in which they reported on their trip to the USA, including a trip to ENIAC and other developments, shows just how advanced their thinking was on the concept of the role of the computer in the "paperless" office. The drawings and the interview list included in the memorandum show the substance of their understanding of important concepts appearing today such as the "virtual office."

An important perspective can be gleaned from this wonderful story and case study of IT innovation. I hope that you, the reader, enjoy as much as I have sharing in the experiences of the pioneering people who were there breaking new ground for many of the computer applications that we take so much for granted today.

Preface to the American Edition

This story first appeared as *User-Driven Innovation: The World's First Business Computer*, and under this title it was a finalist in the 1996 Booz Allen-Hamilton/Financial Times Global Business Books of the Year awards. When it became apparent that the book would attract a considerable readership in the United States, it was retitled to reflect its exciting content more closely. At the same time the text was revised so as to make the book more "reader-friendly" to its American audience.

A feature of the book is that it covers events that happened up to more than 40 years ago. The authors all took part in those events and, despite the passing of so many years, their memories remain vivid, so their instinct was to write in the language and context of those times.

For example, the present-day American reader may be surprised that first names are often missing when referring to people outside the LEO "band of brothers." That is not an oversight; it is as it was. We worked closely with a Mr. Bradley, the administration manager of the Ford Motor Company UK, and always admired his courage in taking his company into the first large-scale business computer service relationship in the whole world, yet it never occurred to us to call him by any other name. We simply didn't know his first name. That was typical. We could research all the missing names, but the result would be unnatural; it was Mr. This and Mr. That in those days. It was a time of different lunch rooms for different ranks and a time when Miss Jones made the coffee and brought it to her boss in a china cup and saucer rather than the present when the coffee comes in a paper cup from the coffee machine.

It was a time when the Lyons teashops seemed to be an indelible part of London life. Started just over a hundred years ago, the chain provided good-quality refreshment in pleasant surroundings such as had never before been within the means of the ordinary man and woman. The housewife could sit down for a cup of tea or coffee in a break in her shopping and the office worker or shop clerk could go in for a quick light meal. Part of the reputation of the teashops had rested on the "nippies," smartly dressed waitresses whose job it was to make every customer feel valued, but the labor shortages of the war had caused them to be removed. In LEO computer days, the cafes had become cafeterias. It seems that Lyons saw Schraffts, S and W Cafeterias, and Stouffers as their nearest equivalent across the Atlantic, though it is fair to say that none of these aimed at the quiet homeliness of the main street tea shop. In Britain there was more than a little derision when "Joe Lyons, the Teashop Company" started to offer computers for sale.

To aid the reader, dollar equivalents have been given for amounts in pounds sterling. It is worth remarking that, over the period of time since the events in the book, the number of dollars to the pound has almost halved. Exchange rates, social customs, and the main street scene have all changed with the passing of so many years. First names have come in and the teashops have vanished. The changes put in perspective how long ago it was that the first business computer started work. We can only ask our readers to forgive us if, despite our efforts, they still stumble over passages here and there that are unfamiliar.

DTC
London, June 1997

Preface

This is the basis and importance of
innovation—adapting the process of
management, and indeed the very nature of
the business itself, to the changing needs.

Innovation is the lifeblood of successful
business management. The past success of
a business can be its own worst enemy.
Conditions change, tastes alter and
new competition springs up. Without
innovation the most successful business will
ultimately become of no more value to the
future than the once fabulous, but
now worked-out, empty gold mine.[1]
        —J. R. M. SIMMONS

In 1949, J. Lyons & Company decided to make the most striking user-driven innovation in the history of information technology. Anticipating this precept of John Simmons, its Chief Comptroller, the company resolved to introduce, before anyone else in the world, what it called an "automatic calculator."

As Britain's best known caterer and a leading manufacturer of foods and beverages, Lyons had played a leading role in feeding the nation during the Second World War, and was now facing the challenges of the peace in excellent shape. The company had achieved an acknowledged preeminence in its field, and the ordinary instinct might have been to let well alone, to continue making only such minor improvements as were necessitated by events or by the equipment enhancements that came along from time to time.

Yet in Lyons there was a contrary reaction. There was a sense of frustration rather than satisfaction, a consciousness of so much still to be done to improve the information service to management, to advance the cohesion of the manufacturing and distributive operations, to contain and reduce the constantly growing burden of paperwork and to enhance the routine-bound working lives of the army of clerks. There was an unwillingness to accept that all that was possible had already been accomplished.

Intimations of the future came with press stories that appeared after the war about the transatlantic wonder of the "Electronic Brain." The first stage in Lyons' user-driven innovation was to recognize from this flimsy material that the computer might provide the way forward for a new advance in the service given to the company as a whole. The second was to decide to be the pioneers. The third was to determine that, as no conventional office supplier appeared to share Lyons' appreciation of the potential revolution in business administration, the company must inno-vate not only as users but as designers and builders too.

It was a source of bewilderment in the business world that a thriving, respected household name, with a reputation for delivering a good cup of tea, and tasty cakes should strike out in this way. True user-driven inno-vation is not a familiar phenomenon. The more conventional pattern is for a supplier to recognize a market, a competitive edge, or a technologi-cal advance or some interconnection between them, and respond through product development. The supplier can check the prospects and the spec-ification for the evolving product with an inner circle of friendly users, perhaps offering preferential terms to those prepared to act as guinea-pigs. There is no isolation in typical supplier-with-users innovation of this sort. The supplier has the opportunity to consult, and the users are able to play their part in the innovation, secure in the knowledge that they have behind them a manufacturer with a commercial interest in their success.

The circumstances in which LEO (Lyons Electronic Office) was designed, built, and brought into regular, time-critical use were very dif-ferent, in that Lyons had to combine both user and supplier roles. There were no other users at that early stage feeling the same urgency, nor did any manufacturers come forward to take on the necessary task of trans-forming a still incomplete mathematical prototype at Cambridge into a machine capable of encompassing the logistically more demanding requirements of office administration.

As this book reveals, this was a situation that Joe Lyons intuitively grasped at rather than flinched from. The firm had grown on the basis of innovation at every stage since its incorporation as a smallish catering company just over 50 years before. It had always been prepared to inno-vate in its own field, and to take on tasks outside its field if the natural suppliers were unready to change their ways and themselves innovate to satisfy Lyons' ambitions. Its board was ready to rely completely on the judgment of its senior officers, particularly John Simmons. There was a built-in understanding of what Peter Drucker[2] later wrote:

The only protection against the risk of exposure to innovation is to innovate. We can defend ourselves against the constant threat of being overtaken by innovation only by taking the offensive.

The twin initiatives of designing and building a business computer and putting it to routine use were two elements of just such a confidently planned offensive.

The timescale of this assault on old office concepts was essentially the twenty-odd years between 1947, the original contact with the "Electronic Brain," and 1968, when the personnel that had been involved in the innovation were disbanded. In surveying these years, this book does not seek to establish some thesis about the characteristics of user-driven innovation in general; the aim is the more modest one of recapturing the motivation, passion, and hazards of this one special case before the picture vanishes in the mists of time. The hope is, nonetheless, that insights may be provided on the general topic. Lyons is not the only innovator in the LEO story. No one should forget the handful of pioneering enterprises that had the courage to take deliveries of systems of their own from the caterering company turned high-technology manufacturers. All risked derision for foolhardiness; the executives who supported the ventures had to be prepared to place their heads on the block.

Among the questions that emerge from this story is whether user-driven innovation on this scale is ever likely to be commercially justified. It may, however, be asked at the same time how many major innovations have ever reaped correspondingly major corporate or personal rewards for those directly responsible for them. Today there are computers in almost every business, and there is a widespread dependency on them for the minute-to-minute transactions of most large enterprises. The fact that the original innovators, both Lyons and LEO, have disappeared save as memories is not unusual. That has so often been the way with innovators; the more way-out and ultimately influential, the more likely the oblivion.

It may be that those who show themselves capable of innovating, and even of managing innovation, are sometimes insufficiently aware of the simultaneous need to manage the wider changes stimulated by their innovations. The relationship between innovation and the management of change might well be a fruitful area for study.

An attendant to innovation is often, as in this case, diversification. When a company feels compelled to set up a facility to design and build for itself what is not conventionally available, it becomes a natural progression to recoup some of the development costs by also building for others. The process continues under its own momentum. Is such circumstance-driven diversification likely to be rewarding? Or is the better strategy to stimulate, then sit and wait? That is another issue on which this account might help to form a view.

According to John Grover, one of the earliest LEO people:

> Brian said "Did you realize that John was one of the very small team responsible for writing the *first* program in the world to run office routines?"
>
> Alan (a very successful 1990s software expert, commuting between London and New York) replied "Well, I suppose someone had to be."

In introducing this collection of memories, no claim is made that what Lyons invented would not have emerged anyway, at some other time or place. The invention of the wheel would have happened again if the original inventor had fallen by the wayside. Alan was correct in responding as he did.

Yet the fact remains that LEO **was** the first computer system in the world to run live office applications to a regular, time-sensitive schedule. The inventor of the wheel is lost to history, but this volume is a tardy attempt to put on paper some feel of the LEO life and times while most of the people who took part are still active and able to check each other's memories.

The perspective of this retrospect is primarily that of those who were concerned with putting LEO to work and then promoting its adoption in the outside world. The engineering aspect of the innovation is no more than touched on, not because it is less significant, but because it has already been so well documented by Dr. John Pinkerton and his colleagues. The award-winning paper on the Lyons Electronic Office that appeared in *Electronic Engineering* in mid-1954 gives a particularly lucid account of the hardware system that they built. This is supplemented, among other papers, by Pinkerton's 1975 audio interview with the Computer Science Division of the National Physical Laboratory, which brings alive the personal and technical environment in which the historic leap was achieved. John's scan of Part One of this book is much appreciated. As always, we turn to him on technical matters!

On the applications side, the task of defining and programming ordinary office work to run on the novel contrivance has gone largely unrecorded. Those involved at the outset did not bring with them the scientist's sense of obligation to make advances known, nor were there the same avenues for publication open to them. In any event there was no momentous sense of innovation at the time; it was to the individuals involved just another step, albeit a large and significant one, in the continuum of refining the company's management systems.

This volume attempts to fill some part of that gap. It does not attempt to be closely researched history; rather it is material for such a history if one ever comes to be written. All the writers took part in LEO's work at some time in the lifetime of LEO Computers Ltd., or earlier, when the innovation was being handled by a small group within the Lyons Clerical Department. Some carried on afterwards into the four changes of name and ownership, as mergers and takeovers pursued each other over the final five years. Most of the writers were once LEO consultants who started out as trainee programmers. Other sections are by members of outside user staffs, who readily came forward to add their recollections.

In editing this work I have been fortunate in the collaboration of three distinguished participants in the LEO endeavor: Professor Frank Land, lately of the London School of Economics and the London Business School; Peter Hermon, one-time Director of British Airways; and John Aris, a past Director of the National Computing Centre. However, each writer takes responsibility for his own paper, and none of us would feel able to confirm or endorse everyone's recollections of what happened thirty or more years ago; nor would we all necessarily agree with all the assessments. As an editorial group we are conscious that it is a human characteristic that, when we are deeply involved, we feel that more of the credit is attributable to us than others might ascribe. Professor Galbraith comments "One too easily claims originality or persuasiveness."[3] What is true of great world affairs holds equally well in the microcosm of computers. So if the reader comes across conflicting claims, that is the way of this book; later historians will have to judge for themselves.

The stimulus for producing this book was provided by Peter Bird's *LEO, the First Business Computer*, which appeared early in 1994 and constituted the first book published on the innovation and what followed. By his searching interviews, references to archives, and his meticulous cross-referencing with the 150 carriers of the "folk history" whom he consulted, Bird compiled a coherent and reliable account of what happened, much of it long before his own time at Lyons. The account he gives of the latter days of Lyons's involvement with computers is particularly valuable, as the relations between LEO and its parent had become tenuous by that time.

A source that has been of great help in placing the LEO story in the context of what was happening in the world of computers later on is Martin Campbell-Kelly's *ICL, a Business and Technical History*. An invaluable source in tracing LEO back to its origins was provided by Maurice Wilkes' remarkably fresh "Memoirs of a Computer Pioneer"; it rekindles the excitement of the earliest electronic computer days. Together these have provided the present writer with a free ride on the back of their exemplary scholarship. Another valuable source has been John Hendry's paper *The Teashop Computer Manufacturer: J. Lyons* in which special attention is given to the "limits of high-tech diversification."

Prime, though, among all the sources is the internal *LEO Chronicle*, compiled by T. R. Thompson between 1947 and 1961. Though his two- or three-line diary entries sometimes seem selective, the sense of loss when 1962 is reached and there is no *Chronicle* is considerable. We are fortunate, too, to have the Thompson/Standingford diary of their trip to the United States in 1947, which gave rise to the LEO project. The particularly relevant parts of this fascinating record are reproduced in this book. Another primary source document is the audiotape of John Simmons's interview with the Science Museum in the 1970s. It gives a vivid picture of the senior executive whose philosophy of management made the computer innovation possible. Again, by permission of the Science Museum, an extended extract is provided here. A further document that is appended is a speaker's script for a mid-1950s demonstration of the Teashops Distribution application.

This enterprise has profited from the penetrating outlook of Leo Fantl in Johannesburg. He would have been a member of the editorial group had he been closer at hand. So too would have been John Gosden, who has made special trips from New York to join in our discussions. Despite the passing of many years, everyone has rallied round in the old way. The editors are especially grateful to John Lewis who with our other old teammate, his wife Diane, has acted as the interface between the publishers and the thirteen far flung contributors!

Apart from the contributors, many others have also contributed memories and comments. These include Mary Blood (now Coombs), LEO's first woman programmer, and Ernest Roberts, who has helped us reconstruct the progress from concepts to implementation of LEO's groundbreaking software system. The project has had the benefit of review by John Grover, the "someone" in the anecdote above, of the passages on the early period. Tony Morgan, an early commissioning engineer, is another to whom we are indebted. Much, too, was gathered in conversations over drinks at a gathering of the LEO Reunion Society—an event which thirty years on shows no sign of flagging.

Though few of them needed it, writers were encouraged to depict the scene frankly, warts and all: not everyone comes out unscathed. That is a privilege I felt it proper to deny myself in the opening narrative, since it is intended to be as far as possible an "I-less" account of events to set the scene for the more personal accounts that follow. It will be seen that the contributions are different in style and size and form. That is deliberate. With the aim of producing a flesh-and-blood picture of times that for most of us were more stirring than any that we lived through later, no format was prescribed, no models were provided, and editing has mainly been directed toward accuracy and clarity. What has resulted forms a passable account of the meteors that flashed across the sky of LEO applications in the 1950s and 60s and then carried the collective experience of this seminal user-innovation elsewhere.

DTC
London, December 1995

Notes

1. J. R. M. Simmons, *LEO and the Managers*, MacDonald, London, 1962.
2. Peter F. Drucker, *The Landmarks of Tomorrow*, Heinemann, London.
3. Professor J. K. Galbraith, *The World Economy Since the Wars* Sinclair Stevenson, London, 1994.

Chronology

1947	May	Thompson and Standingford visit Professor Goldstine at Princeton Institute of Advanced Study
	November	Lyons board agree to provide aid to Cambridge University to complete EDSAC
1949	May	EDSAC completes first live job
		Lyons agree to proceed with building LEO
1951	February	LEO demonstrated to Her Royal Highness Princess Elizabeth
	November	Cadby Hall Bakery Valuations job runs live on LEO and thereafter runs regularly each week: the world's first regular routine office computer job
	December	Calculations carried out for Meteorological Office on service basis
1952	April	Ballistic calculations for Ordnance Board
1953	July	Lyons payroll run for pilot bakeries
	August	L1 Cadby Hall Bakery Valuations job run with full LEO I input/output facilities
1954	February	LEO paychecks used for the first time as payment authorities for Lyons payroll
	July	Decision to proceed with LEO II and to be prepared to produce others for sale or hire
	August	Lyons payroll reaches 10,000 threshold: The limit until backup computer available
	October	L2 Teashops distribution job starts operation
	November	LEO Computers Ltd. formed. Directors: Anthony Salmon, J. R. M. Simmons, T. R. Thompson
1955	April	PAYE tables for 1955/56 produced on Budget Night
	December	Pilot Ford payroll live on LEO I

1

1956	January	L3 Lyons Bakery Sales Invoicing job operational
	February	Extension of Lyons payroll beyond 10,000 starts
		First external order—LEO II for W. D. & H. O. Wills
	July	L4 Tea Blending job operational
1957	May	Railway Distancing job completed after regular 168-hour system working
		Ford payroll running on LEO I reaches 10,000
		LEO II prototype operational
		Pilot running of Stewarts and Lloyds payroll starts
	November	Computer production move to Minerva Road complete
1958	May	LEO II/3 commissioned at Stewarts and Lloyds, Corby
	July	Official opening of Greenwich London Boroughs consortium payroll on LEO II/1 bureau system
	September	LEO II/2 at W. D. & H. O. Wills, Bristol. First LEO with alphanumeric printing and drum. Sales Invoicing
	December	LEO II/4 at Ford Motor Co., Aveley, Essex. Vehicle Parts distribution and stores control
1959	April	LEO II/5 at Hartree House for LEO Service Bureau. First system with magnetic tape
	July	A. B. Barnes, D. T. Caminer and J. M. M. Pinkerton appointed to Board of LEO Computers Ltd.
	August	Army and Air Force Officers payroll for 9000 live on Hartree House Bureau service
	September	Programmers move to Hartree House
	November	LEO II/6 at Ministry of Pensions, Newcastle
		First LEO system for HM Government
1960	July	LEO IIc/8 at Standard Motors, Coventry. First LEO system with magnetic core store
1961	January	LEO IIc/11 at Ford Motor Co., Dagenham, to take over payroll, etc., from service bureau
	May	LEO III available for trials, etc.
		60,000 bargain list completed for Durlachers, Stock Jobbers, on Hartree House service
1962	January	LEO III time-sharing trial for HM Customs and Excise to confirm order
	May	LEO III/1 installed at Hartree House to augment Service Bureau
	June	LEO III/2 at Rand Mines, Johannesburg, as joint service bureau. First overseas LEO installation

		LEO III/3 at Dunlop, Birmingham, for distribution, sales invoicing, stores control
1963	February	LEO Computers Ltd. merger with computer department of English Electric to form English Electric LEO. Sir Gordon Radley (EE) Chairman, Anthony Salmon Vice-Chairman, W. E. Scott (EE) MD
		LEO III/6 to Shell Mex and BP. Then to become LEO's largest private sector user
	April	LEO III/7 with Lector to Lyons
		Prototype LEO 326 operational at Minerva Road works
1964	April	Announcement of IBM 360 range
		First installations for Post Office. LEO IIIs at Charles House, London, and at National Savings, Lytham St. Annes
		Autoelector attached to LEO III/7
	October	English Electric purchase Lyons' holding in English Electric LEO. Becomes English Electric LEO Marconi
	November	Post Office orders five LEO 326s. Largest order for any computer vendor in UK to date
1965	January	Decision to base successor range on RCA Spectra
		Two LEO 326 deliveries to Post Office
		LEO 326 delivery to Freemans Mail Order, London. First installation of this model in the private sector
		Two LEO 326s delivered to Shell Mex and BP
		LEO 360 installed at VLD, Prague. Railway Laboratories. First LEO installation in Europe
	September	Announcement of System 4 as successor range
	December	LEO peak year for installations
1966		LEO 326 installation for Lyons at Elms House, London
		Two LEO IIIs and one LEO 360 with Autoelector installed for HM Dockyards.
1967	March	EELM becomes English Electric Computers on takeover of Elliott Automation
		Last installations of main run of LEO systems at London Boroughs consortium led by Tower Hamlets and Hackney and for HM Dockyards, Portsmouth
1968	July	Merger with ICT to form ICL
		Further orders from Post Office for five LEO 326s. Production line reformed

| 1980 | December | Post Office telephone billing programs emulated on ICL 2960 |
| 1981 | | Post Office LEO 326s taken out of service after 12–15 years of operation |

PART 1
The Story of an Innovation

DAVID TRESMAN CAMINER

1

The World's First Office Computer Job

1951

The world's first routine office job to the run regularly on a stored-program electronic computer started its productive life on Thursday, November 29, 1951.[1] The computer was LEO, a one-off system built by J. Lyons & Co., a leading English catering firm, for its own use. The computer was located in the company's administration office block on the periphery of its 13-acre Cadby hall facility in West London.

The job carried out was concerned with the valuation of the variety of bread, cakes, and pies produced in the several bakeries on the estate and their assembly and dispatch to the company's retail and wholesale channels and to the many cafés and restaurants.

Rehearsals had taken place over the previous month, but from this point the results were regularly delivered to the Lyons Statistical Office for incorporation in the company's weekly management accounts. The results continued to be supplied in this way for many years, with changes in the program from time to time to take account of equipment enhancement.

The LEO equipment employed was closely modeled on the EDSAC computer developed at Cambridge University under the direction of Dr. Maurice Wilkes, who gave full support and encouragement to the

Lyons venture. It did not yet include the enhancements set in motion by Lyons as essential for full-scale office work, and the initial job had been chosen and delineated accordingly. It was nonetheless economically realistic.[2]

Existing clerical labor	50	hours per week
Computer data preparation	8	hours per week
Computer running time	4½	hours per week

When the full facilities became available, LEO was able to do the job in a time much closer to the 30 minutes required for the substantive calculations.

Though small, the job opened the way for the larger and more exacting mainstream jobs that constitute an office workload. Payroll, sales invoicing, stock control, and replenishment all swiftly followed on LEO.

2
The Background at Lyons

1894–1947

The Cadby Hall facility was a very large expanse of factories, dispatches, and office blocks bounded by Hammersmith Road, Brook Green, and Blythe Road. It resembled a fortress, with brick buildings enclosing courtyards in which delivery vans were arrayed. Uniformed staff guarded the wide gates to the facility.

Though architecturally drab on the outside, with small windows, the factories were wonders of mechanization within. They included the dozen specialist bakeries chosen as the subject of the first computer task, kitchens producing precooked meals for later reheating in catering establishments, and a massive ice-cream plant where leading British brands were produced and cold-stored. All had been equipped with the most advanced automatic plant available for the mass production of foods of good quality, though by this time some of the machinery had fallen a little behind because of the slow-down in enhancements during the war and the hard currency shortage that followed it.

The Swiss roll plant, with its long, continuous sheets of dough browning on their slow journey through the traveling ovens and then being automatically cut to size, spread with jam, rolled, wrapped and packaged, was a showpiece, but everywhere there was evidence of the application of mechanical and environmental inventiveness to achieve product consistency and labor efficiency.

The finished goods were conveyed to the dispatches on the ground floors of the buildings. There they were assembled according to the different requirements of the sales departments that had ordered them. For London grocers, the cakes and pies and buns from the bakeries were put up on long wooden trays for delivery by the salesman/drivers of the Wholesale Rounds department. Provincial grocers had their orders delivered by rail in cardboard cartons. A railhead was just around the corner at the Addison Road (Olympia) railway station. In the vicinity of Cadby Hall, ordinary households had deliveries by small vans through the Retail Rounds department.

In 1950 Lyons was also the country's leading caterer. The 150 London teashops were supplied by vans resplendent in the same white, blue, and gold livery as the shops themselves. There was the special requirement that the trays must be stowed in the right sequence for delivery. Time was short on the round, with every shop having to be supplied before opening time. The Teashops out of London had their designated vehicles, as did the famous Corner Houses and the Lyons restaurants. There were deliveries, too, to other outlets, such as the U.S. Air Force, NAAFI canteens, the Olympia exhibition halls across Blythe Road, and for large functions and events such as the Royal Garden Party and the Wimbledon tennis championships. The whole place was alive day and night.

The Task and the Computer

The first task to which LEO would be applied was to value all the output to and from the dispatch center, giving credit to individual bakeries and charges to each of the channels of sale.[1] In executing this task the computer was also required to calculate the "stock balance" for each item, comparing what had reached the dispatch with what had been issued and what was left over. The valuations were made at standard prices; standards were the clock by which the whole company ticked. For each item there were standard values for material, labor and for indirect costs, such as heating. These added up to the Factory Prime Cost for the item, the medium of transfer from department to department. For each channel of sale, valuations were required at this cost together with the standard assembly and distribution costs, and gross profit for each item. Additionally, overall gross profit percentages had to be calculated for each channel of sale, and there were many aggregations to be made.

The main recipient of the results was the Statistical Office, where the results were used to compile the trading analyses presented each week to a precise timetable to the directors concerned and to the management at different levels. Further results went elsewhere; some to the Rationing

Department, which was responsible for the claims to the Food Ministry for flour subsidy. The war was still casting its shadow.

The job was a very small one by later standards, but even so it had its complications because of the computer's limited storage capacity. Everything—instructions, data, tables of prices, and partial results—had to be fitted into the little storage space that was available. In light of the relatively large numbers of different items produced by some of the bakeries, this was by no means straightforward. Detailed maps were kept of the contents of the store compartments, and these were reused as soon as they became available.

The LEO computer at the time of this first job occupied a hall measuring 5000 square feet and had been put together on site. It was an electronic, stored-program system able to accommodate 2048 instructions or 17 binary-bit numbers in a mercury delay line acoustic store.

In all, there were approximately 6000 valves of the kind then used in radios and these were assembled in more than 200 units mounted in 21 tall racks, each with capacity for 12 units. Because of the considerable amount of heat generated by the thermionic valves, the racks were cooled by air drawn in at the bottom and extracted by fans at the top. The whole assembly was mounted on a false floor that provided a platform for the computer.

The time required for accessing a single item of data in the store was 500 μs, and the add time 1.3 ms.

Two input and two output channels were operational at the time of the first run. The inputs were both fed by perforated paper tape. Output was to one perforated tape and one teleprinter.[2]

The whole apparatus was controlled from a console with two video display tubes showing binary images of the store contents. In addition, a loudspeaker provided a sound representation of the instructions being carried out.

The individual items of equipment had largely been constructed by subcontractors, to whom drawings based on the EDSAC system in Cambridge, England, had been sent under the direction of Dr. John Pinkerton, the Technical Manager. The principal subcontractor was Wayne Kerr Laboratories, then at New Malden, Surrey. The very high-precision work on the metal delay lines was carried out by Coventry Gauge and Tool.

Throughout the design and building work, much use was also made of the wide range of expertise within Lyons itself.

Origins

It must have seemed odder to outsiders than to those who already worked in the company that Lyons had decided to build a computer for itself. Since the company had ventured rather reluctantly into catering sixty-odd years before, it had consistently shown vision and frequently faced risks and surmounted obstructions. When no outside enterprise could be found to do what was wanted to the exacting standards it had set, Lyons had generally been ready to take on the job itself. As the years passed, the company had become more and more self-sufficient. It employed its own engineering department, which designed plant lay-outs, ran workshops, and provided round-the-clock maintenance service. There was a Chief Electrician with a sizable staff to define and monitor the heavy loadings placed on the circuits by the forests of machinery. There was an Architects' Office and a Works Department. Lyons had its own Transport Department, which kept hundreds of vans and private cars in good order. In the Laboratory, stringent standards of hygiene were set and a constant flow of random samples of products were subjected to searching tests. Mrs. Thatcher had worked there for a time when, as Margaret Roberts, she came down from Oxford as a young chemistry graduate. Lyons had its own printing plant, laundry, and carton factory. Lyons even employed its own bands and ran its own made-to-measure dressmaking department for its waitresses.

Different activities had been embarked upon with one or two men or women, and then developed and expanded. Sometimes they were taken on as a going concern from outside. There was an enormous confidence pervading the company that it could run anything if the need arose. During the war it had been put to the test by a request to take charge of a munitions works in the South Midlands. The assignment was accepted with enthusiasm, and the company prided itself as having been among the most efficient. T. R. Thompson, a key figure in the LEO story, took a leading part in this venture.

Those who afterwards smiled at the notion of a teashop concern designing and manufacturing advanced electronic equipment and putting it to work were misleading themselves. Lyons was not just a small back room of cooks and waitresses. Technically it was a remarkably comprehensive and self-reliant organization that had long experience of recognizing way-out ideas and carrying them through to timely fruition.

A key to Lyon's success in its disparate activities was the importance placed on organization and planning. At birth it had plunged into setting up transient refreshment facilities, starting from scratch without any existing standing in the trade. By 1925 it had been able to mount a banquet in which 7500 guests sat down at a mile and a half of tables to be served simultaneously by 1250 waitresses.

From the outset, Lyons was run by a single family and its connections. Its roots were in a tobacco business started in London's Soho in the 1850s by two young brothers who had come as immigrants from Germany 13 years before. Their firm, Salmon and Gluckstein, flourished, with retail tobacco shops in many main streets. Then the horizons widened. Through his trips as a salesman, a member of the family became convinced that the catering at large exhibitions was so unappealing that there would be a ready welcome for something better. He overcame reluctance from his relatives only on the condition that the new enterprise would be run under a different name so as not to imperil the hard-won reputation of Salmon and Gluckstein. As a consequence, Joseph Lyons, a cousin of a family member's wife, was enlisted, bringing with him the right exhibition know-how. The catering company established itself in 1894 on a two-acre site known as Cadby Hall, after a piano factory that had previously occupied it.

At first, J. Lyons & Co. was concentrated entirely on widening aspects of catering—first exhibitions, then teashops and restaurants. Larger and larger banquets were undertaken. Other activities were secondary and initially entered into only to utilize the excess capacity of the plants set up to supply the catering outlets. In particular, bread was delivered from a modern steam bakery, installed on the much enlarged Cadby Hall facility, to households in the vicinity. Handcarts and horse-drawn vans were used, the precursors of the Retail Rounds vans, that were still operating when the first Bakery Valuations job was run.

Among the more distant households supplied was Buckingham Palace, for which the company proudly received the Royal Warrant. Similarly, packed tea began to be sold to grocers, who hitherto had scooped out the shopper's requirements from large lacquered canisters. A model tea and coffee factory was opened at Greenford to complement the bread and cakes and, later, ice-cream factories at Cadby Hall. By this time, Lyons had extended its network to almost every grocery store and corner shop in the land. The supplies to Lyons' catering establishments and sales to retail and wholesale customers progressed symbiotically alongside each other.

It was sometimes said in Lyons that expansion took place mainly to match the growth in the family as sons and daughters married and had children of their own to be placed in the business. The children and cousins were given a rite of passage induction, often starting in the kitchens of the flagship Trocadero restaurant after it had opened. Then they were given responsibility as quickly as possible. It could be claimed that they all started at the bottom . . . for a year.

In a sense, the Salmons and Glucksteins were like a government that did not change. Beneath them was a civil service, a very capable body that testified to the family's ability to choose and delegate. At the time of the first computer run of a routine office job, a Mr. Harry (Salmon) was Chairman of the Company and Mr. Geoffrey ran the Bakeries. Members of the family were always known by their first names. There was a Mr. Julian and a Mr. Felix and a Mr. Alfred and Major Monte, and many others as time went on. When it was decided that LEO should become a business on its own, it was Mr. Anthony (Salmon) who was chosen to be its head.

The family was remarkably cohesive. All had their principal offices on the fourth floor of the Administration Building in Cadby Hall, and so "the Fourth Floor" had a meaning of its own. They were in a position to consult each other quickly, and decisions of importance were often made without the paperwork that would generally have been necessary in a more conventional organization. The family prided itself on being as good as its word, even when a disadvantage subsequently revealed itself. In LEO times, a senior Lyons director had great misgivings about doing business at all with a powerful company headed by a most respected figure because it was alleged that some years before he had gone back on an agreement sealed with a handshake.

The Lyons Offices

The Lyons office organization had evolved to reflect the exacting nature of the business. It required the same dynamism to keep up with it. Transactions were very small for the most part, leaving no leeway at all for any lack of economy in the back office. There was a constant movement of goods from place to place that had to be controlled, and a growing army of people handling money. Large bodies of clerks had grown up all over the company to deal with local needs. By the time the company had picked itself up after World War I, it had become plain that something more than common sense and good housekeeping was necessary.

The decision was made to bring in a number of graduate trainees. One of these was J. R. M. Simmons, who came from Cambridge with a splendid performance in mathematics. Under G. W. Booth, who had been Company Secretary since the incorporation of Lyons, Simmons was to transform the offices, especially management accounting. He had the advantage of unwavering support from the older man, who himself enjoyed the deep and almost traditional respect of the family as years passed. For a long time Booth was the only nonfamily member to have a full seat on the Board of Directors.

Back in the 1920s, when Simmons arrived, the ambience was still Dickensian, with clerks standing at tall tables, and occasionally resting themselves on high stools.[3] Vestiges of this still remained 25 years later in the demeanor and dress of some of the older clerks who still remained. There were the residual Bob Cratchits, happy in the few specialized tasks that had not been susceptible to mechanization. There was one still pasting railway waybills into a large brown paper "guard book" and standing to compare them with the invoices when they arrived because that was the only convenient way.

The changes for which Simmons was responsible had many facets. One was to break each office job into its functional parts and then to introduce machinery to handle those parts. It was the equivalent of what was happening in the factories, with precise timing of how long each operation should take. Though pounds sterling was still the official currency, decimalization of cost accounts was introduced, enabling unhampered use of the largely American-sourced calculating and accounting machines. Large open offices were formed with phalanxes of each type of machine. Bundles of transaction notes passed between them. Few people did a whole job that could be identified with a part of the business. It became more like an assembly line than an old-time office. The functionalization was clinically efficient, but, as Simmons said later, it reduced clerks to drudgery. He was more than ready to clutch at anything that could economically produce what was needed without all the repetitive labor.

On another front, Simmons had concluded that the only way in which managers could account for the parts of the business for which they were responsible was with standards for everything. There were standards for each product, composed of costing the required materials and the work that had to be put in, and other requirements such as heating the ovens. Under the systems that were introduced, the actual occurrences were compared with these standards in the fullest detail. Thus commodities taken into each factory were checked both for quantity and price, and similarly for labor and other costs. Managers were told each week precisely what deviations had occurred so they could take corrective action. The computer work carried out in the Bakeries Valuations job for the first time in November 1951 formed part of this process.

On yet another front, Simmons set up what would now be known as an O&M (Organization and Methods) operation to ensure that the most suitable machines were installed and that they were incorporated into comprehensive systems aimed at producing, in a secure and timely way, the information needed by management at all levels to run the business. In the British office management world, Lyons came to be recognized as a center of excellence in everything that concerned office systems and management.

With this background it was not unusual for Lyons to be taking the lead in introducing computers to routine office work.

3
LEO: Idea and Realization

1947–1951

The Trip to America

In 1947 the Lyons offices were back on a peacetime schedule. Men and women returning from the war had been reinstated. The time had come for further advances, but there was an appreciation of the need for something quite new if further improvements of any consequence were to be made. It was in this atmosphere that two senior managers were sent on a trip to the United States to study developments in offices there during the war years. This was the latest in a succession of visits.

Simmons himself had made the journey very soon after his appointment as a young graduate, fresh from Cambridge. On that occasion, way back in October of 1925, the *Business Diary* reports visits to many business machine manufacturers and to businesses with large offices.[1] Among those visited were the Powers Machine Company and International Business Machines, the latter having taken this name only the year before to reflect the enormous ambitions of its dynamic leader, Thomas J. Watson.

Characteristically, though, the report gave special attention to the fact that the American Machine and Foundry Company in Brooklyn, which had relations with Lyons through its bread wrapping machinery, had managed to dispense with bought ledgers to control their payments for supplies. The report outlined the methods employed to effect this saving and also the special American circumstances that made it possible, Sears Roebuck, it was noted, was among other large enterprises that used this approach.

Twenty-two years later T. R. Thompson, who for most of that time had been Simmons' principal lieutenant, led the party of two. He was accompanied by Oliver Standingford, an Assistant Controller. Most of their time was devoted, as usual, to catching up with what had been happening in large organizations with comparable office loads and visiting Lyons' main office suppliers and others to see what was on the way.

In 1947, however, there was to be an additional item on the itinerary. News had begun to reach England about the "Electronic Brain." It seemed to Standingford, who was of a particularly inventive turn of mind, that there was no reason why a device with the characteristics described could not be as applicable to office work as to ballistics. Accordingly, permission was sought to spend time visiting ENIAC and any other research of the same kind.[2] Characteristically, it was G. W. Booth who settled the issue, declaring that "youth must have its head."

On the conventional side, Thompson and Standingford were not greatly impressed. "We did not find any firm," they reported, "which had developed on so broad a front as Lyons, most offices only having tackled a limited number of office problems without having surveyed the whole field." Office systems, they found, were reorganized only when circumstances made it absolutely necessary. Then, they said, "the position seems to be for an office machine company to be called in to review the existing systems and produce one showing a substantial saving, which, of course, involves the use of their machines. The system is then introduced without any consideration of alternatives."[2]

They found that personnel departments seemed large in proportion to the number of staff and concluded that in some cases this was due to overelaboration. In office accommodation they declared that "their best efforts cannot compare with Elms House."[2] Elms House was the Lyons office building erected shortly before the war on the other side of Brook Green to complement the concepts that had been developed for modern, mechanized, large-scale office work. They were particularly irreverent about the Pentagon. "The only thing remarkable about it is its size . . . the time wasted walking between offices must be considerable." Layouts, they thought, were generally poor. As they had expected, punched-card installations were encountered frequently, but they found nothing to dent the accepted Lyons view that in a well-organized office they were of value only in exceptional cases.

Introduction to Computing

If Thompson and Standingford were disappointed by the lack of inspiration on the conventional side, they were compensated by their contacts in the computer field. They were well received by several of the leading figures of the day. At Harvard they met Professor Howard Aiken and found him full of enthusiasm for what he foresaw as the second Industrial Revolution. He was confident about the commercial potential of computers and looked beyond the offices to a time when, as they reported, a factory could be controlled automatically, all the processes being coordinated and made to work in accordance with a predetermined policy.[2] They were impressed by his two models, Harvard I and Harvard II, which were giving reliable service in the laboratories.

However, the Harvard machines were still based on electrical relays, and the introduction to electronic computer that was their objective came from Dr. Herman Goldstine at the Princeton Institute for Advanced Study. Goldstine had been a liaison officer for the U.S. Army during the design and construction of ENIAC at the Moore School of Engineering at the University of Pennsylvania. The computer had since been handed over to the army, and the team disbanded.

ENIAC, they learned, was a vast machine completely dedicated to the task of producing ballistic tables. The stimulus for its construction had come from the part that it might play in strengthening the war effort, but despite a single-minded effort to complete it rapidly, it had been finished too late to make a contribution. A system had emerged with 18,000 vacuum tubes with high heat dissipation, occupying a very large space. It was sufficient to prove, though, that an electronic computer was a thoroughly practical proposition.

Though the Lyons party received permission to see ENIAC at work at its new site at the U.S. Army's Aberdeen proving grounds, this was later rescinded. Goldstine, they said, told them that this was probably because the engineers "must be having difficulty in getting the machine working again."[2]

As well as being encouraging about the ideas they put to him and generous with his time, Goldstine also took the practical step of writing to Professor Hartree, a mathematical physicist at Cambridge University, who had himself spent time studying the developments. Together with his colleague, Dr. Maurice Wilkes, he would, advised Goldstine, be well equipped to give ongoing advice.

While in the United States, Thompson and Standingford also visited NCR and Burroughs, which had supplied many of the Lyons accounting machines, and found that both had formed electronic research sections. These were "highly secret" and nothing was disclosed. IBM, they noted, had already marketed an electronic calculator, but this did no more than replace a mechanical calculator for use in conjunction with other punched-card equipment.[2]

A considerable stimulus was received from the visit to Prudential Insurance in Newark, New Jersey, where they were told of a project to build an electronic machine that would carry out the premium billing of their millions of policy-holders, then occupying a staff of 300. Prudential was also investigating the possibilities for automatically writing contracts, for which there were 2000 standard clauses from which to select.[2]

Cambridge and Pennsylvania

Douglas Hartree's link with ENIAC stemmed from his wartime problem-solving for the Ministry of Supply. That had placed him in official contact with the Moore School from an early stage. He had had his first sight of work in progress in ENIAC very soon after the end of the war[3] Furthermore, soon after the handover to the U.S. Army in February 1946, he had again spent time at the School, discussing nonmilitary uses of ENIAC, and had run a problem of his own.

At around the same time, Maurice Wilkes, in his capacity of acting Director of the Mathematical Laboratory at Cambridge, had written to his Faculty Board:

> There is a big field here, especially in the application of electronic methods, which have made great progress during the war and, I think, Cambridge should take its part trying to catch up some of the lead the Americans have in this subject.[3]

Influential in Wilkes's thinking from this point on had been an opportunity to read a privileged copy of a seminal statement on the future of computers. Entitled "Draft Report on the EDVAC," it had been written by John von Neumann on behalf of the design group at the Moore School, which included the leaders Presper Eckert and John Mauchly. The new ideas had evolved as the work on ENIAC proceeded.[4]

The report propounded the principle of the stored-program computer, with the program sharing store with the numerical data. "I recognized this at once as the real thing," declared Wilkes in his memoirs,[4] "and from that time on never had any doubt as to the way computer development would go."

Armed with this concept, Dr. Wilkes, by invitation, attended the historic course at the Moore School in 1946. Because of the vagaries of immediate postwar transatlantic shipping, his arrival was delayed, but he was compensated by personal discussions with Dr. Goldstine, who had given sections of the part of the course that he had missed.[5]

On Wilkes's return from the United States, he was confirmed as Director of the Mathematical Laboratory, and it was within that organization that EDSAC was taking shape when Thompson and Standingford made their visit. In his project of producing a computer embodying what had become known as the "von Neumann" architecture, he was backed by the firm support of Professor Hartree, who, with his formidable reputation in numerical analysis, had by this time accepted a Chair at Cambridge University.[6]

Return to Cambridge

On their return home, Thompson and Standingford at once took up the invitation awaiting them from Cambridge and visited Hartree and Wilkes at the Mathematical Laboratory. They found the keenest of interest and readiness to cooperate as soon as their own machine was completed. However, they explained, work on what was later named EDSAC was slow. The plans were drawn up, but there was a lack of money. Only Dr. Wilkes, one draftsman, and, temporarily, two vacation students were engaged on the job. "We told them that unless they can proceed more rapidly they may find machines for sale in America before they can complete their first model." The response was that given $6000 they could complete much more quickly.[2]

The account of the visit to Cambridge was appended to the American visit report. The computer section as a whole is a historical classic and those parts most pertinent to the LEO story are published for the first time as part of this volume (Appendix A). TRT, as he was generally known, and Standingford, known in the offices as Sitting Bull, had not only rapidly gained a mastery of the broad outlines of how these systems worked, but were also able to envisage how they might be applied to office work. Sketches are included in the report of how they might be used for sales invoicing, payroll, and also what is now known as word processing.

Action

The report concluded:[2]

> Our first concern is, of course, the advantages which Lyons may gain from the commercial development of electronic machines, but there is a wider aspect that cannot be ignored. This machine may well be a prime factor in relieving the present economic distress of the country. In this latter respect we believe that Lyons occupies a key position; no one else, here, so far as we can learn, has realized the far reaching possibilities of electronic machines.

> We assume that Lyons will want to take full advantage of these machines for its own offices. It is possible to play a passive role by merely keeping in touch with developments, and in due course buying machines as they become available, probably from American sources. But such a role would not enable us to have any influence on the kind of machines built, and without commercial influence they may well be built in a form more suitable to handling mathematical and census calculations . . .

They outlined five possible courses of action. One was to influence Hartree to pursue his work in the required directions, while giving financial encouragement. Another was to put the ideas into the hands of a large electrical company and leave them to exploit the outcome. A third was to collaborate with Electronic Controls Inc. in Philadelphia in the same way as Prudential Insurance had. A fourth was to approach the British government to coordinate research so as to get "Britain first in the field." The final option was to "build a machine in our own workshops, drawing information and advice from Cambridge and Harvard Universities."[2]

Simmons, to whom the report was presented, accepted readily that Lyons had a special role to play. The options were weighed and a number of exploratory approaches were made. He speaks about this period in the transcript of an archival interview for the Science Museum that is also appended[7]. By the end of the period all but the final option were judged to be undesirable or impractical. Simmons then submitted the report to the Board of Directors with a covering note in which he advised:

> We believe that we have been able to get a glimpse of a development which will, in a few years time, have a profound effect on the way in which clerical work is performed. Here for the first time there is a possibility of a machine which will be able to cope, at almost incredible speed, with any variation of clerical procedure, provided the conditions which govern the variations can be predetermined . . . .

After estimating possible costs and savings, the memorandum went on:

> We feel, therefore, that the company might well wish to take a lead in the development of the machine . . . .

He warned that unless organizations such as Lyons, the potential users, played their part, "the time at which they became commercially available will be unnecessarily postponed for many years."[8]

Perhaps he was underestimating the inexorable march of events in the United States once technological change became manifest. Nonetheless, he was able to win the immediate support that Cambridge University needed to expedite their work. This was seen as providing a basis for a Lyons system once EDSAC had proven itself. Three weeks later a delegation, led by Booth, the veteran Company Secretary, then in sight of his 80th birthday, visited Cambridge and made an offer of $8400 and the services of an electrical assistant in return for guidance in constructing a computer for Lyons' own purposes.[8]

The World's First Practical, Stored-Program Computer

The offer was gratefully accepted and played a valuable part in enabling EDSAC to become the first stored-program computer to operate in a practical way. This it did on May 6, 1949, when it calculated a sequence of prime numbers, the mathematician's touchstone, and printed the results. The program was written by David Wheeler, who later became a professor at Cambridge.[9]

Wilkes's success in reaching his goal of providing a practical system for the use of the very large computing community at Cambridge had been made possible by his early decision to avoid all experimentation that was not strictly necessary. From the outset he had adopted mercury delay lines as the medium for the vital stored system, doing so because their feasibility had already been proved in use for other purposes during the war. He has since commented that although the *Draft Report on the EDVAC* did not specifically refer to this method of storage, Presper Eckert and John Mauchly had always envisaged proceeding in that way.[10]

Further, Maurice Wilkes had decided on a conservative specification for the EDSAC storage. He says in his memoirs:[11]

> I would have been entirely prepared . . . to accept the challenge of working at I Mc/s, and this in fact was what most designers of machines using electronic memories were doing. I had, however, other objects in view besides solving problems in electronic engineering. I wanted as soon as possible to have an electronic computer and to experiment with the writing of programs to solve real problems.

Both in the United States and in Britain there had been many laboratories at work on producing a working embodiment of the stored-program computer. ENIAC and the von Neumann report had lit a torch. In America, work had been proceeding under the auspices of the Eckert-Mauchly Corporation, the vehicle chosen by the two ENIAC engineers to further their vision of commercially available electronic computers. They had found, however, that it was much more time-consuming to design a generalized system that could be made repetitively as compared with a specialized one-off system, and had not yet been able to realize their ambitions.[11] Later, problems in financial backing led them to the Remington Rand Corporation, where their system emerged under a name that became famous: UNIVAC.[12]

As anticipated, the Eckert-Mauchly memory was, like EDSAC's, based on mercury delay lines. Additionally, the system utilized magnetic tapes in the way that had so much attracted Thompson and Standingford several years before. Like all computer systems of the period, UNIVAC utilized several thousand vacuum tubes, and though the designers had learned a great deal from their experience with ENIAC, it was still very large.

In Britain, the parallel effort to produce a working system was in progress at Manchester University, which had succeeded in 1948 in demonstrating "the Baby," showing the stored-program principle in live operation. In this experimental system, a cathode ray tube devised by Professor "Freddie" Williams was employed as the storage medium. Later, the Baby led to a commercially available system manufactured by Ferranti, the Manchester electrical and electronics company.

However, Wilkes's strategy had paid off. He had met his objective of producing a practical system as soon as possible to meet the needs of the "clients" of the Mathematical Laboratory of which he was head. One of his first actions after EDSAC had done what was asked of it was to telephone the news to Cadby Hall. As it happened, the Lyons Board was holding its regular biweekly meeting. A note was passed in asking for confirmation that full-scale work could proceed now that the EDSAC determinant had been achieved. Within a few minutes an affirmative response came back from the Chairman, Mr. Harry.[13]

People

Having been given the official blessing, the embryonic Lyons computer received the name LEO, an acronym for Lyons Electronic Office. Simmons, who invented it, was an austere man, and it was never known whether he had Leo the Lion in mind. Later, when successors came along, this machine became known as LEO I.

Responsible for the construction of LEO and bringing it to a condition robust enough for it to be entrusted with time-critical office work was Dr. John Pinkerton, a young physicist who was hired by the offices for the task in anticipation of the board decision being a favorable one. Only 32 when the first routine job was run, he had spend much of World War II in the Government's Telecommunications Research Establishment engaged in radar research vital to the effectiveness of the Royal Air Force. His principal assistants were Ernest Kaye, an even younger engineer, who brought industrial experience, and E. R. (Len) Lenaerts, whose previous civilian experience had been wholly in the Lyons offices.

Pinkerton's career background had been wholly in research and development. Though he had successfully built radios since boyhood, electronic engineering on this large scale was something very different. That had been true, too, of Dr. Wilkes, and it seemed reasonable to believe that this new field required a new kind of man. In any event, Pinkerton fitted the bill admirably, combining a theoretical understanding in depth with a shrewd practicality and a boyish glee in getting contraptions to work.

Pinkerton's principal assistants were Ernest Kaye, an even younger engineer, who brought industrial experience, and E.H. (Len) Lenaerts, whose previous civilian experience had been wholly in the Lyons offices. After graduating from Imperial College in London, Kaye had spent the latter part of the war at GEC Research Laboratories, starting off with work on the electronics of underwater homing torpedoes. After participating with Pinkerton and Lenaerts on the circuit design of the new machine, he was given the responsibility of interfacing with the subcontractors who were manufacturing the individual units. With the team still coming to grips with some of the details of the not always clear Cambridge design, he sometimes found himself having to send units back for modification as soon as they arrived.

Lenaerts had already been involved for some time. He had arrived at Cambridge within days of Lyons undertaking to provide assistance in return for guidance and information. Before the war, "Len" Lenaerts had been a supervisory grade clerk, although his inclination had always been toward electricals. In the service he had been able to follow his bent and became a sergeant in the RAF's radio counter measure operations. Whatever the expectations were at Cambridge, he proved to be more than another pair of hands there. His service orderliness and his firm determination to get on top of a subject that was largely new to him, together with his natural inventiveness, all contributed to the project. At the same time he kept Cadby Hall in touch with frequent reports, giving a clear exposition of the almost undocumented work that was going on. He did not allow even the shortage of paper that beset postwar Britain to stand in his way. Among others who played a valuable part in the design of LEO and putting it together were Raymond Shaw, Gordon Gibbs, and Wally Dutton, an electrician transferred from Lyons.

At Cambridge, Lenaerts was joined for a time by Derek Hemy, who was sent there to pick up what he could about the infant art of programming. He joined the Lyons offices as a management trainee in 1939, and during the war served first in the Chemical Warfare unit of the Royal Engineers and later in Signals Intelligence for the Royal Corps of Signals. He did not stay for long periods at Cambridge, but came to and fro like a bee carrying pollen so that those back at Cadby Hall could stay in touch and make their own contributions. With this prewar office experience and a knowledge of methods and procedures that he gained in the Systems Research Office in his return from military service, Hemy was able to participate positively in the definition of the instruction set. He went on to work side by side with a talented young Cambridge mathematician, David (later Professor) Wheeler, on the problem of "bootstrapping" into the EDSAC system the few initial orders that constituted the rudimentary operating instructions.

The first three programmers to learn their trade from Hemy were Leo Fantl, John Grover, and Tony Barnes. After war service in the RAF, Fantl had worked for a time in the Lyons Labor Planning Office, which was responsible for work measurement and labor efficiency techniques in factories and other workplaces. An early talent search had brought him to LEO, where he went on to exert influence in many different fields.

Grover was a volunteer for flying duties in the RAF who had joined the Lyons office as a management trainee in 1947 after deciding against a long-term air force career. In LEO he was given responsibility for the coding of the Bakery Valuations job, the world's first, described earlier in the book. Working with him, sometimes impulsively leading, sometimes restlessly in step, was Barnes, yet another management trainee from the offices. After graduating in mechanical sciences from Cambridge, he had served as an Instructor Lieutenant in the Royal Navy.

My own role as Programming Manager sprang directly from my previous post as Manager of the Systems Research Office. The aim from the time that Simmons had established the function, as far back as 1931, had been to build totally integrated systems from the ground up. Mention has already been made of the employment of conventional office machines as they became available; it was a cardinal principle that they should not be introduced without the system as a whole being reexamined. There was no question of leaving the system as it stood and merely mechanizing those aspects that most readily presented themselves. The computer was to be considered in that same way. Accordingly, my own part in the Bakery Valuations job was to select, specify, and chart it. My background was as another prewar office management trainee, followed by war service in the Green Howards, a northern England infantry regiment.

Heading the LEO activity as a whole was T. R. Thompson, to whom Pinkerton and I reported. A Cambridge mathematics graduate with a first-class honors degree, he had been Chief Assistant Comptroller of Lyons, where he had worked as Simmons's principal assistant for almost

20 years. For a time he regarded his LEO duties as just an exciting add-on to his normal job, but after a while he left his high-level post, as I did my more modest one, and we both took our places in the full-time team.

Oliver Standingford must also be named. Having made his striking contribution at the start of the whole concept of computing for office work, he participated for a while in what followed, while continuing in his post as an Assistant Comptroller in the offices. Later he became a Director of associated companies within the Lyons orbit and was encountered again only when he commissioned a job from LEO for one of them.

Requirements for Office Work

Before even the go-ahead was received, there had been considerable thought among the original group to determine all that was needed to fit the EDSAC design to office work. One major requirement that presented itself very early was the need for multiple inlets and outlets. Studies on payroll indicated that three parallel input channels were required to follow the logical pattern of the work. One was needed for the "permanent data" of each employee's wage rate, etc., another for the hours worked each week, and a third for bringing forward previous totals to date for the year so that PAYE could be calculated. On the output side there was a requirement for at least two channels, so that information for printing paychecks could go on one and the updated carry-forward totals on the other. Some inkling of this had already appeared in the American visit report, but work had to be done to fill this out and to see how the principle applied to other procedures.

A second problem that required study was how to cope with the vastly greater volume of data and results that occurred naturally in office work. At the extreme, a mathematical program could just live on itself, without needing to be fed again once set in motion. The initial job on EDSAC was such a one where, having calculated one prime number, no new data at all was needed at all to calculate the next. On the output side, only a single number needed to be printed on each cycle, though in between the calculations were becoming longer and longer. The calculation phase was completely dominant, but this situation never applied in clerical work. Study soon showed that in the general case the time taken to feed information into the computer was going to be at least as long as the time taken to carry out the relatively trivial calculations. The indications were that the output might take longer still. Thus, while the computer might be operating at the "almost incredible speed" of which Simmons had written, the whole operation was going to be slowed down to the pedestrian unless something could be done about input and output speeds.

Part of the input/output problem was that the data entering the computer system and the results leaving it were not in the same notation as were operated upon internally. Input and output were in some form of digital representation on whatever medium was transporting them, while numbers inside the computer were in binary mode. There was the impediment to overcome that the conversion of data and results from one mode to the other might take at least as long as the substantive calculations to be effected. There was no problem about the EDSAC design being able to carry out the conversions, but the inroad into the inherent speed would again be substantial.

Another concern that emerged was that, unless great care was taken, the labor of preparing data in the form that the input mechanism could read could well amount to an unacceptably high proportion of the keypunching effort previously expended on calculating or accounting machines. On the conventional side, this effort had already been researched down to a minimum. It was plain that applications for the computer had to be defined in such a way that an item of data, once taken into the system, must automatically be used and reused for every purpose in which it played a part. It was also recognized that for some office tasks, like adding up piles of restaurant bills and comparing them with service issues, the computer had little to offer as long as the data from them still had to be key-punched.

A further product of the experimental coding that was carried out was the realization that while clerical calculations might be simple, there tended to be a great many choices to make. This meant that clerical programs would tend to require more instructions than were being provided for in the EDSAC store. Fortunately the address capacity of the instruction set enabled LEO to service a store size double that of EDSAC.

Implementing the Enhancements

Work on physically building the LEO engine went ahead briskly after the go-ahead. There was no delay for second-guessing what Cambridge had done. As Pinkerton engagingly said later, "The first machine we built, LEO Mark 1, was based on the logic of EDSAC Mark 1. The philosophy we had was that we would not change anything if we didn't understand why it was done the way it was. So to start with, since we didn't understand very well why it was done the way it was, we didn't make very many changes at all."[14]

Be that as it may, there was an additional task to be carried out in parallel with the construction of the central units. That was to implement enhancements to give effect to the additional requirements that had been identified. On the architectural side there was first the need to meet the extended input/output arrangements. In the Thompson/Standingford report, magnetic wire had been postulated as the medium of transfer.[15] By this time, magnetic tape had replaced this technologically, and a manufacturer was sought with experience in this medium who would be prepared to design and build what Thompson and the engineering team had in mind. The natural first choice was Standard Telephones (STC) which had recently installed a central telephone exchange at Cadby Hall and was already developing equipment for use with their own teleprinters.[16]

The schema developed with Standard Telephones was based on having subsidiary devices associated with each input and output channel. The data would be fed into the input device on magnetic tape and there automatically converted to binary form. When the computer was ready to make use of it, the converted data would be transferred unchanged into the main store. There would be electronic buffering between the external device and the store, so the computer would never be kept waiting. Similarly, when the computer had results ready it would transfer them to a buffer and then to the output device, and arrange them in the required format for magnetic tape.[17]

Conceptually, the assembly went as far as was logically possible toward enabling office programs to enjoy as full use of the computing speed of the computer as scientific programs. There was inevitably a price to be paid for the enhancement, quite apart from the cost of the design of the equipment and of building a device for each of the inlets and outlets. There was the risk of delay, since the computer would be incomplete without the enhancement. There was also the danger of an effect on overall reliability with additional equipment operating inline with the computer itself. On the other hand, the enhancement was seen as a necessity; without it the project would be meaningless.

The timetable agreed with Standard Telephones was for the auxiliary equipment to be completed by May 1951; the computer was to be tried and tested by then. Furthermore, the timetable for the preparation of application programs was geared to that ready-for-service date.[18] But through no lack of effort on the part of the contractor or of cooperation from Lyons, the project was never achieved. In logical terms the design was satisfactory, but several of the components were relied upon long before they were ready for so demanding a task. When the auxiliary equipment, already late, was connected, it did not function reliably. The project had to be scrapped.

However, by this time a replacement scheme was already in place. As the delays extended and doubts grew about the eventual reliability of the

STC equipment, it had been decided to pursue a fallback solution in-house.[19] Internally, the substitute approach was known as the "Consolidation" project, and work proceeded on this while STC continued to make repeated efforts. The replacement system provided for the three input channels to be fed by punched cards and paper tape, and the two output channels to be served by a line printer and a card punch. Conversion and reconversion to and from binary would now not need an external device, but would be accomplished by single orders added to the computer's instruction repertoire. The paper tape would serve for current data, such as "hours worked," and the punched-card feeds for permanent data, such as "wage rates," and carried forward data, such as "totals to date." There would be on-line printing of results and the output punch would provide for totals carried forward. Logically there would be similar buffering arrangements to those previously envisioned.

The supply of punched-card equipment was negotiated with British Tabulating Machines and the paper tape readers from Ferranti. When the linkages were completed, the assemblage as a whole constituted LEO I.

Commenting afterward, Simmons expressed the view that had LEO concentrated on one innovation at a time and used conventional equipment for the enhancements at least two years could have been saved.[20] In his sympathetic paper, "The Teashop Computer Manufacturer: J. Lyons," John Hendry, then of the London Business School, disagreed. He argued that Simmons was being too hard on himself and his colleagues because the growth in the speeds of paper tape and punched-card machines had been so considerable in the interim that little time was lost in the end.[21] It is unlikely, though, that many concerned with LEO at the time would echo that assessment. It was frustrating to be delayed in getting live work onto the machine, whether the optimum speed was achieved or not.

Almost the only outlet for programmers at the time was constructing computer test programs. A searching repertoire was constructed in compliance with the engineers' (particularly Lenaerts's) requirements. Building on their close relationship going back to their days at Cambridge, Hemy and Lenaerts were largely instrumental in initiating the suite under Pinkerton's overview, but later Fantl played a major part in developing it. Though the wry phrase "It is a poor machine that can't do its own test programs" had probably not been coined yet, he quickly became aware that the battle with the computer gremlins was a subtle affair and adapted his programs accordingly. When live running of application programs did eventually begin, the computer was subjected to the whole suite of test programs with marginal electrical conditions applied before the runs were allowed to proceed. It was a notable day when it was felt safe to proceed without this overhead.

A significant feature of the test programs was that though each of them had only a small number of instructions, they observed the same disciplines as were being developed for application programs. Their content was agreed upon with the end customer, the engineer in this case. Then they were charted and coded on the specially designed coding sheets. The coding was checked by another programmer. Fair copies were prepared of both the charts and program sheets by my secretary, Miss Hyam. Corrections or changes were made to the charts and coding sheets, and then a check was made as before. No change was too small to escape the checking rule. Computer time was so precious that the aim was always to present *correct* programs to the computer for *confirmation*, rather than to use the computer as an instrument for finding errors. Changes to programs at the console were frowned upon, even though the few programmers quickly became adept in this regard.

Running a Live Office Application

Though the test programs provided a chink of window into the real world of live running, they were an unsatisfying substitute for the programming team. Consequently, when it became unlikely that the STC equipment would be ready by anything like the planned date of May of 1951, the proposal was made that a suitable application be run using only low-speed input and output. The Bakery Valuations job was delineated for this purpose. It was chosen to be low in data volume though still making a useful contribution to the week-by-week management accounting operation of the company.

There was no great enthusiasm for this project outside the programming ranks.[22] Anything that diverted computer time from improving reliability or from testing the auxiliary equipment as it became available was frowned upon. As will be seen from the Simmons interview (Appendix B), the view at the top was that if a job could not be run with the full facilities required for office work in general, its contribution would be very limited. Nonetheless, it was eventually agreed that the job could go ahead. To make it possible, additional slow-speed equipment was added to the system, resulting in an overall complement of two perforated tape readers, one paper tape punch, and one teleprinters. The coding was supervised by Hemy and the definitive version of the program was produced by Grover with the participation of Barnes. All took part in the checking and testing of the job.

In June of 1951, Simmons wrote to Geoffrey Salmon, the Director in charge of Cadby Hall Bakeries, informing him that, "We are proposing as an experiment to use LEO in the job of valuing the Cadby Hall Bakeries output and sales. This is one of the major tasks that we have to do in order to prepare the departmental accounts." He went on, "Although we are running this simple job as an experiment, we must, of course, try to get the conditions which are likely to exist when LEO is in full swing." Mr. Geoffrey was accordingly asked to ensure that the work of reporting quantities and notifying new and deleted lines would be executed accurately in accordance with the timetable to be agreed upon with his people.[23] A main board director would never normally have been approached about details such as this, but it was felt imperative that there should be the fullest awareness at the highest level of this first excursion into live office work.

The normal Systems Research procedures were followed in preparing the job for running. A Method Summary was circulated to those concerned, backed by specimens of the forms to be used for reporting the data and schedules of the results that would be produced.[23] Times for passing data of different kinds were agreed upon, and fallback arrangements were made, to be invoked if the computer failed to perform.[23] Special care was taken over documenting the data preparation arrangements, even though these were to be carried out by members of the programming team.[23] No automatic paper-tape comparing and correcting facilities were yet available, as it had been assumed up to this time that entry would be by magnetic tape. Consequently, preparing the data was regarded as potentially one of the most fallible parts of the whole exercise.

Operations, too, were in the hands of the programmers. The internal timetable for Friday, November 17, 1951, read:[23]

P23	11 A.M.	Last data received	
	12 noon	Perforated	
	12:45	Checked	Grover
			Miss Hyam
P2	2:00	On calculator	
	3:30	Completed	Barnes
P3	3:30	On calculator	
	5:00	Completed	Barnes
Later Work:	Friday		Hemy
	Saturday		Hemy

There was also a contingency plan with an alternative program approach if a particularly fault-prone unit of the computer were to give trouble. In the event, although there were machine faults in both the first and the succeeding week, by November 28/29 the whole timetable had been shifted forward, the results produced by early on Friday afternoon.[23]

The experience of the subsequent week-by-week runs was invaluable. Quite apart from rooting out frailties in the circuitry that the test programs could not reach, the job helped to establish the checking equipment that was required for the perforated tape that was to remain the main input carrier for variable data. It also revealed how very fallible the data supply could be, even after the most careful of precautions. In the past these errors and omissions had been masked by clerks at all levels reacting when something like a price was missing or a quantity looked palpably wrong. It has been appreciated that perfection could not be expected and that it must be contrived so that, even though some elements of garbage came in, the programs would neither come to a halt nor put garbage out. The need for this precaution was borne out by events. It provide to be a long struggle to obtain fully complete and accurate data even from this small field. In personal terms, Mr. Geoffrey was accustomed to receiving a Trading Analysis that he could rely upon at a set time each week. If it failed to appear at the right time, under the new arrangements it would not appease him to be told that it was because his own bakeries had sent in false information to the computer.

Above all, there was the encouragement that this had been a real job and not just a demonstration piece, of which there had been many. It has been noted that, up to this time, no more than 20 people, including clerical assistants, had carried out the whole LEO task in computer design, construction, application design, and programming.

The application had integrated three different tasks hitherto carried out separately. It had:

- valued output from each of the different bakeries at standard material, labor and indirect costs and total factory cost

- valued issues to each of the different channels of sale at standard factory costs, distribution cost, sales price and profit margin

- calculated and valued at standard factory cost the Despatch stock balances for each item arising from differences between receipts from bakeries and output to the several channels of sale

Previously these calculations had been carried out separately and, frequently, incompatibilities had given rise to tedious reconciliation investigations to bring them into line before routine submission of Trading Analyses to management.

4
Loading LEO I

1951–1954

Scientific Service Work

Apart from the ongoing Bakery Valuations job, the wait for the full input/output facilities was made productive by work from a quite unexpected quarter. As soon as it became known that LEO was working, first the Ordnance Board,[1] the government department responsible for artillery for the British forces, and then others with scientific calculations, approached Lyons with a view to having work done on a service basis. At the beginning, the customers brought their formulas and it was the LEO programmers' job to express them in program terms and then carry out the operations. Again Hemy with his fertile imagination responded to the challenge, taking the slim volume of Cambridge subroutines as his starting point. Later some outside users brought their own programs and the LEO programmers guided their implementation. Hemy was joined in this work by Leo Fantl, who quickly became the LEO mathematical programming expert, able to transmute the algorithms of scientists into finished results, produced more rapidly than was ever possible before.

Fantl was a self-trained mathematician. Arriving in England as a child refugee from Czechoslovakia, before he was old enough to enlist in the RAF he had worked as a farm worker, educating himself with books borrowed from the public library. Then he carried on with correspondence courses while in the services.[2] (Turn to Chapter 14 for Fantl's own account of his work with LEO.)

Ballistics tables for the Ordnance Board were a natural first for the new service, and this was followed by work on weather forecasting for the Meteorological Office, guided missile trajectories for De Havilland Propellers, and many others.[3] The LEO programmers took quiet pleasure improving the work of the Cambridge mathematicians by speeding up a key sequence used in differential equations. It was the nature of the mathematical work that the same sequences were repeated many, many times, so eliminating one instruction could easily mean saving an hour on a long tabulation. It therefore became a practice to pass much-iterated sequences from hand to hand to try to save an order, and then another and yet another. It became like an ingenious endgame, and in the atmosphere that prevailed, one logical problem was much the same as another.

Closer to the home office, calculations were commissioned by the Institute of Actuaries, and new tables were produced for joint and last survivor values.[4] Other work followed for insurance companies. All the work was billed on a formal service basis for each component. Useful revenue was obtained at a time when otherwise there was little but outgoing expenses.

There was a limit, though, to the extent that this could be expanded. Other equipment aimed specifically at mathematical work was beginning to become available as manufacturers followed up the experimental work that had been proceeding, in parallel with Cambridge, at other British universities and at the National Physical Laboratory. While LEO was pricing its services on a basis that sought to provide a reasonable return for the services provided, computer time could sometimes be found elsewhere more cheaply. An internal note recorded sometime later that, "The Meteorological Office are now trying the Ferranti machine because they can get cheaper terms."[5] However, though a target was developed for a significant income from scientific work, it was never seen as more than a bridge until such time as the main revenue was provided by large-scale, regular, clerical work. A special attraction of the scientific work for the future was that it was generally not closely time-dependent; it could therefore make way where necessary in favor of more urgent office applications.

Quite apart from the revenue that was obtained, this service work also made an invaluable contribution to the experience of live running. Some of the runs were very long. Ballistic tables, for example, automatically stepped on through one small change after another in projectile dimension or elevation. Sometimes they ran right through the night, and by now the computer was altogether more reliable. Early in 1952 a reliability test run, at the initiative of the programmers, had repetitively produced tax tables for two and a half days with an operational efficiency of 87 percent, a remarkable figure for the time.[6]

The discipline of the live long runs contributed considerably to the techniques of rapid recovery after faults. Provision was made for clean restarts at prearranged checkpoints so that the minimum of productive time was lost.

Initially this was still using only two slow-speed inputs and two slow-speed outputs. For most mathematical and actuarial work, the loss of efficiency was negligible.

Recruits

There was a very modest recruitment of programmers following the success of the Bakery Valuations job. In another sweep through Lyons, several more candidates emerged. These included Mary Blood and Frank Land, who both became core members of the group. Candidates were invited to take part in Lyons' very first Appreciation course. This was approached with very considerable trepidation. Blood and Land both recall the rigors of the concentrated one-week course, in which they were taught everything from how the computer worked to binary arithmetic and basic programming in packed days, followed by homework in the evenings.

Mary Blood (now Coombs) has described her pleasure at being the first woman accepted. Her father was the formidable Lyons Chief Medical Officer at the time. She studied modern languages at university and became interested in joining the computer activity through the conversations between her father and senior colleagues around the bridge table. She went on to take a prominent part in many LEO applications, starting with the Lyons payroll. Her misfortune was to join at a time when, outside the Teashops, few women achieved even supervisory status within the Lyons empire, and she did not receive the advancement that she might have otherwise.

Frank Land had been a child refugee from Germany and followed his graduation from the London School of Economics with a year's research there. On joining Lyons he was placed in management accounting for the provincial bakeries. He went on to take responsibility for LEO's first incursions into stock control, as well as production control and other fields of application, including the Stock Exchange.

Some months later, another recruit made a major contribution. John Gosden's studies in mathematics were so undistinguished that only his disarming candour saved him. After an apprenticeship under Fantl, working on scientific and other service jobs as they came up, he quickly became a senior programmer.

The Lyons Payroll

The first large-scale office job prepared for Lyons was payroll. From the start it was intended that the programs be available as soon as the full equipment was ready to run them. Lyons by this time had many thousands of employees, and weekly pay for most of them was calculated in the accounting offices in Elms House on batteries of calculators and accounting machines. In an Organization & Methods sense the requirements were very familiar, and there was no problem in producing a comprehensive specification of what the system had to do. Hemy had indeed sketched an outline payroll program to establish the parameters of an office machine in the earliest Cambridge days.

The aim was to fit into a connection set of runs *everything* that had to be done, from the point of receiving details of the hours worked, as recorded on time cards, to that of printing the paychecks. The same data would be used to carry out all the other calculations and listings that customarily had required separate jobs. PAYE was specified to be calculated on the fly after the gross pay brought forward from the previous week had been inserted by accounting machine clerks by reference to tables mounted on screens in front of them. Holiday and sick pay were also calculated in the same run. The cost of National Insurance stamps was deducted, and at the same time listings were prepared for the authorities. The same was done for club and society subscriptions. Another deduction was for the repayment of loans, and these were automatically terminated when the loan had been repaid. Care was taken that deductions did not carry the net pay below a prescribed minimum, in which case only the statutory deductions were made. Labor statistics were accumulated, and a coin analysis carried out to arrive at the total number for each denomination needed to complete all the pay envelopes for each department. There were further refinements as time went on, such as the agreement with the workforce that cash payments should be rounded up or down and the balance carried forward. This significantly reduced the number of coins handled, thus making another labor saving and speeding up the whole process.

The one component of pay that was calculated externally was the premium bonus, the payment for achieving or exceeding production targets. These were based on the performance of changing groups of workers, and one employee might participate in several groups in the course of the week. Because of the logistical complications arising from the very small computer store available for working space, this calculation was excluded and the amounts for each employee submitted as another item of data. It was then, and remained, a LEO systems and programming maxim that a project, although as fully embracing as possible, should never be put at risk by trying to cross a bridge too far.

Having put all this down on paper in nontechnical terms and the requirements and accompanying pro formas approved by the Wages Office management, the flow charts of the job were finalized: first, over-all charts showing the several computer runs and the linkages between them; then the progression from one stage to another in each run; and finally, small logical charts for each of the 20 or 30 instruction stages into which the runs were to be divided. The charts were nontechnical and uncluttered in their presentation. At an early stage it had been decided to replace the rather complex, Greek character-strewn "chartology" that seemed to be emerging by something much simpler that could be under-stood and commented upon by any intelligent lay person associated with the job.

No more detail was included in the charts than was necessary to con-vey the procedures that had to be transformed into instructions. The emphasis was on branchings rather than the calculations that gave rise to them. Care was taken to cover every contingency in the same way that junior clerks might spot oddities and refer them to their supervisors, and to provide for the nonfeasible as well as what was to be expected. There was a sharp consciousness that the pay envelopes had to be completely accurate as well as on time.

While producing the charts there was a step-by-step assessment of the logistics of the job. From early experimentation it was clear that there would need to be some overlaying of the store contents, and this was worked out on a store layout chart. Where a sequence looked as though it might be crucial, the actions were rapidly jotted down by Hemy, who had a gift for making sound off-the-cuff approximations of the space and time required. On the output side, the layout of the paycheck was arranged so as to minimize the number of lines to be printed while still presenting an easy-to-read and uncomplicated account of the company's one regular communication with its employees.

Much of the coding was carried out by John Grover. Most of the other programmers took part in the checking. A feature of the programs was the extent to which they policed both the operation of the computer and the functioning of the programs themselves. Wherever possible, reconcil-iation accounts were inserted to check consistency. Most were obvious, such as checking that the aggregates of gross pay less the aggregates of each deduction equaled the aggregates of net pay. Another was checking that the loan balances carried forward were equal in total to the loan bal-ances brought forward plus new loans minus loan repayments for each unit at a time. The numbers of employees on the payroll were similarly checked. The computer was, in fact, used to the fullest for what it was best at—carrying out simple calculations and comparisons. Multiplications that could not be checked in this way were in some instances subjected to a multiplier-multiplicand reversal and a comparison was made. The overhead of all these checks was not great, but it served to engender a much heightened sense of security. There was always satisfaction when a column of zeros appeared at the end of a run, signifying that all reconciliation accounts were in order.

In July 1953 the programs were complete and two small pilot bakeries had their payrolls run successfully.[7] An immediate step was to place Barnes in charge of Operating, which became a separate activity for the first time.[8] He had working with him two very disciplined characters, Peter Wood and Sid Jenkinson. Between them they established the practices that came to be followed both by the LEO Service Bureau and by outside users when they acquired their own machines. Wood, with a remarkable war record in which he had become a battalion commander in India and Burma, came from the Wages Office. Jenkinson came from the company's car subsidiary, Normand.

Another member of the operating team was Marjorie Coles. She had been leader of a large accounting machine section in the Accounts Office and was carefully chosen to build what was foreseen as a vital component of the whole operation—data preparation. The time had passed for secretaries and whoever could be pressed into service to perform what had become a routine job. Marjorie Coles's experience had prepared her to play a key part in staff selection and training on the new equipment that had taken the place of the jury-rig efforts that had fueled the first production runs. The "comparator" data preparation device now enabled checking and correction to be carried out altogether more rapidly and securely, and operator speeds were built up to match. The LEO Data Preparation Section may have been the first anywhere to undertake the task as a discrete operation. Miss Coles, as she was generally known in those more formal days, brought calm to what were sometimes hectic situations, and her helpfulness became a byword.

The pilot runs were followed by parallel runs of the payroll for the whole of the Cadby Hall Bakeries Department, with the orthodox method still used for payment purposes.[9] Since this was the first major job affecting people outside the offices to be run on LEO, any erring was on the side of caution. However, on February 12, 1954, the LEO paychecks were actually used for the first time to make up pay envelopes, which went into the hands of the bakery staff, 1670 men and women on the other side of the Cadby Hall estate.[10] There was an emergency system in case of machine failure, but in fact neither LEO I nor its successors ever failed to meet their obligation for producing the payroll on time. By the summer the numbers had reached almost 10,000, the cut-off point until a standby arrived.[11]

A payroll on this scale was another world first for LEO. Because of the care that had been employed in constructing the programs, the computer time was 1½ seconds per employee as compared to 8 minutes of human time that it had taken using one of the most efficient precomputer systems anywhere.[12] The speed was twice as fast as had been estimated several years before when a case was still being made for building a computer.

Celebrations and Demonstrations

It was time for a celebration. LEO was featured in a TV newsreel shot on the day of the historic run. There was a demonstration for the press, and Pinkerton gave a talk on *BBC Calling Europe*.[13] The success had been anticipated by Simmons with an internal announcement immediately after the start of the parallel running that LEO is "now virtually complete and within the next few weeks should be capable of undertaking full-scale clerical jobs under regular working conditions." He accompanied this with the very welcome announcement that Lenaerts and Hemy were forthwith to become assistant managers, the former reporting to Pinkerton in Maintenance and the latter reporting to me on the programming side. Barnes was confirmed as Operational Supervisor.[14]

The bald announcement does not convey the full force of the management appointments. The LEO activity was still part of the Lyons offices, and management appointments in the offices were very infrequent. Under the grading system Simmons had pioneered there was a supervision grade, F, with graduations F1 to F3 and, rarely, F4. This covered all senior staff in charge of operations on the ground. To climb as high as their job permitted in the supervisory grade was almost invariably the limit of their promotion expectations or even hopes. Management trainees came in with the expectation that if they fulfilled their promise there were management potentialities, but no time scale was placed on it. Partly the difficulty of making the jump was caused by the few management posts in the organization chart; partly, it was sometimes said, it was because of the shortage of places in the managers' dining room. Including his war service, Hemy had been with Lyons 14 years since being recruited as a management trainee. As for Lenaerts, he had truly risen from the ranks after what had been a quarter century since joining the Lyons offices as a young man.

The seal was set on the occasion with a splendid dinner at the company's Cumberland Hotel, given by the Board:[15]

> to celebrate the inauguration on Christmas Eve 1953 of the first high speed truly automatic electronic calculator to be designed and built for general commercial work and the successful taking over of its first full-scale clerical job, the payroll of Cadby Hall Bakeries.

The triumphant presentation to the press of the payroll job in live operation was just the most significant in a sequence of a great many demonstrations that had taken place ever since there was sufficient of LEO assembled to provide any demonstrable output at all. Among the earliest from outside the company to view this new phenomenon was the then Princess Elizabeth, though at this time in February 1951[16] no more than a test program could be exhibited.

In the same period many internal demonstrations were given to Lyons' staff, from Directors to members of the Clerical Staff Committee. Later there were on-site visits by the entire clerical staff of 2000, who came in parties of around 25 until everyone had had an opportunity to see "the calculator," as it was still known, at work.[17] A decision had been made that no one was to feel that his or her job or status was threatened by what was going on,[18] and many of the early demonstrations were rudimentary as a result. Indeed, more than a few of those who came to the show with high expectations must have gone away wondering how so large a device could produce so little. Sometimes what was shown could be preempted without difficulty by anyone in the audience with the very rapid mental arithmetic speed common among the office supervisors and others. Nonetheless, it was firmly believed that it was imperative to keep staff in personal touch with what was happening rather than let the computer be feared as a Frankenstein creation taking shape behind closed doors.

As time went on, politicians and statesmen paid their visits, together with members of learned societies, industrial and government scientists, business people, and administrators of all kinds. One such visitor in the 1950s was Mr. McPherson, a vice president of IBM. He declared himself impressed, but quite certain that his chief, Tom Watson, the dominant leader of the company, would never accept a course of action that would imperil the highly profitable ongoing trade in punched cards.

Thompson took a very special interest. Whenever he could he introduced the demonstration. Though to others it became a chore, he enjoyed very much showing off LEO's prowess, and like nothing better than to stand on the platform of false flooring and share his enthusiasm with an invited audience. The arrival of the Lyons payroll as a going concern increased outside interest, of course, and the demonstrations became more frequent than ever.

The Growing Load

It was in some ways unfortunate that the arrival of this new demonstration piece came at a time when loading the single computer was becom-

ing more and more crucial. There was only the one machine to serve all
purposes. As routine Lyons office work added to the load, regular service
jobs made their demands, and engineers continued their development
work, the time available for program trials was inevitably squeezed.
Programmers became accustomed to carrying out much of their work at
night, at weekends, and at whatever time could be made available to
them. Often this came at short notice. Sometimes management was consulted when the need seemed indisputable, but generally programmers
responded to what became "the law of the situation," and they ferreted
out trial time for themselves when their own small entitlements were
exhausted.

In all LEO's short life as an organization, the only discord of any note
between sections of its personnel was that arising from divisions
between programmers and engineers on this question of trial time. Each
had objectives that they were determined to meet and they each had to
extract their sustenance from a cake that was laughably small. The engineers were irritated when fault conditions were encountered and the
programmers would not relinquish the system rapidly enough. For their
part, the programmers were sometimes convinced that it would be faster
to trace a machine fault by examining store compartments through the
twin oscilloscopes rather than by clearing the system and running test
programs and applying electrical margins.

Disagreement on the point of handover gave rise to a very rare
involvement by Simmons in the day-to-day working of the project. With
his positive belief in the division of labor, he insisted that there be no
blurred lines.[19] The detection of faults was the responsibility of the engineers and the handover must be immediate. However, in spite of its
authority the directive was sometimes honored in the breach.

Because of the excess time often spent in nonbusiness hours, an effort
was made at one point to obtain overtime pay for staff in special circumstances. Accordingly, payments of less than one dollar per hour were
given to staff working authorized overtime beyond a given threshold. A
record that remains from a period in which payroll programs were under
reliability trials shows two programmers, two operators, and the maintenance engineering supervisor enjoying this concession, with a senior programmer clearly working off the clock.[20] Later, regular shift work became
common when longer service jobs needed many hours of running, but
for what could be described as "random" trials the usual practice was to
follow the Lyons supervisor custom of finishing the outstanding work
without extra reward. Even though this tradition had to be stretched at
times, it did give the programmers the freedom to decide for themselves
when they would win their trial time, without the constraint of having to
record time for payment purposes.

Although most programmers found it satisfying, it was not an easy life. The expectation was that they would be at their desks at the normal time the next morning, for it was a cooperative effort and the absence of one could hold up others. One compensation that loomed very large in what became a way of life was the privilege for programmers and operators to eat at night in the managers' dining room, on the top floor of the Administration building. There was a camaraderie among the bakery, kitchen, and dispatch managers on the night shift that put the cares that beset the computer staff into perspective, and they generally emerged with a lighter step than when they went in.

5

The Second LEO and LEO Computers Ltd.

1954–1957

Little time was allowed to elapse between the successful start to the Lyons payroll and the formal decision to build a LEO Mark II. It had always been regarded as axiomatic that there must be a standby if any large volume of time-critical work were to be entrusted to the new medium. Now, with payroll running live and other applications upon which the company would depend for its smooth operation well underway, the need was urgent.

The general approach to the design of a LEO II had been agreed upon within the LEO team a month before the switchover to live running of the pilot payroll, and by May of 1954 Pinkerton had submitted a firm outline of the design.[1] LEO I had intentionally been closely modeled on EDSAC I, but now there was the opportunity for independent engineering, though time was again of the essence. There was the constraint, too, that the prime reason for the new machine was to provide cover for the load on LEO I. Consequently there was a limit to which facilities could be enhanced, notwithstanding the advances in technology and the operational experience that had been gained.

One important improvement in the design was to make store access more rapid. A striking proposal by Lenaerts was adopted that enabled the mercury delay line storage tubes to be reduced to a quarter of their former length.[2] This not only made a welcome inroad into the onerous space requirements, but also considerably increased overall speed. There were also improvements to the arithmetic unit, with more fast registers being provided.

Another enhancement was to increase the word size, thus making it possible to address a four times larger store if so desired. The programmers had quickly come to learn that the LEO store capacity, though double that on EDSAC I, was still inadequate for most clerical applications, giving rise to a great deal of work on store management. Others not so closely involved sometimes found it difficult to accept that twice what was sufficient for abstruse scientific computations was not enough for run-of-the-mill data processing. There was a suspicion that unnecessary complication was being allowed to intrude.

Additionally, care was taken by the engineers to ensure that further peripheral attachments could be made. This facilitated the connection of magnetic tape and magnetic drums when suitable equipment became available.

The Go-Ahead for LEO II

With the outline design agreed upon, Simmons made a detailed report to Isadore Gluckstein, a Managing Director, in which he recommended that the go-ahead be given for building not one but two (or possibly three) LEO IIs.[3] He listed statistics for the group of Lyons jobs on which programming work was in progress and was able to show that they exceeded the normal hours capacity of a single machine and also provided a very satisfactory financial return. It was calculated, in fact, that the net savings on the seven Lyons jobs listed would be almost equivalent annually to the total capital cost of building a LEO II. This, it was pointed out, was "quite apart from the value of the additional and quicker information that will be provided . . ."

At this point the attitude seems to have changed from one in which a LEO II would provide cover for the LEO I to one in which the LEO I would be phased out, leaving two LEO IIs to provide cover for each other. In the event, LEO I, for all its relative slowness and fallibility, remained in service with Lyons for another 10 years.[4]

In making his recommendations, Simmons went on to discuss the possibility of LEO IIs also being supplied to outside users. He declared,[5] "The likelihood of our going to be able to get orders for machines either in this country or elsewhere is difficult to assess. As far as we know, ours is the only machine which at the moment is doing clerical work, but we know that a number of manufacturers of office machines and other electrical apparatus, particularly in the USA, but in this country as well, are spending a lot of money to get machines for clerical work into the market."

He went on to warn that, "There is a special difficulty that we have to contend with, that, because Lyons are not manufacturers of office machines or equipment, potential customers will go to those companies that are, rather than to us." He continued. "This impression of amateurism is being accentuated whenever we are asked whether we intend to build LEOs for sale or hire (as we are almost invariably asked after every demonstration) by our present indefinite attitude."

On these grounds he recommended that, "the time has come for a definite declaration that we are ready to build LEO IIs for sale or hire and that our tactics should be framed against the background of this fundamental policy." He went on to urge that "having a third model in being, or at least in building, would make it easier to find a customer—since otherwise any prospect would need to be told that he would have to wait 12 to 18 months for delivery. And even if the worst came to the worst and we did not find a customer for a sale, having a third machine would enable us either to use it ourselves or, better still, to set up a LEO service for hiring time to other commercial users."

In what had become the customary way, Simmons was given the Lyons Board approval to go ahead with building LEO II within a week. After a boardroom discussion on June 30, 1954, it was agreed that "we should let it be known that we are prepared to build other Mark IIs for sale or hire." There was also agreement to a recommendation that a subsidiary company should be formed. "This would help to professionalize the project," said Simmons, "and help to get rid of our amateur status."[6]

In addition to what was anticipated from the employment and supply of computers and of computer time, there was a belief at this time that there might also be a return from royalties on the input/output innovations, for which patent applications had been filed.[7] In considering the sales prospects, the view was that, in the U.S., it would be better to license one of the existing companies and not to compete with them in that market since, in Simmons's words,[7] "the big companies have already spent millions of pounds on electronic calculators and are currently ready to spend millions more."

However, it emerged some time later that a U.S. electronics company had applied for a patent for a similar approach two years earlier than Lyons had. The fact that LEO I had provided the first practical embodiment of the buffering of input and output was irrelevant, and any dreams that existed of large royalty returns from across the Atlantic were dispelled.[8]

Teashops Distribution

After payroll, the first on the list of applications that had been submitted to the Lyons Board was that for Teashops Distribution.

From the time that a computer was first discussed there had been thinking about how it could be applied to the work of the teashops. This was the Lyons activity with the "lowest-spending power" per customer, and profitability depended on the utmost economy in all the supporting services. In the past, a monumental clerical effort had to be expended on cash control in the two hundred or more prewar teashops. Now, with waitresses replaced by self-service, the main target for efficiency measures was the replenishment phase. Almost everything was ordered daily by the teashop managers, using a thick pad of preprinted order forms. Some products, like bread rolls, were delivered more than once each day in order to maintain the reputation for freshness and crispness.

To achieve the turn-around of daily orders and deliveries, the clerical work both in the teashops and the offices was intensive. In a very few hours the orders from all the shops had to be collated so that requisitions could be forwarded to the bakeries and kitchens and other departments. Then the orders had to be valued and the goods assembled and loaded onto the waiting distribution vans.

In evaluating the contribution that the computer might make to this process, the major obstacle that presented itself was the sheer mass of the data represented by 180 teashops, each ordering 250 lines. Quite apart from the cost of the data preparation labor represented by the system as it stood, the need to wait for it to be completed ran counter to the unchangeable urgency of the job. It was apparent that if the computer were to play a productive part, an altogether different approach was required.

That approach was discovered after a great deal of searching through heaps on heaps of order forms to unearth an ordering pattern. What surfaced was that while orders from each teashop varied from day to day, there seemed in most cases very little difference between the orders on any one day and the same day in other weeks. The idea therefore emerged of having each manager place a standard order for each day of the week and then to notify of changes if necessary.

This was a long, long time before on-line working became practical, but the existence of punched cards as one of the input media gave feasibility to the idea. What was arranged was that the managers would be telephoned at a set time each afternoon for their last-minute changes. These were punched directly into cards by the telephone operators, who wore headsets to free their hands. The cards would then be sorted into teashop order and run in parallel with the standard order file to give the computer information necessary to process the modified orders for the day. There had, of course, to be arrangements for the managers to make permanent alterations to their orders when the seasons or pattern of trade changed. There had to be provision, too, for management to override orders at the last moment: by changing some hot dishes for salads if a heat wave was forecast, for example, or making substitutions if there was a kitchen problem.

This was a revolutionary scheme, and it is remarkable that it was accepted by what was by nature a very traditional, conservative part of the Lyons organization. The family directors, Mr. Julian and Mr. Felix, had to decide whether to place the whole supply side of their business, not just accounting, in the hands of a computer organization that still could scarcely be described as mature. Live running started on October 20, 1954, ahead of the timetable indication given to them. Forty-two teashops were involved to begin with.

After the job had been running for only a few days, the daily report from the Wembley Teashop contained the entry:[9]

> The head staff at this shop would like to give thanks for LEO. This is a wonderful timesaver, work saver, and we are grateful for it.

Teashops Distribution has always been regarded as an archetypal LEO job, combining, as it did, creative O&M work with what again needed to be intricate programming in the logistic sense. A full account of it is given in a contemporary demonstration script, which appears in Appendix C.[10] It was rescued from oblivion by Colin Tully, once a member of the LEO programming staff and later a senior lecturer at York University.

A user's view of the impact of the computer on the Teashops organization is given by Ralph Land in Chapter 18.

In a reminiscence written after a long and distinguished career in systems and computer management and management consultancy, Donald Moore recently declared:[11]

> I look back with regret that LEO did not survive, the team and the machine were models of achievement at the time and the teashop application illustrated the value of the integration of the user management, the system designer and the various operators, computer, van delivery, etc. It was done then by voice over ordinary telephones and I question how much better are the results today with modern technology.

Formation of LEO Computers Ltd.

Within a few days of the start of the Teashops Distribution application, LEO Computers Ltd. was incorporated.[12] Its purpose was to give substance to the decision "to be prepared to build further LEO IIs for sale or hire." Anthony Salmon, who had been involved in the patents venture, was appointed as a family presence on the board, and with him Simmons and Thompson were named. Initially the share capital was only a nominal $300. Five years later, Pinkerton, Barnes, and I were also appointed as directors; by this time the capitalization had reached a level more appropriate to the scale of operations.[13]

At the outset, there were no exaggerated expectations. No numerical estimates of computer sales had been forecast in the Simmons report that triggered the formation of the subsidiary, and no steps were taken to equip the company for a higher scale of activity. Rather, the progression was more of a see-how-it-goes nature. A second machine was required as the standby for the first. Given that these would prove out the designs and that to build them the manufacturing facilities would have to be in place, it seemed reasonable to capitalize on these assets by offering further copies to outsiders.

The computer market as a whole in Britain in 1954 was not visualized as large; few companies were seen by Lyons as having the background Organization & Methods (O&M) resources and experience required to carry out the systems analysis necessary. Equally, few companies were believed to have the top management backup called for if significant change were to be effected. While there was good reason to believe from the informal inquiries that had been received that a solid potential market existed, it was not thought of as being, in office machine terms, large-scale.

Accordingly, though the formation of the company was an important statement of intent and a significant signal to the outside world, it at first made little difference to organization within the LEO operation. One change, perhaps too little recognized at the time, was in the relationship with the Lyons Board. In the past, Simmons had made his recommendations directly to the Chairman or a Managing Director, and, because of the trust in his judgment and his care in timing, quick agreement could be expected to be forthcoming. Now there was the intermediary of a family member able to form his own views based on his experience in the core activities of the company, to follow his own intuitions, and, as time went on, to take personal control of segments of the business where he judged that to be appropriate.

LEO had grown out of being the internal Clerical Department sideline as it had been born.

Sales Force

Another change was to put LEO Computers Ltd. on a conventional business footing by appointing a marketing person. Geoffrey Mills was transferred from his post as Personnel Manager of the Clerical Department of Lyons.[14] He brought with him the credentials of having played a creative part in the revolutionary "Recordak" invoicing job for the wholesale bakeries 20 years before.[15] This use of film as the only retained copy of the customer's order, delivery note, and invoice was to provide the essence of the successor LEO application, which is referred to later (p. 56). Mills did valuable work in commissioning clearly written brochures and an attractive film. He also provided what was then the comparative novelty of "Executive Courses" to enable Senior Management to grasp the essentials and practicalities of computer systems, and to enable them to feel that they were not being "blinded with science" when those they had appointed reported to them. However, time proved that this was not truly his forte. The task on hand was to convince management that full-scale, program-stored electronic computers were worth all the expense, risk, effort, and potential upheaval that they seemed to entail. A "No" vote at any level could be sufficient to outweigh all but the most enthusiastic support elsewhere. In these circumstances, anyone who had not been directly involved with mounting successful computer applications was at a severe disadvantage, and the appointment was terminated.

Anthony Salmon's own view, based on his experience in Lyons' mainstream activities, was that a good salesman could usually be successful whatever he was selling. Accordingly, he moved an area manager from his own Confectionery Department and set him to follow up leads and to make cold calls to likely contacts. "Hank" Levy was instantly likeable and a very good bridge player, able to argue the theory of the game with the best. However, while he played a useful part in bringing in a number of bureau customers, his lack of both computer and office knowledge stood in the way of his making a positive contribution in the wider field. Among the applications staff there was always the fear that he would reinforce the image, so assiduously cultivated by competitors and relished by journalists, of Lyons, the Teashops firm, being too unlikely a supplier to be entrusted with the nervous system of any other business.

Another salesman, a wartime naval officer, John Masters, was more successful. Having learned endurance through having two ships sink beneath him, he was able to exhibit patience and pertinacity in relationships with the senior staff of potential customers that would have been beyond the capability of his more volatile colleagues.

Regrouping

There was a setback soon after the establishment of the new company, when Hemy left to join the emerging computer activity at EMI. Coming later onto the scene, EMI aimed to leapfrog LEO technologically, and started with the advantage of being an established electronics firm. The opportunity that arose enabled Hemy to again be in the forefront of development for office computing needs. The pioneering experience he had gained was an invaluable asset to take with him. He had made a great contribution to LEO's success in harnessing the dynamo of EDSAC to the special needs of office work, and went on to play a key role in the design of EMI systems that, not surprisingly, exhibited many of LEO's characteristics.

The move came at an inconvenient time, but the ranks closed at once and no hiatus was experienced. Fantl went from leading the service activities to taking over Hemy's payroll responsibilities and was aided by Mary Blood, who had been working on the Lyons payroll for some time. Grover and Land took on an increasing variety of other office applications. Gosden, too, played an important part in ensuring that there was no slackening of tempo by quickly picking up Hemy's role as liaison with the design engineers. Although he had never worked with Hemy, the change took place in a seamless way and the programmer-perspective input into the instruction code definition and other aspects of the embryo LEO II was uninterrupted.

The growing scientific and actuarial load was passed on to two talented mathematicians who had recently been recruited for that purpose: Jim Smith, who had graduated from Imperial College, London and gone on to become senior programmer, and Ernest Roberts from Oxford University who became his deputy. Together they built a unit able to hold its own with specialists anywhere.

By the end of 1955 the Programming Department was thus on a structured basis, with seasoned staff providing a firm basis for expansion as LEO II reached completion. The team leaders possessed strikingly different temperaments and came from many different backgrounds, but all showed the way by the example of the quality and vigor of their own hands-on work. The only shortcoming was that, strong as the chiefs were, there were very few Indians to support them. An "end of term" survey just before the start of the August 1955 holiday season indicated that the total programming staff numbered no more than twelve, with three trainees. They were responsible for eight new Lyons applications, three major external office applications, programming external market research mathematical and scientific assignments as they were won, maintaining existing programs and recoding them for LEO II, and preparing courses for LEO II. This was in addition to ancillary tasks, such as involvement in recruitment and teaching.[16]

The report warned that, "it is not at all impossible that during this period work for Lyons might have to be delayed in favor of work for external customers." Notice was also given that the time was approaching for a new group to be established, with the special task of maintaining existing Lyons programs. The request for additional staff was still couched within the frugal ambience of early LEO organization. Five extra staff were called for by mid-1956 after allowance had been made for one departure. The need for assistant managerial appointments from among existing staff was stressed. The pressure under which the leaders were themselves working constituted a brake on the rate at which newcomers could be absorbed and contributed considerably to the very narrow horizons for recruitment.

The operations side was also becoming stretched by the need to prepare for LEO II, and Ted Rowley, an experienced Wages Office manager, was transferred to take charge of existing operations, freeing Barnes to spend more of his time on preparing operating procedures for the new equipment.[17]

Return Visit

With LEO I regularly processing large-scale office jobs for Lyons and the construction of LEO II under way, a return visit was made to the United States to check on progress there and to gather new ideas.

Much had been accomplished at home in the eight years that had passed. The special input/output arrangements essential for integrated office applications had been brought into spectacularly successful operation. The techniques for secure programming, enabling accurate results to be produced to a tight timetable, had been firmly established. The Lyons payroll served by LEO I had reached the 10,000 upper limit insisted upon until a standby was available. The Teashops were being supplied under the LEO distribution system, and other key jobs upon which Lyons' day-to-day operations depended were on the way. All this had been backed by the development of strong maintenance and recovery techniques to ensure that faults were rapidly tracked down and the system brought back into service close to the point reached in the work upon which it was engaged. The Operations unit was running both in-house and outside work in a professional, routine way.

There was little corresponding achievement in office computing elsewhere in Britain. At the Office Management Association Conference on "Computers in the Office" held at Eastbourne in May of 1955, 11 manufacturers were listed as being ready to supply electronic computers.[18] Of these companies, six were British and the remainder were from the United States. In all, 17 models were offered, though in the event three of these failed to reach the point of delivery. Almost all were basically scientific systems without provision for the special needs of clerical work. None, whatever their specification, had yet been delivered to users in Britain. Of those that could be identified as directed toward data processing, the very low-capacity BTM 1201, the Powers Samas PCC, the Elliott 405, and the IBM 650 were still months away from installation in the UK. That was equally the case with what was presented as the general-purpose Ferranti Perseus.

Such electronic devices as were in use were no more than adjuncts to punched-card systems. Among these was the BTM 542 multiplier, which, drawing on IBM patents, had made an immediate impact and had secured over a hundred orders in 1954 alone. It was, however, little more than a faster electronic counterpart of established mechanical punched-card multipliers. The more versatile PCC was on its way, but still relied on a conventional punch-card machine plug board for its instructions.[19]

It was therefore with some confidence that the follow-up visit was embarked upon. On this occasion, Thompson was accompanied by Barnes, leaving Pinkerton and myself to run the shop at home. They were soon struck by the general acceptance in the United States that computers were the wave of the future. Large enterprises, both commercial and governmental, were making substantial investments in computer equipment and in the applications to run them. Prominent among them was the Bank of America in California, where an enormous investment had been made in a custom-built system engineered by the Stanford Research Institute. The aim was to maintain the clients' accounts and to carry out ancillary tasks such as overdraft listings, stops, and the rest. It was an ambitious scheme at this stage. However, ERMA, the computer employed, with its wired-in program, was not a system with general application. At the Metropolitan Life Insurance Company in New York they were shown such a general-purpose system, a million-dollar UNIVAC computer, that was being wholly devoted to a single actuarial application. They also saw experimental census tabulations at the Bureau of Census in Washington D.C., where the high cost of transcribing data onto cards was leading to determined work on mark-sensing. In the industrial field, they saw UNIVACs on payrolls and other tasks at United Steel in Pittsburgh, and preparations for a similar installation at General Electric in Louisville. At other plants they saw rather small-scale office work being carried out on IBM 702s that had been installed for scientific rather than business applications.

Apart from the technical quality of equipment and the degree of market acceptance among large organizations, Thompson and Barnes were less impressed.[20] On the systems side they noted the continued adherence to punched-card methodology. Series of runs were being employed to complete jobs that, with the facilities available, should have been accomplished more straightforwardly. In his summary report to the Lyons Directors,[20] Thompson declared:

> It can be said that despite a prodigious expenditure in time and money in the USA the amount of use of automatic computers on office work is negligible. There appears to be no example of regular use of a computer in the way LEO is used.

He went on to add:

> Nowhere did we see a computer which was doing jobs to a regular planned schedule.

The comments on the return visit to the Pentagon were particularly caustic:

> There is one UNIVAC in the Pentagon, not really in use, and there are more computers on order. There seems to be ample evidence that they have no real idea of organizing a job for a computer.

This was not for lack of resources, they declared:

> Judging from the number of Colonels of the Army, Captains of the Navy, and other high ranking officers and even higher ranking civilian personnel . . . involved in trying to use electronic computers for controlling the supply needs of the forces, there must be at least the equivalent of a division of men and women involved in this operation.

In the tour of the large administrative and business industrial installations, much more had been seen of UNIVAC than IBM. The reactions of the party to what they were told and shown at the IBM computer showrooms and plant is, therefore, particularly revealing. Discussing business computing with a vice-president at the Madison Avenue showrooms, they discerned no enthusiasm for the development. His view was that payroll could not be done economically on electronic computers. The payroll in the IBM computer plant at Poughkeepsie did not pay off, he told them. However, the impetus behind computers in general and the investment backing it were clearly enormous. They were able to watch customers' checking out programs on IBM 702 and 650 systems in the facilities provided at Madison Avenue and, at, the factory in upstate New York, they saw for themselves the production lines of the more advanced IBM 704 and IBM 705. Many systems were being assembled and checked-out concurrently. There were more than a hundred orders for these powerful and, by British standards, prohibitively expensive models. Though many of these were for the mathematical 704, the general-purpose 705 was also clearly in demand. A technical aspect that made an impression was the use of magnetic core storage with the 705 system. It was noted, too, that though the 705 was a decimal system its programs could be tried out on the supplanted 702.

Most significantly, Thompson reported to the Lyons Board:

> There is evidence that the fundamental requirements for putting information into the computer and for taking it out are gradually being realized. IBM has just announced that they are to make a modification to their 705 model, which will enable multiple input and output equipment to work simultaneously with computation within the machine.

At one time it had been believed that this was an essential architectural feature for which LEO held the rights, and that the use by others would, at least, yield royalties. But the hopes had faded by this time and now LEO had to look forward to eventual competition of an altogether more formidable kind.

Another feature of the American scene that made a deep impression on the visitors was the rapid advance in education and training. At Harvard there was already a Masters' course on Electronic Computing, with students spending a year working on Harvard Mk II. At a lower level, their estimate was that the number of people who had been put through a course to prepare office jobs to be done on automatic computers "probably exceeds 10,000." For all the disparagement of much of the work on business applications, a major message was that, with so much investment and commitment and acceptance in the USA, LEO's lead must be in danger of slipping away. This was, though, intended as a call for renewed effort rather than as anything like an acceptance that the days of LEO preeminence were numbered.

Ford Motor Company

Thompson and Barnes arrived back to fresh encouragement. While they had been away, a payroll suite commissioned by the Ford Motor Company had completed its check-out on LEO I and its pilot runs had started. Instrumental in the project was a Mr. Bradley, an old colleague of Simmons in the Office Management Association, who was in charge of office administration at the Ford UK headquarters at Dagenham, Essex. Bradley did not give the impression of being an adventurous man, but he had so much faith in Simmons that he probably did not even feel one in embarking on this pioneering project.

The Chairman of Ford UK had been one of the earliest outsiders to see LEO at work on the Lyons payroll,[21] and a request for a proposition for similar work to be carried out for Ford followed swiftly. Bradley's surprise at the two thick blue-bound volumes that were handed to him as the draft specification of the payroll requirements for the Dagenham hourly workforce was an indication of the common underestimation of the detail that goes into the fabric of most large-scale office jobs. He declared that it had certainly not been as complicated when he had been closely involved.

Responsible for the implementation of the payroll was Fantl, together with a very small team that included Mary Blood, who had the benefit of experience on the Lyons payroll. The speed with which the project was brought to fruition was remarkable. Though LEO I had been tamed by now, it was far from user-friendly in the facilities that it offered, and it still exhibited a youthful temperament from time to time. The report was handed to Bradley in May, the order was placed by Ford in August,[22] parallel running started in November,[23] and the first live run took place at the beginning of December 1955, when paychecks produced by LEO I were used to pay the first batch of 700 employees.[24]

A significant contribution to the slickness of the operation was the very small amount of computer time used to check out the programs. Great care was taken to ensure that the programs were accurate when they were presented to the computer for the first time. When, as was almost unavoidable, errors still occurred in the trial runs, the corrections, however small, were checked by another programmer before the program was returned to the computer. It was not enough to find an error; what was corrected had to explain fully what had gone wrong. It was not a matter of hierarchy; junior checked senior as much as the other way around. As a result, the whole trial process was completed in only part of the time that has since become habitual, notwithstanding the introduction of more sophisticated tools than the two spyholes into the binary interior provided in the LEO I console.

Partway through the brief programming period, two recruits, Peter Hermon, an Oxford mathematician who had joined after a period of research there followed by teaching at a grammar school, and Arthur Payman, a Cambridge philosopher, were assigned to Fantl. They were put to work at once, and not surprisingly their recollections of their rapid immersion bear little resemblance to the orderliness with which the principal programs were completed. Both learned their programming on this job and went on to become leading figures in LEO applications. An account of Hermon's baptism on the Ford payroll job is given in his own reminiscence (see Chapter 17).

The backing of a strong O&M organization at Dagenham facilitated the move into live running after only two weeks of parallel running. There was concern at the brevity of this period in the LEO organization and caution was advised, particularly as Ford's emergency arrangements in the event of a failure to produce the payroll on time were rudimentary. Bradley was prepared to repose greater confidence in LEO's ability to produce regular timely results than even the home team itself. His confidence was not misplaced, and the Dagenham payroll soon became the largest full-scale office job to be run so far on a service basis anywhere in the world.

Major Lyons Jobs

Further major jobs followed for Lyons. Hard on the heels of the Ford payroll came an invoicing system to handle all the paperwork for Lyons' largest sales and distribution organization, the Wholesale Bakeries Rails Department, responsible for cake and pie supplies to shopkeepers all over Britain. A special feature of the system was that only one piece of paper served as order, packing note, delivery note, and invoice. No paper copy was retained either in the dispatch or in the offices. Instead, a film copy was retained that could be referred to if any query arose. The orders were taken by a salesman, who also collected the cash on a one week's credit basis, so that there was little in the way of an accounting system.

The system had originally been introduced in 1935 to cope with a considerable increase in the wholesale bakery business. The contribution of Geoffrey Mills and the Systems Research Office has been referred to earlier (see p. 49). In his book, *LEO and the Managers*, Simmons explains:[25]

> The existing quite orthodox system was proving too clumsy to cope with the speed of operation desired. The system was breaking down simply because of the volume of paper . . .

The challenge faced, he stresses, was:

> Not merely to carry out an existing operation as efficiently as possible, not merely to make the best use of conventional office machinery. . . .

With only a reel of film left in the office and only the total to be paid added to the original order to form an invoice, Simmons stresses the courage of the General Management—that is, the family directors—in being prepared to go along with the scheme:

> The company, which had long enjoyed a reputation for being enterprising in its own fields of catering and food manufacture, was evi-

dently equally prepared to experiment in a purely clerical field, even though it would strike across the accepted procedures on the so-called productive side of the business.

"It was quick and economical because there was so little to it" was his summing up.[26] The new challenge in seeking to transfer this system to LEO was therefore more severe. The job had already been pared down to the bone, but LEO was still able to pay its way by heavily reducing the key-punching and by absorbing subtasks surrounding it.[27] As by-products of the invoice calculations, LEO automatically produced instructions as to which of a range of cartons was to be used for each order, calculated the assembly trolley loadings in the dispatch and the standard time allowance for packers and loaders, and checked the carriage-free-of-charge thresholds. It also provided each salesman with a cash collection list, incorporating amounts not yet paid for previous weeks' deliveries, checked the cash banked, and provided a variety of statistics to serve management at all levels. In the background, the programs effected feasibility checks and made the now standard provision for rapid restarts. In all respects—method of delivery, efficiency of loading, and dispatch, salesman interface, and in paper economy—it remained a model system in which LEO played a thoroughly integrated part. Grover was again in the lead in the execution of the programming.

The next big Lyons job concerned the company's tea stocks at Greenford. Frank Land was responsible for this job, and the application that resulted must have been near to another first in its treatment of large-scale stock control. Deeply implanted in the business that it served, the job maintained control on the thousands of chests of tea, classified for different flavors, colors, strengths, aromas, and other characteristics, and followed them as they were mixed in prescribed proportions to produce the company's famous packeted blends. There were also the usual valuations to check that the permitted cost for each blend had been adhered to and to arrive at the overall value of stock. Additionally, the computer application provided senior management with rapid information about stocks that had never been available before.

Among other stock control jobs for which Land was responsible in this period was one related to the company's Reserve Stores of raw materials for the manufacturing units. These had been set up during the war and scattered around Britain to achieve the utmost security of supply. The job determined the appropriate store from which each requisition was to be shipped in order to achieve the utmost economy.

Further new ground was broken with a production control application for a clock manufacturer in which there was a "family" interest. Oliver Standingford had been placed in charge of its administration in an effort to repair its failing fortunes. The task of fitting the "breakdown" of products into their many components and subassemblies within the tiny store space available was one of the most mind-breaking jobs that any of the LEO range ever attempted. The project succeeded, but the company's malaise was too far gone, and only experience survived from this exercise. Land was helped in this exercise by Betty Newman, another of the increasing number of young women programmers joining the team.

6
LEO II in the Field
1957–1958

Building LEO II

After the Office Management Association's May 1955 Computer Conference (see p. 51), Simmons reported:[1]

> It was noticeable that almost all the questions of fact about the use of computers were left to Mr. Thompson. The result was that there was a general impression that all the other companies were still hoping to be able to do something suitable but as yet had nothing to offer. On the other hand, though they were prepared to accept everything that was said about LEO as definite fact they were still unable to accept the idea that LEO Computers was really intending to manufacturer and install computers for other people.

Simmons stressed the importance of getting LEO II into operation if this disbelief was to be dispelled. However, the system was already beginning to fall behind its original timetable. In the request for agreement to proceed with building that Simmons had submitted to the Lyons Chief Executive Mr. Isadore, in 1954 he had forecast that a "LEO Mark II should not take more than 18 months to complete from the date of starting."[2] Later, Thompson had produced a detailed month-by-month itinerary for a second LEO II aiming to be ready to start testing individual units by June of 1955, and completing the machine by the end of the year, providing that all the components and auxiliary equipment could be obtained from manufacturers when needed.[3]

There were two major impediments. One was that the engineering resources were, if anything, even thinner in relation to their commitments than those of the programming wing (p. 50).[4] The other was that, in addition to completing the urgently needed basic standby for LEO I, there was a cloud of demands for the consideration and implementation of additional features and auxiliaries.[5]

At the start of 1955 the design and production personnel were much the same as those who had constructed LEO I with remarkable economy. There were two design engineers, Shaw and Gibbs, reporting to Pinkerton, who was again personally leading that aspect of the work. Lenaerts continued to contribute, though he was heavily engaged with his responsibility as head of maintenance. This little group was also responsible for any changes that became necessary to LEO I and its ancillary equipment. They were assisted by an instrument maker, a drawing tracer, and an apprentice. Production was, as it had been with LEO I, in the hands of Kaye, whose total staff consisted of a supervisor (Dutton), a circuit inspector, two part-time wirers, and two people controlling the scheduling and ordering of components, issuing documentation to the subcontractors, and inspecting the units when they were received. Here too the proposals for expansion were extremely modest. They consisted only of two trainee engineers to cover both design and maintenance requirements, three semiskilled staff for production, and two additional apprentices.[6]

By August of 1955 the fall behind the original timetable was causing severe concern to the programming management. The loading of LEO I was proceeding inexorably. Gaps left by limiting the expansion on one key job were filled by the insertion of another. The extent of the dislocation that would be caused by a breakdown of a day or two for whatever reason was increasing all the time, notwithstanding such emergency arrangements as were in place for most time-critical jobs. Additionally, time was slipping by for being in a position to press home the decision to interest outside organizations in acquiring systems of their own. It was urged that getting the prototype LEO II designed, built, tested, and running remain the main task and, to that end, after a final review, the facilities and logic design should be frozen.[7]

"Floating point" was cited as an example. "It may be very desirable indeed in subsequent all-purpose models," ran the Programming submission, but it "should not be allowed to occupy the time of any engineer who could make a contribution to the basic LEO II."

There were a number of significant additions to the engineering strength in 1956, on both the electronic and mechanical sides, but progress inevitably suffered from the earlier underestimation of the resources needed to add new features and the distraction caused by them. There was a natural desire to meet the perceived and anticipated requirements of potential customers already aware of the facilities available in one or other of the generally less sophisticated systems spoken of at the Eastborne Conference. The needs for an auxiliary drum and a high-speed printer were particularly pressing, but there were no specialist staff available for them. Similarly, Lyons O&M had made a very strong case for a mark-sensing document reader to relieve the drudgery of data preparation, and work was proceeding on this, too, drawing time and thought from technical management, on whom the completion of the basic system depended.

Additionally, the need was perceived for dedicated work on magnetic cores if the new model was to hold its own for long in the marketplace. IBM, it was pointed out, already had machines in the field employing this development. Again, the need for additional skilled engineers able to take the initiative was urged by the Programming Manager in a rare call across the fence that divided the two specialties.

Given that so much was attempted with such slender resources, it is not surprising that LEO II was not fully operational until May of 1957.[8] However, Simmons's fears that there would be no orders until the prototype was in operation were not borne out. The continued high performance of LEO I, the intimate discussion of outside user's applications, and the evidence of progress on LEO II were sufficient to bring in several orders along the way.

Tobacco, Steel, and Cars

The first organization to take the plunge and sign a contract for a LEO II of its own was W. D. & H. O. Wills,[9] then a leading cigarette and tobacco manufacturer. It was part of the Imperial Tobacco Group, which has itself since been absorbed into a diversified conglomerate. The introduction was through Anthony Salmon, who drew on the family's long-standing connection with the tobacco industry. The application concerned the invoicing and distribution of a wide range of products, from Gold Flake cigarettes to chewing plug, produced by the Wills factory in Bristol.

The study had been started by Grover, but at an early stage he left to join his old colleague, Hemy, at EMI. With his firmly disciplined approach, Grover had played an outstanding part in the earliest applications for Lyons, and he had been a senior figure to whom newcomers could be allotted for training with confidence that, however exuberant they might be, they would be allowed no shortcuts around LEO modalities. His place was filled at very short notice by Hermon, with his first senior appointment. Over the period that followed, Hermon made a searching in-depth analysis, and at the end of it could be said to know at least as much about the minutiae of packing practice and the tangle of special terms as any one person in the Wills organization itself.

On the detailed programming side, Hermon was given the help of a very able young assistant, Bob Brett, whose only shortcoming was that for sometime he was still largely engaged on the completion of the Lyons Bakery invoicing job.[10] Brett later moved to Wills and remained with them for the rest of his career. For implementation on site there was again close cooperation with the customer's own efficient O&M organization.[10] There is more about this in Hermon's reminiscence (see Chapter 17).

A valuable outcome of the Wills installation was that LEO acquired alphabetic printing. Hitherto, Simmons's radicalism had insisted that, given preprinted stationery, there was no necessity for alphabetic characters, especially as these must inevitably give rise to more expense or loss of speed. The responsible manager at Bristol was an imposing character named A. G. Wright, but he was almost universally known as "The Master" because of his magisterial bearing. He made it clear that, ingenious as Lyons might be in managing with numerical characters only, this would not be acceptable to Wills. It was a matter of "no alpha printing, no order."

The Samastronic printer manufactured by Powers Samas appeared at the time to be the only candidate[11] to achieve the required speed with these additional characters. It offered a wide range of characters produced by a matrix of needle styluses. Functionally this was adequate rather than ideal, because it needed only minimal maladjustment for characters to become distorted. Lenaerts worked wonders in devising maintenance techniques to keep up the quality required by Wills for their invoices, but as soon as an alternative became available from Machines Bull in Paris, the Samastronic was dropped from the catalog with considerable relief.

The second order was from Stewarts and Lloyds,[12] an old family firm that had built a new steelworks and integrated tube production plant outside Corby in Northamptonshire, bringing down much of the skilled workforce from Scotland. Responsible for the whole computer project was Neil Pollock, Stewarts and Lloyds' youthful O&M manager who reported to Bill Castle, the Company Secretary, who had considerable authority over all administrative matters in the company.

Pollock sent down parties of potential programmers and operational staff for aptitude tests and, where successful in crossing that hurdle, for training.[13] The programmers, led by Bob Caldwell and Hamish Archibald, worked under Fantl alongside LEO staff and absorbed the same ways and practices. It was a firm contractual commitment that the order was conditional upon the payroll programs being ready for the delivery of the equipment.[14] The steelworks payroll had more than its share of complication, with gross pay (comprising cost-of-living bonus, piecework pay, allowances, and one or more production bonuses) per employee having to be allocated to 5000 cost accounts, but the programs were ready as soon as the prototype LEO II became available and well ahead of delivery of their own system. Commenting on their choice of payroll for their first application, Stewarts and Lloyds declared:[15]

> Payroll was chosen . . . because it is a good test of a computer's capacity and reliability. It is a recurrent task that must be carried out on time, its results can be predetermined, and it is subject to a critical scrutiny by its customers—the employees.

However, payroll was seen only as a beginning and work "to associate LEO more and more with the company's productive operations" went ahead in parallel. Among the targets were engineering and operational research applications, and on these LEO continued to play the leading role through Jim Smith's scientific section. A key job that was ready by the official opening day was pipe stressing to guide the fabrication of steel tubes to withstand high pressures.[16] The aim was to be safe but not extravagant. A fascinating job was to decide where best to dig each day's iron ore from the neighboring open-cast deposits. Regard had to be given to the chemical composition of each dig and the particular types of steel for which iron was required, as well as to many logistical factors. A great deal was learned about the almost insurmountable difficulty of obtaining in advance the full parameters for determining heuristic decisions of this sort. There were more "ifs and buts" than in exception-strewn office work, and the one or two proud experts were scarcely conscious of the instinctive reactions that led them to their optimized conclusions. In a shorter time than it seemed possible, though, the computer was able to take over the job and so relieve the company of succession problems that had been causing concern.

A third machine order in 1956 was from the Ford Parts Depot at Aveley in Essex. This was a huge warehousing facility that maintained supplies of parts for the wide range of Ford vehicles, past and present. In competition with what it regarded as pirates for the parts in most demand, it needed to maintain a rapid and reliable response time and to assure this with timely but economic replenishment. The initial study was carried out by Gosden, and the work was then taken over by Land, who by this time had become LEO's stock control specialist.

The order was particularly significant, because approval for capital expenditure on this scale had to be obtained by the local Ford management from their headquarters in Detroit. This took rather a long time, and for a while there seemed no certainty that the UK subsidiary would be allowed to go its own way.[17] However, systems work proceeded in the meantime and in this Land was well supported by the local personnel. As with other installations there was the advantage of a strong O&M activity on site, though LEO analysts sometimes felt it inhibiting that they could not reach right back to the "ultimate customer," the management on the ground. Prominent among the Ford O&M staff was Peter Gyngell, a giant in both stature and vitality. Later he made a career move that was the reverse of the usual and joined the colleagues he had worked with at LEO.

There was promise of several other early orders, but with the severe caution of the times and the still forbidding bulk of LEO II, these did not come quickly to realization. Generally, the option of a start in bureau mode was more appealing. Among those that chose this option were The Ever Ready Battery company, Kodak, and Tate & Lyle.[18] Mostly they followed the example of the Ford Motor Company and Stewarts and Lloyds and decided on payroll as their starter. With past program specifications and sequences such as for PAYE to draw on, the task was well understood within LEO and a succession of user programmers came to learn their trade under Fantl's leadership, working beside LEO programmers, who steadily moved on to run projects of their own. Each payroll had its own twists and turns that had evolved with the circumstances of the company; with the constraints of the small LEO store and the still relatively low speed, the time had not yet arrived for standard programs. Each application had to be crafted separately for there was no room for the inefficiency in machine resource usage that is an inevitable accompaniment of standardization.

Sources

These first commercial "prospects" had in the main been drawn from two sources. The first was Simmons's circle in what was then the Office Management Association and later became the Institute of Office Management. Simmons's work on office organization and gradings and on the use of office machinery, combined with his radicalism in business systems, had gained him enormous respect as a colleague and leader. He had been elected Chairman and then President, and members of the organization were among the earliest to make the pilgrimage to Cadby Hall as soon as LEO I became open to inspection.

On occasion, though, Simmons was not the best of interfaces. His integrity and quiet, courteous candor were such that a chief executive, accustomed to deference, could be frightened away. There was an occasion when Boots, the British pharmacy chain was interested in acquiring a computer, and Dennis Greensmith, the company's O&M chief at the time, brought his Chairman, Arthur Cockfield to see LEO. A first study had been done, but this conflicted with the pattern as seen by Boots itself. When Cockfield pointed this out Simmons remarked that if Boots did not feel able to make use of the benefit of Lyons' experience, then there was nothing more that could be done. It was typical of him to presume that the recommendations of his own staff must be well-founded. It could be said, though, that the assurance that "we" were right and the unwillingness to bend to circumstances could well be regarded as LEO's Achilles' heel in its relation with the less logical world outside.

The second source of prospects was the family's large circle of business and personal acquaintances, among them the leading suppliers in the food industry. They, too, came in considerable numbers to see the computer at work and were generally entertained by Anthony Salmon, who was a most accomplished host and knew precisely the right moment to have the LEO expert present to launch into a very short stretch of business aimed at obtaining an entry for something more serious after the visit.

As potential customers, there were also all the other people who found their way to LEO's demonstrations or attended the occasional lectures and seminars on business computing, such as those at the Northampton Polytechnic, now known as the City University,[19] and at such bodies as the Institute of Chartered Accountants and the British Institute of Management, at which Thompson, Pinkerton, Barnes and I took our turns at delivering papers from time to time.

There were also occasional write-ups in management and business journals, though they were not always as supportive as one in the *Economist* entitled "The Electronic Abacus."[20] It appeared shortly after the payroll demonstration and commented shrewdly on the conflicting attitudes of Lyons and the conventional suppliers. Of the latter, the author wrote:

> The business machine companies argue from their long experience of the market that the more complicated and versatile computers are unnecessary unless the most abstruse calculations are involved and they offer instead—or will shortly offer—calculators . . .

By contrast, the article continues:

> The exciting feature of an electronic office is its flexibility: the computer is an all-purpose machine that can switch from one type of work to another in the time which it takes to erase the pulses of the old job from its memory. It will do all the work of a business, its scientific calculations, its routine office accounting . . . and it will take in its stride all the awkward exceptions that crop up on any batch of routine calculations.

Despite the highly influential standing of the *Economist*, it must be said that this article did not bring new prospects thronging to Cadby Hall gates. Possibly the title gave the wrong impression.

As for the applications staff, they published little on what they were accomplishing, either in the very early days when novel work was being done in the mathematical and actuarial fields, or later when the office jobs began to flow. There was no management objection to publication, but the programming staff did not bring with them the discipline of scientific publication, so that little about their work was recorded at the time.

Another source of encouragement that might have been expected was the government, but this had not yet made itself felt. At the end of 1955 a member of Parliament asked the Chancellor of the Exchequer:[21]

> In view of the advances toward automation made by Messrs. Lyons in the use of the electronic device named LEO, will he consider the use of similar methods in the Treasury and Civil Service generally to enable the nation's business to be carried out more expeditiously and more economically?

The Chancellor of the day, R. A. Butler, replied:

> Several electronic computers are already in use within the Civil Service for mathematical work and less elaborate apparatus is used in some departments on clerical work. The scope for further use of electronic computers is continuously studied by the Organization and Methods Division of the Treasury and other Departments.

So far there had been little sign of much emerging from these studies.

Recruitment and Selection

The loading of the succession of ground-breaking jobs on LEO I and the commissioning and rapid utilization of the prototype LEO II in May 1957 were accompanied by recruitment in all parts of the organization. After searches in the Lyons offices, most programming staff now came from the universities, some through the annual "recruitment tour" and others through the helpful activities of appointments boards. Because of the continued novelty of the enterprise, there was considerable interest among some of the brightest of the new graduates. They were not all mathematicians (though many were), but none of them arrived at Cadby Hall with any knowledge of programming or systems analysis whatever. These were not yet topics to be found in British universities, save, by exception, at the seminar level.

When a need was felt to step up recruitment, it was made known that graduates could present themselves on Saturday mornings. Two of the top university recruits, Alan Jacobs and John Lewis, were netted on one Saturday. Another Saturday recruit was Paul Dixon, who came from Czechoslovakia. Among others who arrived in this way was Jeremy Isaacs. He was made an offer on the spot but was awaiting a callback from the BBC, where he had also applied. He later became the first Director of Channel 4 Television and then General Manager of the Royal Opera House. He was regarded as "the one who got away."

The normal selection process was based on the aptitude test that had been used with the earliest recruits. Short talks were given on simple office tasks and on the instruction code followed by the group being set to work to carry out the coding. They were free to ask questions of the demonstrators, who would also intervene to help if anyone seemed to be in difficulty or appeared, from a look over the shoulder, to have gone astray. Afterwards there was a little more complicated session along the same lines. At the end those running the exercise would make their assessments of ability to pick up new ideas and of responsiveness to guidance and to general intellectual acuity. Those who seemed to match up to what was required were subsequently interviewed at management level.

In this next interview, reaction to the exercise was discussed first, followed by the candidate's outside interests, be they athletics, the theater, or whatever. There would follow an explanation of what LEO was trying to do and the atmosphere in which the team worked. Because of the quality of those who had reached this stage, it was as much a matter of selling LEO to the applicant as of the applicants selling themselves to LEO. No time was lost, and offers were generally made at once. The others were thanked for coming and sent on their way; there was no institutional suspense to be suffered. All the demonstrating and most of the interviewing was carried out by existing members of the programming staff, some of them themselves comparative newcomers. At times, but not always, professional personnel from elsewhere in the Lyons organization participated in the interview process. When Lyons employed a psychologist to assist in senior staff selection, his overview was added to the proceedings, but usually his views coincided remarkably with those of the home team.

One aspect of the job stressed at the final interview was the pressure under which those who joined the team would be expected to work, and the dedication expected of them. They were told that they would need to be physically resilient and able to understand mental stress. What was offered was the chance of rapid promotion in a growing field, the opportunity to be in the front line of something entirely new. There was also the prospect of camaraderie and intellectual excitement. These were enough to attract most of the more able people who were interviewed.

Mr. Booth, the fatherly Company Secretary to whom Lyons' clerical management annually presented their already approved lists of raises always emphasized in his homilies the preeminence of character in recruitment and advancement. Ability is imperative, he would say, but before even that must come character, and that was always in mind at the final interview.

Brian Edwards, who became Chief Programmer at the Ford Motor Company HQ at Dagenham and Colin Davis, a programmer at Wills, have commented in a memoir:[22]

> For us the LEO aptitude test remains the most effective ever. Unlike others, which are variants of IQ and numerical competence tests, the LEO version tests applicants in the very skills that they are to exercise in the job. Consequently the results can be taken as serious evidence of relevant competence. Moreover the applicant has the opportunity to experience precisely the sort of thinking that programming is going to call on, even if at an elementary level. If anyone finds it intimidating or trivial this can be a useful guide to their suitability.
>
> The defect of the LEO test in its day was that it was relatively expensive in person time; it required a day from a qualified and preferably working programmer to administer. In our view that was compensated by the greater predictability of success, and by the fact that a subsequent interview could be based more thoroughly on real issues about the substance of the job.

There was also some mileage still to be made in Lyons. A notable recruit from the offices was Doug Comish, a Cambridge mathematician who had played wartime football for the university. He had spent a longer time than most in the Clerical Department and had derived great confidence from this for his many later encounters in the business world. Another recruit from Lyons was Sam Waters, who was no more than a boy when he was recommended by the manager of the Lyons Treasury, which oversaw all money transactions. Sam could be described as the one and only apprentice in LEO programming history and was so successful that in retrospect it is a wonder that more was not made of this avenue at a time when a much smaller proportion of young people had the opportunity to go on to higher education.

Training

The formal training of newcomers was confined to an intensive five weeks in which they received lectures on coding technique from different members of the programming staff.[23] These culminated in a trial job which, as computer time was made available, was tested and corrected and tested again in a realistic way. Thompson always placed giving the introductory lecture above his other priorities and expected the other part-time lecturers to do the same. The lectures were nonetheless carefully scripted so that they could be handed over to another speaker in an emergency. Giving a good example of care and organization on the course was regarded as training in itself. Trial job scenarios changed from time to time. Sometimes they were concerned with an imaginary business. At another time they turned to cricket batting averages, an area of considerable interest among several senior members of the programming staff.[24]

Colin Davis observes:[25]

> The enthusiasm and detail with which everything was explained and the obvious relevance of the subject to the instructors (as it was part of their everyday life) was never repeated in many years of computer training.

It was considered a pity when it became expedient to pass the programming training into the hands of full-timers. However, as these trainers were themselves selected from members of the staff who had shown special aptitude for this branch of work, there was still a continuity of experience in the teaching, and there was no gulf between what was taught in the lecture room and what was encountered outside. John Smythson, a very capable programmer himself, was made responsible for this work when it became full-time.

Training on systems analysis and report writing followed the programming course. Here there was no formal script. Newcomers were allotted to a senior who would throw them into a problem and induct them into the theory and practice of business organization and methods as they went along. Reading the specification of the job being coded provided an induction into both programming strategy and the way in which information had to be presented. Every specification had, itself, been closely scrutinized. Newcomers were not always consciously aware of what they were learning or how fast. Above all, there was always a close person-to-person relationship in passing on the ethos of responsibility, commitment and cooperation.

Apprenticeship

Programmers and systems staff from outside users, both those using the service bureau and those using or awaiting LEO computers of their own, received their initial training on the same courses as the LEO recruits. Many of them stayed behind for a time to gain working experience in the LEO teams. Generally they would take part in the programming of applications for their own enterprise, as was the case with the Stewarts and Lloyds team (see page 62), but sometimes they would work on other jobs that provided relevant experience for the applications that were still to be enacted at home.

Brian Edwards had termed the arrangement "apprenticeship." He writes:

> The customer's trainee programmer would stay on at LEO for some months getting hands-on experience of writing and testing real programs, under the close supervision of a project team. No money changed hands; but LEO had the benefit of free, albeit slow, labor; and the customer had its programmers trained free in a well-disciplined shop. Once again, the peculiar circumstances of early LEO . . . enabled a service to be given that could not always be emulated by other manufacturers in different circumstances.

Consultants

Notwithstanding the initiative with salesmen, sales remained largely in the hands of the programming wing of the business. Selected senior programmers acquired by usage the title of "consultants" to recognize their role, which was as much advisory as technical when dealing with the outside world. It had become natural to say, after an ice-breaking lunch with a visiting director. "I'll send a consultant to see your people," and no description could have been more appropriate. At the time prospective users knew little about how full-scale applications could be mounted in their enterprises beyond what had been gleaned in visits, articles, and the two- or three-day courses that were beginning to appear. They still had to be shown how computers could meet their particular needs, what the obstacles were, and how they could be overcome.

A characteristic of the LEO consultants as a sales force was that they worked entirely without the bonus incentives that were the norm in the office equipment field. This was also the case at English Electric and possibly other capital goods firms that had entered the computer market. The matter never became an issue at LEO Computers because selling and implementation were so closely intertwined. The concern of consultants was more with enterprises that received their analyses and then proceeded to use extracts as the basis for lesser-scope applications on other equipment. Even users tentatively committed to LEO would use the report submitted by their consultant as the basis for obtaining market testing competitive bids.[26] In the beginning some surveys were charged for, but this practice died out as market norms asserted themselves.

The golden age of LEO consultancy was in the late 1950s, when they were all assembled in what was known as the "goldfish bowl" in Elms House, the custom-built Lyons office building near Cadby Hall. They occupied a very large room with wide windows along the sides and a glass wall dividing them from the remainder of the open office floor. There can scarcely very have been such an array of computer talent in one room. It was a profoundly committed group. With unending demands on computer time, they found no relief from the daytime famine that had beset LEO I. Much of the program testing on the LEO II installed beyond the partition still had to be carried out in begged or snatched hours at night.

The great solace remained the managers' dining room, where they were able to dine in the middle of the night and, if they were still around, to have an early breakfast. Most consultants and programmers of the time have nostalgic memories of the walk across the Cadby Hall yard, the bustle of the trucks being loaded and the bright lights in the dark, and the sweet scent of ovens baking.

Some of those who became consultants have already been mentioned, among them Fantl, Land, Smith, Gosden, Hermon, Payman, Lewis, Jacobs, and Comish. Together with others who followed they make a long list for what was still a small organization. There was always a particular cluster around Fantl's desk, where he sat with his back to the window; many had their induction there to the succession of payroll applications. Brian Mills, Geof Pye, and Ian Crawford were others of the era who quickly came to acquire their independence through coding under his direction.

Elsewhere in the goldfish bowl there was George McLeman, who acquired the reputation of being the fastest and most accurate coder of them all. With him at one stage was Paul Dixon, the Saturday-morning recruit of Czech origin, who spoke later of the sheer frustration of having to check "Mac's" work and never finding anything wrong. Others were Mike Josephs, Roger Coleman, and John Aris (LEO's solitary classicist), who sat face to face with Sam Waters, the young man from the Treasury who became his protégé.

With Smith in his corner over Hammersmith Road there were Roberts and, toward the end of the stay in Elms House, Helen Clark, another talented programmer who went on to lead the service bureau programming as it grew to become a separate entity. She married consultant Mike Jackson, continuing a trend started by Mary Blood and John Coombs. Over the years there followed several more marriages between members of the consulting community.

It was a sociable world. There was the tennis team of which Gosden writes in his memoir (Chapter 16) and an occasional cricket team in which Comish, a regular weekend player when he could get away, was a leading light. At one point a team drawn from all parts of the LEO organization won the coveted Lyons Club pennant against all the other departments competing on a single day in everything from football to athletics and swimming to bowling and rifle shooting. Pale-blue turbanned Sikhs from the "works" showed unsuspected hockey skills, and I am remembered for my exhortations in the tug of war team. Later on, the LEO team, of which Pinkerton was a member, won the Lyons Club quiz championship in a knockout competition against 15 other departments. But mostly it was work.[27]

The "family" became wider than those employed by LEO alone. Brian Edwards and Colin Davis, both of whom went on to careers in IBM in Bristol, say:

> The feeling that LEO customer people had for the supplier was probably unique; we were very much included in the community of LEO people . . . and I am glad to say we still are.

7

End of the First Generation

1958–1960

Third Trip to America

In March of 1958 it was time for another trip to the United States, partly to see whether the sleeping giant was stirring in the application field and partly to keep abreast of the technological advances that were being monitored at a distance. In Britain, beyond the continued progress that LEO had registered, there had been little change since the last visit, two years before. On LEO I the Ford Motor Company payroll had emulated Lyons in reaching 10,000;[1] the overnight distribution to teashops was running as though the new method had always been the obvious way; shopkeepers all over the country were receiving their almost paperless deliveries of cakes and pies; and the massive Lyons tea stocks were more accessible than they had ever been before. Many service jobs were being executed or prepared for a wide spectrum of users, including the largest single service job so far: the calculation for freight charging purposes of the distances from each railway station in the UK to every other station. This had been completed in a succession of 168-hour weeks.[2] Especially encouraging were the three orders for LEO II from leading industrial enterprises. Pilot running for the payroll of one of them was already in progress. To match the new status as a supplier, the design and production wings had completed a move into more appropriate quarters at Minerva Road in Park Royal.[3] Their previous home had been in the stable block once occupied by the horses that had drawn the retail rounds carts around West London.

Elsewhere in Britain the population of electronic computers of any kind was still small. The number of full-scale, live office applications was even smaller. The only other system dedicated to data processing was the increasingly out-of-date BTM 1201, of which there were 12. From the United States there was a single IBM 650. Additionally, there was a scattering of general-purpose and scientific systems installed by Elliott Automation, Ferranti, and English Electric.[4] In the office field, LEO continued to be way out ahead both in capability and in employment. The task was not just one of convincing others of the superiority of LEO II over its rivals; it was rather more one of winning credence for what in Britain still remained a way-out idea.

This time it was the turn of Pinkerton and myself to cross the Atlantic. There was a coast-to-coast itinerary that drew on the advice of John Diebold, the leading U.S. computer publicist of the time, the New York office of the Westminster Bank, and others. What was found was more of what had been encountered on the previous visits. We, too, were struck by commitment of everyone—government officials, suppliers, and users alike—and we, too, encountered enormous investment without the equivalent quality of work being performed. Above all there was a vitality that was scarcely visible in the British scene.

It was noteworthy how in all sections of the economy it had become the thing to take at least the first steps into electronic computing. Though there was little evidence of a grass roots movement, the deployment of electronic devices was of an altogether higher order, even allowing for relative population size, than in Britain. Everywhere there seemed to be more equipment on order.

At U.S. Steel, where the Pittsburgh installation was in its infancy at the time of the Thompson/Barnes visit, there were now 22 systems spread around the country.[5] A powerful IBM 705, two Univac IIs, and no fewer than 19 punched-card IBM 650s were in use. On order were an additional Univac II, eight more card 650s, and two of the new RAMAC 650s with large-capacity backing stores. In this one company there was overwhelmingly more office computer power than in all British industry and public administration.

There did not however appear to be output to match. At the National Tube Division of U.S. Steel where the operations were studied in some detail because of its affinity with the Stewarts and Lloyds tube works at Corby, it was reported; "It would not be possible to justify the cost with those jobs in the UK."

At Ford and Kodak there was also the special interest of home associations. An IBM 705 was about to replace another large IBM system at the main Ford plant at Dearborn. One comment was that "the payroll did not go as far as the Ford UK job." At the Ford steel division there was an IBM 650 with an extended input/output facility being largely occupied by a monthly payroll for only 1100 members of staff, together with daily incentive payment calculations. Again, after noting the high reliability, the verdict was, "By UK standards the work at present being done could not begin to justify the cost of an installation." Among other Ford facilities visited was the Central Parts Depot, with a function similar to that of the Aveley Depot, for which an LEO II order had been taken. It was noted that the job was less than that for Aveley in that it is completed after the event and after orders have been calculated. Otherwise there would be real trouble at the moment."[6]

At Kodak, one of the first IBM 705 users, there was now a second system in use "rather to provide a cover for what they regard as an essential operation than to provide additional capacity." Here, too, it was noted that the main job, invoicing, was carried out "after the event" in contrast to the Lyons Wholesale Bakery job, where the delivery note and invoicing functions were satisfied in a single "before the event" operation. Of their payroll application it was noted, "Payroll is done Gross to Net only and does not produce the full range of Rochester [U.S. HQ] statistics as carried out by LEO."[7]

The message was much the same everywhere. At Wrigleys, the chewing gum giant in Chicago, it was reported that "they were going about the job of billing customers and maintaining some rather unsophisticated sales statistics efficiently. However, it seems remarkable that such an elementary job of low volume could justify the cost of comparatively advanced equipment." The system in use was the first IBM RAMAC in the mid-West.[8]

There was an air of anxiety not to be left behind. We were told over a Bankers' Club lunch on Wall Street of a leading bank where a recommendation had gone forward for a small machine as a beginning. It could be justified, it was said, only because of the "high current costs of the present cumbersome system, which management are disinclined to alter."[9]

All this coexisted with technological advance and innovation. The forward march of semiconductors everywhere made a deep impression and reinforced the conviction that developments in their use at home must be accelerated with the utmost vigor. At RCA the model 501 under development could be compared to the elephantine BIZMAC, built on a similar scale to the LEO systems. The size reduction that could be achieved was evident.[10]

Other innovative projects revealed the liveliness of the U.S. computer scene. Character recognition was being pressed forward for the Bank of America, with check sorting as an immediate target. At the Bureau of

Census there was advanced work on mark sensing. Particularly exciting was a project at Higbee's, a large Chicago department store, where point-of-sale terminals were linked by cable to a central BIZMAC computer that returned the bill value and retained a copy for credit accounts, stock issues, and statistics. The point-of-sale devices were described to the visitors as begin prohibitively expensive, but the project was proceeding nonetheless in anticipation that with encouragement something would in time emerge at an acceptable price.[11] They were correct, of course.

A feature of American computer life often mentioned in the report was the cleanliness and tidiness both in supplier's workplaces and at installations in the field. At the end of a visit to an office machine manufacturer only recently entered into electronics, the wry comment was that "Minerva Road looks like a pigsty by comparison."[12]

The Scene at Home

It was a different world to which the party returned: one in which the level of investment, the degree of acceptance of change, and the relative costliness of equipment in relation to salary rates placed British manufacturers at a great disadvantage compared with their U.S. counterparts in the respective home markets. The immediate tasks, though, were concerned with more tractable domestic issues. On the engineering side the task was to push ahead with the outline designs of an all-semiconductor LEO III and at the same time doing what was possible to modernize LEO II to enable it to hold out in the market until the second-generation system came to the rescue.

At Stewarts and Lloyds, Wills, and Ford the task was to bring the first deliveries of LEO systems to the field into rapid productive operation. This was accomplished smoothly from the first installation onward. At Corby a specially designed air-conditioned building had been erected—almost certainly the first for any office computer in the UK. Despite the size of the system, with more than 7000 glass valves of 30 different types, the Stewarts and Lloyds system, the first LEO delivery outside Lyons, was recommissioned as though it was a matter of course. In their attractive open-day brochure, Stewarts and Lloyds declared:[13]

> Because of the careful preparation that had been done, LEO was in productive operation within three weeks of the packing cases arriving at Corby. By making the satisfactory running of the first job prior to delivery a condition of the contract for the equipment, there was no delay between installation and productive work. Since then the payroll has run smoothly from week to week.

The engineer responsible for this first external delivery was Stan Holwill, who had earlier been involved in general design and production and engineering. The pattern was already forming of a Senior Commissioning Engineer being responsible for a system in the works and then taking it out to the user site. It was sensed that each system had its own personality and profited from being accompanied by an engineer familiar with its ways.

It was a considerable undertaking to move one of those massive early systems. The 12 or more tall racks had to be electrically disconnected and unbolted for the journey and reassembled on arrival. The valves were left in place in the racks, but not all could be expected to survive the journey, however much care was taken. A particular hazard was posed by the very high-precision acoustic delay lines, which provided the store, registers, and buffers. The tubes were drained of their mercury for dispatch and refilled on arrival. Then they had to be brought back into their precise millisecond time alignment with each other.[14]

The tribute from Stewarts and Lloyds is a worthy record of the calm, skill, endurance, and professional pride of the teams of commissioning engineers who, throughout the lifetime of the LEO marques, invariably set a standard for everyone else associated with the systems to follow.

However, it was the job rather than the machine that was the test. It was recorded by Stewarts and Lloyds that the time taken to calculate each employee's pay and to produce the paycheck took 2.4 seconds. Cost accounting programs added 1.2 seconds to this figure "and thus the nominal speed is 1000 employees per hour."[15]

The Bureau

A great deal of attention was devoted to the next installation, another for the London Service Bureau, which was already bursting at the seams. The conviction had been growing among some senior members of the LEO management that in Britain there was only a limited number of users with the capital resources, investment policies, O&M capability, and readiness to embark on an entirely new approach to their office work. Many more, it was felt, would want, at least for the medium term, to take advantage of bureau services, which would lessen the risk and yet lead to the same results in terms of work executed.

To give the Bureau a sharper identity—up to that point it had been more a capacity-filler for the Lyons machines than an enterprise in its own right—it was decided to install the system outside Cadby Hall.

There had been a strong lobby for prestige premises in the center of London,[16] but in the end there was compromise, and in April of 1959 a home was found by the Lyons Estates department, another of Anthony Salmon's responsibilities, on an upper floor of the Whiteley's department store in Bayswater. The site had the virtue of providing a great deal of inexpensive space and, when renovations had been completed, the bureau system was joined by the whole of the programming department and the LEO Computers Ltd. headquarters. The suite as a whole was given the name Hartree House, in affectionate memory of the far-sighted Cambridge professor whose encouragement had meant so very much when the Lyons venture was still up in the air. As soon as everyone was settled down, Hartree House was visited by the Duke of Edinburgh, to whom the LEO II/5 performance included the sailor's hornpipe.[17] The Duke went on to visit Minerva Road on the same day.

The closeness of the association of LEO Computers with Lyons was inevitably reduced by the move. A feature of the relationship in the past was that the LEO engineering, applications, and operating managements had met each other and some of their principal customers every day in the managers' dining room. However lighthearted the banter might seem, they had been left in no doubt about how the Lyons user world was reacting. Equally, the LEO managers had had the informal opportunity of keeping each other in the picture on what was going on and what the problems were. It meant that there could be few wholly unexpected surprises, and it gave a considerable sense of togetherness. The moves to Hartree House and Minerva Road were the price that had to be paid for an independent identity as well as for adequate space. They marked a coming of age.

A feature of the new system was that it was the first LEO equipped with magnetic tape. It constituted a formidable assemblage for the times, with its magnetic drum backing storage and fast alphanumeric printers, as well as paper tape and punched-card input and output, both in binary and decimal mode. Later Kimball tag input was added to meet the needs of the fashion trade.

George Manley, who was the first but not the last to have an unfinished building to contend with, was responsible for the commissioning of the system. A young engineer who had showed prowess as a rugged forward in the Lyons rugby team, Manley was well chosen for the task. Because of the variety of ancillary equipment, every available commissioning engineer was assigned to his team. A natural leader with infectious good humor, it was to him another uphill game on a difficult pitch. Tony Morgan, a member of the team, recalls, "It was a matter of all hands to the pump . . . in the long hot summer of 1959. Although the machine was force-cooled there was no air-conditioning for the room and temperatures in the aisles, where all the value circuitry was, had to be experienced to be believed."[14] Later Manley became a leading figure on the

manufacturing side of LEO's successor businesses and remains an enthusiastic off-field figure in the rugby club to this day. The name of Morgan,
another keen rugby player, turns up time and again in recollections of
LEO installations.

Officers Payroll

The extended features were employed from the outset to carry out an
assignment to produce the Army Officers Payroll for Glyn Mills Bank,
acting as agents for the War Office and Air Ministry.

It was a job that could not have been reasonably attempted without the
extra facilities. However, it meant that LEO was undertaking a highly
sensitive time-critical task for an old established city institution with an
enviable reputation for soundness in all respects, with equipment that as
an entity had never seen action before.

The consultant entrusted with the task was John Lewis, a senior member of Fantl's group. He brought with him programming experience covering a wide field, from matrix manipulation for aircraft design to grading cows and goats at the Olympia Dairy show, and, more to the point,
on working on sections of the Stewarts and Lloyds payrolls. Lewis and
his team took what was for LEO another pioneering job in their stride.
Program trials were carried out at Minerva Road, where the engineers
were still testing the new facilities. Here, too, the programmers found
themselves carrying out much of their trial work at night. They lacked
the comfort of the all-night dining arrangements to which most of them
had become accustomed at Cadby Hall, but they improvised an alternative. Lewis, in charge of a large group for the first time, led an outstand-
ingly happy team. Intellectually tough and committed to detail, he could
be relied upon to try out the suite with the fullest rigor before it came
under the fire of live running. It came through with flying colors. Three
more marriages followed. (An account of the project is given by Lewis
himself in Chapter 19.)

Though LEO was awarded the Officers Payroll project by a merchant
bank, the much larger contract for equipment to run the payroll for the
other ranks had already been placed with IBM by the British government
itself. The system ordered for the Royal Army Pay Corps was a model
705, more powerful and several times more expensive than anything yet
in use at home or available from British manufacturers. There had been
no advance consultation, and though LEO put up a tenacious fight to
match speed and ancillary facilities by systems skills and ingenuity, the
contest was inevitably one-sided. The completely dispassionate evaluation that took place with Treasury participation could reach only one

conclusion for a task of such magnitude.[18] The equipment procurement that it entailed would have given LEO enormous impetus had there been readiness to await the necessary development, which was already along the road with the magnetic tape-equipped LEO II/5.

Instead, relatively large, highly skilled LEO resources were tied up in an intricate job that because of its modest scale, could not be remotely as financially rewarding for all that it marked a new stage in LEO's progress. At the time, little assessment took place in LEO of the worthiness of projects in terms of resources tied up. So long as the client was prepared to pay the charges and to accept the analysis of what needed to be done, the work was accepted on a first-come, first-served basis; whatever resources were necessary were assigned to it.

Another job that was undertaken near the start-up at Hartree House was one for the Hudson Bay Company, which ran periodic auctions of karakul lamb fleeces in what is now Namibia. LEO was awarded the highly time-critical job of allocating the proceeds of all the many lots over all the farmers participating in each of them. A hitch occurred soon after live running started, and an increasingly desperate effort ensued to track down the fault and make corrections soon enough to meet the expectations of the farmers. The specter of farmers lining up in the hot sun thousands of miles away hung over Hartree House for what seemed a painfully long time. The target was met in the end, but at the cost of senior staff being completely occupied when their time would have been more profitably employed on bigger things.

A more significant assignment later on was from Durlachers, then one of the leading stockbrokers on the London Stock Exchange. When it had reached full-steam ahead in May of 1961, a load of 60,000 bargains was handled in a single run. The implementation was carried out by Frank Land after his short but intensive immersion in the affairs of the Stock Exchange. He was guided by an enthusiastic partner in the firm named John Bennett.[19]

First Government Order

It was a matter of great satisfaction when an order for a LEO II for a government department did eventually arrive.[20] This was for the vast Ministry of Pensions paperwork center outside Newcastle, where it had been decided to start with payroll before essaying the altogether greater mass of work concerned with payments and records.

There had been previous government assignments to LEO, but these had been for bureau work alone. They had included the production of the full range of 1955–56 PAYE tables for the Inland Revenue, but after one thoroughly successful year even this had been discontinued because a lower cost had been found elsewhere, possibly at a research establishment with less stringent accounting.[21] There had also been work for the Ordnance Board and the Transport Commission, but these were all locally authorized jobs. Now with the background of the payroll work that had already been done elsewhere, it was a very simple matter to respond to the Ministry's invitation to train and guide their team in implementing the application. A close relationship was struck with the civil service team in the north, which even devised its own LEO II/6 tie to signify its allegiance. For all the success of this installation, however, it was still another four years before a further central government LEO system was implemented.

The Last LEO IIs

Among the remaining LEO II installations there was a second system for Wills and another for Ford Motor Company to take over the payroll for themselves in their Dagenham offices and to augment it with other work that had been discussed with LEO consultants. There was also a system for Standard Motors, then a prominent name on British roads. The system was used for factory loading and other production control tasks, transforming the orders received from dealers into shop-floor tallies. Another industrial implementation was for Ilford, where the on-site LEO team was led by Joe Crouch. He worked alongside an ex-LEO consultant, Roger Coleman, who had joined Ilford as Computer Manager.

Of all the LEO IIs only one was less than very successful, measured by the one meaningful rule, the output of ongoing reliable, productive work. That was for British Oxygen at Edmonton. LEO consultants were responsible for guiding new users past potential pitfalls, and the failure to achieve the planned results at Edmonton made a deep impression. The application was production control and the interface between the two companies was a knowledgeable Works Chief Accountant, who had all the enthusiasm and drive to make an intricate operation succeed. Programming went well, and there was every reason to believe that the application would have erected another landmark had it not been for a major organizational change of which there was no warning whatever. The structural basis of the job was destroyed. The need to make certain that there was sufficient awareness and support right up to the decision-making top of any organization entering into computers was painfully reinforced.

Ownership

In the case of British Oxygen nothing resembling it had been experienced before. The mistake had been, in present-day terms, in not identifying the correct "owner" of the system. As the number of systems grew, problems of "ownership" were also beginning to arise between wings of an organization in places where customers had already taken over full responsibility for their own systems.

Brian Edwards, chief programmer at Ford, Dagenham in this period has commented on the competitive atmosphere there:[22]

> There was little conception among us in those days of the now familiar ideas of business ownership of systems and system projects. In this, I think, there was some carry over of LEO/Lyons attitude. It is highly likely in the LEO/Lyons case that the Systems Office or whatever had established adequate credibility with the business, but that was certainly not true in Ford. We did not spot the need to build this up.
>
> Ford also suffered from an extreme case of the then fashionable organizational concept of "staff and line." Systems and Computing were part of the Administration Staff, which was cordially detested by the rest of the organization.

On a more positive note, the aging LEO II was given a much needed facelift for the last four installations. Two years after the Pinkerton/ Caminer trip to the United States a magnetic core store was made available. This replaced the mercury delay-line coffins and made arithmetic performance a third faster and some operations faster still. Above all, the new store technology reduced the size of an assemblage and gave it a more modern appearance. However, hard valves were still used for the logic units; consequently, LEO II remained basically a first-generation machine.

Punched-Card Merger

In retrospect, the outstanding event in 1958 on the British scene was the announcement of the merger of the two home punched-card manufacturers. The new organization was named ICT (International Computers and Tabulators).[23] Both BTM (the British Tabulating Machine Company) and Powers Samas had formerly had close, if uneasy, relationships with American partners, but at this stage both had been independent for almost ten years.

The BTM connection had started as far back as 1904 in an arrangement with Herman Hollerith at a time when the U.S. punched-card pioneer was seeking ways to broaden the base of his operations following his census successes.[24] Under the arrangement, the especially formed "Tabulator Limited" had access to Hollerith patents and the right to import machines into Britain at cost plus an acceptable premium.

Later, the Hollerith interests were swept up into CTR. In 1924 the early conglomerate became IBM under Thomas J. Watson and the association continued, with BTM having full rights to the British and other designated markers.

The Power Samas link to the United States was with Remington Rand, the other punched-card leader. The original connection had been formed by a user, the Prudential Assurance Company. The "Pru," a household name in Britain, had assured itself of security and continuity when it found itself growing increasingly dependent on its punched-card installations. Its supplier and later its partner was the Powers Accounting Machine Company, formed by James Powers, an engineer turned businessman with experience as technical adviser on the U.S. census. A joint British company was set up in 1919 with similar patent, supply, and territory arrangements to those between BTM and Hollerith. Here, too, when the Powers organization was gathered up into the newly assembled Remington Rand in 1927, the arrangement with the junior British partner continued.[25]

Thus, in terms of U.S. equivalents the merger agreement between BTM and Powers Samas represented the coming together of two giants. In practice the impact was very much less. Both partnerships were discontinued in 1949 when negotiations for the future had led instead to the abrogation of the long relationships. No tears were shed on either side. Freed of the constraints of territory allocations, an immediate response from IBM was to form its increasingly powerful World Trade Corporation.[26]

Left to themselves the two British companies had been unable to match the R&D investment of their old partners which had grown much more rapidly over the years. Nor, with markets thriving in the postwar reconstruction years, did adventurousness seem appropriate. As a consequence, when the two British punched-card manufacturers came together in 1958, they had little to show in terms of stored-program computing as LEO interpreted it. Their commitment was judged to be wholly to punched cards and punched-card methods. There were certainly no 705s or Univacs to be seen upon their respective horizons.

Contacts between LEO Computers and the two companies had been largely concerned with peripherals such as card feeds, punches, and tabulators stripped of their adding mechanisms to provide printers. No interest had been shown by either of the companies in closer involvement in the work in which LEO had been engaged. In 1960, two years later, H.V. Stammers, a Deputy Chairman, reported to the ICT Board:[27]

> They [IBM] believe as we do that the discontinuance of orthodox punched-card equipment is not yet in sight, and I gather that they are experiencing some feeling of relief and added security now that they have introduced the 1401 in a defensive role.

The British Scene

An insight into the British scene in this period is provided by an account of decision-making in a public corporation regarded as progressive in its adoption of computers for office purposes.[28] The conclusion arrived at was that pay was too sensitive to risk being entrusted to their IBM 650 installation. The Pay Officer "was unfailingly courteous and supportive, but the earlier problems of reliability had made him very nervous of computers."

The total amount of office work being executed anywhere in Britain remained limited. LEO II and the venerable LEO I continued to handle the lion's share of the load. By the end of 1961 there were still few stored-program computers dedicated to this end. Of these most were punched-card oriented, with the long outdated ICT 1201 and the new arrival, the IBM 1401, accounting for most of them.[29]

The extent to which the UK lagged behind the United States in large systems is illustrated by comparative statistics for 1962. By then IBM had made several hundred deliveries of the large 700 series systems in the U.S. but only a handful had come to Britain, where their price disqualified them for most applications.

New installations everywhere were predominantly of second-generation models, with both logic units and main store constructed from semiconductors. By the time LEO II was retired from its delivery life it had been overtaken in numbers by the EMIDEC 1100, produced by a late-starter, EMI, the electronics and record company.[29] More significantly, it had also been passed by the second-generation IBM 1401, which by the following year had multiplied its British numbers four times.

IBM had truly entered the British scene. An IBM UK subsidiary had been established immediately after the break with BTM in 1949, but its progress over the first few years had been relatively slow, despite a generous capitalization. Now it was beginning to bear out the caption in the U.S. business magazine, *Fortune,* in November 1960:[30]

Q. What grows faster than IBM?

A. IBM Abroad

With compatible access to much of the ICT punched-card population as well as the customers it had won for itself, IBM's strategic thrust was now into upgrading to electronic computers. They were following the path set by Dick Watson, President of IBM World Trade, who had forecast that by 1964, four years away, some 40 percent of World Trade's revenues would be from electronic data processing equipment, "compared perhaps with the 10% it represents today."[31]

In Britain it was very much the 1401 that was the spearhead of the advance. From its announcement in 1959 it had been well received in

Britain, with its short delivery times and its attractive access to advanced peripherals. The received wisdom, though, within the LEO organization was to dismiss the new arrival as not being designed for full-scale, integrated office work. In practice, the model met a perceived need in Britain just as it had in the United States. It provided continuity with what was already at work in mainstream offices together with a ring of technological updates. An IBM 1401 might cost a little more than a LEO II and do a lot less, but it struck a chord. In IBM's classic PR words, it represented "Evolution, not Revolution." By 1962 there were already more than 4000 installed worldwide.

8
Arrival of LEO III
1960–1963

Meanwhile, work had pressed on, with the aim of restoring LEO's vanguard position. The overall architecture for a LEO Mark III, with multiple buffered inputs and outputs, had been established on the earlier models, and Pinkerton and his team were well-informed on the semiconductor scene. There was experience now of magnetic tapes and magnetic drum backing stores and of the routines necessary to control them.

Design over the years had diverged from the original Cambridge work, but one innovative feature of EDSAC II was incorporated in LEO III thinking from an early stage. That feature was *microprogramming*, by which instructions were broken down into their elements rather than each being hardwired.[1] Progress in technology now made it possible to implement the concept using magnetic core matrices to represent the microprogrammed instructions, which facilitated the addition or alteration of instructions as design proceeded. Complex instructions involving a number of basic operations were particularly well served by this technique, which reduced the number of main store references for both instructions and data. Using microprogramming, the LEO III repertoire was enriched to around 90 discrete instructions by the time the design was completed.[2]

A second major feature was *multiprogramming*, or time-sharing: the ability to run two or more programs concurrently and independently of each other. Gosden recalls Stanley Gill, who played a major part on EDSAC and later with Ferranti, bringing back the concept from the United States. Pinkerton attributes the germ of the idea to Manchester. Its significance was clear in the context of office work where, even with buffering, the avoidance of inefficiency through unbalanced input, output, and calculation was not always achievable with a single throughput system.

Now, with several independent programs able to run at the same time, balancing the strands became less onerous, though it was still desirable for optimal loading to keep overall input, computation, and output broadly in line with each other. The basic arithmetic speeds of LEO III had grown ten times over those of LEO II, and keeping up with the arithmetic unit remained as essential as it had ever been.

To ensure that interference between programs did not occur, there was a simple system of store tagging to check that nothing had strayed into forbidden territory. Its task of policing the time-sharing facility was effected with little of the design complication and operational overheads associated with some virtual machine systems that came later. Up to 13 concurrent programs were provided for, though in practice the limitations on input and output channels generally restricted the number of programs running together to five or fewer.

The applications wing again participated, with John Gosden continuing the work that he had been engaged on with LEO II. Early attention was given both to the instruction set and to editing and manipulating information within the system. The word *software* had not yet become common in the British computer world, but Gosden's activities went on to embrace the delineation of an operating system to cover all aspects of input, output, device control, and multiprogramming. There was the enormous advantage that the design engineers were themselves familiar with the requirements of office work by this time. Additionally, a high-level language, CLEO, was sketched to supplement a lower-level but very handy Intercode. Glimpses of this period appear in Gosden's memoir (see Chapter 16).

Taken together, the innovative features that were built into LEO III (time-sharing, microprogrammed instructions facilitating common clerical functions such as merge and sort, and mixed radix arithmetic) produced an overall system performance well beyond the basic speed parameters. This served the system well when it was judged against well-constructed, work-based criteria.[3] Embarrassment to a user was caused toward the end of the lifespan of the system when an intrinsically much faster machine from another supplier encountered very severe difficulty in taking over a LEO workload.[4]

The definition of LEO functions and the implementation of them both in hardware and software were very much within Thompson's personal interests, and as work developed Gosden was moved over to report directly to him. He was joined by Ernest Roberts, who was transferred from mathematical programming to specify the Master Routine and Intercode as soon as the foundations had been laid. This done, the numbers rose in a short time to 16. Some of these came from the applications programming side, but others were comparative newcomers, drafted in after their basic training. Heading the principal teams were Adrian Rymell and John Forbes.[5]

Along the way, Jim Smith, hitherto in charge of the mathematics section, became manager of the software effort, replacing Gosden, who had accepted a very attractive opportunity in the U.S. Again the change was effected without trauma. It has been estimated that the LEO III software suite occupied 140 years of programmer effort over the five years from 1960. By LEO standards this was completely unprecedented.

Looking back at the human and machine resources essential to produce a reliable operating system and a high-level language compiler, and the length of calendar time required to accomplish either, it is remarkable that the relatively small LEO software team could have achieved what they did in so short a time. Partly this was because nothing was included that did not seem strictly necessary and nothing was attempted that had not been thought through beforehand. Thus, in defining the CLEO language, care was taken from the start that the compiler would not be rendered too elaborate. But it has also been commented that they simply didn't realize how difficult it was and took it in their stride as a consequence.

Whether it was wise to choose CLEO as the high-level language is open to question. It was characteristic of the LEO ethos to go its own way and follow its own judgment rather than incline to what was happening elsewhere. By this time generalized high-level languages (COBOL for commercial work and FORTAN for mathematical work) were taking root in the United States. They were not confined to individual manufacturers of individual models, but were directed toward being applicable to the universality of systems. In theory, a program written in one of these languages could be transferred from one manufacturer's systems to another's or from a smaller system to a larger one. In practice there were dialects that betrayed the origins of different versions, and years of standards committee work had to pass before either language could be said to have reached its substantive definition.

Nevertheless, a COBOL programmer for one system could readily read and understand a COBOL program written for another, and a COBOL program could easily be adapted to run on a different system, though not always with the same efficiency. LEO chose to stand outside this growing family. It rejected the possibility of additional compiler complexity and recoiled from an underuse of LEO's special capabilities, such as the sterling arithmetic feature and some of the other macro-instructions produced by microprogramming. There was a firm belief at the very top that the company's experience and field achievement were still preeminent and that therefore there was no good reason to accept as a model what had been devised by others.

Absence of Government Support

By 1961 the construction of LEO III had been completed. It was a remarkable achievement by John Pinkerton and his not very large engineering team. The software implementation was following closely on the availability of equipment for trials. LEO III preceded the IBM 360 announcement by three years. Drawing on one hand from what had been learned of the practicalities of using computers for office work and on the other from the closely monitored technological advances over the years, the new system promised to be smaller, less heat-generating, faster, logically more sophisticated, more user-friendly, more reliable, and, in terms of productivity, several times less expensive than what had gone before.

With its time-sharing, or multiprogramming feature, LEO III was right in the forefront of logical design for commercial work. This had been achieved without government support or, indeed, any R&D support other than that which Lyons itself had been ready to inject. The National Research and Development Corporation (NRDC) set up by Harold Wilson when he was president of the Board of Trade in the postwar Attlee administration,[6] had continued under Churchill, Eden, and Macmillan, but nothing had come LEO's way despite its pathfinding role in the burgeoning world of commercial data processing. Disbursements to others had been small, but despite this lack of encouragement there had been seven or eight British firms each making their own separate and competitive R&D investments into computers of different kinds.

It is fair to say that Lyons as a parent was complaisant to this neglect. One of the five options for progress presented in the 1947 U.S. visit report had been to invite the British government "to coordinate the research in this country and make resources available to get Britain first in the field." [7] But this found little favor at Lyons, which cherished its independence above all things, [8] and there was no initiative from elsewhere. Each company and laboratory went its own way, and there seems to have been no informed appreciation anywhere in Britain of the likely rapidity of change in electronics and peripherals and the daunting amount of R&D investment that would be required to keep pace with it.

By contrast with Lyons, IBM in the U.S. been more than happy to involve the United States. Foreseeing the enormous potential R&D cost, it took on the Defense Department as a very active partner. For its part, the Department recognized early on the probable importance of electronic computers to national security. During the 1950s, when LEO was making its own frugal pioneering way, R&D contracts worth almost $400 million had been awarded by the U.S. armed forces to IBM.[9] Similar contracts, though not on the same scale, had gone to other U.S. companies developing computer equipment.

Much of the work had a valuable fall-out for commercial system development and the contracts made an enormous contribution to the ability to move on a wide front, exploring many possibilities concurrently. Over this formative period, the value of U.S. Government contracts amounted to 60 percent of IBM's total R&D spending.[9] Even had LEO sought and been awarded financial support as others had, the total amount at NRDC's disposal was no more than $15 million to cover the whole of British industry. [9]

Launching LEO III

LEO III was not announced with a fanfare of trumpets. Instead, information was passed quietly to those who had already shown an interest in acquiring a system of their own. In the meantime, work was pressing ahead with preparations for using the first production system as the latest addition to the London Service Bureau. To emphasize the importance that he personally placed on the Bureau business, Anthony Salmon now took over its direction himself. There were two schools of thought at the time. Some believed firmly that, in spite of the slow start in the United Kingdom, there were many larger businesses, government departments, public utilities, and local authorities with workloads sufficient to lead them eventually to systems of LEO III power. The view of others was that this would be restrained by natural conservatism and lack of internal resources, and that organizations were more likely to turn to hand-held bureau services as their entry into electronic data processing. Whichever the inclination, everyone in management agreed that the first LEO III must be devoted both to providing a service of this kind and for all other requirements. These included program trials for clients, who were still being firmly encouraged to have a workload ready for delivery of their equipment, and training facilities for programmers and operators. John Lewis , who had been conspicuously successful on the Glyn Mills implementation, was to head the augmented London Bureau. He was supported by Helen Jackson, who was already in position as programming manager, and by Ralph Land, who was responsible for marketing bureau services; with them were Wood and Pye, whose job it was to manage the operations at the two main sites. Ralph Land, twin brother of Frank, had had exposure to LEO as a management accountant in the teashop headquarters. Mrs. Jackson's appointment was noteworthy because she was the first woman promoted to that level in LEO. Hitherto, without any conscious expression of policy, the instinct had been to shield women from the rigors of night work and other pressures associated with the life of a senior programmer or consultant. Limitations had grown accordingly on the way they were considered for leading roles. However, Mrs. Jackson by this time had spent several years as a mathematical programmer and had shown herself to be extremely well-organized and well-equipped to lead the team, which now grew rapidly to meet the anticipated demand.

LEO III was installed alongside the LEO II system in Hartree House in April of 1962.[10] The policy setting up the first system to obtain in-depth experience of its operational behavior under load proved to be more than justified. The processor performed well, but there was an irksome period of wrestling with the whole range of bought-out peripherals, and especially with the Ampex magnetic tape drives, which had been imported (like the Anelex printers) from the United States.[11] Brake shoes failed and caused tape slippage, oxide coating from the tape clouded the read-write heads, cooling fan failures led to overheating of the tape control circuits, and creasing of tapes made some of what was written unreadable. At one stage, there were even cases of spools falling off drives. None of these faults occurred very often, but they were frequent enough to be disrupting.

A great deal of machine time had to be devoted to postdevelopment engineering work, and bureau commitments fell embarrassingly behind,[12] but the faults were steadily rectified. Among other measures, operating speeds were reduced, a later model of the tape decks was introduced, and the plug connections were upgraded. At length, the Bureau was ready in September 1962 for full-scale business. By that time the second system had already been sent out to Johannesburg.[13]

The First LEO Overseas

Almost everywhere in early computer history, a brave individual must have sufficient faith in his or her own judgment and sufficient enthusiasm for new vistas to carry colleagues along and win their agreement. Here such a person was Mike Hay, a senior officer of Rand Mines, which operated a number of gold mines in South Africa. Applications foreseen were not only the conventional tasks, such as payroll for the very large body of mineworkers, but also advanced management aids, such as mapping of reserves and other technical studies. To LEO, the installation was also seen as providing an on-the-spot demonstration for the other gold-mining houses and for large-scale administration and industry throughout southern Africa. To both partners, the market potential for straightforward bureau work seemed considerable.

The prospects were heightened by Lyons' strong presence in South Africa through its sales of packet tea to shops everywhere in towns, townships, and the countryside. Among its local directors was Arthur Hopewell, politically prominent as Chief Whip of the United Party, which formed the opposition in the South African parliament. He had set up the contacts leading to the deal and had provided introductions for Thompson, who, following the Rand Mines invitation, had explored the ground and significantly advanced the relationship.

Two engineers were sent out to install this first overseas LEO in May of 1962: Tony Morgan, by now an experienced commissioning engineer who had been a member of the team installing the first magnetic-tape LEO II (p. 78), and Arthur Clements, a mechanical engineer who had run the model shop in LEO I days.[14] Clements was proud of being a Freeman of the City of London by servitude—a survival of the old British guild system—having completed his time with the Goldsmiths and Silversmiths Company. He was a taciturn character who was said to win all his arguments by unbreakable long silences. Morgan was equally quiet and unflappable. He had commissioned the first LEO II with magnetic core store at Coventry, and the fact that the Johannesburg system was being installed almost in parallel with the very first LEO III in London in no way disconcerted him.

The task of setting up the bureau and getting the Rand Mines work running on it was placed on Leo Fantl, who had prepared the original proposal. His was a daunting task. He had to start by helping Rand Mines to select staff, while honoring their pledge to give all of their present office staff the opportunity to present themselves for assessment. He was then responsible for training the staff, analyzing and sifting prospective jobs for the system, specifying and programming them, and controlling operations, There was also the quite different responsibility of marketing services and attracting new computer customers. Fantl had arrived in June 1960, within two or three weeks of my signing the agreement in Johannesburg with the Rand Mines board.[15] He was one of the most talented, experienced, and resourceful of all LEO Computers' consultants, and his achievement in this new scene was again outstanding, building a new body of "LEO people" around him and aided from time to time by experienced consultants from the United Kingdom.

When operations began fitfully, even he had his doubts for a while as to whether the system would stand up to all that was planned for it.

Through his skills and resolution, it did (A penetrating picture of what was needed to accomplish this is given by Fantl himself in Chapter 25.)

Warm Reception at Home

Despite the rather low-key approach, the reception of LEO III was warm, particularly in technical circles, where its continued logical innovation was much admired. The first orders came rapidly. Ten systems were marked down for delivery at the end of 1962 and in the first full year that followed.[16] That was almost as many systems as had been installed in the whole lifetime of LEO II. There was the danger that the response would overwhelm the capabilities of the company. Production, recommissioning on site, field maintenance, and systems support all had to be at an altogether higher level. A staggering uplift in output was required from Minerva Road. The site had never been designed for "clean environment" assembly or for a rapid succession of systems undergoing checkout. It was not air-conditioned, and weather invaded the premises at times. Insufficient money had been spent, in fact, to remedy the adverse comparison made in the 1958 Pinkerton/Caminer U.S. report.

Now Minerva Road was being called upon to be the production base for what had suddenly become a full-scale electronics enterprise based on semiconductor circuits specified to run in closely controlled environments. Somehow the production force under Barnes contrived to meet the challenge, but it was never easy to explain to customers who visited Minerva Road why their own site preparations had to be so costly.

In addition to the two bureaus there was another installation in 1962, which was particularly significant in that it was for an industrial giant whose implementation fully embodied the LEO precepts of full systems analysis and integration. The customer was Dunlop, then Britain's leading tire manufacturer but since swallowed up into the conglomerate BTR. The order had been won after a protracted battle with IBM and was a heartening victory for a comprehensive system, covering all aspects of distribution and sales over a punched-card style solution offered on an IBM 1410.

Dunlop's headquarters were at Fort Dunlop, a massive building that can now be seen under a different name from the M6 highway outside Birmingham. The main production and stores were situated there, and there were several other factories and base stores as well. All supplied a network of local depots throughout Britain. Dunlop manufactured 10,000 products, ranging from inflatable tires for giant earthmovers to tires for bicycles and solid tires for industrial equipment. Separate covers, rims, wheels, and all manner of accessories were also manufactured and distributed.

There were five separate markets. One supplied vehicle and cycle manufacturers (the OE market), and another supplied replacements for vehicle users to dealers and garages. There were other markets for government and for export. The fifth was the "mileage market" for large fleet operators, to whom tires were rented on the basis of a charge per mile traveled. Each of the markets had its own, sometimes intricate, pricing structures that had grown up over the years.

The senior consultant assigned was Hermon, who had the benefit of having handled the corresponding application at Wills with a similar tangle of pricing arrangements. His report to Dunlop gave ample evidence of his broad appreciation of the life of the tire company in all its aspects, and went far beyond the existing practices in the offices. The system proposed not only to replace the existing clerical tasks, but also to use the data employed in them to add such innovations as automatic replenishment down the supply chain and a wide range of statistical reports to facilitate better informed management. The report submitted to the Group Financial Controller also contained outline charts and brief nontechnical descriptions of the group of programs that would accomplish all this.[17]

After much costly negotiation, the order for a LEO III was received from Dunlop, but there was a heavy price to pay for it. It had been confidentially agreed during a "family network" intervention that Hermon would be part of the package, although he was unaware of the arrangement. When the order arrived, it was duly announced that he would become a member of the Dunlop management.[18]

This was a severe loss, coming as it did at a time when the skies were bright after a down time and when every experienced member of staff was needed to fully exploit renewed opportunities. Behind the "firing line" the extent of the loss was inadequately appreciated. There was pride in having "good people" but there was the belief that the company had found them and trained them and there was no good reason why more could not be found and trained in the same way. The fact was that even if the company could always enjoy its good fortune in attracting such outstanding people (there were competitors now), training on the job and experience-gathering took time. With the accelerating tempo in the computer world, time was a commodity that LEO did not have too much of if the qualities of LEO III were to be fully exploited.

Meeting the Potential

Any loss was felt the more because of the way in which LEO Computers continued to operate. The consultants used their accumulated experience to analyze customer needs before a sale and to guide the detailed system design and program preparation afterwards. Once attached to a new user, the consultant was committed to ensuring a productive load when the system was recommissioned on site. The consultant gave what time was necessary to the installation until the purchaser became sufficiently self-reliant.

Engaged in this way, after the necessary regrouping, were Frank Land, who reported to me as Chief Consultant, and Comish, Mills, Aris, Jackson, and Payman, who formed a powerful group of Senior Consultants. Alongside them were Mike Josephs, responsible for Technical Support and for liaison with Design; McLeman, who provided an essential backing service in installation programming; and Jacobs, who in addition to other consultancy duties had been given the special assignment of promoting the use of Lector, a mark-sensing device for which there were high hopes.[19]

Additionally, Dan Broido had been put in charge of what was seen as a potentially fruitful European market. He was a native-born Russian who had joined LEO Computers as Chief Mechanical Designer in 1956, and in that capacity had been closely involved in the Lector development. He had become convinced that there was a ready market for computers behind the Iron Curtain, and not unnaturally saw himself as the spearhead. Beside being an inventive engineer, Broido was a remarkably persistent man and he eventually was given the go-ahead, first in Germany and then farther east.

LEOs horizons were expanding. The London Service Bureau under Barnes and Lewis had significantly increased its equipment resources, and the Johannesburg Bureau was also in operation. In addition to the prospecting in Europe, where Broido was necessarily given consultancy support when interest was aroused, there had also been activity in Australia. This latter had culminated in an agreement to install a LEO III in Sydney to be shared between Tubemakers, a steel company, and another LEO Bureau. Again, senior consultancy resources were required to prepare for the loading of this system.

At home, in addition to providing for their other calls and the leap in sales that had attended the introduction of LEO III, several of the consultants had to spend almost all their time with customers to whom they were already committed. There was little time left for responding to others. Proactivly seeking new prospects became exceptional. There was inevitably a brake on the rate of further growth.

The constraints were partly the legacy of an insufficient reaction to the new demands of the entry into the marketplace with LEO II (p. 48)., but there had also been developments in organization. Ten years before, the structure could not have been simpler. Pinkerton was responsible for producing an efficient, reliable machine to meet office needs, and my task was to put it to work. It was part of our job to gather the staff and to train them. Above us was Thompson, who though it was a bit grandiose a title for so small an operation, was Chief Executive. Presiding over the whole was Simmons, who while avoiding involvement in day-to-day affairs, embodied the ethos of what we were about and argued our case authoritatively at court.

Since those days in the early 1950's the expansion of the workforce from a handful to hundreds had been accompanied by a departmental-ization to match. At the top, Thompson had relinquished control of Production and the home Service Bureau to Anthony Salmon, who had, in effect, become joint Chief Executive. In these responsibilities he was assisted by Barnes.[19] Simmons was now largely concentrating his still lively computer interest on integrated applications within Lyons itself. Below them were separate departments for the whole range of activities, backed by an efficient and responsive Training Department managed by Bob Gibson, an experienced engineer who gave invaluable service to all wings of the enterprise. There was also a Personnel department.

A recognizably more conventional organization had evolved, very dif-ferent from the less orthodox ambience in which the consultancy organi-zation had been established at the outset (pp. 66–70). The early applica-tions staff had themselves been front-line programmers informed by a firm grounding in Organization and Methods principles. They had administered the aptitude tests to applicants, carried out the interviews and selection, designed and lectured on the training courses, and trained the newcomers on the job, covering not only the technicalities of the craft, but also the relationship with the businesses whose needs were being served. Trainees were rapidly pulled up the ladder to a position of self-reliance where they soon found themselves inducting the latest LEO arrivals and trainees from outside companies.

What was straightforward in a small operation would not have sat as comfortably in the larger one. It would not have been easy for senior consultants embroiled in the tougher open marketplace to continue to give the time necessary to recruit, train, and develop their successors Nonetheless, the functionalization that came naturally to Lyons meant that the almost organic growth, free of departmental boundaries, with which the consultancy function had evolved could no longer be relied upon.

However, for all the strain, enthusiasm was high and commitment unabated. The end of 1962 saw an order book more than double any that LEO had ever known. The main problem was how to fully exploit the new potential that LEO III had opened up and to reap the fruits of the long cultivation of many leading companies in the service bureau.

9

The Merger with English Electric

1963

The first LEO III installation to a British client went well, but then there was a bombshell. It was announced in February of 1963 that Lyons and English Electric had agreed to merge their computer businesses at home and abroad. The machinery leading to this was a considerable increase in the share capital for LEO Computers Ltd., which was to be owned equally by the two companies.[1] Two months later the revised name, English Electric LEO (EEL), was introduced.

In the atmosphere of the successful launch of LEO III, the announcement caused something between disbelief and dismay to staff at all levels. It was clear from the appointment of Sir Gordon Radley from English Electric as Chairman that the great electrical engineering company had been given the leading role. With English Electric as one of the two or three most powerful organizations in its field, there could be little doubt that whatever the legal terminology, a virtual takeover had occurred. Anthony Salmon was to be the Vice-Chairman,[2] but he could not fail to feel technically lightweight compared to Sir Gordon, a former Director General of the Post Office and already in charge at Marconi, the technologically very advanced subsidiary of English Electric.

From his conversations with Anthony Salmon, Peter Bird states in his book, *LEO: The First Business Computer*, that the evidence was that at this stage "Lyons had no intention of divesting themselves from the emerged company. On the contrary they were determined to stay with computer manufacture. The change of heart, declares Bird, was caused by legal problems that arose unexpectedly when the time came for the computer interests of Marconi, too, to join the new company.[3]

English Electric LEO
Organization

The perception that English Electric was in control was confirmed by the appointment of W. E. Scott, the head of the computer division at Kidsgrove in Staffordshire, as Managing Director. Raymond Thompson, who had been in day-to-day control of LEO since its inception, was given the post of Head of Marketing, though his interests were wide-ranging and, if anything, more directed toward the way in which systems were attuned to clerical work than toward marketing them or devising applications to run on them. In a formal statement, Thompson's sphere of responsibility was promulgated as:[4]

> to establish a powerful and effective sales force; to determine the detailed requirements of future customer applications and, in the commercial field, to provide specialist training courses.

Most of the top jobs fell to the English Electric incumbents. The merged bureaus' organization was placed in the hands of Cliff Robinson at Kidsgrove, and this included the new LEO III bureau at Hartree House. In field maintenance, Derek Royle, from English Electric, was put in charge. His was the challenging task of achieving satisfactory reliability standards on three newly introduced and disparate systems and four other models of varying vintages and design. Under his leadership this was probably the most successful area of the merger. He melded the two sets of engineers, each with their own loyalties, into a cohesive EEL team that was both technically and financially effective.

John Pinkerton, who had successfully brought LEO I and LEO II to fruition and had directed the design of LEO III from scratch, became responsible for product research and planning jointly with Colin Haley from Kidsgrove. Both had new introductions on their hands as well as thoughts for the future.

In the sale field there was a similar arrangement, with Don Kilby, whose background was on the conventional engineering side, representing the English Electric interests. Tony Barnes, besides continuing to run the Minerva Road works, was given the additional job of coordinating the two production units. However, he did not fit naturally into the Kidsgrove manufacturing scene, and his stay there was relatively short.

The immediate shock within LEO was the greater because negotiations leading to the merger had been cloaked in such complete secrecy. There had been suspicions that "something was up," but there had been no sounding of views with the three staff members of the LEO Computers Ltd. Board of Directors, Pinkerton, Barnes, or me. Whether Thompson was consulted at this stage may never be known. Certainly he was deeply upset by the outcome, though he kept it very much to himself.

The way in which the deal was conceived, negotiated, and concluded was in keeping with standard practice at Lyons, however much the LEO people might have thought they were a special case. Business strategy, as opposed to operational management, had always been the preserve of the family. Strategic decisions were "handed down" from the suite of offices on the fourth floor of the Administration Building on the edge of the Cadby Hall estate. The family prerogative was the *quid pro quo* for the kind of very rapid collegiate decisions that had approved the initial grant to Cambridge and the investment in LEO. Now, though, there was an air of "the Lord giveth and the Lord taketh away."

Had the need to justify the deal occurred to anyone, there was no lack of arguments to deploy. With a total payroll approaching 500,[5] LEO was by no means a sideshow financially. Whatever the promise of the future, the subsidiary had been trading at a loss almost consistently since its formation, and this had had a depressing effect on the performance of the Lyons company as a whole.[6] It has always been a matter of pride for the Lyons Board to arrange matters so that an increase profit could be presented to the shareholders every year, but progress since the war had been bumpy; over the past four years there had actually been a decline, to which increased losses by LEO Computers Ltd. had contributed.[7]

The year ending in March of 1962 had been particularly fraught, with LEO II sales tailing off as it was overtaken by second-generation systems from both sides of the Atlantic. Within LEO itself there was still unshaken confidence; with the completion of LEO III they again felt ahead of the competition, the world over. But it had come too late to affect the decision. Lyons badly needed all its resources and management attention to acquire new ventures in order to give fresh impetus to its stagnant core businesses. The ongoing cost of development in the computer field, including the demanding new systems software side, was better understood now, and steps had already been taken confidentially to find a partner in Britain or continental Europe to share the burden.[8]

The Culture Shock

A sharp difference of business culture revealed itself between the London-based LEO organization and their English Electric colleagues, with their base in the North Midlands. The one was a rather idealistic group with a sense of mission to bring efficiency to the office, buoyed by the conviction of "knowing best" about their area of expertise. The vision of the paperless office beckoned way ahead in the future. Even when systems were sold, the LEO team retained its sense of responsibility for them. The new owners must be guided and trained to provide a good home for what they had secured.

At Kidsgrove, not many miles from the English Electric fastness at Stafford, the computer division was made of grittier stuff. It was highly conscious of being part of one of Britain's prime engineering organizations. In English Electric, computers were equipment, just as giant transformers were equipment.

Each side brought its baggage. From the English Electric side the prime contribution was a scientific computer, the KDF 9. Just as Lyons had used the Cambridge Mathematical Laboratory's EDSAC as its springboard, English Electric has obtained its start at the National Physical Laboratory at Teddington and had built on the Alan Turing-designed ACE. Their Chairman, Lord Nelson, served on the NPL Executive Committee.[9] From ACE, the English Electric engineers had derived DEUCE, which after first appearing in 1955 had gained a solid reputation as a medium-sized scientific machine within the pockets of university and other scientific establishments. From the first-generation DEUCE came the second-generation KDF 9 at about the same time as LEO III succeeded LEO II. There was no conflict of interest here. The KDF 9 was as positively dedicated to scientific work as LEO II was to commercial. It was equally innovative in that it introduced the concept of the "stack," which enabled computations to be carried out without the need for store reference to put away partial results and then to operate on them again. This further speeded what was, for its time, an inherently fast machine.

A much smaller computer, the KDN 2, was aimed at linking computer-driven controls to English Electric's far-ranging equipment catalog. It introduced automatic control to ships' engine rooms, power stations, and steel mills. Informed by the intimate knowledge of the processes to be harnessed, the KDN 2 was almost as pioneering as LEO I had been in the office field. Led by a large man named Matt Delahunty, the little team was equally committed to the end results. The KDN 2 met the essential requirements of being compact, rugged, and to a considerable extent impervious to engine heat, vibrations, and atmospheric conditions. It had to be reliable to an extent that was unnecessary for an office computer. An office building would not blow up if some clerical work went awry.

Another small system being offered by English Electric was the KDF 6, which sought to bridge the gap between the process control and commercial worlds. Sometimes, though, it was not sufficiently rugged for the former, and the "new boys" soon decided that it was rarely powerful enough to be cost-effective for the latter. This led to differences on occasions; there was sometimes a feeling that the KDF 6 was being offered more because it was affordable for the customers than out of conviction that it would handle their work.

However, it was the fourth item in the English Electric portfolio that gave rise to the major problems—an office computer known as the KDP 10. This was a British version of the RCA 501, which had been manufactured under license for two or three years at the time of the merger.[10] The RCA 501 had built up a good reputation, but by now it was growing older. Pinkerton and I had seen it under development during our U.S. tour, and it had been announced as far back as 1958, at roughly the same time as the deliveries were made of the earliest LEO IIs.[11] It was a machine whose quality was primarily in the professionalism of the engineering rather, even then, than in logical innovation. In Britain the first KDP 10 delivery had been made in 1961, but with the rapidity of change the system was now well past its prime.[12]

LEO III and KDP 10 were aimed at precisely the same market, and it became frustrating to the LEO consultants that they found themselves incapable of proving to some of the English Electric salesmen that, job for job, the new LEO System would generally be the more cost-effective. Their counterparts were equally tried by what they saw as a failure to value sufficiently the reputation that the RCA 501 had won and the appeal that the KDP 10 therefore held out for potential users who wished to avoid all unnecessary risk.

The success of the merged company had inevitably to be closely related to what it proposed to make and sell. A decision on this might reasonably have been made during the merger negotiations. Whether it was ever raised in the talks, in which Lyons was guided by merchant banker Lazards is not known. Certainly no decision emerged, nor was any direction given by the new board once the merger had been effected. Wilf Scott, always conscious of the fall-back value of the licensing arrangement with RCA, was reluctant to weaken the relationship, represented for the present by the KDP 10, in any way. For his part, Thompson felt such a distaste for arguing any matter with Scott that the matter went by default. He viewed Scott as an altogether inferior chief to Simmons, to whom he had been accustomed for so long, and found it difficult to defer to the new Managing Director in any way.

As a positive outcome of the merger, English Electric LEO Computers became equipped with a number of regional offices—in London, Birmingham, and Scotland—to reinforce the bases in Hartree House and Kidsgrove. However, because of the haze regarding product policy, the full fruits of the partnership could not be harvested. In London, as one example, where the success of English Electric in banking and insurance provided a solid foundation for building with the most up-to-date equipment available, the opportunities were diminished by the partisanship that was inevitable without a firm direction from the top of the company. A manager was moved across to take charge of this office, but it was not easy for common modes of assessment to be established. (An account of this period is given by Ralph Land in Chapter 26.)

A severe obstacle to unification was that nationally the merged forces operated on radically different lines. In English Electric there was a conventional organization with separate sales and systems staff. In LEO the combination of both functions in "consultants" was a cardinal feature. Nothing was made easier by the founding announcement's appointment of joint sales managers, one from each tradition. After several difficult months this dichotomy was resolved by my being given responsibility for the whole of the home market. Eastern Europe soon followed. However, there remained an unreadiness to rock the boat by objectively reassessing ability and experience across the board as a whole using a single set of criteria. Relative seniorities for the most part stayed in place. On the LEO side this inhibited the rapid promotion of those who made their mark, which hitherto had been a distinctive feature of the organization. Equally, on the English Electric side it was irksome to some of the salesmen to go for training in skills that had previously been assigned to assistants.

Where the opportunity arose, staff were moved in order to bring more commonality. Mike Gifford, a high-flyer who was a late recruit to LEO from the Lyons Works Department, used the commercial experience he had already gained to carry through the successful implementation of a KDP 10 for Schweppes. Neil Lamming went to New Zealand with an English Electric KDF 6. In general, though, it remained an uphill task to reconcile the two traditions. Frank Land, responsible to me for field work in a major part of the market, bore a heavy burden. He was a naturally patient man, but this was a new experience for him. It was especially trying that the "sizing" methods (again, the word was not yet current) that were habitual in LEO were not accepted by what sometimes seemed like "the other side." The differences were eventually hammered out on the ground, but with resources thin in any event, the process was wasteful and bruising and much impetus was lost.

LEO III in the Field

Notwithstanding the upheaval, LEO III installations of orders already taken went ahead smoothly in 1963. They represented a cross-section of the markets and applications toward which the model was directed and provided a firm base to build on. Four systems were installed for industrial and commercial users, including one bought by Lyons for their own use, two for government departments, and two for local authorities; there was also the installation in Australia.[13]

Among the early industrial installations was one for CAV, a subsidiary of the Lucas group, with its works at Action. Prominent in the world of the electrical car accessories used in many British private cars and transportation vehicles, CAV had over a period developed a varied portfolio of service work. They had started as far back as 1956, when programs were designed by Leo Fantl to their specification to carry out exploratory work on the design of engine pumps.[14] The programs aimed at making use of the computer's speed to carry out partial differential simulations of what happened inside the pumps, a process almost prohibitive in time-cost using hand methods. Other product design problems followed, building up over the years a repertoire of utility programs directed toward understanding and improving the behavior of the company's products. Heat and pressure characteristics of engine cylinders and cold start and fuel injection systems were among the performance aspects covered by the suite.

Service time was used on LEO II as well as on LEO I, and the scientific applications were joined by payroll for the works. The two wings developed side by side. CAV's own programmers, led by Fred Bishop, were almost part of the LEO team, and they were well qualified to convert the existing programs for running on LEO III and to continue to build up the load.[15]

Smith and Nephew, the Birmingham-based manufacturer of market-leading health and sanitary products, was another industrial firm to take the plunge. Their office manager, John Hargreaves, learning of the joint venture in South Africa, had gained the support in principle of his board for a similar enterprise to tap the rich market for service work in the Midlands and to make use of their extensive contacts there.[16] Though it was not possible at this stage to make further capital investment, Smith and Nephew was assured of LEO Computers' cooperation and decided to proceed on its own, starting off with its considerable load of distributive and sales work.

However, in the commercial field the most important installation of this first full year was Shell Mex and BP. The potential load was huge. The company was a marketing consortium joining the retailing activities in the UK of the two great oil producers. Again, the bread-and-butter tasks were invoicing on a very large scale and the sales statistics that sprang from the invoices. Additionally there was pressure from a backroom member of the management team that equal support should be given to operational research studies involving mathematical statistical computations. The clerical content of the report was very well received, and it was accepted that LEO Computers was by now thoroughly at home with work of this sort and competent to guide the implementation of their main load. The company, though, had little to offer by way of standard statistical subroutines, and misgivings were expressed by the economist as to whether LEO could match what was being urged on them by competitors. In what became a difficult situation, Raymond Thompson was brought in to "front" the group of Shell Mex executives, and after a whole cluster of consultants had been deployed the order was eventually secured.[17]

The Shell Mex and BP systems were installed in a new office block in Hemel Hempstead and Brian Bowden, one of their rising stars, was given the opportunity to prove himself. He was responsible both for the loading and operation of the computers and for the interface with his demanding colleagues in the field and at Shell Mex House. Later came Donald Moore, who had previously encountered LEO as an officer in the Royal Army Pay Corps. Later still he was prominent in management consultancy at Peat Marwick. Moore was much impressed by the untypical zeal of the supplier in ensuring that operations and applications were running to plan even after the checks had been signed. On one occasion, after giving a warm testimonial to representatives of another large enterprise visiting the site, he concluded, "But be careful to make it clear to them that it's your computer and doesn't belong to them any more."

Installation for Lyons

Lyons had long since taken responsibility for the work on their own LEO II at Cadby Hall, and the vigorous O&M department looked forward to realizing far-reaching plans on a much more powerful LEO III. This was also among the first-year deliveries.

Lyons had taken over the initial jobs programmed by LEO staff, such as the payrolls, teashops deliveries, wholesale bakery invoicing, and tea blending, and had added other jobs of its own. The later arrivals were not always as successful, partly because they were beginning to invade territory where almost independent divisions were increasingly resistant to inroads into their way of life.

In mapping out the future, Lyons O&M now possessed something of a bible in John Simmons's *LEO and the Managers*, which had appeared in 1962, and they were determined to work their way to the realization of its objectives. Lyons was very much a customer now and completely certain that "the student is as good as his teacher." There were no longer the informal personal contacts that had occurred before the departure of the LEO people to Minerva Road and Hartree House. After the effective takeover by English Electric, the two wings could best be described as "separated." When the gap seemed to be becoming too wide, Simmons asked for a senior consultant to be appointed and Aris added Lyons to his other clients, but the relationship was inevitably different from that with less knowledgeable users coming fresh to computers.

An important innovation attending the LEO III/7 installation was the Lector document reader,[18] with which LEO consultant Jacobs was concerned in the outside market. This enabled marks on forms, representing numbers, to be read by a photo-sensing device and converted into perforations on paper tape. The process was slow, since the forms had to be fed by hand and the tape was read into the computer at relatively slow speed, but to Lyons it represented a first step toward reducing the new chore of data preparation that had replaced some of the mindless repetitive work that Simmons had criticized in his book. The device was initially used to read the Bakery salesmen's order forms. This represented a further advance in the Wholesale Bakery Rails application, which had been in the forefront of office systems worldwide for more than a quarter of a century. By eliminating the task of perforating the item numbers and quantities, three hours were shaved off the job and the whole business cycle was advanced.

The potential of the mark-sensing technique was well appreciated by the LEO consultancy organization, but the obstacle to wider introduction was the need for studies within organizations—not only of the jobs on which it might be employed, but also of the management relationships. It was becoming less common by this time for LEO consultants to have the luxury of such an investigation, and there seemed to be very few potential users prepared to make a study on their own.

It had been intended that Lector would be connected on-line to the computer, thus cutting out another manual operations. The online version, Autolector, was completed a year later, replacing Lector on the Lyons installations.

Installation in Australia

Tubemakers, who received the first LEO in Australia,[19] were an affiliate of Stewarts and Lloyds at Corby, whose LEO II had been operating for some years. There were close personal relationships between the managements of the two organizations. The Australians had kept in close touch with the implementations of succession of applications at Corby. Neil Pollock, the Midlands company's O&M manager, was well satisfied with progress and had been a firm point of reference.

The arrangement with Tubemakers was that they would operate their work by day, allowing service bureau work to be run during the evening and at night. Peter Gyngell, who had joined LEO Computers from the Ford Parts Depot at Aveley, was assigned to head a new offshoot in Australia, from which he could give support to Tubemakers as well as carrying out similar operational and marketing responsibilities to those of Fantl in South Africa. Gyngell had worked closely with the senior consultant, Frank Land, in implementing the parts distribution system on the Aveley LEO II, and had proved to be a responsive and congenial colleague, and a fast learner. A massive Welshman, he settled happily in New South Wales and became well known there. Even though Gyngell had spent only a short time at LEO Computers he was well equipped by the intensive experience at Aveley; his enthusiastic temperament was a lively advertisement for LEO overseas.

LEO III to the Government

The two local government installations in 1963 were for the London Boroughs Joint Computer Committee and Manchester Corporation. The former was remarkable in that it was based on a consortium of six southeast London boroughs who had come together to make an investment that none of them could justify by themselves. They were led vigorously by officers from the Greenwich Borough Council, which had been running a sizable payroll as a LEO II bureau job for some time. Bermondsey, Southwark, and Woolwich had followed them in bureau work, and later Camberwell and Deptford completed the group.

Greenwhich played its part through an excellent officer named Derek Schartau. Again the system was starting with a full load as soon as it was installed. The only problem was that the computer room wasn't ready yet, and the system had to start its life in cramped quarters that were a relic from an innkeepers' charity. Those who worked in the installation remember the four stone fireplaces and the oak panels listing the benefactors.[20] Environmentally the premises were grossly substandard, but the equipment was recommissioned and work was run nonetheless. Perhaps its beginnings at Minerva Road had conditioned the assemblage to weather adverse conditions.

The breakthrough to central government was made with installations for Customs and Excise and the Board of Trade. Neither appeared at the time to be among the larger departments in terms of computer potential, but they were a welcome start. The only previous order received from the government was for the then Ministry of Pensions, where a LEO II had been installed four years earlier. Successive governments had not gone out of their way to encourage LEO's pioneering efforts in a field that was now promising to be a major factor in world industry and trade.

It has already been noted that there was an absence of the kind of R&D contracts from which U.S. manufacturers had profited so much. The problem now was not so much to which company orders were placed as one of the government placing orders for advanced office systems at all. As seen from English Electric LEO, there seemed to be little recognition of the potential contribution to office efficiency and the economy or that therefore the government had a duty to promote the British computer industry. There was no priming of the pump, nor did there appear to be any sense of urgency in instituting studies to identify suitable projects.

There was no evidence of government recognition that it could influence the direction of computer development by indicating what might most profitably be tackled from within its own mountain of paperwork. Instead, possible projects dribbled in and, where technically endorsed by Treasury O&M and the Technical Support Unit, they still had to pass an economic evaluation as stringent as if computers had been current for half a century. The whole process could have been speeded up very considerably had LEO been asked to supply consultants to sketch out the likeliest propositions.

It was not within the nature of the protocol for there to be shortcuts. The intention to place an order for a LEO III for Customs and Excise had been made known by telephone on December 14, 1961, by Her Majesty's Stationery Office,[21] which was responsible for the formalities of procurement for computers just as it was for paper clips. The order was conditional on an exacting trial of the time-sharing feature on January 2, 1962. The trial involved, among other features, a bank of magnetic tape drives providing and receiving a concurrent flow of data and results. The trial was devised to test the limits of LEO's capacity in multiprogramming, and had to be checked meticulously; there was no reason to expect any indulgence. It meant that consultancy, software, and engineering staff saw the New Year in hard at work. Anthony Salmon, learning of the effort, acted as Santa Claus and appeared unheralded with food and champagne. Private cars were not as common in those days, and he also commandeered blankets and pillows from the Cumberland Hotel. The trial the next day was successful, and installation at Southend was the fruit of it.

High Hopes at the Post Office

If the central government was moving slowly, there were more encouraging signs from the General Post Office (GPO), which then comprised not only the postal services and National Savings Department, but also the telephone services (now privatized as BT) and others. The GPO had its own very powerful O&M Branch and its own Post Office Engineering Department, strong in all aspects of electromechanical design and maintenance and with a growing presence in electronics.

The O&M Branch was under C. R. (Nick) Smith, an Assistant Secretary with long experience in many parts of the Post Office. There was an enormous amount of clerical work to be done, including on the one hand Telephone Billing, reputed to be the biggest invoicing job in the world, and on the other the accounting for the Post Office Savings Bank, where at that time almost every man, woman, and child held an account. Having decided that the time had come for an infusion of computer power, Smith paid visits to every candidate supplier, including what had become the almost ritual pilgrimage under IBM World Trade auspices to Poughkeepsie.[22] Here, as in all his other work visits, Smith was accompanied by colleagues from PO Engineering. After relating what was available to applications, the Post Office decided on two pathfinding applications, one for each of the two wings. They were to be LEO IIIs.

The plan in Smith's mind was that the work would largely be carried out in the bureau mode, following the LEO pattern. One service would be based on the National Savings Department (of Britain) although other work would be undertaken if it meshed in satisfactorily. The other service would cover the enormous load of the telephone service and other Post Office departments, and provide a general resource for government. This approach developed further, and later Smith was instrumental in having legislation passed to enable outside work to be undertaken as well. The eventual organization was named the National Data Processing Service (NDPS).

In making the initial implementation, C. R. Smith leaned heavily on LEO support. Hands-on experience of office applications was still rare, and the confidence displayed by the LEO personnel was infectious.

To support the implementations there was a succession of high-quality consultants to guide and assist the Post Office in every way. First came Mike Jackson, who led the small team that prepared the response to invitation and went on to set the initial applications in motion. He brought with him five years' experience, starting with engineering programming on the Stewarts and Lloyds "anchor problem" and including the pilot schemes for production control at Renold Chains and CAV and consultancy on the initial applications at Customs and Excise. He was followed by John Smith and then by Ninian Eadie, with whose help many of the Post Office aspirations reached maturity. There was a relationship that was classically in the LEO mode, at the same time professional and personal. The young consultants, as well as being able to guide applications analysis, were all capable programmers (and intellectually and physically lively). Jackson's off-work interest was in sailing and racing dinghy design, where his ambition was to reach the limits of inherent speed within the regulation dimensions. Eadie was also a first-rank sailor who had represented Britain internationally. They were regarded by C. R. Smith as being as much his resource as LEO's, and he looked upon them as a complement to his own staff, whose exposure to the ways of the commercial world was limited. Additionally, a great deal of my own time came to be devoted to meetings with Smith and preparing for them. In return he made it clear that if equipment, software, and programs behaved well and if cooperation continued, LEO could expect to be a front-runner when the hoped-for expansion took place.

Commissioning LEO 326

While the merger negotiations with English Electric were proceeding there had been progress on a faster version of LEO III that took advantage of fresh advances in technology. Logically identical to the basic model, its store access speed was more than five times as fast and its add time almost seven times as fast. Additionally, instructions were assisted by faster microelectronic logic than before. The increased arithmetic speed made it possible both to run individual programs faster and to run more programs concurrently.[23]

When commissioned, LEO III/12 (as it was numbered in the works) remained an experimental system. For the first time there was the luxury of a production system staying in the hands of the engineers for further development.[24]

As a model for sale, the system was named LEO 326. It quickly attracted attention from the still relatively few office managements with very large volumes of data processing and a readiness to consider changing their methods sufficiently to justify the employment of a comparatively large computer. The Post Office had been made aware of the 326 project at an early stage, and this played an important part in their decision to install LEO III systems, which it saw as compatible forerunners. It was obvious to Nick Smith that the basic LEO III would need to be replicated many, many times to cope with the enormous Post Office loads. Shell Mex and BP had similar considerations. A LEO 326 was altogether more space-effective than a number of the smaller systems providing the same overall power. Lyons, too, was keenly interested.

It now became possible for the first time for large LEO users to try out their work at the basic level and then switch their load to the higher level without the burden of program modifications.

10

The Range Revolution

1964

Following a mixed bag of shocks, problems, and successes, 1964 opened promisingly. The population of LEO systems in the field had more than doubled; bureaus had been established on three continents to sustain ongoing support in the LEO way; the time-sharing facility had been conclusively demonstrated and heavily used in practice; installations had been made in the fruitful local government market and in central government; there were high hopes at the Post Office; and the solitary LEO III had grown a much bigger brother. Then came several major events, each one sufficient in itself to make the year decisive in LEO's subsequent life story.

The IBM 360 Range

The most significant event was the wholly unexpected announcement of the IBM 360 range.[1] Up to this time IBM's mainstream commercial products had been essentially sophisticated extensions of their punched-card lines. At the very expensive top there was the arithmetically very fast but comparably very expensive 700 series. While attractive to the largest scientific users, these systems were well outside the price range for most commercial enterprises, even in the United States. This was all the more true in Britain, where the Royal Army Pay Corps (p. 79) was a remarkable exception.

For most users the less ambitious systems had enabled the large family of punched-card users, which included most large enterprises and administrative centers, to test the water of computers without altering the structure of their clerical work. There was the attractiveness of not having to venture in too deep. This meant, though, that IBM had been unable to compete on equal terms against LEO III for that minority of users that was prepared to contemplate major change. The IBM 1401 and its upgrade, the IBM 1410, were able to efficiently execute parts of a job, but were incapable of handling the integrated job for which the whole succession of LEO systems had been devised. Now, suddenly, on April 7, IBM announced not just a single model but an unprecedented small-to-large compatible range. There were to be six processors and thirty peripherals of differing speed, capacity, and capability.

The internal report in which the range was proposed had been code-named SPREAD. Presented in January of 1962, it had been kept completely secret for two years, which was remarkable given the sizable number of very capable "IBM watchers" who were anticipating some move and watching out for a sign.[2] The kernel of the report was the principle that once committed, users would be securely "locked in" to the new range. Users would be able to start with a small model, and as their workloads grew they could move higher and higher up the range with no conversion restraints. Originally, though, IBM's intended introduction tactics had followed the usual pattern, with care being taken to protect the existing rented market base. The new models were to be phased in over something like two years. There were more than eight thousand 1400 series systems in the field or on order by this time.

This plan was shattered by the announcement in December of 1963 by Honeywell of the H 200, cheaper and four times as fast as the 1401, to which it was architecturally almost identical.[3] Furthermore, it was claimed that by using "Liberator" software, the H 200 could automatically take over programs already running on the 1401 in the field. There was no alternative to moving fast, and with its dramatic riposte IBM was able to reinforce its domination in world markets. The wry comment, "No one was ever fired for recommending IBM" become commonplace.

Soon there was the challenge of not one, but two, compatible ranges. Alarmed by the IBM announcement, ICT in the UK rapidly resolved its uncertainties about what was to follow the modestly powered 1301. Only five months later it countered with a seven-model range of its own.[4] The range was based on the Canadian Ferranti Packard FP 6000, which had been under observation for some time. The two central members of the resultant 1900 range were closely derived from the Canadian development, and this enabled attractively rapid delivery to be offered. ICT's highly competent manufacturing division undertook delivery of these virtually copied models within four to six months, whereas IBM's precipitate announcement had given rise to 18- to 24-month delivery times.[5]

Both ranges were competitively priced. IBM had taken advantage of the emergency as an opportunity to shake off the "seven dwarfs," as its U.S. rivals were dubbed. ITC necessarily followed suit, and its 1900 price list was closely related to that for the IBM models.

The New Marketplace

The announcement of the new ranges inevitably affected the makeup of the British marketplace. From now on, English Electric LEO would always find itself in at least a three-way competition for any new installation. Hitherto, it had been possible to make a case that what was offered by the two market leaders, and especially ICT, was ill-attuned to full-scale integrated data processing. Now, while there were still shortcomings in the two ranges that betrayed their finalization in haste, the weaknesses were less obvious than the attractiveness of the corporate strengths behind them.

Over the years the nature of the office computer world had changed in character. At the outset, LEO had worked closely with users in specifying the scope of the applications and the detailed needs to be satisfied. "Joint studies" was the term that was often used. Sometimes these had to be at arms length through a resident administrative or O&M function, but whenever possible the contact was with the productive or distributive operations on the ground. This latter approach was time-consuming and expensive and swallowed up the experts involved, but it was much more likely to uncover the real needs rather than the presumptions enshrined in existing office procedures.

It had never been common for any supplier to be given a free run of an enterprise in this way, and as alternative equipment, such as the IBM 1410, became available, such in-depth studies become the exception. Now, with the arrival of multimodel competing ranges, they became almost unknown. The sharp distinction that had been forming between the roles of management consultancy and equipment manufacturer became firm. An organization was expected to be either one or the other.

So far as the office machine companies were concerned, it continued to be a "caveat emptor" world. They made sure their equipment would have the facilities and perform at the speed and with the reliability that they specified. It was the prospective user's responsibility in the last resort to judge whether these facilities and speed and reliability were adequate to process the work that the customer had in mind.

For all that new users were generally and almost by definition wholly inexperienced in computer planning or implementation at this time, it fell to them to specify their requirements and for the several invited suppliers to respond. What emerged frequently reflected the constraints of an existing conventional system. This practice was not only normal among commercial enterprises; the government, with its departmental and central O&M resources, had for some time been presented its specifications in this way.

It was a more mechanistic two-sided world in which LEO and its English Electric partner were now competing. It was not the environment in which they had grown up, and it offered fewer opportunities for professional satisfaction than before. On the other hand, the market had grown profusely and there was no alternative other than to observe the prevailing reactive conditions rather than the proactive conditions that would have been preferred. However, the raised level of interest engendered by the two ranges was recognized as increasing opportunities at least as much as the competing machines increased the challenge.

Within English Electric LEO, there was every belief that with their application skills and the user-friendly architecture of their systems they would continue on the steep upward climb that had attended the introduction both of the data processing LEO III and the mathematical KDF 9.

Successor Studies at English Electric LEO

Meanwhile, in what had become the industry norm given the rapid improvements in technology, English Electric LEO had started studies for replacements for LEO III and KDF 9 not long after their first-year deliveries. A "state of the art" system, code-named KLX, was emerging.[6] Under the leadership of Pinkerton and with the assistance of an erstwhile member of the consultancy staff, Mike Josephs, the architecture had been mapped out in some detail, and software had been broadly specified. In hardware terms the system was to employ the new integrated circuits as used by Marconi in their Myriad process control and military command computers, introduced in 1963. By the time of the ICT announcement, work had advanced as far as the construction of engineering prototypes.

In the radically changed computer world, Scott felt the need to take action more quickly. Quite apart from the standard that had been set for multimodel ranges, he was convinced that only a new range would unite the two wings of the company, which were still separated as much by their system allegiances as by the geographical distance of most of them. But however much effort was put in, KLX was still a long way off. There were uncalculated financial burdens to be faced in converting the experimental work so far into a full range of equipment and software, and there was no certainty that the parent company would be ready to make the huge investment that might be required.

It was in this situation that privileged information was received about the advent of yet another new range. RCA, English Electric's closest associate technically, had also taken action. Finding its 501 model base in danger of erosion by the IBM 360 announcement, RCA, too, had looked at what it had in the planning stages and had decided to go the same way.[7] Invoking the licensing arrangement with RCA that had earlier given rise to the KDP 10, Scott at once decided to dispatch a team to RCA headquarters at Camden, New Jersey. I was appointed to lead the team, and the other members were Colin Haley, the remarkably knowledgeable head of engineering at Kidsgrove, and Denis Blackwell, head of software there. There was no delay; everything else had to be dropped. It was made clear that what RCA had developed was to be assessed as a likely successor range for English Electric LEO.

The team arrived in the United States in November of 1964, just before the range announcement, though the imminence of this was not known in advance. The range was named the Spectra 70, and there were to be four members. The two larger members, the 70/45 and 70/55, were constructed with integrated circuits, technologically similar to those in the Marconi Myriad. RCA, rich from its triumphs in color television, had spared no expense in their development. These models were equipped with very large multilayer integrated circuit boards.[8]

Like the other two ranges, the different parts of the Spectra 70 range had been put together hurriedly. The two smaller members were much less impressive. They employed discrete circuitry but, though compatible with the larger models, offered only reduced instruction sets.

Architecturally, the Spectra range had the advantage over other ranges in its provision for time-sharing and in concern for online working in the larger models. In this sense it related well to the characteristics with which LEO had established itself.

In software the picture was less satisfactory, despite what seemed to the visiting party to be an army of experts and programmers. What was prepared or planned did not appear adequate to handle the multistrand workloads that appeared to have developed further in the UK than in the U.S.[8] There was criticism, too, of the upper limit of the range, for it was clear that the 70/55 at the top would not satisfy the aspirations of the LEO 326 user in the future.[8] Oddly, RCA executives were not conscious of the shortfall, though it made them vulnerable to at least three models at the top of the IBM range. They continued to aim at their existing RCA 501 "middle market" though even the true middle was moving upwards.

A detailed report was completed in the United States and presented to Scott for his Christmas reading. It drew on a close examination of what had been achieved and the ongoing work in the research and development laboratories, the software development, and the manufacturing plant at West Palm Beach in Florida. The party also had talks with those responsible for the marketing and financial affairs of the computer business, despite launch preoccupation's.

The report concluded that Spectra 70 was indeed suitable for adoption as the basis for a replacement English Electric LEO range, but there were two firm provisos. The first was that it would be necessary to introduce a new top-of-the-range model to compete with IBM and ICT at the upper end of the commercial market. The second was that a new operating system would be required to support the logical facilities that the team thought essential.

The report also highlighted a significant possible ground for misgiving, which was that RCA had very deliberately chosen to meet IBM head-on and to employ the IBM 360-byte notation and its instruction code.[8] With the widespread use of high-level languages this would impact the ordinary user a great deal less than it would have five years earlier. However, it might still present itself as more a handicap than a help in Britain. Detailing the concern, the report ran:

> A prospective customer might well ask why, if there is no essential difference between our model and IBM's, they should not go to the originator. The simple answer is that so far as we are concerned these are industry standards with which we have no quarrel, but in the practical case we should be able to say that . . . throughout the range we give better cost/performance curves than IBM and we will back our equipment with better service in the field.

Despite the diverse composition of the team, drawn from senior members of both the LEO and English Electric wings, the report was completely unanimous.

New High in LEO Installations

While all these momentous events were transforming the computer world, life proceeded in the field with LEO installations edging above the 1963 level to a new high. Reliability had still not reached the desirable state where faults could be regarded as very exceptional, but Derek Royle and his growing force of maintenance engineers were coping well with their greatly expanded coverage in the UK and abroad. Customers were meeting their objectives and time targets by employing feasibility checks, reconcilations, restarts, and other safeguarding techniques with which they had been inculcated in their learning stage.

New domestic installations in 1964 included the second system for Shell Mex and BP at Hemel Hempstead and others to such British household names as Cerebos, the domestic salt manufacturer, and Heinz, which had decided to go along with LEO rather than follow their parent company in the United States.[9] Doug Comish, the forceful Liverpudlian, became very close to both managements and set the companies securely on the right road. Another installation was to British Oxygen, with uncommonly intricate sales statistics a principle objective. Perhaps most adventurous of all in the commercial field was Kayser Bondor, a no more than medium-sized manufacturer of ladies' hosiery and underwear, which it distributed to its own boutiques and other outlets. There were doubts within LEO as to the economic justification for such relatively expensive equipment, but the enthusiasm of the management at Baldock in Hertfordshire for the business benefits that they hoped to gain carried the day.

There were also two more installations in Australia, both in Melbourne. The first was Shell Australia, which could be described as a spin-off from what had occurred at Shell Mex and BP, although there was only a very loose association between the two companies in that they shared a common parent.

U.S. manufacturers had mounted an intensive assault on the Australian market, and Shell had the whole spectrum of models to choose from. An exhaustive study was made, but in the end the promise of the same quality of support in Australia as was evident in the UK had played a significant part in their decision. They were inevitably going to be a long way from the headquarters of whichever supplier they chose and they needed to feel secure. A passage from the Study Group's report read:[10]

> LEO Computers have established an excellent reputation in the UK for successful installations of computers and have been known to refuse to supply where they considered the chances of success were not good. The people we have dealt with here have impressed us more than representatives of any other company, and we know that a similar impression has been registered with other potential users with whom we have had discussions.
>
> The report submitted by LEO Computers was by far the best of any, confirming the favorable impression we had gained of local personnel. Its content demonstrated imagination as well as computer knowledge and hard work.

The second Australian installation of the year was for Colonial Mutual Life. This was LEO's first insurance installation anywhere, though the English Electric wing had been more successful in that area. Colonial Life came to the venture with the experience of having been the first

Australian life insurance company to augment its punched-card installation with the early small-scale computer equipment. This was the first fruit of Gyngell's responsibility for attracting new users as well as serving and guiding the two he had inherited.

Around this time the company made a further staffing investment in the antipodes, when Neil Lamming, a young man trained as a junior consultant, accompanied a KDF 6 out to New Zealand.

There were also stirrings in Eastern Europe. Dan Broido's efforts (p. 95) were beginning to yield results. Born in Siberia, where his parents had been political exiles, and a graduate of the prestigious Berlin Technical Institute, he was completely fluent in both Russian and German and as a natural linguist he was able to pick up other Slavic languages quickly.

Czechoslovakia had emerged as the most receptive target in Eastern Europe. There was interest both in the government service in Prague and in the coal and steel belt in the east of the country around the town of Ostrava. There was, however, an impediment in that LEO III was too small to meet the needs of any of them, while there was the danger of the LEO 326 falling under the prohibitions of the COCOM regulations imposed by the United States. These had been framed to prevent the Soviet Union and China and their satellites from obtaining or developing any equipment that could advance their military capability. Not only U.S. entities came under this embargo, but also equipment manufactured abroad under U.S. license, or including components such as, in the case of computers, peripheral equipment manufactured in the U.S. The declared end purpose was not regarded as relevant. The perception was that wherever it was installed a computer could be used for prohibited purposes; it could even be moved elsewhere.

The solution was found with a reduced-speed version of LEO 326, which fell within the COCOM limits but was still powerful enough to perform satisfactorily in the contexts that had been discussed. It was rather oddly designated the LEO 360 to incorporate the 6.0 μs store cycle time in its name.[11] The model was geared down to operate at less than half the speed of the LEO 326, but it was still nearly three times faster than the basic LEO III. It led to LEO's first orders from continental Europe.

The new model was also attractive to a number of home users to whom it was revealed. Compared with the two range explosions of the year, this was the "miniest" of ranges, but the step-by-step ease of movement that it offered was welcome nonetheless.

The Largest Order Yet

The two planned installations for the Post Office were duly effected partway through the year, one at a modern office building, Charles House, in

West Kensington, London, and the other at a new Savings Bank building at Lytham St. Annes, close to Blackpool. Applications work was quickly begun and the outcome was promising enough for orders for "bulk" systems to follow, though only after a thorough assessment of what was now available and a determined onslaught on the rather mechanistic maintenance tariffs of what was now English Electric LEO Computers, Ltd.

An important evaluation tool introduced by the Post Office was the Post Office Work Unit (POWU), which was based by their O&M and programming staff on representative sequences from programs that had already been implemented or sketched. The microprogramming feature in the LEO III range was of assistance in responding to this assessment in that it enabled additional instructions to be added that corresponded to the requirements identified by the Post Office. They were also, of course, of value to other users. The enhancement defined by Mike Josephs was made possible by the continued close relationship between the consultants and design.

At the press conference announcing the order at Post Office headquarters at St. Martins le Grand in London, the Postmaster General (PMG) Tony Benn, MP declared:[12]

> We in the Post Office have very strongly believed in the computer as the most powerful tool of our modern age in the business of increasing our efficiency, and we have devoted a very great deal of study indeed to the problems they have posed for us in economics, techniques, and organization.

After stating that five large LEO 326 installations was the largest order for general-purpose commercial data processing so far announced in Europe, the PMG went on:

> I am pleased to say that we have been able to place this order with a British manufacturer after a most stringent examination of the tenders which have been made to us directed toward finding the machine which offered the best value for money . . . It is very encouraging that the British computer industry is currently capable of standing up to and beating on its own merits the competition from overseas.

In the course of his address Benn referred to the telephone service as providing "the largest load for our future." In words reflecting the impact that the LEO concept already had on Post Office thinking, he declared:

> The words *integrated data processing* are very freely bandied about in the computer world, but on the wall behind me you will see a diagram illustrating what we think is an extremely sophisticated scheme for integrated data processing in the telephone manager's area. The idea is that data relating to any single occurrence shall be fed only

once to the computer and retained within the machine. The importance of all this is that having thus designed our master plan we can develop its elements one by one in the certain knowledge that they will all fit together properly.

Telephone billing was, in fact, in an advanced stage of preparation by this time. Mike Jackson and his team, aided by efficient specification work by Post Office O&M, had actually completed the programs, including those for the taking on of the enormous subscriber records, in three months using only four programmers. Consequently, after the most exacting trial run to satisfy Nick Smith's injunction *"Il faut les torturer,"* the programs were fully ready for loading the London and Regional NDPS systems as they were delivered.

With the Post Office embarking on its computer expansion, Ninian Eadie took over responsibility for providing the LEO consultancy service. He brought with him experience with LEO in South Africa as well as at home and, forging a remarkably close relationship, was able to give guidance and support as one large project after another was brought to fruition. He gives an account of these years in his reminiscences in Chapter 21.

More Innovations

At Lyons, too, progress was being made. The LEO III was being loaded with old and new jobs, but the urge to make inroads into the new drudgery of data preparation was undiminished. Earlier in the year, a firm step had been taken toward the "no hands" office that increasingly came to be seen as a realistic goal. An Autolector document reader and a Xeronic printer represented complementary innovations in input and output.[13] They followed sustained endeavor by the LEO design engineers with the senior consultant, John Aris, closely involved. He had been particularly concerned with the printer assessment, at Lyons' request, and had made important contributions to its eventual design.

The Autolector was the automatic feed and further developed version of the slow, hand-fed Lector that had been delivered with the Lyons LEO III. Forms marked by salesmen with quantities could now be used to initiate deliveries and invoicing without manual intervention other than to place a pile in the feed. It was clearly a development with potential in many data capture areas. One that seemed particularly inviting was for recording meter readings by gas and electricity staff. There appeared to be many inviting possibilities. For Lyons it became the linchpin of its major office systems.

As always, John Pinkerton played a prime part in creating the device, assisted for part of the time by Daniel Broido, wearing his Chief

Mechanical Engineer hat. The automatic feed component was built by a Bristol firm, Parnall, part of the Avery group, who had the task of constructing a mechanism that could cope with forms that had spent time in the field and could not be expected to be increased. They already had relevant experience. Unlike Lector, which had been restricted to perforating paper tape for later entry to the computer, Autolector was directly connected to its LEO input channel.

To complement Autolector a fast, clean printer had been envisaged by Lyons, capable of producing customized pro forma documents that could be read back automatically. The concept was that the printer would produce, say, an order form with both item descriptions and corresponding coded marks representing identity numbers. A salesperson would complete the form in the field by entering marks to denote the quantities ordered, and then feed it back into the system. Similarly, attendance sheets could be printed in each payroll run listing the employees and their coded key numbers in marks. They would then be completed in the departments with marks denoting the hours worked.

In experimental runs it soon became apparent that no amount of tuning would fit LEO III's standard printer, the Anelex, to this role. It could not print unambiguous marks within the tight tolerances upon which the Lyons turn-round operation depended. Attention moved to a development based on the Xerox printing technique. Rank Xerox had been working on such a printer for some time, and collaboration had led to the emergence of a Xeronic printer that could be activated by magnetic tapes produced by LEO as output. The Xeronic was much faster than any other printer that had so far been employed in a computer system, and it also promised to be consistently clean and clear.[14]

The two developments gave a great impetus to Lyons's plans. However, on the LEO side they involved a great deal of effort that could not be regarded as mainstream to the essential task of consolidating the niche that LEO III had won in the larger commercial systems market. They represented another thrust ahead at a time when the advance so far still had to be made secure. In particular, the Xeronic printer, though functionally attractive, was also extremely expensive, and little market outside Lyons had been identified for it. Without the special relationship that still existed with Lyons in regard to technical development, it is very unlikely that it would have figured in LEO's activities at this stage.

Lyons Disengage

Notwithstanding the close technical association, the time had come for Lyons to disengage financially. It was announced on October 2, 1964, that

English Electric had agreed to purchase the Lyons shareholding in English Electric LEO Computers Ltd.[15]

A press release declared that "Lyons have achieved their main purpose of developing computers to meet the requirements of their own business and the consideration agreed approximately covers Lyons' total expenditure on the LEO project since its inception." The amount that changed hands was a little under $11 million, with the greater part in cash but with a balance in English Electric shares, which Lyons undertook to retain for the time being. Anthony Salmon was to remain on the board of the new company, which was to be called English Electric LEO Marconi Computers, Ltd. (EELM). This extended name gave recognition to the company's access to Marconi's valuable know-how in online computing and microelectronics.

The announcement neither internally nor externally created the same friction as the merger announcement of the year before. Business continued with the same structure and personalities. The new development had merely given financial effect to what were the clear implications of what had gone before. The new name, though, was a challenge to the newly appointed stylists, who cut their teeth on it before moving on to greater things elsewhere.

If everyone had not been quite so busy at this time, the language of the announcement could well have seemed more than passingly insensitive. The LEO personnel in all parts of the company had given so much over the years without expecting or seeking recompense that they felt instinctively that what had been built up from nothing was as much theirs as Lyons's. There were few of them who had not worked far, far beyond the call of duty. Indeed, sometimes they had performed their overtime work *sub rosa* because of the fear that the Lyons's management would fail to understand why quite so much effort was necessary. But there was so much still to do and look forward to that no one had time to dwell on the sadness of the disengagement.

The Government Takes a Hand

Late in the year of the "range revolution," there was also a reaction from the British government. In October of 1964, Harold Wilson led the Labour Party to office after several years of noninterventionist conservative administrations. The "white heat of technology" had been the keynote of his campaign[16] and he was particularly concerned about the prospects for the computer industry in the light of the new developments.

Wilson wrote subsequently[17] that he had become concerned in opposition that:

> if no action were taken quickly, the British computer industry would rapidly cease to exist, facing, as was the case in other European countries, the most formidable competition from the American giants.

It was apparent that, though the British manufacturers had met the technical challenge from across the Atlantic remarkably confidently, the financial strains were becoming more than they could bear. There was a clearer realization now of the extent of investment both in R&D and in product-line setup that was necessary to keep abreast of the flow of technological advice. Wilson recounts how he told Frank Cousins, his first Minister of Technology, that the British computer industry "must be his first priority."

Within two years this directive was to have a profound influence on the structure of the industry and on the individual companies within it.

11
The 1965 Paradox

1965

1965 produced a paradox for LEO. It was the year of peak installations, but it was also the year of the announcement of the new range destined to replace it.

Almost twice as many systems were installed in that year as had ever been achieved in the past, and these included the first appearances of the new faster models. All or almost all of these resulted from orders taken after the announcement of the IBM 360 range. In spite of the challenge, LEO was holding its own.

Repeat Orders

A sizable proportion of the year's installations was for users already employing LEO III systems who were by now sufficiently confident to extend their use. Among them was Shell Mex and BP, to whom the LEO 326 offered the power uplift required to cope with their massive invoicing and sales statistics load. Two LEO 326 systems were installed at the main production center at Hemel Hempstead on the outskirts of London, and the systems already installed were moved up to Wythenshawe, near Manchester, where they were rapidly recommissioned.[1]

At the Post Office, too, LEO 326 became the standard model, and after a time the LEO IIIs already installed were relocated to other users with less exacting burdens. Two LEO 326s were installed in London during the year, enabling the vast telephone billing job to reach an unprecedented scale for computer-based invoicing. A third LEO 326 brought additional power to the National Savings Department at Lytham St. Annes, and Premium Bonds joined the National Savings Bank and National Savings Certificate accounting in the NSD workload.[1]

Another repeat installation was at Dunlop, where, as was to be expected, there was a rapid appreciation of the cost-effectiveness of the LEO 360 model. Here, too, the existing processor was sold off to a new user.[1]

At all these organizations extending their computer activities in 1965, LEO consultants had worked closely with the home teams, delineating the applications, defining the systems structures, and bringing the applications into timely, efficient, secure operation. Peter Hermon was at Dunlop, John Aris had provided the service at Shell Mex and BP, and Ninian Eadie had taken over as Senior Consultant supporting the Post Office.

Catalog Mail Order

The GPO led the way with the LEO 326, but they were closely followed by a London mail-order company, Freemans, who were equally attracted to the ability to handle very large volumes.[1]

Freemans carried on its business through catalog selling by agents reward by commission on their sales. The agents were generally women selling in their own circles of neighborhood acquaintances or at work. It had been built up to to its present considerable size as a private company and was just becoming public.

To cope with dispatching all the orders and accounting for them, a small army of packers and clerks had to be assembled at their South London headquarters, near the Oval cricket ground. Many of them were part-time workers. The computer offered the prospect of being able to function with less strain from peaks of work, and the very lively family-led management, with Anthony Rampton at its head, was quick to recognize the potential benefits. The Freemans system was probably the most powerful taken on by any British commercial organization up to that time. Freemans as an organization had no experience at all with computers and asked whether a consultant could join them. As it happened, Mike Jackson, who had been working on the Post Office project, wanted to become thoroughly involved in achieving the business objectives of a large system rather than to continue moving from project to project. He readily seized the opportunity that presented itself and, despite its comparatively high cost, the system more than realized Freemans high hopes. To English Electric LEO Marconi, though, the loss of a senior consultant was severe. Jackson gives a vivid account of his subsequent work at Freemans in Chapter 23.

In a retrospective review of the project some years later, Freemans described the task as applying "a computer not just to the work of our offices but [also] to the work of hundreds of thousands of housewives. The large bulk of our information originates in kitchens, sitting rooms, and on door steps. A large proportion of the originators have never experienced a commercial environment."[2]

In evaluating the results of the implementation, in which the importance of the sensitivity of the interface to this army of nonprofessional salespeople cannot be overstated, the company declared:

> For each pound of company turnover we now employ one half of the staff in dealing with agents' orders and one half of the staff for dealing with agents' accounts and stocks. There is a reduction of well over one thousand staff.

Additionally, it was stated that the:

> capital cost was more than covered by the delivered reduction in capital required for stocks and debtors.

With the flexibility engendered by the computer's "intelligence" there was also a corresponding uplift in management control of the business, which had enjoyed little support from the displaced massive punched-card installation. A vivid picture of the thought processes behind this remarkable business application is given by Jackson himself in Chapter 23. As he records there, the installation later took on the *extra* task of controlling and providing for the rapid issue and replenishment of the 150,000 separate catalog items held in the mail-order company's warehouses.

First Installation on the Continent

Although the needs of Eastern Europe had given rise to the LEO 360, only one of the four installed in 1965 went there. Other prospects took longer to satisfy the tortuous administrative chain and came to fruition later. The installation that led the way was that at the Czech railway research offices, the Vypocatni Laborati Dopravy (VLD), where the responsible official, Mr. Sebek, appeared to be better connected than others working their way through the stringent procedures for obtaining technical and expenditure consent and then approval for the use of hard currency.[3]

VLD provided its own engineering maintenance team as well as the programming and operational personnel. There were problems at times with the very academic approach of the highly qualified engineers. Following their training in Britain they still tended to treat each equipment fault as a scientific event rather than as a probably repeated occurrence to be recognized by experience.

Nevertheless, the installation was efficiently run and relationships were remarkably close, with Ralph Land joining Broido in Eastern Europe to play a major role with his buoyant bonhomie. He was backed by his solid experience as a user at the Lyons Teashops Offices, as Manager at the English Electric LEO City office, and by his subsequent training in implementation and operation at the London Bureau. Despite their ever-present desire to be independent, the Czechs reacted well to the obviously competent and well-intentioned consultant from abroad. As a courtesy, business was carried out in German, despite the extreme reluctance of most Czechs at that time to use the language of the Nazi invaders.

Mr. Sebek, a firm supporter of the communist regime, deployed the system very capably and exhibited it proudly both to his own countrymen and to visitors from other members of the Soviet bloc. Nevertheless, he missed no opportunity for soundly berating visiting LEO management for any shortcomings he perceived.

The Take Off

While the two larger models were making their impact, implementations of the basic LEO III took off in 1965. Leaders in British commerce and industry were again included. Among them was Allied Suppliers, a grocery chain giant, with whom early talks were held on the possibilities for mark-sensed data capture at checkout. Others included Colvilles, the Motherwell steel mills, and British Insulated Callendar Cables.[3] Overseeing implementations at all of these companies and ensuring that standards were maintained was Frank Land, in his role as Chief Consultant.

Another installation that year was at EverReady, the electric batteries firm, where Doug Comish had again formed the close personal ties with senior management that came naturally to him. The company was by now one of the very longest-standing LEO bureau users. There was also LEO's first UK insurance company (Phoenix Assurance), its first bank (Royal Bank of Scotland,) and its first public utility (South West Gas Board).

To the LEO organization, where the interest in application innovations was unabated despite the move into a much larger scale of business activity, an exciting installation was that at Renold Chains, Manchester-based engineers. The major task was to effect the machine loading of the great open shop floor. It was a considerable intellectual challenge, and Jackson and Hermon reveled in it at different stages. To make a contribution to the already sparkling efficiency of this Swiss-founded wonderland was an opportunity that was grasped gratefully.[3]

There was an important local government installation at Coventry Corporation, another responsibility of Comish following his earlier implementation at Manchester. There was also a LEO III installation for what promised to be in time a major central government user, the Inland Revenue, though for the present the envisioned application fell far short of their long-term ambitions for computerizing PAYE.[3]

There were two pathfinding installations at HM Dockyards at Portsmouth and Devonport, both of which were strategic bases for the Royal Navy in the 1960s. The principal task was very much in the LEO mold of integration, with labor dockets being used to produce ship and project cost records at the same time as payroll. A particularly innovative feature was that Autolector was employed to feed and read the code-marked dockets into the computer systems. Here, the senior consultant was Aris, who had gained unrivalled experience of Autolector and its ways through his work as liaison to Lyons. The two LEO IIIs were supplemented a year later by two of the more powerful LEO 360s with similar ancillary equipment. One was installed at Chatham and the other at Portsmouth, allowing the initial computer there to be moved to Rosyth.[3] An "insider" view of this project is provided by Reg Cann, the leader of the RN Dockyards staff, in Chapter 24.

New Range Announced

For all that LEO had reached an installation peak, the British market as a whole was growing even more quickly. Though the 360 range was not yet being delivered in the UK, suppliers from across the Atlantic were by now enjoying almost two-thirds of British sales, with IBM selling more than all the home manufacturers together. ICT was fighting back with the 1900 series and by the spring of 1965 had already taken more than two hundred orders.[4] Most of these were for small systems, but they represented a powerful springboard for the future.

Among the Americans, NCR and Burroughs had also grown into a powerful presence, capitalizing on their deep roots in accounting machine installations all over the country. Of the early British manufacturers, Ferranti as well as EMI had been swallowed up by ICT by this time.[5] Elliott's position had dwindled in the commercial field. Apart from English Electric LEO Marconi, the market now was very much in the hands of the conventional office machine suppliers (accounting machines as well as punched card).

EELM's response to this situation was to announce its own new range, with models reaching down to the smaller entry level. The decision to base this new range on the RCA Spectra 70 had been made early in the year. The recommendations of the team that had visited the United States shortly before were accepted rapidly and almost in their entirety (pp. 115). There was to be a stronger software regime than that devised at Camden, New Jersey. It would employ the experience gained on the LEO III range and KDF 9 as well as that of RCA, and would place special stress on time-sharing and online connections. There was also to be a much faster top-of-the-line model, sufficiently powerful to carry users forward from their present ranges. It was decided to name the range System 4, as an indication of the succession from LEO III.

The performance and cost parameters for the top-of-the-line 4/70 were quickly determined. They were aimed at providing a significant cost-performance improvement over the corresponding IBM model, as well as achieving the necessary upgrade in power. At the same time, a check was made to ensure that what emerged would also have a clear advantage over what was promised in the 1900 range. IBM, however, was seen as the principal competitor. The uplift from the 70/55 at the top of the RCA range was substantial, but the young Kidsgrove engineer assigned to the task, John Bowthorpe, undertook it with assurance. A stage was soon reached where the announcement of the range as a whole could proceed with confidence.

The one deviation from the team's recommendation was a decision to use integrated circuits for the lower end of the range rather than to copy RCA and make as little development effort as possible in the first instance. It was found that the Marconi organization, which was given the task, could not achieve the required cost limits using the advanced technology; first one[6], and then the other small system was dropped from the range.[7] This was ironic, as the rapid availability of a compatible range scope comparable to those of the two market leaders had been one of the particular attractions of the venture.

The launch of System 4 took place in September of 1965. It was on an altogether more aggressive scale than had attended earlier announcements. The whole commercial and industrial establishment was invited and attendance was high. Presentations lower down the echelons went on for several days. Inevitably the announcement terminated the active marketing life of the LEO III range, although it had been in the field for only three years and the larger systems for only a matter of months. With the announcement pending and rumors being vigorously fostered in the field, orders had already been seriously inhibited, and it was a considerable relief when at last the secret was officially out.

A Departure

By now commercial office machine business practices had taken over the market. There was little expectation that the role of the computer sales force would be very different from that of the tabulator and accounting machine sales force, whatever supplier they came from. It tended to be overlooked that it was unlikely that a full-scale system could be set up with that same dexterous manipulation of plug boards or control bars that had often been a source of admiration in the past.

In the heated atmosphere of 1965 it had become commonplace to detail someone "to look into computers," and as often as not it would be a representative of one of the big battalions referred to earlier (p. 127) that would provide the first interface. Assurances were rapidly accepted that what others had accomplished "you, with all your high-quality people, can do." Office machine sales forces were never notably lacking in flattery.

There would, as always, be forward-looking expectations, but the fight for System 4 sales was in general to take place on different ground from that on which LEO consultants had made their way in the past. It was dominated by arithmetic and peripheral speeds, inventories of standard subroutines and packages, worldwide sales, and corporate R&D investment statistics, rather than by how quickly and securely effective systems could be brought into operation or what management information could be extracted. It was not altogether surprising, therefore, that alongside the elation of the lively presentations of System 4 there was also the wound of a departure—that of the Chief Consultant, Frank Land. The scene had changed radically since he had joined LEO to learn programming 13 years before. The opportunity to take up an appointment at his old college, the London School of Economics, where he could pass on what he had learned to new generations of students, was too inviting to turn down.

12
LEO Winds Down

1966–1968

LEO had ended its growing days. The name was vanishing and the promotion of System 4-now became the main focus of activity. As a recent historian relates.[1] "The large System 4/70 was a considerable triumph. Unlike the IBM 360 it had been designed in the expectation that the future growth in large-scale computers would be in real-time and multiaccess systems." In 1966 and 1967, many of the most prestigious computer orders went to this system, which had emerged as a contemporary embodiment of all that LEO had been striving to achieve in each rapidly succeeding computer generation. It was judged to "completely outclass" its ICT counterpart[2] and offer to the more venturesome user more exciting possibilities than the IBM 360 range. In the public field the new National Giro Bank (established by the Post Office), Electricity Boards, and the UK Atomic Energy Authority, as well as universities, placed orders for the System 4/70 within a short time. There were also important successes in the business field, and a very high level of interest was generated in Eastern Europe, where the IBM compatibility made a special appeal (see Chapter 26).

As for the LEO range, there were still installations to be effected, though most of these were the result of positions taken before the announcement of the new range. Three of them were repeat installations for HM Dockyards, five more went to the Post Office. Two went to Czechoslovakia to follow the system working well in Prague. The NHKG steelworks in Ostrava and the Social Service Ministry in Prague had by now contrived to obtain their scarce hard currency. Another powerful system went out to Shell in Australia, and in London a second consor-

tium of boroughs, this time led by Tower Hamlets and Hackney, had a
system installed to share together.

There were also installations by organizations that were preparing
themselves by bureau work. One was for Consolidated Glass in South
Africa, who had been employing the Johannesburg bureau set up by Leo
Fantl. Another was for Wedd, Durlacher, the leading London Stock
Exchange stock broker who had explored the ground with searching
large-scale bureau work on LEO II several years before. It was the fore-
runner of the later all-embracing computer development on the Stock
Exchange.

A notable feature of LEO's last implementation phase was that two-
thirds of the systems were for the larger models.[3] A firm platform had
been constructed upon which the System 4 was able to build.

The Last LEO for Lyons

Among the 326 models installed in 1966 and 1967 was one for Lyons. The
LEO III at Cadby Hall was fully loaded on a three-shift basis, and the 326
offered the power required to implement the master plan that John
Simmons had enunciated and to which their O&M management, led by
the creative and determined A.K. Robey, still strongly adhered. Together
with Autolector and the Xeronic printer they now deployed the resources
to make the next steps toward their goal of complete integration.

The philosophy of the master plan had been expressed in Simmons's
"LEO and the Managers" four years before. It was closely interlinked
with the complementary vision of management self-sufficiency. In a large
or medium-sized business, the theory ran, the responsibility for overall
planning and control must lie with top management, but this must be
coupled with the delegation to first-line managers of the responsibility
for making their own plans for attaining their specified objectives.
Simmons held that a high-speed automatic computer could play a crucial
role in fulfilling these twin management responsibilities.

"In short," he declared, "a highly centralized piece of computing
machinery like LEO III paradoxically enables a forceful but controlled
decentralized business organization to be established."[4]

Accordingly, the master plan aimed at transportable but suitably modified applications in each of the trading divisions, with them all linked to
produce the final company results and top management information. A
very considerable inroad was foreseen into the still very large clerical
forces, while providing still more responsive service to each of the local
managements.

However, a severe setback occurred only a year after the installation of the LEO 326 system alongside the LEO III in Elms house. A fire broke out in the computer hall when paper in the Xeronic printer overheated in the middle of the night during routine operations.[5] The printer was destroyed and the older system was severely polluted by the fumes and charred particles. In a remarkable effort, the reinforced maintenance engineers brought the LEO 326 back into service the next morning, though it was not fully reliable for a time. The LEO III suffered greater damage, and a large number of engineers had to clean it, board by board. It remained out of action for some time, but fortunately the National Data Processing Service run by the Post Office was ready to step in by providing facilities at its nearby center in Charles House. Though not without dislocation, operations were able to continue.[6]

An inevitable outcome was that the credibility of the Lyons computer operation was severely dented within the company. Although all essential services were maintained, the policy of holding all the computer eggs in one basket could not fail to be questioned. It was not unnatural for people to feel that if the first-line managers held delegated responsibility for achieving their objectives, then the choice of what computing facilities they deployed should be delegated too.

Formation of ICL

From 1965, the Ministry of Technology (Mintech) had been pursuing the conviction that the only hope for the British computer industry was consolidating its warring elements into a single organization. The efforts to this end were completely behind the scenes, but it has emerged since that at first English Electric was looked upon as the likely senior partner in such a coming together. As the third largest British electrical engineering company, with an annual turnover in 1960's money of $560 million a year, English Electric was seen as the only player in the field with sufficient resources to fulfill this role, if it could be persuaded to do so.[7] The others, now whittled down to ICT and Elliott Automation, were for different reasons, in financial difficulties.

A first outcome of this approach was the absorption of Elliott automation by English Electric LEO Marconi Computers two years later in 1967. It was an event of no great importance in operating terms, as Elliott was now only a shadow of the organization that had been so prominent in the early pioneering days. The merged company was called simply English Electric Computers and all the constituent parts, including LEO, were subsumed in this name.

Work toward unifying ICT and English Electric continued, despite an unfavorable report by Cooper Brothers, who had been called in by Mintech to report on the prospects. The report declared:[8]

> The 1900 series and System 4 are incompatible and each company is convinced of the technical superiority of its project . . . It would be . . . impossible for one system to be evolved from a joint operation except on a long term, basis . . .

Mintech was undeterred, and in 1967 Tony Benn, who had become Minister of Technology, called together the Chairmen and principal executives of the two organizations. Much-needed financial help was offered, but only if a merger was effected.[9] In these circumstances a technical working party was formed by the two companies to consider whether a joint product line was feasible within an economically reasonable time. The working party, which included among its members John Pinkerton, veteran now of three generations of computers, answered positively.[10]

By this time, ICT, having battled its way through the financial crisis that attended the introduction of the 1900 series, was in an altogether stronger condition and had taken over as the presumptive senior partner if a merger were to take place. Though there was no enthusiasm in that company for the new commitment when things were going relatively smoothly, it was accepted as unavoidable. After an interval in which other powerful suitors suddenly appeared, a "white paper" was presented to Parliament by Mintech outlining "The Computer Merger Project," This was followed by a press conference announcing the impending creation of ICL. After the enactment of the Industrial Expansion Act, which provided the promised funding, the new company was vested in July of 1968.[11] Among those who had expressed an interest, Plessey took a significant shareholding, but control was firmly placed in the hands of the old ICT company.

After the Merger

LEO people already had experienced a merger, but the previous one was on much more nearly equal terms than this one. ICT were now so much stronger in terms of data processing turnover, systems installed, and staff numbers that the coming together could only take the form of a takeover. Whereas the 1900 system was firmly established, the LEO III series and KDF 9, which had been the strength of the other partner, were already being phased out. Its contribution depended wholly on timely deliveries of the System 4 built with state-of-the-art technology in a new works by a new force.

Consequently the merger was seen in ICT more as a distraction than as an acquisition of strength. Arthur Humphreys, appointed Managing Director of ICL, described what he had been handed as "the largest range of incompatible computers in the world." He made no secret that having steered ICT through the eye of the storm he would have preferred the company to have continued on its way alone.[12]

There was no pretense of equality in the management structure. From English Electric only Cliff Robinson from Kidsgrove was appointed to the ICL Board of Directors, and his stay was short. There was no representation at all from the LEO stream. Of those who had been the executive directors of LEO Computers Ltd. nine years before, only John Pinkerton and I now remained. Raymond Thompson and Tony Barnes had left in the English Electric days. Pinkerton and I were both assigned to background posts where it was argued that our long and broad experience could most valuably be employed.

Pinkerton's role led into the increasingly important field of international computer standards, where he represented with distinction what was effectively the British computer industry. For me a new Market Planning Organization was created from which it was envisioned that as its director I would be able to disseminate those firm principles in analysis and sizing which had characterized the LEO approach. I was joined by John Aris and a very able professional from the ICT side, Hugh Macdonald. After a short time, though, I was prevailed upon by Humphreys to move over to the New Range Organization, set up to realize the Mintech concept of the "ultimate" unifying range for the British computer industry.

Dispersal

On the marketing side, LEO management had held the upper hand in the previous merger, though it had made positive efforts to be fair. Now they and their teams were simply recruits joining a fully established organization with management already in place. Past contact had been limited, since IBM rather than ICT had been the more common LEO opponent.

When it came time to allot positions, I met with my inevitably better-placed opposite number, Lyon Lightstone, Marketing Director of the new company, to go through the names. He was genuinely sympathetic, but there was little that he felt able to concede. At the principal Divisional level nothing could be made available to the newcomers.

At the Divisional management level only that for Local Government was awarded to a newcomer. Doug Comish was appointed to that job.

He had been a leading LEO consultant since the very early days and had won and implemented key municipal accounts against entrenched ICT opposition. At the Regional level below there were just two appointments. The London North West Region where many national headquarters were situated went to Mike Gifford, who had been especially singled out as a high flyer. He had joined LEO from Lyons in the middle period. The Midland Region with its high concentration of engineering enterprises was taken over by Peter Benstead.

Other consultants and programmers were scattered, not unkindly but with the aim of disturbing the existing battle-hardened setup as little as possible. Their task now was to adapt themselves to the way of life and practices of their new home. The opportunities to introduce any distinctively LEO approach were limited. Many of them must have felt abandoned in the early days, but mostly managed to adapt themselves to the essential disciplines of a large organization still fighting for its life in a competitive international market.

The ICL Product Line

In deciding what the new joint marketing offering should be, it was recognized within the dominant ICT camp that System 4 had significant advantages at the larger and more forward-looking end, Arthur Humphreys' first thoughts were directed toward producing a "bridged" range in which users would progress up to the very successful 1904A model and then cross over to larger System 4 models based on the 4/70.[13]

This compromise became less attractive, however, in light of the difficult migration path between two systems of entirely different number composition, instruction code, and operating systems. There were also other factors that largely came to light after the merger. Most important was the fact that the production difficulties referred to earlier were continuing to impede deliveries, and, furthermore, reliability problems had surfaced in the field leading to the expensive replacement of soldered connections. Additionally, examination of the books had revealed that at this stage System 4 cost more to produce than had been provided for.[14] Though serious, all of these could be described as a teething troubles arising from a rapid and not sufficiently prepared entry into the large-scale utilization of the new multilayer board technology; once corrected, both production and reliability became satisfactory. However, the outcome was to confirm the 1900 range for the upward progression of all customers other than those with a positive interest in real-time applications.[15] To provide a performance and price spread, several adaptions of the 4/70 design— the 4/60, 4/65, and 4/75— were developed.

A crunch came some time later when it was felt that a decision had to be made on a single top-of-the line model, and a knife-edge decision by Humphreys went in favor of a further 1900 speed-up and against a 4/85 design that incorporated additional logical advances, this time toward a virtual machine architecture.

The Customer Base

The customer base represented by the LEO, KD, and System 4 models was necessarily distributed around the firmly structured ICL sales organization in the same way as the programmers and consultants, though there could not always be a match.

In many cases ties had been very strong, but it was not now feasible to maintain the close contacts to which the customer had become accustomed. The danger was that by way of a rebound some organizations would feel that the reason for their attachment had ended and would desert the British computer industry when it came time to make a change. Several did.

Prominent among the early customers was Stewarts and Lloyds. They had taken delivery of the first LEO computer to be installed on a user's premises and their supplier's loss of independence was felt particularly deeply there. A rather bitter speech by Neil Pollock, their O&M manager, at the closing ceremony for their LEO II gave expression to their feelings.[16] He declared:

> Inevitably this is a mildly emotional occasion . . . not necessarily because we become attached to hardware . . . but because to most of us here, the computer represents a major part of our lives. To quote from the Ancient Mariner, and together with the Lyons team, "we were the first that ever burst into that silent sea." Not absolutely true, but near enough and I, for one, cannot pay enough, tribute to the skill, energy, and foresight of that original LEO team which designed and built the machine and, above all, gave us of their skills in the design of systems to be run on it.
>
> It had been a success story and much of the credit goes to them. It was a black day for the British computer industry when that team was dispersed by people who should have known better . . . and, perhaps because they didn't, were dispersed themselves.

In the course of the occasion, to which Thompson came out of retirement to join me, the operating statistics over the 12-year period were distributed. "They are impressive," said Pollock, "by any standard and show what remarkable service has been given by the equipment and its maintenance engineers. I don't suppose we shall ever again keep a computer in service as long as this one and this, in itself, will be an additional record which the designers may hold with quiet satisfaction." At the close of the ceremony, mounted panels from LEO II were presented as a memento "to each of our two visitors late of Joe Lyons."

Disintegration at Lyons

"Joe Lyons" was itself among the customers distributed around the ICL areas, and what remained of the special relationship after the English Electric years evaporated. The individuality of the main manufacturing divisions was becoming more and more assertive, and with the old guard of the ruling family relinquishing the reins, Lyons became a very different company. The catering side, with which the company had started out in 1894, was dwindling. There were fewer teashops and the contribution from those that remained and the famous Corner Houses was insignificant compared with their site values. In 1965, the Trocadero, the family's favorite "watering hole" for generations, closed its doors.

The bakery, ice cream, and tea businesses had always been separate. Each had its own factory, management, and sales force. They often delivered to the same customers, but by different transport, and submitted different accounts in different ways. Personnel rarely moved between them. Their managements were aware now of the availability of smaller systems and standard packages within the financial range of their separate divisions and there was growing resentment toward a centralization that prevented them from going their own separate ways.

While Simmons remained there was no change in the senior management of the Lyons computing arrangements, but after he retired in 1968 they were placed in the hands of a new subsidiary, Lyons Computing Services Ltd., with directors representing the main user divisions.[17] As Bird describes it in an enlightening passage of his book, the new directors had dual responsibilities, but their main accountability was to the divisions that paid their salaries. The operating divisions wanted the cheapest computing systems for their own operations, "but the cheapest for them was not always the cheapest from a corporate viewpoint."

When in the following year the feeling prevailed that *something* must be done, it was decided to acquire a replacement mainframe, though why this decision was made in the light of the situation is unclear. A mechanistic points evaluation system with no fewer than 80 parameters. all painstakingly weighted, was put together to ensure a "no-hands no-ties" objective judgment.[18] Quality of support and the experience of the supplier played little part. The general inclination was that if they were going to stick together, then it was best to join the mainstream, where both small and large were available.

By this time Lyons was an ordinary, not especially fruitful, customer in ICL's eyes. There was no sentiment on either side. When close to the midnight hour a senior manager with a LEO background was called in to try to redress the situation, the points had all been added up and it was much too late. The pioneering company in British commercial computing dispassionately went over to the American giant. However, the new arrangements soon fell apart. In Bird's words. "The demand by Lyons' operating divisions to assume complete control of their data processing and to install nonstandard equipment was overwhelming."[19]

The LEO III service bureau at Hartree House continued its work after the merger, first as part of ICL, then, as "unbundling" became fashionable, as part of International Computing Services Ltd., and finally in 1970 as a constituent of BARIC, a joint service company formed with Barclays Bank. Among the customers, the Richard Shops chain, which, as Ralph Land relates in his memoir, had suffered severely in the bureau's birth pains, was still using the service when LEO III was replaced by an ICL 1904A ten years later. Those LEO programs that were not rewritten for the new system were transferred to the GPO's National Data Processing Service.[20]

More at the Post Office

The Post Office had taken over from Lyons as LEO's home ground. Around the time of the formation of ICL, Nick Smith retired and his place as Director of NDPS was filled by Murray Laver, who returned to the Post Office as a member of the board from his influential position as Head of the Computer Division of the Ministry of Technology. Among his first actions was to review the computer capacity at his disposal in light of the increased traffic in all the principal services. His decision was to mop up whatever LEO 326 systems became available in the field and to order five new systems.

By that time production of the LEO III range had ceased and the team had been redeployed. There was reluctance to risk the dislocation of current production. However, a price was negotiated that covered the additional costs and, for all its inconvenience, the order was plainly too compelling to be turned down. The additional systems were installed in centers in Glasgow, Derby, Bristol, and London in 1969. By this time the System 4/70 had been set in motion for the new GIRO Bank, which was dear to the heart of the then Prime Minister, Harold Wilson, and opened by him. For the ongoing Post Office and Savings Bank applications, though, the LEO 326 remained the workhorse. Among its acquisitions the Post Office took over the Lyons 326, with which it had long had a mutual help arrangement. Nothing could have highlighted more vividly the role reversal that had taken place. A final precaution by the Post Office to ensure adequate capacity was to commission an emulator so the suite of LEO programs could run on an ICL 2960 two ranges later.

Murray Laver contributes his own impressions in Chapter 22.

The Wake

Almost the last major effort to swim against the tide was in 1967, when a LEO 326 was displayed at work in a Moscow exhibition in Sokolniki Park, following the presence of the same installation a year before in Prague. Both exhibitions were supported by the deployment of many of the senior LEO consultants. The hope was that, although interest in the LEO III range had largely died at home because of the onset of System 4, the Soviet bloc would continue to be ready to acquire these systems since they were just inside the COCOM embargo limits on exports of strategically critical equipment. Hopes of selling the system off the Moscow stand however, were misplaced. With hard currency so short, unwillingness to invest in a system that was about to be replaced was at least as great there as at home, and the equipment had to be shipped back.

There was a grand farewell Moscow dinner at which all the Russians who had helped on the stand, from interpreters to cleaners, were entertained. Many, many toasts were drunk, with Broido indefatigably interpreting both ways. It was a fitting wake for LEO, though under continuing LEO-led management System 4 took over and enjoyed a period as a leading name in several countries of the Soviet bloc. It achieved and held its place as much because of the quality of support as the excellence of the equipment. A graphic picture of the times is given by Ralph Land in Chapter 26.

Conclusion

The last group of LEO computers finished their work in 1981. Several of them were LEO 326s that had been carrying some of the heaviest loads in Britain for 15 years. In all, 82 LEO systems had been engaged on office work over the years since the world's first regular job was run in 1951. Mostly these were from the LEO III range, in which the ideas culminated. The number was not great compared with the growing stream of systems that was entering the field as LEO left it, but the standard of achievement was almost uniformly high. Not more than two or three of the installations failed to reach the level of consistent productive loading that was recognized as LEO's standard. There were no enormously expensive calamities, which have come to be recognized as fellow travelers with progress, and programs were from the outset devised so the common excuse, "It was the computer's fault," seldom had to be invoked.

The ethos lived on, but perhaps the most fitting epitaph for LEO as an organization was written by Dr. John Hendry in his paper, "The Teashop Computer Manufacturer: J. Lyons":

> In the end, they were perhaps too strong on the applications side. Carried away by their own sophistication and obsessed by the pioneering spirit, they failed to understand the social and psychological needs of ordinary customers with ordinary muddled systems and ordinary resistance to change.

13
Postlude

Almost 50 years have passed since the trip to the United States that gave rise to LEO and the world's first regular office job entrusted to a computer. Change has been dramatic over this half-century. The arithmetic power and storage capacity of that air-cooled giant are now surpassed by the resources of any laptop computer. The institutions involved have been overtaken by a "twilight of the Gods."

Lyons is no more. After finally divesting itself of its LEO interests in 1964 in order to concentrate on its core businesses, the company fell on hard times through injudicious ventures in Europe and was itself taken over by Allied Breweries to form Allied Lyons. Now, even the *Lyons* part of the name has been dropped, as have several of the food businesses, in a process of divestment. The family, which was so potent in the creation of the company and so supportive of LEO at the outset, has disappeared from the scene. Cadby Hall itself is gone. The once teeming facility is now occupied by modernist, glass-sided offices and apartments bordered by shrubberies.

English Electric, too, has gone, swallowed up by its long-term rival, GEC. Maps are no longer drawn showing Stafford as the center of the world, as they were when LEO was absorbed. The proud London office building at the foot of the Strand has been taken over by an American bank.

LEO's final repository in ICL has also had its changes. Formed under government pressure to provide a British computer entity strong enough to hold its own against incursions from the U.S. it is now part of Fujitsu, the Japanese electronics giant. Happily, the company retains its operational independence and has continued to trade profitably while computer firms everywhere have suffered severely from the erosion of margins.

But this LEO story is intended to be at least as much about people as about companies and competitors. It is fitting to look back at some of those who contributed over the years.

Raymond Thompson died in 1976 and was buried quietly, having gained nothing like the recognition in the wider world of administration and business to which his pioneering vision and unflagging vitality entitled him. He had been with LEO from before the first day and must have looked forward to leading it to greater and greater success for the rest of his working life. His interest covered every aspect of computers and their application to office work, and because of his mathematical background he enjoyed being involved with that aspect, too. His greatest interest, though, was in making computers logically more effective, in both hardware and software, and in the marriage between them. When the merger with English Electric relegated him to what he regarded as a subservient position and confined him to a limited sphere of responsibility not of his choosing, he felt betrayed. He was no longer the gadfly who had been the source of so many anecdotes. In 1966 he left English Electric LEO Marconi to undertake consultancy at Shell Mex and BP. He was still only 59 and physically and mentally in good shape, but his time had passed in the British computer industry, to which he had made a unique contribution.

The succession of mergers took their toll of consultants, many of them left to pursue their interest in applications, following the path trodden by those who had transferred to LEO customers. Some went on to teach what they had learned to a wider public in academia. Others went into professional consultancy. A deep loyalty to LEO remained, whatever the new name, and very few ever joined another supplier.

On the consultancy side no one gave more over the years than Frank Land. As Chief Consultant, he had been indefatigable after the merger with English Electric, traveling up and down the country, sorting out the differences in perception and still contriving to keep a clear mind and an equable response no matter what the provocation. At the London School of Economics (LSE) he rose to become Professor of System Analysis, and during this period also acted as advisor to the parliamentary select committee monitoring the computer industry. Later he was appointed to a chair at the London Business School.

Among others who chose an academic life was Sam Waters, for whom the "Goldfish Bowl" in Elms House was something of a further education with tutors at hand at the drop of a hat. He is now Professor of Computer Science at the University of the West of England. Colin Tully, who among other programming assignments had taken part in the development of software of LEO III, joined the LSE as a Research Fellow and later became a senior lecturer at York University before making available his unusually wide range of computer expertise as a consultant.

One of those who moved into the user field was Peter Hermon. He attracted a powerful ex-LEO kernel of his own. After building up the computer activities at his old customer, Dunlop, he went on to British Airways (BA), where he devised and implemented their world-renowned reservation system, among other applications covering the whole range of the airline's activities. Later he relinquished his computer responsibilities to become Managing Director of the European Division and a full member of the airline's board. He was joined there in his computer years by John Lewis, Alan Jacobs, George McLeman, and George Hayter, all with strong LEO consultancy experience. At one stage Lewis was senior manager for batch development at BA and McLeman was senior manager for real-time development. Jacobs went on to succeed Hermon as Head of Computing and then made a further move to become Head of Computer Services at Sainsbury. Hayter, after heading an influential development study group at BA, became Director of Computerization at the London Stock Exchange, and the first market-wide online systems were introduced under his management. Others with LEO experience who joined the Hermon scene were Jack Warriner, who was appointed to run the computer operating force, and Bernard Pierce, a senior programmer.

For all their ability and drive, few computer people have "been able to leave" information technology and achieve directorship of a major enterprise. There has been a widespread perception that computer people are too specialist and too backroomish to be entrusted with the more pragmatic world of business.

But another LEO man to be recognized in the wider field is Mike Jackson, who won board-level line responsibilities in Freemans mail-order house, which he computerized. Yet another to make this leap was Mike Gifford, who for some years had been the redoubtable Chief Executive of the Rank Organization. After being recruited from Lyons, Gifford became a very capable consultant in the early English Electric LEO days. His first move out of computers was to the Australian wing of Schweppes, for whose home organization he had led an impressive implementation. His lieutenant on that job was Tim Holley, who more recently headed the successful Camelot campaign for the British National Lottery contract. Gifford has commented that "After LEO everything else was a piece of cake."

Several LEO consultants have made their mark, giving guidance in the world outside. Prominent among them is John Aris, another contributor whose round-up of the LEO professional ethos concludes this book. After a period running the IT affairs of the Imperial Group, Aris served as a distinguished Director of the National Computer Center before moving to head a private consortium of several leading enterprises. Another in the consultancy field is Mike Josephs. Brian Mills has used the insights that LEO consultancy gave him to pursue a career in venture capital.

Others have carried the LEO stamp abroad, among them Leo Fantl, who probably trained more LEO consultants and user programming staff than anyone else. After firmly establishing the joint service bureau venture with Rand Mines in Johannesburg, he returned to the UK for a time to head Product Planning at Kidsgrove, but then went back to South Africa to take up the reins of one of the country's leading computer bureau services. Among his closest colleagues was Joe Crouch, another LEO consultant who had joined him in the early days. In Australia, Peter Gyngell became well-known for a cultural program on Sydney radio as well as for his rugby refereeing and computer consultancy. Others in the antipodes are Neil Lamming and Ian Crawford. Lamming became Director of the whole Pacific Region for ICL, including Australasia and Hong Kong. Crawford, after returning to his native New Zealand with EELM, later enjoyed a successful career in consultancy there. Jim Smith used the experience he had gained in actuarial service work in a later career with a leading insurance company that took him to South Africa. Arthur Payman runs a consultancy practice in the Netherlands and John Forbe's career took him to Canada, which is also the base of Paul Dixon, who rapidly rose there to become head of Massey Ferguson's IT operations worldwide. John Gosden's career in North America has included chairing the committee to determine the IT services to be provided to the President of the United States.

None, though has traveled more often than Ralph Land, who, after a period in the ICL European Division, later employed his special knowledge of the Eastern European market to direct Rank Xerox's penetration there. His outstanding service to British exports won him the decoration of the Officer of the Order of the British Empire (OBE). This was later raised to Commander of the Order of the British Empire (CBE) to recognize his continued guidance to British exporters in a very active "retirement."

Among LEO consultants and programmers who weathered the successive takeovers and won recognition in their new environments are Doug Comish and Ninian Eadie. At ICL, both found John Grover awaiting them in a senior position. He had already reached the company by a different merger route. Comish became Director of International Division at ICL and Eadie became Group Executive Director responsible for ICL's Technology businesses. He retains a nostalgia however, for his years as senior LEO consultant to the Post Office.

Of the initial informal Lyons group of five that worked on the concepts of the use of computers for office work, only John Pinkerton and I remained with the successor companies until normal retirement age, and we both went on to consultancy work with the group thereafter. Of the others, Lenaerts continued to exercise his innovative gifts with research on computer speech recognition, but felt a lack of encouragement and chose to leave early to pursue his other interests, which included an early PC. As has already been told, Hemy left to join EMI, where he made a notable contribution to one of the world's first second-generation machines. Later, like so many other LEO people, he went on to join a LEO user, where he gave consultancy to a large group internationally. Thompson's early departure has already been touched on.

Though no longer at the helm, as he had been with the LEO system design, Pinkerton became a leading figure in world standards, and in the latter part of his career chaired the Telecommunications Policy group of the Business Computer Technology Association. With his remarkable ability to keep thoroughly abreast of developments, he followed this up in retirement with editorship of the *ICL Technology Journal* and its successor, *Ingenuity*.

My own final period of work before formal retirement was as Project Director for the implementation of a very large computer and communications system for the European Commission in Luxembourg and Brussels, with tentacles to other European capitals. The task included the takeover of the substantial load from the previous IBM machines. I was very grateful to ICL for being allowed this self-indulgence after years of planning, guiding, and monitoring.

This list of consultants and programmers who made a marked contribution is a long one but it still does not name them all. That is equally true of design, commissioning, and maintenance engineers, training staff, operators, and the secretaries and others who looked after us. Remarkably, those who moved elsewhere and those who had retired continue, with those who remain, to form a cohesive group of LEO oldtimers. An unshakeable empathy exists between us and there is a feeling of "Once a LEO-type, always a LEO-type." The stay, measured in years, was often short, but the imprint has proved to be indelible.

Notes

Main Sources

The following abbreviations are used throughout these notes for the major sources quoted:

BIRD	*LEO: The First Business Computer*, Peter Bird, Hasler, 1994
CAMPBELL-KELLY	*ICL, A Business and Technical History*, M. Campbell-Kelly, Clarendon Press, Oxford, 1989
DTC Papers	Original LEO memoranda and other papers collected by D. T. Caminer
HENDRY	"The Teashop Computer Manufacturer: J.Lyons," Dr. J. Hendry, *Business History*, 1986
JMMP	Dr. J. M. M. Pinkerton, interview with National Physical Laboratory Computer Science Division, recorded, in 1975
JRMS LEO	*LEO and the Managers*, J. R. M. Simmons, MacDonald, 1962
JRMS Science	J. R. M. Simmons, interview with Science Museum, recorded in the 1970s. A transcript is included as Appendix B
LEO Chronicle	Chronicle of events concerning LEO maintained by T. R. Thompson, 1947-1962
RCA	Report of visit to RCA, 1964, by D. T. Caminer, D. Blackwell, and C. Haley
USA 1925	Business diary of J.R.M. Simmons' visit to United States, 1925
USA 1947	Report of visit of T. R. Thompson and O. W. Standingford to the U.S. in 1947. Reproduced in part as Appendix A.
USA 1955	Diary of visit of T. R. Thompson and A. B. Barnes to the U.S. in 1955

| USA 1958 | Diary of visit of D. T. Caminer and J. M. M. Pinkerton to the U.S. in 1958 |
| Wilkes | *Memoirs of a Computer Pioneer*, M. V. Wilkes, MIT, 1985 |

I am also indebted to talks and correspondence with contributors to this volume and to many other members of the LEO staff and users of LEO services. John Grover, Mary Blood, Ernest Roberts, and Tony Morgan have been particularly helpful with their memories and comments.

References

Chapter 1: The World's First Office Computer Job 1951 pages 5–8

1. DTC Papers (P1/3 file): "LEO Cadby Hall Bakeries job" T. R. Thompson memo, November 28–30, 1951
2. DTC Papers (P1/3 file) "Calculation of Sales Statistics for Cadby Hall Bakeries," October 1951

Chapter 2: The Background at Lyons 1894–1947 pages 9–15

1. DTC Papers (P1/3 file): Bakery Sales Valuations, London Bakeries Statistics Office, Lyons, June 1951
2. DTC Papers (P1/3 file): "Use of Electronic calculator . . . with only slow speed reading and recording, "p.2, T. R. Thompson, December 1950
3. JRMS Science

Chapter 3: LEO: Idea and Realization 1947–1951 pages 16–32

1. USA 1925
2. USA 1947
3. WILKES, p. 108, EDVAC now forseen as the successor to ENIAC
4. WILKES, p. 109
5. WILKES, p. 122
6. WILKES, p. 117
7. JRMS Science
8. BIRD, p. 38, quoting J. R. M. Simmons, October 1947
9. Joyce M. Wheeler, "Applications of the EDSAC," IEEE, *Annals of the History of Computing* Vol 14, No 4, 1992
10. WILKES, p. 121
11. WILKES, p. 129
12. WILKES, p. 166
13. JRMS Science
14. JMMP
15. USA 1947
16. BIRD, p. 64

17. *LEO Chronicle*, July 13, 1949: "It is suggested by Wright that there need be no discontinuity between the conversion of data and its feeding to the calculator nor between the feeding out of the calculator and the reconversion but there should be an annex system . . . outside the control of the coordinator"
18. *LEO Chronicle*, January 31, 1950: Timetable agreed to finish assembly of calculator by June 1950, its testing by January 1951 and the connecting of the auxiliary equipment by May 1951
19. *LEO Chronicle*, October 5, 1931: "In view of the delay... Simmons, Thompson Pinkerton, Kaye and Caminer discuss possibility of developing other input and output systems: a program of development is drawn up."
20. JRMS Science, p. 11
21. HENDRY, p. 84 (note 38)
22. JRMS Science, p. 12: "We tried to do too much. If we had been content to use already existing systems we could have saved at least a couple of years time and a great many headaches."
23. DTC Papers (P1/3 file)

Chapter 4: Loading LEO I 1951–1954 pages 33–42

1. *LEO Chronicle*, November 16, 1951: "Brigadier Hinds writes . . ."
2. BIRD, p 48, and correspondence with Fantl
3. *LEO Chronicle*, January 14, 1952, Ordnance Board; March 19, 1952, Meteorological Office; July 16, 1952, De Havilland etc.
4. *LEO Chronicle*, November 7, 1952, etc.
5. DTC Papers: LEO Report No. 11, Appendix 3, LEO Outside Work, June 1954
6. *LEO Chronicle* January 10–12, 1952: "The test ran over 59 hours and during 51¼ hours useful work was produced"
7. *LEO Chronicle*, July 21, 1953: "Payroll results for the pilot, Bakeries produced for the week ending July 10th using tabulator"
8. *LEO Chronicle*, July 29, 1953
9. *LEO Chronicle*, December 4, 1953: "Parallel running of L1 commenced"
10. *LEO Chronicle*, February 12, 1954: "LEO payslips used for the first time as payment authorities"
11. *LEO Chronicle*, August 19, 1954: "Number of staff on the LEO Payroll 9,921"
12. BIRD, p. 92
13. *LEO Chronicle*, February 16, 1954
14. DTC Papers: Clerical Department announcement, December 7, 1953
15. *LEO Chronicle*, May 27, 1954
16. *LEO Chronicle*, February 12, 1951
17. JRMS Science, p. 13: " . . . we came to the conclusion that the only thing to do was to take them into our confidence right from the beginning, and long before we ever got permission to go ahead with the computer we had [meetings] ... to tell them what was in the wind"
18. JRMS Science, p. 13
19. DTC Papers, Simmons, October 22, 1951: "If he [Pinkerton] wishes to have the help of programmers, he should say so. Otherwise they must log the calculator as unserviceable and retire . . ."
20. DTC Papers: "Night work on LEO, April 22, 1953

Chapter 5: The Second LEO and LEO Computers Ltd 1954–1957
pages 43–58

1. *LEO Chronicle,* January 14, 1954 and May 4, 1954
2. *LEO Chronicle,* August 19, 1953, "Lenaerts submits proposals for a future LEO mercury delay line store using shorter tubes in which pulses would be ¼ microseconds in length . . .
3. DTC Papers: LEO Report No. 11, June 30, 1954
4. BIRD, p. 179: "At 6 pm on Monday 4th January 1965, after a full day's work and 14 years of continuous service (LEO I) was quietly closed down."
5. DTC Papers: LEO Report No. 11 , Appendix 4
6. *LEO Chronicle,* July 6, 1954, "At a Board room discussion on policy, instructions are given to proceed with the building of LEO II as soon as possible."
7. DTC Papers: LEO Report No. 11, Appendix 4: "If the patents hold then we should be able to obtain royalties from any company that uses our ideas."
8. BIRD, p. 195: "On 3rd August 1965 the Patent Office cited certain Raytheon computer patents against the claims of LEO . . . On 13th September 1956 Lyons abandoned the patent application for LEO."
9. *LEO Chronicle,* November 5, 1954, quoting Teashops general report from Wembley teashop
10. LEO: Teashops Demonstration script, 1955 (from C. Tully papers)
11. From a memoir contributed by Donald Moore entitled "Some recollections of LEO 1956-1965." Colonel Moore was responsible for the implementation and management of the Army pay system at Worthy Down, Manager of Computer Systems for Shell Mex and BP and Partner responsible for IT consultancy at Peat Marwick Mitchell."
12. *LEO Chronicle,* November 4, 1954: "Incorporation of new company, LEO Computers Ltd."
13. BIRD, p. 102, "On April 16, 1959, a further issue of 249,900 ordinary shares was made bringing the total share capital of the company to £250,000."
14. *LEO Chronicle,* July 25, 1955, "Steps to be taken to set up a formal sales organization to exploit the contacts Lyons have to get clerical as distinct from mathematical work."
15. JRMS LEO, p. 21, Wholesale Bakery invoicing reorganization
16. DTC Papers: "Meeting the programming requirements for extended LEO activities." DTC, August 5, 1955
17. DTC Papers: "Management of LEO Operations," T. R. Thompson, June 17, 1955
18. CAMPBELL-KELLY, p. 182
19. CAMPBELL-KELLY, p. 162
20. USA 1955, quoted by BIRD p. 102 *et seq.*
21. *LEO Chronicle,* May 4, 1954 "Visit of Sir Rowland Smith to see LEO. Possibility of doing their payroll on a service basis raised."
22. *LEO Chronicle,* August 8, 1955 "We hear from Bradley of Fords that they have decided to go ahead with having their payroll done on LEO."
23. *LEO Chronicle,* November 14, 1955
24. *LEO Chronicle,* December 2, 1955
25. JRMS LEO, p. 21

26. JRMS LEO, p. 22
27. DTC Papers: L5 Wholesale Bakery Invoicing Output specimens

Chapter 6: LEO II in the Field 1957–1958 pages 59–72

1. DTC Papers:JRMS note of OMA Conference, May 27, 1955
2. DTC Papers: JRMS LEO Report No. 11 to I. M. Gluckstein, May 17, 1955
3. DTC Papers: T. R. Thompson, Tentative timetable for construction of a second LEO
4. DTC Papers: JMMP, "Staff policy for LEO Technical section", January 5, 1955
5. DTC Papers: DTC, "Comments on the General Situation, August 5, 1955
6. DTC Papers: JMMP, "Staffing Policy," January 5, 1955
7. DTC Papers: DTC, "General Situation," August 5, 1955
8. *LEO Chronicle*, May 20, 1957
9. *LEO Chronicle*, "Formal order from ITC received."
10. PMR Hermon paper, Chapter 17
11. *LEO Chronicle*, May 15, 1956 *et seq.*
12. *LEO Chronicle*, May 18, 1956
13. DTC Papers: Stewarts and Lloyds Open Day brochure, November 1958
14. DTC Papers: Stewarts and Lloyds Open Day brochure, November 1958, p. 10, "Payroll"
15. DTC Papers: Stewarts and Lloyds Open Day brochure, November 1958, p. 14
16. DTC Papers: Stewarts and Lloyds Open Day brochure, November 1958, p. 15
17. *LEO Chronicle*, June 1956, "Fords decide to order LEO II for their parts job at Aveley."
18. *LEO Chronicle*, May 4, 1955 "Bayliss brings Directors of EverReady to see Teashops job": July 6, 1956, "Kodak agree to joint study of their payroll application"; February 22, 1957, Booth of Tate and Lyle . . . has recommended to his Board . . . payroll for 2600 employees at Plaistow on LEO.
19. DTC Papers: Resume of papers by J. M. M. Pinkerton, D.T. Caminer and A. B. Barnes at Seminar at Northampton Polytechnic (now City University) on "The Application of Digital Computers to Accountancy and Management Control"
20. *Economist*, March 13, 1954, "The Electronic Abacus" believed to have been written by senior staff writer Mary Goldring, who had witnessed a payroll demonstration.
21. House of Commons *Hansard*, December 20, 1955, Question by Commander Maitland MP, quoted by BIRD, p. 107
22. From a memoir (1995) contributed by Brian Edwards and Colin Davis entitled "LEO Computers: customers' views covering the period 1958-1961. Edwards was then a programmer with the Ford Motor Company and Davis a programmer at W. D. & H. O. Wills, the tobacco company. Both left those positions to join IBM at Bristol, where they first met. They are now partners in an IS consultancy.
23. DTC Papers: A typical course program, undated
24. DTC Papers: The Cricket Averages model job, undated

25: DTC Papers: Stewarts and Lloyds Open Day brochure, November 1958, p. 4
26. *Lyons Mail*, Magazine of the Lyons Club

Chapter 7: End of the First Generation 1958–1960 pages 73–85

1. *LEO Chronicle*, May 6, 1957, "Ford payroll reaches 10,300"
2. *LEO Chronicle*, December 11, 1956, "Plan submitted to LEO I staff for 168 hours per week operation so as to be able to complete the Railway Distancing job in time to meet the statutory commitment of the British Transport Commission of which we had not been informed . . . "
3. *LEO Chronicle*, November 6, 1956, "Production staff move to Minerva Road"
4. HENDRY: Appendices on numbers of installations etc., sourced from *Computer Survey and Computers and Automation*
5. USA 1958, p. 8, 1 April 58, Pittsburgh
6. USA 1958, p. 10 *et seq.*, April 3/4, 1958, Deerborn, Michigan
7. USA 1958, p. 15 April 7, 1958, Rochester, New York
8. USA 1958, p. 25 May 14, 1958, Chicago
9. USA 1958, p. 5, March 27, 1958, Lunch at Bankers Club, Wall Street, with Westminster Bank and Chase Manhattan
10. USA 1958, p. 7 March 31, 1958, Camden, New Jersey
11. USA 1958, p. 18 Higbee's Cleveland
12. USA 1958, p. 27 April 10, 1958, NCR, Los Angeles
13. DTC Papers: Stewarts and Lloyds Open Day brochure, November 1958
14. Tony Morgan memoir, 1995
15. DTC Papers: Stewarts and Lloyds Open Day brochure, November 1958
16. DTC Papers: "Possibility of installation of the first LEO II in the West End"
17. *LEO Chronicle*, May 28, 1961
18. Conversation with Col. Donald Moore, who was in charge of the RAPC installation, 1994
19. *LEO Chronicle*, May 28, 1961
20. *LEO Chronicle*, June 12, 1958
21. *LEO Chronicle*, April 21, 1955."PAYE tables for 1955/56 are successfully produced on Budget Night; January 13, 1956, "We hear from Beale that for financial reasons only we shall not in future be asked to produce the PAYE tables."
22. Edwards and Davis memoir, 1995
23. CAMPBELL-KELLY, p. 189/190
24. CAMPBELL-KELLY, p. 18
25. CAMPBELL-KELLY, p. 45
26. CAMPBELL-KELLY, p. 140
27. CAMPBELL-KELLY, p. 193, quoting from a report to the ICT Board after a trip to the USA, January/February 1960
28. *BABS, BEACON and BOADICEA, A History of Computing in British Airways and its Predecessor Airlines*, p. 27, Brian Harris, Speedwing Press, 1993
29. HENDRY, Appendices
30. CAMPBELL-KELLY, p. 202, quoting R. Sheehen, Fortune, November 1960 p. 116
31. CAMPBELL-KELLY, p. 206, quoting R. Sheehen, Fortune November 1960 p. 241

Chapter 8: Arrival of LEO III 1960–1963 pages 86–96

1. JMMP, p. 15, "By this time Wilkes had invented microprogramming. We decided that LEO Mark III should be based on microprogramming facilities. This would enable us to have a much more sophisticated instruction code than LEO Mark II.
2. BIRD, Appendix 7, Program Actions on the LEO III computer
3. The reference is to the Post Office Work Unit (POWU) devised by the Post Office systems and programming staff to provide a realistic representation of the office work with which they had to deal.
4. The reference is to the replacement of the Shell Mex and BP system by a UNIVAC 1108.
5. Correspondence with Ernest Roberts, 1994
6. CAMPBELL-KELLY, pp. 166, "NRDC was announced by Harold Wilson, President of the Board of Trade, in May 1949 with the stated aim that it would foster the patenting and the commercial exploitation of British inventions."
7. USA 1947
8. JRMS Science: "We had experience of Government in this kind of thing and this we didn't think was very likely."
9. CAMPBELL-KELLY, p. 239
10. BIRD, Appendix 9, Sales of LEO III computers
11. BIRD, p. 127
12. Ralph Land memoir, Chapter 18
13. BIRD, p. 128, "The first LEO III service work carried out in September 1962", p. 129, "Commissioning work started [in Johannesburg] on May 22, 1962.
14. Correspondence with Tony Morgan
15. DTC Papers
16. BIRD, Appendix 9
17. DTC Papers: LEO report for Dunlop Rubber Company, January 1959
18. BIRD, p. 130
19. LEO Reunion Society papers, "LEO organization as presented to English Electric visiting party, March 1963."

Chapter 9: The Merger with English Electric 1963 pages 97–109

1. BIRD, p. 175, "To give effect to this merger the issued share capital was increased to £2 million of which Lyons and English Electric would each hold 50%."
2. BIRD, p. 175
3. BIRD, p. 179: Bird reporting on discussion with Anthony Salmon. Hendry had concluded from his own research that Lyons had intended to divest themselves completely of computer manufacture.
4. BIRD, p. 176, quoting General Notice 1/63 dated May 1, 1963.
5. BIRD, p. 102
6. BIRD, p. 170, Table 6.1: Loss for year end March 31, 1962, £258 000
7. HENDRY, p. 99, Note 73: Net Profit 1958 £1 143 000; 1962, £1 070 000.
8 BIRD, p. 175: "Anthony Salmon and Sir Gordon Radley . . . jointly toured Europe and had preliminary talks with Olivetti, Phillips, Siemens and Bull with a view to encourage them to join a computer consortium."
9. CAMPBELL-KELLY, p. 165

10. CAMPBELL-KELLY, p. 203, Table 9.5
11. USA 1958, p. 7
12. HENDRY, Appendices
13. BIRD, Appendix 9
14. *LEO Chronicle,* April 9, 1956, "CAV accept proposals for our help in preparing programs on mathematical applications."
15. Correspondence with Mary Coombs (née Blood), 1994
16. *LEO Chronicle,* February 23, 1961, "Hargreaves of Smith and Nephew visits us to discuss possible cooperative service bureau business in Birmingham."
17. *LEO Chronicle,* December 5, 1957, to October 31, 1960, meetings with Shell Mex and BP, July 4 1961, SMBP "inform us of their decision to buy a LEO III"
18. BIRD, p. 146; illustration of mark-sensed form, p. 147
19. BIRD, p. Appendix 9
20. Correspondence with Mary Coombs and John Lewis
21. *LEO Chronicle,* December 14, 1961,
22. DTC Papers: photograph of GPO party at IBM Poughkeepsie, New York
23. BIRD, Appendix 14, Summary of LEO characteristics
24. BIRD, Appendix 9

Chapter 10: The Range Revolution 1964 pages 110–122
1. CAMPBELL-KELLY, p. 226, "On 7 April 1964 IBM announced System 360"
2. CAMPBELL-KELLY, pp. 226-9
3. CAMPBELL-KELLY, pp. 226-9
4. CAMPBELL-KELLY, p. 235, Table 11.2
5. CAMPBELL-KELLY, p. 230, Table 11.1
6. CAMPBELL-KELLY, p. 240
7. CAMPBELL-KELLY, p. 232
8. RCA, visit report
9. BIRD, Appendix 9
10. Shell Australia Study Group report, July 1962; quoted by BIRD, p.117
11. BIRD, p.258, Appendix 14
12. DTC Papers: GPO Press Notice, December 16, 1964, "Post Office buys five computers. £2½ million order.
13. BIRD, p. 149 *et seq.*
14. BIRD, p. 158
15. BIRD, pp. 177/8
16. Ben Pimlott, Harold Wilson, p. 348, Harper Collins, 1992
17. CAMPBELL-KELLY, p. 246 quoting The Labor, Government, Harold Wilson, p. 8 Weidenfeld and Nicolson and Michael Joseph, 1971

Chapter 11: The 1965 Paradox 1965 pages 123–129
1. BIRD, Appendix 9
2. "Computers for Profit" Paper presented by Freemans at Conference organized by BIM, CBT and ICT at Queen Elizabeth Hall, January 22, 1970
3. BIRD, Appendix 9
4. CAMPBELL-KELLY, p. 250, Table 12.1: "Market Shares 1964–1969"; "The launch of the 1900 series had been a major success. With over 200 machines on order by Spring 1985 which ensured ICT's medium term survival."

5. CAMPBELL-KELLY, p. 218, "July 9, 1962, ICT acquires EMI's computer interests"; p. 223, "Agreement in principle for ICT to acquire Ferranti's Computer division was reached in July 1963."
6. CAMPBELL-KELLY, p. 243, Table 11.4: Model 10 cancelled
7. CAMPBELL-KELLY, p. 270, "It was decided to axe the 4/30 (and the 4/40) in favor of the small 1900's."

Chapter 12: LEO Winds Down 1966–1968 pages 130–140

1. CAMPBELL-KELLY, p. 243
2. CAMPBELL-KELLY, p. 243
3. BIRD, Appendix 9, Sales of LEO II computers
4. JRMS LEO, p. 94, "LEO as a management tool"
5. BIRD, p. 165, "At 2 am on July 12, 1967 a combination of circumstances resulted in the paper catching fire."
6. BIRD, p. 167, "This arrangement continued for several weeks and in this way almost regular service . . . was maintained."
7. CAMPBELL-KELLY, p. 256, "During 1956 when ICT had been at the height of its financial crisis Mintech had proposed a merger scheme for English Electric to take control of ICT."
8. CAMPBELL-KELLY, p. 257, quoting Pears Report on "Rationalization of certain companies in the British computer industry"
9. CAMPBELL-KELLY, p. 259
10. CAMPBELL-KELLY, p. 260, "We are agreed that there is no *prima facie* reason why it should not be possible to plan a range of systems meeting the basic requirements of competitiveness and of acceptable compatibility with the current ranges of both companies."
11. Government white paper, March 21, 1968, "Industrial Investment: The Computer Merger Project; quoted by CAMPBELL-KELLY, p. 263
12. CAMPBELL-KELLY, p. 263, based on Humphreys interview with Babbage Institute, February 26, 1971
13. CAMPBELL-KELLY, p. 270
14. CAMPBELL-KELLY, p. 263, "It was only when the merger process had been agreed that he [Echo Organ, the Production Director] had the opportunity to examine the manufacturing costs of System 4 and he found them to be even worse than he had suspected."
15. CAMPBELL-KELLY, p. 271, "To make the most of the transaction processing market it was decided to enhance the upper range System 4 by introducing several new models . . . which would sell to big real-time users."
16. DTC Papers: Note of Neil Pollock's speech at closing down of Stewarts and Lloyds LEO II
17. BIRD, p182/3. "In December 1969 a subsidiary, Lyons Computer Services, was formed. Directors were executives from Bakeries, Tea, Ice Cream, etc"
18. BIRD, p. 183 "Some 80 separate measuring parameters were used, each having previously been allocated a weighting index."
19. BIRD, p. 186, "Users progressively began to install a variety of equipment."
20. BIRD. p. 184

PART 2
Pioneers

14
The Early Days
LEO FANTL

Planning Office

I joined Lyons sometime in 1948 as a trainee in the Planning Office at Cadby Hall.

Our function was two-fold: advising management on the introduction of new methods and techniques, and time and motion study. The latter activity involved detailed observation of each step in a repetitive operation, timing it and also recording an estimate of the degree of effort that went into each step. These observations were then worked up to arrive at an overall estimate of work content. This was not merely a matter of averaging, but of agonizing over excessive divergence in our results. Sometimes studies would be repeated by our training supervisor or even the section manager.

The method might seem hit or miss, but it was in fact extremely sound. By demanding from each planner a personal assessment of effort expended, our supervisors were soon able to establish a rating for each planner's judgment—tight or loose. By employing several different planners and operators on the same operation at different times, very fair judgments were made most of the time.

A few examples will demonstrate the diversity of our activities. In the 18 months or so that I was in the department I was involved in analyzing the passenger traffic in the elevators at the Cumberland Hotel, ice-cream deliveries, tray wash in Elms House, operations at the Hayes Laundry, and production in the jam factory, as well as operations in the

Cadby Hall Kitchens and Bread Bakery. There was also a study of office cleaning. In order to avoid the friction with the cleaners that would have arisen had we watched them at work, we trainees did the work ourselves before the cleaners arrived early in the morning and studied each other.

The practice of labor planning at Lyons was recorded in a little yellow book, called rather surprisingly the Yellow Book, written by J. R. M. Simmons. A truly masterly presentation of a complex subject, it was a planner's bible. Little did I know then that I was to meet the great JRMS in person before long.

Arrival at LEO

After some months we trainees were standing outside Mr. Warner's office (Mr. Warner was manager of the department), having our tea when he poked his head out of the door and said, "Anyone here know any-thing about electronics?" I admitted to having done some electronics in school physics and that was that. The months passed and I had all but forgotten the incident when I was asked to see T. R. Thompson.

TRT seemed to know everything about me; he certainly asked me not a single question about myself. He took me through a huge chart that represented the structure of LEO. I understood absolutely nothing. Then I was shown the computer by John Pinkerton. It seemed like a battle-ship. Huge racks, steel gray, with nothing inside them standing on a platform of wooden boards, mostly upended to reveal the delay lines underneath: cobwebs of cable everywhere. I realized then that whatever electronics I had done in school bore no relation whatever to this new world.

There were no other interviews and some time later I transferred to LEO, on the second floor of WX block. Derek Hemy was there and Joan Hyam. David Caminer wasn't; I suspect he still had his office at Systems Research and moved across a few weeks later. John Grover also joined LEO shortly after, followed by Mary Blood and Frank Land.

Derek had written an excellent Users' Guide to LEO, and he took me through that with one or two lessons every day. I remember the thrill of being introduced to the new world of digital logic, the fundamentals of programming, and of applying all of this to actual day-to-day processes. It was tremendously exciting. Derek was an outstanding teacher, and I soon realized my good fortune in being taught by him. One of my first tasks was to write a chapter for the manual on the subject of how the computer did arithmetic. Seemingly trivial, this turned out to be a challenge. The structure of LEO's register was such that numbers behaved like fractions.

But this went against the common sense of a clerical mind, which was used to counting in integers. So numbers held in the machine had to be visualized as being scaled by factors that would turn them into fractions.

Early on I helped Derek and then took over organizing our library of the Cambridge EDSAC subroutines. These routines were written at Cambridge by people who were using the EDSAC computer. At that time most of them were of little use to us, but later, as our activities in the field of scientific computing intensified, they became invaluable, and I went to a course run by Stan Gill where I gained valuable insight into their programming methods.

Test Programs

One of my early tasks was writing test programs, which became an important tool in the battle with a temperamental system. We had a comprehensive set of programs designed to regularly test all the major functions, including input, printer, and memory. Whenever a malfunction was identified, the circumstances leading up to and surrounding it were built into our test programs. For example, certain binary patterns could be used to expose latent problems when running under marginal conditions (e.g., voltage variations). These tests were run at least once every day and more often when particularly crucial or long projects had to be run. We even identified certain program combinations that could sometimes give warnings of impending problems when run in combination with particular data. These, too, were included in the suite.

As the list of features grew, so did the time taken to run them, and any test run that did not reveal a fault ate into our running time. Therefore, the frequency and duration of running test programs called for quite a fine judgment at times.

Service Programming

It will be clear from the above that in the early 1950s LEO was by no means fully ready for routine commercial data processing, yet there arose a lively demand for our services in the technical and scientific fields. Initially it fell to me to support these activities, having dabbled in mathematics over the years. Later, as demand intensified, we recruited a number of graduate mathematicians, first John Gosden, then Jim Smith and Ernest Roberts.

Some of the projects I was involved in are described below.

Weather Forecasting

Busby, of the Meteorological Office, did most of the system, and Derek Hemy did a lot of the initial programming and liaison. I came in when Derek went on to payroll and engineering liaison full-time. The work basically involved second-order partial differential equations using relaxation (finite differences) with complex boundary conditions. It was frustrating in a way, because even with a system much more powerful than LEO I, I think that the "forecast" could never have done better than say what the weather ought to have been. It's just as well that we now have satellite views of the globe and the clouds. Even I can predict the weather now.

Crystallography

This was for the Lyons laboratories, done by Miss Brown, I think, and her partner—two wonderful, dedicated people. It was basically a three-dimensional analysis job using "steepest descent." I did the program according to their definition. It was not all that easy on LEO I, but with modern technology it would be about half an hour's work. Papers were written, but sadly I think they ran out of money. It was a really worthwhile application at the time.

Tax Tables

The Department of Inland Revenue was responsible for producing the tax tables, a job that invariably required a large printing volume but unpredictable system changes. Budget details were of course closely guarded secrets and no one was allowed to see what was coming, so any changes had to be implemented in a hurry and machine time had to be available to support programming and to run off all the tables. Hence, we were required to stand by not only to modify programs as necessary but also to run them if need be. Frank Land, I think, joined us at that stage, and this was perhaps his first job. I probably learned more about digital accuracy on this application than on any other. There were many different tables, including those for sailors, all based on different criteria.

Matrix Algebra

This was done for Hawker Siddeley, Armstrong Whitworth, and de Havilland—mainly guided missile work. It was basically all matrix algebra and some numerical integration, hence Runge-Kutta techniques were used (see below). We had no matrix algebra library, but we got eigenvalues and the associated routines from Cambridge. John Gosden and later

Ernest Roberts did sterling work here. Matrices were the sort of application that really stressed LEO's weaknesses—lots of data moving in and out and not much one could do to assure accuracy.

Actuarial Work

The Institute of Actuaries publishes life tables linking life expectancy statistics with annuities for men and women jointly and separately. We were asked to do the first publication by computer. I had never been involved in actuarial mathematics and found it hard going. It was quite a big job and one of the tables was wrong. I think I programmed the wrong cut-off date for a joint annuity. That cost us about 17 hours, I think, and unkind things were said, but I got invited to a dinner by the society somewhere in Piccadilly and I had the time of my life. They were incredibly gracious and appreciative.

Guided Missles

This was done by Jim Smith for de Havilland. It was highly classified and I was precluded from clearance, being a naturalized alien, but after Derek's initial involvement it came under Jim Smiths' "control." When the job ran, we had to string a colored cable around the computer to warn everyone off. It was on this application that we first encountered Runge-Kutta techniques. These are basically an adaptation of Taylor's theorem for multi-equation systems; Runge and Kutta postulated the basic approach, which was adapted by Stanley Gill at Cambridge to provide accuracy tracing algorithms. In its infancy at that time, not much was known about the technique, and we were pioneering once again, with TRT insisting on clear, basic-principles-type expositions. (This was an invaluable lesson. If someone doesn't understand what they are supposed to do, make them explain it to the whole world.) We had lots of fun streamlining the Cambridge subroutine.

CAV: Pump Design by Simulation

CAV designed oil pumps by practical benchtesting, which was a long hit-and-miss process. They looked around for theoretical simulation methods and Eric Knight was responsible for designing a very sophisticated system. The idea was to define systems performance in terms of the number and location of air bubbles generated inside the pump; the more bubbles, the lower the efficiency. The process involved solving a number of second-order differential equations, again using relaxation, but it was far more complex than the Met Office job. We made progress, but funds ran out and we moved on to administrative systems, which were as complicated as the pump job.

Chebyshev Polynomials

Moving to LEO II and then LEO III required redesigning all subroutines based on power series because the size of the numbers increased. Most of these functions were already economized with Chebyshev polynomials (a way of ensuring that a power series delivered errors of similar size throughout the allowed range rather than minimal errors at specific points, for fewer terms than an ordinary power series would have employed). Regenerating the terms of the reduced series would have involved much manual effort and it was therefore decided to automate the procedure. Ernest Roberts and Eric Kavanagh carried on after I went on to payrolls when Derek Hemy left.

Ford Payroll

Derek had launched this, our first big external administrative job, as I recall, and when he left I moved across from technical work. leaving John Gosden in charge. I had had some exposure to the Lyons payroll, where Mary Blood, Derek Hemy, and DTC had given me a good grounding before becoming involved on the technical side.

From start to finish the project took under three months, except for labor statistics. American-controlled organizations overseas even in those days tended to place heavy emphasis on head counts, which made for complicated personnel statistics. I don't think we ever finished the personnel statistics, but everything else worked on D-day. The job was simple enough and there was no labor costing allocation. But even so, two and a half months was not bad going. I recall not being home in daylight for what seemed then like the whole project time. I certainly felt like a zombie at the end. This was the first and last occasion I was paid a bonus—$70. I bought a Stanley power drill and still have some of the parts in my garage now.

The chief problem with the project was machine time. I clearly remember one of those exceptional Sundays when I was home doing a bit of gardening, when who comes along but Lenaerts, from the engineering team, asking whether I wanted to go on the machine. I nearly wept! However, Ford's reaction was a rich reward. I know that at the higher levels too there was much enthusiasm. The main benefit seemed to arise in the dramatic reduction in queries. A clear and well-presented earnings record reduced tax queries and found ready acceptance by the workforce. It all but eliminated the lines of people at the pay offices with questions about their taxes.

My team comprised some outstanding talent: Mary Blood, Pat Cooper, Betty Newman, and toward the end Geoff Pye, Peter Hermon, and Arthur Payman.

Other Payrolls

Our performance on the Ford payroll was actually quite astonishing, even by today's standards. It was indeed a trendsetter and, not surprisingly, payroll became one of LEO's main administrative applications. We diversified into the principal payroll requirements quite soon after, namely labor statistics, costing, extensive incentive schemes by trade, qualifications, and type of work, and of course the multiplicity of rules and procedures arising from trade union agreements. This diversity undoubtedly led to the many powerful payroll packages that began in earnest in the 1970s.

Many of the companies mentioned here came to our bureau service initially with the intention of moving on to their own LEO installation later.

I was involved in the following applications:

Stewarts and Lloyds, Corby

This was far more complicated than Ford, with costing and pay structures that even by today's standards were complex. Pay documentation was far more involved too, but we had tremendous support from the Stewarts and Lloyds manager, Neil Pollock, and his team, and I still recall the enthusiasm with which our first operational run was received in Corby. Our programming team was mainly the same as for Ford, but I recall John Lewis and Pat Cooper coming on board. Bob Caldwell and Hamish Archibald from Corby joined us also. This marked the introduction of the concept of building users' teams on our premises under our management, working on their projects, and going back home with the machines and the main applications to get things going—a brilliant strategy. Many times later I saw the contrast between this approach and the more aloof approach, which kept the user away from the nitty-gritty.

Kodak and Tate & Lyle

We were by now (1956–57) thoroughly familiar with the main requirements of payroll processing, including particularly the housekeeping aspects, which are so essential in a tight, high-accuracy operational environment. Building on the original Lyons and Ford team, we created new teams of systems designers and programmers under John Lewis, Geoff Pye, Ian Crawford, and Alan Jacobs. Thinking back to those exciting, eventful years, I am amazed at how many of our star performers earned their colors in the payroll field. I wish I could name them all. (Pat Cooper comes to mind easily enough, being now Pat Fantl, and Betty Newman, her sister-in-law.)

MPNI and Greenwich Borough Council

This was my first introduction to government departments and municipalities. Both were very complex applications because of the elaborate staff structures and remuneration. Both organizations sent staff to us for training. I was in both cases struck by the high level of competence and determination at the users' end.

Technology Developed

We had, of course, nowhere to turn for help with the many operational problems we encountered, so we had to improvise. Some of our problems were transient, being primarily equipment-related, and so our solutions too were phased out as soon as possible. An example is checking on printer performance before the advent of parity checks. But quite a few techniques remained, and indeed were reinvented elsewhere later.

A few recollections follow.

Checkpoint Restarts

We first used the Checkpoint Restart technique on the CAV pump design job. Once the program was working, we decided to run it in earnest, doing a live run. When I worked out how long it would take to run, I triumphantly announced the glad news to DTC: it worked, we were ready to run, it would take three and a quarter hours, we would make lots of money at last, and would he fix it with the engineers? (Even an hour was hard to get and required DTC's intercession.) But far from sharing my elation, David grunted; how on earth could we keep the machine going for that length of time? I hadn't thought of that, so we had to improvise fast. The answer is still with us today; do a store dump every 15 minutes or so. We had no answer then (as we don't now) to the question, "How did we know when things started to go wrong?" But at least we could resume quickly after a system had crashed.

Debugging

Of course, we knew nothing of syntax checking in those days, and although we had learned the paramount importance of independent visual checking of code, finding bugs was never easy, particularly on scientific work, where results could be invalidated at any one of a series of obscure points. So early on in one of the ballistics/guided-missile jobs I hit on the idea of checkpoints in the program, which could be activated selectively and key variables examined and checked. Today, many of the more sophisticated compiler debuggers still employ the basic thinking of those early days.

Error Detection

Another vital technique was devising algorithms in our systems, which helped us verify results. John Gosden did excellent work here, stimulated by DTC, when we found that hours of work on a large latent root job had been invalidated by a system malfunction. Basically, the idea was to create additional sum vectors and relate those to the result. More and more we had to devise techniques like these to overcome the otherwise insoluble problem of how to finish a job correctly given that the machine could not consistently run long enough without some fault or other. Other examples included backward integration to check a step function (a well-known technique in manual computing), alternative methods to check the main procedure (or at least establish confidence limits), and, when all else failed, running the job twice.

Flowcharting

We had early on developed and applied the discipline of hierarchical flowcharting to enable us to plan, partition, and control the implementation of programs. It soon became obvious, however, that one of the most powerful benefits of good flow charting arose in preventing errors in the logic of a program, as well as in tracing errors that got through. As a last recourse, if more experienced help had to be called in to solve a problem, the flowchart was an invaluable tool for explaining what was going on in the program. The same, of course, applied to "on the job" fault-finding. Quite often, programs might come up for machine verification long after they had been written. Indeed, authors might have moved on to other projects, and machine testing would be carried out by others. Here in particular the ease of finding out what was happening or supposed to happen by means of a clear flowchart was of immense help.

All these applications led us to improve and adapt the techniques we employed in designing flowcharts to improve their effectiveness. For example, programmers deeply immersed in a chart to resolve a problem at their desk obviously know the direction in which they are moving on the chart. But programmers attempting to locate a problem quickly while the machine is standing idly by need all the help they can get to guide them through the chart. This led to the introduction of techniques that showed at a glance the direction in which the logic of a chart was progressing.

Although I am familiar with modern techniques, I still employ the old LEO methods when drawing a flowchart.

Reconciliations

On running clerical applications, I realize now that perhaps our most powerful tool was the application of traditional accounting methods. David Caminer devised rigorous checks and balances, which we called "reconciliation accounts." They were quietly cursed by all, but helped us survive the worst hardware and software problems. In our context, reconciliations were really a logical extension of basic accounting techniques, but in practical computer work they posed a formidable problem. This was due to the fact that any nontrivial reconciliation account required the accumulation of many component elements in many different places slotted into various aggregate totals. All of these factors had to be identified and catered for in advance—to build these things into a program after it was finished was in those days very messy.

This meant that reconciliations had to be planned in detail at the outset and programmed as the work progressed. This forced people to become really conversant with a new application right from the start, a very good thing in itself, but troublesome for impetuous young programmers.

A Strictly Personal Note

I have sometimes wondered whether some of the early pioneers were not motivated more by an urge to be in the forefront of progress than by a balanced consideration of what was good for their organization at that time. Names that come to mind are Polley of the Ministry of Pensions and Pollock of Stewarts and Lloyds. There was also Hay of Rand Minds, of whom I speak in Chapter 25. Perhaps this is more true of outfits that bought machines when they were in their infancy than those who came to the bureau.

And was it not true of ourselves? It can certainly be asked whether TRT, DTC, and (less so) JRMS were driven for Lyons or by their own agendas. It is more likely that no corporate goal can ever succeed if it cannot also provide the ambitious individual with the challenge of extraordinary difficulty and the promise of self-fulfillment.

Whether or not ambitions as they developed were strictly justified in a business sense, there was within LEO a dedication that was unwavering. In the 30-odd years after I left the UK, not counting the five years at EELM and later ICL, I was exposed to vast amounts of indoctrination and most of the catchphrases of the times, and I found that nothing had so much meaning, relevance, and truth as the set of values I saw in the early LEO days. Whether we managed to spread that gospel, I don't know.

How did those values come about? Is there some alchemy here that a future historian could prescribe for another challenge in uncharted territories? For what it is worth, I think it happened this way because of the personal qualities of two people: DTC and TRT. They were not comfortable people to work for. TRT was able to be brutally frank, and he unthinkingly made me suffer for my nonscientific background and do-it-yourself education. He was inclined to proclaim to a visiting party, "Fantl is the worst kind of mathematician . . . self-taught." I don't suppose that anyone realized how hard it was to keep up with applied mathematicians by brushing up on calculus the night before a meeting or writing reports with a dictionary constantly by my side. Yet TRT could be very kind at times.

With the determination to reach objectives that had never been reached before, the LEO management style could seem intimidating, with TRT's cold frankness often more painful than David's outbursts. Closer to the work in hand, David was the hardest, most relentless driver of all, though at difficult times he could always be relied upon to help as effectively as he could without sparing himself or taking credit. They were very different people, but remove them from the scene and the innovation in its thoroughness could never have been achieved.

15
The Widening Field

FRANK LAND

In the 1940s and 1950s, J. Lyons was one of the most successful business-es in the country, with its products and establishments—Lyons Tea, Lyons Cakes, Lyons Ice Cream, and the Teashops and Corner Houses—being household names. The company had built its success on quality products and services sold to a mass market and a constant striving for value-adding innovation.

Selling to a competitive mass market required tight control over costs and margins, and a sensitive response to customer preferences and market movements.

John Kay,[1] in his study of what makes businesses successful, suggests that "architecture" is one of the important ingredients. The distinctive architecture that Lyons had developed over the years was the way information was passed from operations—manufacturing, selling, distribution, as well as the concomitant operations concerned with invoicing and payments—to the decision-making senior management. Each of the many businesses (Tea, Teashops, Ice Cream, Bakeries, Kitchens, etc.) had it own groups of clerks and managers. The vast mass of transaction data stemming from these operations was summarized and compared with preset standards, forecasts, and budgets. The resulting information was analyzed by the junior manager in charge of each group who was responsible for explaining any important variances.[2] The junior manager had a direct line to the senior manager, often a Lyons Director, responsi-ble for that activity, and had to explain the functioning of that activity. At the same time the senior manager could ask the junior liaison manager to undertake investigation of the "what if" type. Suppose we want to increase the production of Swiss rolls by 10 percent and reduce the production of cupcakes by 3 percent: what would be the effect on gross profit? The arrangement ensured direct access by senior management to information originating at the operating level, and bypassed the more usual filtering though layers of middle management.

This architecture provided the company, long before the advent of computers, with both an almost real-time management information system and a decision support system of considerable sophistication. In addition, the architecture and system provided senior management with a detailed picture of the week's trading on the Monday of the following week.

The management had seen the need to innovate, not only in new products and services, but also in "business processes" as early as the 1920s. As described in Chapter 2, they engaged a top-ranking mathematics graduate from Cambridge[3] to oversee the office functions, which already were seen to be the source of information for management. He established a Systems Research office whose function was to analyze primarily office operations in order to see how processes could be improved to provide better control and to reduce costs.

The Systems Research Office, working with line mangers, produced a stream of business process innovations from the time of its establishment. Examples include the notion that sales representatives, each having a customer group of many small retailers, would be responsible not only for selling to their customer group, but also for the accounting, credit and payment functions conventionally carried out at arm's length by a separate accounting office. The introduction of "traveler-covered credit" was a radical business process innovation that increased efficiency and the effectiveness of the representative.

Yet in many other ways the company was deeply traditional and conservative. It operated on a strictly hierarchical basis. At the top were the owners: the founding family. They ran the company with the help of a very few employee directors. Each grade of management had its own dining room. Separate toilets divided managers from the rest. Trade unions were discouraged, though the family took a paternalistic interest in its staff.

This was the company I joined in 1952 as a recent graduate in economics. My first job was as a clerk in the Statistical office—one of the major offices compiling and checking transaction data for posting to the cost accounts of the various operating units. I was responsible for keeping the costs accounts of the Provincial Bakeries and the Lyons laboratories for further analysis and interpretation by the junior manager, Alec Kirby. I learned then that the established routine for almost all staff, down to the lowest clerk covered only a portion of the time available. Much time was spent in tracing errors and various forms of troubleshooting. The more senior clerks and junior managers seemed to spend most of their time in that kind of activity. As in much of British manufacturing, "project chasing" kept the wheels turning.

At that time Lyons had already embarked on its pioneering adventure with computers. In retrospect the move into computers is not so surprising. The Systems Research Office had investigated the possibility of coping with the mass of transaction data by some kind of mechanization or automation for many years. They had started to investigate the possibility of devising a document reader for transaction data before World War II. They had researched the possible application of unit record systems based on punched cards but rejected these as too localized, too constraining, and too costly. Lyons had only one punched-card installation, and that had a very limited application. Instead they had installed alternative types of office mechanization based on accounting machines and calculators. Computers, it was reasoned, had the capability of overcoming the limitations of the unit record equipment then available.

I knew nothing of the experiments going on with the LEO computer. But as the LEO group expanded, the company searched for possible recruits from its offices. It was suggested that I might like to learn about LEO to see if I was interested and fitted their requirements for computer programmers. I was put on a one-week LEO "appreciation" course. The course taught us the rudiments of binary arithmetic, programming, and how the computer worked. It was tough. Each evening I would go home, sometimes in despair, and together with my wife[4] work at the homework to master the exercises. By the end of the week I was still in a fog but felt that joining the LEO group would be a most exciting challenge, and certainly an improvement over the by then rather boring Provincial Bakeries.

In 1952 I was selected to join the LEO group. At that time the first LEO (LEO I) was being commissioned in its final form. Magnetic tape, though still standing around, had been abandoned for the time being. Punched cards and paper tape were the main input devices, though it was possible to intervene directly from the console to change the program or data, or to single-step one's way through a program when debugging. Output was also on punched cards and paper tape, but also in printed form directly onto a line printing tabulator. The computer was by present standards very unreliable, and the combination of programming errors, data errors, and an unreliable machine made the log entry "passed point of previous stoppage" a particular joy for the operators and programmers. Nevertheless, a substantial amount of work was being carried out.

The first application to provide experience of what was involved in running a live, time-critical office job with a precise weekly schedule had gone live three or four years earlier. Now the team[5] was working on the various Lyons payrolls (L1), and beginning to plan the teashop ordering job (L2) and the reserve stores allocation job (L3). In addition, the machine was being utilized as a service bureau with work, principally of a scientific nature, being carried out for a number of external organizations. Some of these involved programming on the customer specification by a member of the LEO team, but others were programmed by the customer's own staff and LEO merely provided machine time.

Although the Lyons applications were some of the earliest business systems on a computer, a pattern of planning and development had already been established, and for any application a kind of standard of "good practice" had been established. Many of these standards are as relevant today as they were in the early 1950s.

Selecting and planning the use of LEO for business processes that might benefit from the use of computers was in the hands of the senior LEO management (T. R. Thompson and David Caminer) and the Systems Research Office,[6] working with senior Lyons managers—often directors—and line management from the business area affected. To be selected, an application had to provide clear cost savings against conventional methods, or had to make the business process more effective as well as show savings in costs. The planners would look for opportunities to improve the business process in a way that would not have been possible with alternative methods.

There are many examples of such improvements. The teashop distribution job (L2) is described elsewhere in this book (Chapter 18 and Appendix C). It provides a number of instances of the way the job was designed to achieve a range of business improvements. These included the developments of standards—via the standard menu—that added value by reducing the workload of the teashop manager, who could pay more attention to matters such as the presentation of the food and staff management. The standard menu provided the production management with the means of planning production and with a way of dealing with emergencies. It also gave time to a manager to think what an appropriate menu should look like for the teashop. At the same time, the use of LEO enabled changes to be made later and hence closer to the business situation that gave rise to the changes. In other words, the response to market conditions became closer to real time. The teashop distribution job made possible a major business process innovation.

Another early application again illustrated the focus on using the computer to achieve extra value. In 1953 food rationing was still in force, and Lyons, as a food manufacturer, had to rely on a great variety of materials, including substitutes for the natural raw materials. For example, a substitute for sugar used in the bakeries was sweetened fat. The substitute materials were held in so-called "reserve stores." An application was planned and developed for maintaining the inventory records of all the material held in the reserve stores and allocating these to the manufacturing centers, bakeries, ice-cream plants, and kitchens, on the basis of orders received and manufacturing schedules. The computer received manufacturing schedules as data, and consolidated and allocated material from reserve stores according to the availability of transport in order to keep distribution costs to a minimum. As with all LEO jobs, the automatic procedure could always be overridden by management action. Costs were calculated for each store and charged out to the manufacturing departments. The reserve stores allocation job ran successfully for only a short time, as it was abandoned once rationing was ended and material could be ordered from suppliers on something close to a just-in-time basis.

While the focus of the more senior LEO management was on business processes and the selection and planning of applications, those of us involved with getting the work onto the computer lived and dreamed the technical problems of getting the programs to work. Each job presented major problems of fitting the tasks required into the small computer store and at the same time getting the job to run efficiently. The trade-off between saving instructions by tight programming and saving time in execution was a constant problem. Saving the execution of one instruction in a loop was a triumph and was reported and discussed at mealtime and coffee breaks. Programming so a transaction could be fully computer-checked within the time it took to read a punched card was good; missing the cycle by a fraction of a second could double the execution time of a job with thousands of transactions to be dealt with. Every day produced new tricks of programming and avid discussions of how the trick was done.

At the same time, the standards of good practice already in force were maintained and supplemented. Senior management kept a tight discipline that ensured high quality and safe applications. No program was allowed on the computer for debugging without it having been checked by a colleague. This practice helped the learning and spread of "best practice" among the team. All applications had built-in reconciliation procedures that were based on good accounting practice and that not only ensured accurate work from the computer, but helped to pinpoint mistakes when they occurred and demonstrated to the business user the integrity of the work done on the computer.

In the year I joined the LEO group, the Lyons payroll and teashop distribution jobs were rolled out and became jobs routinely carried out on a weekly or daily basis. Having routine jobs required the computer to be run by a cadre of professional operators. Hence a new operating section with initially two computer operators and a number of data preparation staff was set up.

By now what had been regarded by the outside world as a perverse experiment was reality. Knowledge about what was happening at Cadby Hall began to spread, largely through the Office Management Association of which John Simmons, a Lyons Employee Director, was president. Visitors were frequently taken around the computer and told about the applications. As a result, inquiries about the possible use of the computer for their own businesses began to arrive. For the LEO and Lyons management, this suggested the possibility of making LEO an independent business, manufacturing and selling computers and running computers as a service bureau for other companies.

The requirement to continue to develop applications for the Lyons group and to provide for the planning, development, and implementation of applications for an outside market increased the need for programming staff, and a period of recruitment and expansion followed. For the group already in place it meant that the lessons learned from the successes of the Lyons applications and the standards of good practice, which had been absorbed into the way of working, had to be rapidly applied to a range of new jobs on behalf of outside clients. Of these the biggest to be carried out on a regular basis was the weekly Ford Motor Company payroll for over 20,000 workers. In terms of developing operational practices, providing regular secure delivery of outputs to a host of service customers provided a major challenge, which the LEO team met successfully.

But to some of us the real challenge was to understand and master the business needs of a very diverse group of customers covering almost all sections of British (and, in later years, East European) business. The fact that this offspring of a food business could sell systems to a wide range of blue-chip companies and government departments is an outcome of the quality of the team recruited by the LEO management, but even more of the good practices they had inherited from the Lyons pioneers. Many of those involved in the early days have risen to high ranks in industry and academia, reflecting the important role of the LEO venture as an educator, almost as a business school.

My own progress was hesitant at first, but under the tutelage of my peers—Derek Hemy, Leo Fantl, and John Grover—I began to acquire some skills as a programmer. Among my contemporaries, John Gosden in particular made spectacular progress and began a whole series of programming innovations.

At that time all of us worked on a wide range of applications. Some of these involved systems programming. One of my earliest jobs, working under Derek Hemy, was to make some small alterations to the LEO I initial orders. Later, working with Leo Fantl, I helped to prepare the routines for the calculation of tax tables for the Inland Revenue. The application was carried out once a year only—immediately after the Chancellor of the Exchequer had sat down in the House of Commons after his budget speech. We waited at Elms House for the courier to come with the data describing the tax changes to be incorporated in all the tax tables. We had no idea what the Chancellor would propose but hoped that our system was sufficiently flexible to cope with any changes he might bring in. The programs could easily cope with tax rate and allowance changes, but if the Chancellor wanted to make basic changes in the tax structure we could have been in trouble. Of course, the civil servants who briefed us had a fair idea what was likely to be in the Chancellor's package. Nevertheless, Budget Day had a rather special meaning for those of us involved with the tax table production.

The first job for which I was primarily responsible was a service bureau job carried out for a Liverpool clock manufacturer, J. D. Francis. The job entailed a weekly calculation of production costs using standard costing and computing variances of the rather complex product—complex when compared with an equivalent task for, say, the Lyons bakeries. This required breaking down production orders for the end product (clocks and watches) into the parts and subassemblies needed to complete production. With the very limited computer store available, this involved an ingeniously designed computer program, in particular as the job also had to do the reverse process of building up actual product costs.

The requirements for the job were specified by Oliver Standingford, who by that time was working as a Director of J. D. Francis. The job broke new ground in providing management information for a complex group of products. I was helped in bringing the job into operation by Betty Newman, a quiet, unassuming young woman who became a first-class programmer. The J. D. Francis job appeared to achieve the objective set by Standingford: to bring the manufacture of clocks under rigorous control. However, it could not save the company from eventual bankruptcy, illustrating the important lesson that, however good and effective the support activities of an enterprise are, they cannot save the enterprise if the core operations—in this case the manufacture and marketing of a range of clocks—are not equally well managed.

Gradually the emphasis of our worked changed. From primarily programming applications designed in essence by someone else, I became involved, first, in designing a system as a group of linked programs and later in establishing directly with users what the system as a whole should do, and what part the computer could play.

My first major application in the first sense was the Lyons Tea Blending job. This was largely specified by members of the tea management working in conjunction with the Systems Research Office and senior LEO people. But I came to the job at an early stage in its specification.[7] The job was concerned with the tea purchased by the company each week and its blending and packaging. Some was bought at the auctions held each week at Mincing Lane, the London center of the tea trade. Other supplies were contracted for directly with growers in India and Ceylon. Allocations to blends and stocks were valued according to an average price formula. The application commenced working in 1954 and continued very much as specified for the next 25 years. As with all other LEO jobs, it combined information relevant to the efficient running of the tea business at the operational level with management information to help in the longer-term planning of that business.

The Tea Blending application was the first of a number of jobs I worked on that had stock control as a central feature of the application. These applications varied enormously in scale and scope. At one extreme was the parts ordering system for the Ford Motor Company, who acquired a LEO II computer for the task. The number of parts stocked was vast—well over 40,000 discrete items. They ranged from parts originally used in the Model T to the newest release of a component for the latest Ford model. Model T engines were still in use in the 1950s, not in cars but in old pumping engines. The number of transactions to be handled on a daily basis was also vast, primarily orders from the thousands of Ford dealers plus deliveries from Ford's own factories and suppliers like Lucas. The objective was to turn around orders quickly, to prepare picking and packing documents for the Aveley warehouse within 24 hours of the orders being received and to deal with emergency orders—that is, orders for immobilized vehicles—almost as soon as they had been received. At the same time, the application warned stock controllers of items that were at risk from stock-outs and suggested reorder quantities.

A number of LEO people worked on the design of the application, cooperating with Ford's own staff. I took over the LEO liaison with the Ford staff from John Gosden. On the Ford side the senior man in charge of managing the implementation was Stan Woods, who had previously been responsible for a very large punched-card installation at Aveley. That experience enabled Stan to understand and manage the huge task of preparing the data, which had to be made ready for LEO each day. The designated method was to use a very large pulling file. This permitted much of the data to be prepunched, thus avoiding the problem of having to prepare the vast volume of fresh data each day. However, he found it more difficult to appreciate how the computer could do tasks that were impossible (or impractical) on unit record equipment. Hence we were faced with many battles on how best to exploit their LEO.

The situation was eased by the arrival at Aveley of Peter Gyngell as systems manager. Peter was a somewhat larger-than-life figure. He had arrived at Aveley from his native Wales, having studied philosophy, played rugby, and narrowly decided to join the world of business rather than becoming a preacher. He rapidly saw what could be done with a computer and was willing to work very closely with the LEO people. The success of the Aveley project owes a great deal to his skill. Later Peter joined LEO and became the manager of LEO in Australia.

A very different stock control application with which I was involved was a service job carried out on a LEO III on behalf of Lightning Fasteners, a subsidiary of the ICI company's Imperial Metal Industries (IMI). Lightning Fasteners was then the major supplier of zippers in Britain. The company was facing increased competition from abroad and had to improve its efficiency to survive. On the one hand it needed to reduce costs by reducing its inventory of finished goods, while on the other it needed to improve its service to customers by reducing the incidence of stock-outs. Both requirements might be met by finding a way to more accurately predict the demand for fasteners. The LEO application was based on recording all stock movements each week and then using a statistical technique only recently developed—exponential smoothing—for predicting stock movements. The application appeared to be a success, achieving the goals set by IMI management. It could not, however, save Lightning Fasteners, who found the competition from the Japanese fastener company YKK unbeatable, and rather rapidly IMI (by then separate from ICI) decided to abandon the zipper business.

The job that taught me most about stock control as a business process was a pilot service job developed for the central stores of the North Thames Gas Board. The Gas Board ran a central store to supply its service departments with items needed for construction and maintenance. Items of stock ranged in value from a few cents to thousands of dollars. Some were highly specialized, manufactured only for the Gas Board. For others, the stock held was a lifetime stock. Many items were issued to user departments on a fairly regular basis, while others moved only occasionally and erratically.

The business problem was the classic one of achieving a high level of stock service with a minimum investment in stock. The operational problem was to deal efficiently with a large number of varied transactions in a sufficiently reliable way for the book stock to be a good indicator of physical stock. The North Thames manager responsible for Central Stores was a Mr. Ryan. He had worked with Central Stores for many years and knew what went on—both the formal rules for operating the stores and the informal shortcuts that are used to make any system work. Ryan saw the possibilities of using the computer, and strongly supported the notion of setting up a pilot system to evaluate possibilities. We established an excellent relationship and as a result were able to specify a very comprehensive description of what had to be done.

In practice we were forced to make some compromises. The timetable for getting the pilot running was tight. As a result we decided not to implement some of the less frequently occurring transactions. This is a course of action that is frequently advocated under the Pareto principle. Pareto had shown that in many situations 20 percent of the possible types of occurrence account for some 80 percent of the activity. Hence, if the computer system could cope with the right 20 percent of transaction types, it would cover a very substantial part of all the activity. The advocates of the Pareto principle point to the large difference in costs between implementing a system based on the most active transaction types and creating one that is comprehensive and aims at achieving close to 100 percent of all activity.

In the case of the Central Stores we were able to deal with very many of the possible transactions. The moment the system cannot deal with all transactions, it becomes necessary to develop independent noncomputer systems to cope with the residue. Inevitably this leads to synchronization and reconciliation problems. The practical outcome is that even if the fraction of transactions dealt with outside the computer system is very small, there may be differences between physical stock and book stock on some stock items each day. It does not take long for the stores staff to distrust the computer-based system and to start keeping their own manual records.

In many ways the pilot program was a success. It showed that a computer system could cope with a very large number of stock items and stock movements, and produce valuable management information enabling the stock controller to keep a good balance of stock. However, at the time North Thames Gas Board decided not to go for a full-scale implementation of the system.

As the emphasis shifted from serving the parent company to doing jobs for prospective users of the service bureaus and prospective purchasers of first LEO II and later LEO III computers, the content of our jobs changed, too. Our role was still to understand and interpret the needs of users, but the object was to sell LEO computers. The transition from a primary emphasis on systems analysis in order to develop computer systems to systems analysis designed to demonstrate the merit of buying into LEO to potential customers was gradual. Our marketing strategy was based on our ability to convey to potential customers that they would be buying into an organization that could understand their needs and leave no stone unturned to help them launch their computer systems.

At that time, to get senior management to accept the use of computers required very strong championship, usually from one individual. Later, as the use of computers became more widespread, the procedures for acquiring computers became more formal, with offers and formalized evaluations. In the earlier times it required the champion's enthusiasm and willingness to overcome obstacles in order to make progress with computers. I believe one of the strengths of the early LEO team was its ability to work closely with and to support these champions.[8] But sometimes that could lead to trouble. In practice the champions were very different from each other. Some had vision but also saw the need to prepare carefully, keep the rest of the organization in the picture, and work at a pace the organization could take. Others were visionary but could not foresee possible difficulties and opposition from "counter champions." A number of the failures that we had to accept involved champions of the latter kind. Their enthusiasm carried us with them. Sometimes we saw the danger ahead but allowed the champion to block access to others in their organization who might have provided needed balance. Perhaps we should have seen that we were building on sand.

Of course, we too made mistakes. A particular fault was our expectation that other companies could change at the pace of the fastest movers. Somehow we assumed that having seen what we took to be the needs of an organization and having understood the business problems they faced, developing and implementing the system would be straightforward.[9] On the other hand, a paper in the *Computer Journal* of 1958 by David Caminer[10] points to the difficulties of getting applications into operation and provides guidelines as relevant today as they were then. We had a confidence in our ability to understand what was needed that sometimes made us appear arrogant. But we too were capable of missing a real requirement or misjudging a situation.

Over the course of many years working as a consultant with LEO, I had the opportunity to visit and study a large number of companies from many industrial sectors. Some decided to come to LEO, and acquired LEO computers or used the LEO service bureaus. Many others went elsewhere. Competition in the late 1950s and throughout the 1960s became intense. As consultants we had to understand not only what potential customers needed, but also what hardware and systems advice our competitors would offer. Some of the hardware features offered by competitors were difficult to match—in particular random-access storage—and it took LEO some time before we could match competitors' capabilities. Thus I could claim to have a better grasp of how, say, NCR would use their random-access store than the NCR salesman I was in competition against. In the meantime we had to demonstrate that we had a clearer understanding of what was needed, and that we knew better than our competitors how to translate requirements into effective systems.

The opportunity to see so much of British industry—private and public—provided an unrivaled insight into the strengths and weaknesses of the British economy. Perhaps the weaknesses left a more lasting impression. Possibly the most obvious, for someone trained in the Lyons tradition, was the very widespread failure by senior management's to have any detailed knowledge of how the business processes, and in particular the support processes provided by the offices, on which the effectiveness of the business depended actually worked. There are many examples.

For instance, a potential customer was one of the UK's premier machine tool companies. It had a world reputation for the advanced design of its products. I was shown around the company by the chief executive. He talked at length and with enormous insight about their product line and new product developments. That was clearly where his interests lay. But a visit to the works showed very quickly that the production management system, based on punched-card equipment, was not in control. It was being bypassed by a variety of informal procedures. Only the ingenuity of the progress chasers kept the factory going at some level of effectiveness. But overhead costs were high and schedules were not adhered to. The managers of the support procedures was poorly paid and held in low esteem. Senior management did not seem to be aware of the problem. The company decided to go to IBM, but computer systems could not save them, and soon afterwards they went bankrupt.

Another company, later a LEO customer, an important steelmaker, ran its offices almost as an independent division, working at arms' length from the manufacturing division it was supposed to serve. There was considerable rivalry between the engineering division, which was also responsible for supporting the steelmaking functions, and the office division, which was more concerned with the accounting functions. Some support functions, for example payroll, were divided between the two divisions. The engineering division and the office division independently requested bids for the supply of computers to carry out, among other tasks, payrolls. Each of the divisions favored a different supplier. LEO was chosen by the engineering division, while the office division chose ICT as its supplier. In business terms this made no sense, but senior management seemed to be scarcely aware that there was a problem.

Another company we studied, a multinational, was the leading brand name for a class of goods that owed its dominant position in the marketplace to soon-to-expire patents. However, its lead position had made it complacent. I visited the company with Ninian Eadie. We were astonished to find that the manufacturing site was like a museum of the industrial revolution. The production process utilized banks of belt-driven, old-fashioned, machine tools. The factory was totally vertically integrated. They produced everything themselves, including hardware items such as screws, nails, and bolts, lubricating oil, and the oil cans delivered with the product to the consumer. We were shown around the works by a young man—the first and only college graduate the company had ever employed. When the patents expired, the company could not match the new competition from Japan.

Visiting German manufacturing companies underlined the problem. The basic support services in German manufacturing companies were not very different. The difference lay in the fact that senior German management appeared to have a very thorough understanding and interest in the operation of these services. Hence they spotted weaknesses much earlier and seemed to be ready to invest in providing solutions.

I worked for LEO between 1952 and 1967. I started as a naïve recruit, scarcely understanding how to make computers work. I finished in 1967 with the title of Chief Consultant, responsible for the company's regional offices and much of the British marketing organization. By that time LEO had become part of English Electric and the joint company disputed the title of premier British computer manufacturer with ICT. In 1952 there were only a small handful of computers worldwide intended for white-collar work. In the UK, J. Lyons and LEO were without doubt the pioneers. A few more were beginning to be used to control industrial processes and the majority—still only a tiny number—were used for scientific and technical calculations.

By 1967 there were few major companies or government departments in the industrial world that were not using computers for some business functions, or at the very least planning to use them. Companies that had in the early 1950s scoffed at the idea of computers playing any major role in business were now planning ever wider use. It had become fashionable for computer managers to have vast diagrams on the walls of their office, with an often very detailed master plan for achieving the totally integrated management information system. The number of computers in use had risen to thousands. The number of personnel engaged in computer work of one kind or another had risen to hundreds of thousands. The business machine companies that in the 1950s had entered the computer business reluctantly and doubtfully now competed for the growing market with the utmost vigor. The largest of them, IBM, was on course for becoming the largest business enterprise in the world. Governments were beginning to use computers on a large scale, to support and replace the work of civil servants. At the policy level the computer industry was regarded as an important national asset, which had to be strengthened through direct government intervention. In the UK this led at the end of the 1960s to combining the fragmented computer industry into first two groups and then one major group.[11]

Over these years our own perceptions and style of working changed. When I started, the dominant influence was that inherited from the Lyons tradition of systems research. This focused on the whole business, and the function of planned change was to improve the business as a whole. This needed an intimate feel for and understanding of the relationships, interconnections, and power bases in the company. But without a powerful champion who had won the esteem of his peers at the highest level—John Simmons—it would not have been possible to win over the line management of the productive parts of J. Lyons to the stream of radical changes of which the introduction of LEO and some of the key applications were good examples. It is interesting to note that many of the ideas we put into practice at that time are now trumpeted as the latest solutions to the problems of intense business competition.

As interest in LEO and the potential value of computers to business rose, we increasingly became involved with the outside world. At first, those who approached us were themselves companies with good organizations and an innovative spirit. We were encouraged by at least some of them to behave as "experts" and to provide advice on how a LEO might be used within their organization. This gave rise to the term *consultant* for the group of senior programmers and systems analysts who gradually took over the role of selling LEOs or LEO bureau services to the outside world. Nevertheless, we soon came up against restrictions that in Lyons we would have had encouragement to overcome. For example, working with Dunlop, it seemed out of bounds to suggest that the tangle of sales terms that had grown up was counterproductive and that simplification would serve the business as well as ease the implementation of the computer system. Any such suggestion would almost certainly have raised the suspicion that we wanted simplification because we could not cope with the complexity of the pricing system.

Over the LEO II and early LEO III years the way we worked changed only slowly. For many potential customers we still carried out firsthand systems studies and provided them with detailed job plans. But as the number of customers each senior consultant had to deal with rose, the pressures on us became greater and we allowed ourselves to accept more of what the potential client described as the needs of the business. After all, we received no payment for work for which management consultants now charge large sums. In any case we were most frequently only one of many competitors vying for the business, and the opposition sales forces worked very differently. More and more often we were expected to respond to a defined specification. From the point of view of the customer it was easier to evaluate offers where each contender responded in an identical form. Putting our own gloss on what we thought the needs were was not always welcomed.

Some of the people we worked with from other organizations thought that as vendors of computer equipment our style of selling was amateur. Our enthusiasm for understanding the business and using computers in a radical way to improve the business may have seemed amateur compared to the hard-nosed sales representative from our competitor, whose effort was solely confined to selling boxes using whatever means were necessary to get the order.

The merger with English Electric underlined the differences. We joined up with a group of people whose culture was completely different. It was based on a divide between the sales representative, who fronted all negotiations with a customer, and a backroom systems analyst who provided a service to the sales representative working under the control of the latter. By contrast, the success of the LEO III range and its sales was largely based on winning approval from our customers by means of our application-led mode of operation. The conflict between the cultures was never completely resolved.

For me, the years 1952 to 1967 were largely exhilarating. We often worked at a frantic pace, and at times the pressure became immense. We felt that we were leading the world in the application of computers to business, and for a time we were in the forefront in technical developments. By 1967 the world had changed. The pace of work and what was expected of individuals was, if anything, still accelerating. But by that time we had become bit players in the global computer business. We had had little time or opportunity to reflect on what we were achieving. I left the company in 1967 to set up the study of computer applications at the London School of Economics, partly because I felt the need to think more clearly about the way computers should be used. It is interesting that today's rhetoric[12] suggests that the way ahead lies in following the precepts we learned with J. Lyons and which we implemented with Lyons and our LEO customers over 30 years ago.

Notes

1. John Kay, *Foundations of Corporate Success*, Oxford University Press, Oxford, 1993.

2. In the Lyons grading structure, these people were placed in the "F" or supervisor grade and not deemed managers. Many of them rose to manager rank in their subsequent careers, and some reached the very top of the organization.

3. The company engaged John Simmons, who subsequently played a major role, in the development of the J. Lyons style of management, backing the LEO venture and giving it direction.

4. Ailsa Land, now Emeritus Professor of Operational Research at the London School of Economics.

5. The team at that time comprised T. R. Thompson at the head, David Caminer as head of programming and systems development, and John Pinkerton as head of engineering and design. The programming group (application and systems software) comprised Tony Barnes, Derek Hemy, Leo Fantl, John Grover, Mary Blood, Elizabeth Newman, John Gosden, Eric Kavannah, Ernest Roberts, and me. Derek Hemy, Leo Fantl, and John Grover had been with the LEO project longest and were, together with David Caminer, my mentors.

6. The Systems Research Office was renamed the O&M office when it became fashionable to have an O&M function in an organization. The manager of the O&M office at the time I joined the LEO team was Frank Blight, who when he left Lyons was succeeded by George Robey.

7. I still have the draft job specification, entitled "L4 Tea Blending," dated October 18, 1954. Other correspondence suggests that by that time the L4 job was already working, though some requirements had not been fully implemented. An earlier note, dated August 1953, from David Caminer sets out a number of questions regarding the tea blending requirements. An outline of L4 must have been clear in his mind.

8. A number of these champions come to mind. Those with whom I was involved included Neil Pollock of Stewarts and Lloyds; Oliver Standingford, who championed the J. D. Francis job; Bradley of the Ford Motor Company, who helped to give LEO a foothold in that company; John Hargreaves of Smith & Nephew, Price of Smith Clocks and Watches; Jim Barclay of British Oxygen Engineering; Olav Hoeg at Kayser Bondor, Jackson of Renold Chains, Ryan at North Thames Gas Board; Atkins and later Wilkinson at CAV; Potter of the stockbrokers Nivison; and John Bennett of the stockbroker Durlachers. Each of these (and many others) had to carry their organization with them and sometimes put their own career on the line.

9. I remember vividly a meeting with T. R. Thompson. David Caminer and I had been working for a number of weeks with the Ford Motor Company at Dagenham, trying to get a grip on their production planning and control procedures. I had finally reduced the complex procedures to a series of block diagrams that I believed to be a fair but rather simplified representation of Ford practice. At that stage we did not yet see how the job could be organized given the limited resources of the computer. To us, the diagrams served as a first step toward getting the understanding necessary to start eliciting detailed requirements. We were summoned to explain the situation to Simmons and Thompson. I "walked" them through the block diagrams. Thompson congratulated us and assumed we had provided a solution rather than a way of describing the problem. All that was now needed was

an implementation of the systems. In any event we decided not to go forward with making a bid for the Ford contract.

10. D. T. Caminer, - - - - - - And How to Avoid Them, *Computer Journal*, 1(1) (1958).

11. In practice the 1969 rationalization was only partial. The computer suppliers working primarily for the Ministry of Defense held out against the formation of a single all-embracing computer company. As a result the defense computer divisions of English Electric (Marconi Computers), Plessey, GEC, and Ferranti remained outside the new company, ICL. A great deal of expertise at the frontier of computer application and design was lost to ICL. I believe that this held back the progress of ICL for a considerable period.

12. The current orthodoxy is that the way to achieve competitive success is through business process reengineering (BPR). Most of the management consultancies now have teams of consultants advising companies on ways to reengineer their business. The methods suggested are often brutal in their operation. A recent survey suggested that over 60 percent of companies are currently engaged in BPR. The failure rate of reengineering efforts is said to be about 70 percent. Much of what J. Lyons preached and practiced, but without the brutality, would now be called business process reengineering.

16

Toward System Software

JOHN GOSDEN

Looking Back

Today even a modest desktop PC has 100,000 times the power and 100,000 times the storage that LEO I had in the early 1960s. The increase in software support to users is even more dramatic. LEO I had a simple assembler-loader and a set of subroutines to do floating-point arithmetic, various mathematical functions, and primitive debugging aids. Today a typical desktop PC contains a complex operating system, tens of utilities, and several major packages (typically spreadsheet, database, word processing, communications, and graphics). These take up several megabytes of storage. LEO I could hold only about 6000 bytes.

During the seven years that I spent as a member of the LEO team, I observed and took part in the transition from the primitive beginnings to the arrival of early programming languages, multiprogramming operating systems, and new hardware such as drums and magnetic tape. I began in an era in which programmers necessarily had to be very aware of the actual mechanisms of the computer. When I left, seven years later, we were developing environments where programmers were able to give more of their attention to what the applications were required to do, and less to how the computer could achieve this. At the start, system software was a part-time job for one person. When I left in 1961 there was a team of some 15 people, which was growing.

At LEO, I personally took part in preparing a great variety of applications, large and small, for the system—first scientific and actuarial and then for business as LEO's facilities matured. This firsthand experience provided the basis for arriving at the aids that would be needed to control all the new facilities as they became available. There were few examples to draw on and we grabbed at good ideas from elsewhere, such as drum addressing. Generally, though, we were truly working from first principles, solving our most urgent problems (probably in parallel with others) and often reaching unique answers derived from our clerical applications perspective.

This chapter traces something of my and LEO's progress toward a complete software system. It is written from the perspective of 34 years spent in the heady information technology atmosphere in the United States, and is inevitably colored by that experience, which included:

- developing and editing the Standard EDP Reports, 1961–62
- building an early multicomputer operating system, 1962–65
- participating in U.S. and ISO programming language standards, 1961–70
- database planning for the Joint Chiefs, 1966–70
- various teams reviewing large government systems, 1969–93
- VP and Technology Officer at Equitable Life Assurance, NY, 1970–86
- installing and converting a major online system, 1972–75
- research fellow at New York University, 1986–present
- database and PC consultant, 1986–present

Starting at LEO: 1953

In some ways it seemed to be my destiny to join what was to become LEO Computers. In my last year at Cambridge I was taken to see the EDSAC computer in the Mathematical Laboratory by my friend Colin Reeves. He was one year ahead of me and doing research that used EDSAC. The Mathematical Laboratory at Cambridge was one of the pioneers in computers, and EDSAC was their first computer. They also had a close relationship with J. Lyons, who had supported them with money and help when their progress was slowed by lack of resources in 1947.

Reeves encouraged me to consider computers as a career. As a result I mentioned my interest in computers when I visited the University Appointments Board to start looking for a job. They responded with two computer-related possibilities, one of which was J. Lyons. They had no supporting material and my knowledge of J. Lyons was limited to the Teashops and Corner Houses. As a result I did not take Lyons seriously and did not follow up. I did go to an interview with the War Office, an intimidating session in front of a "board" of some dozen people. I was told very little because the work was top-secret. I was offered a job "related to my interests" if I got at least a second-class degree. This would be because I had only a second- and a third-class rating in my exams so far.

I was also the first person to apply to take the Numerical Analysis Diploma being started by the Mathematical Laboratory in 1953. I was interviewed by Maurice Wilkes, who was the Director of the laboratory and responsible for the EDSAC effort. He, understandably, rejected me.

Meanwhile my mother was a live-in registered nurse and housekeeper for an elderly bed-ridden gentleman who frequently changed his will. On one occasion his solicitor stayed to dinner with my mother and me before returning to London. He asked what I was thinking of doing when I graduated. I mentioned computers, including my dismissal of J. Lyons. He was a friend of Tony Barnes, who was an early pioneer at LEO. He set me straight about the quality of the Lyons computer effort and insisted that I pursue it. He got in touch with Tony and it was arranged for me to go to an interview at J. Lyons headquarters in Cadby Hall in Hammersmith, London.

I am vague about the early part of the interviews at Lyons. I think I started with TRT, as T. R. Thompson, the manager of the LEO group, was known. My recollection is that, once he discovered that I played bridge, TRT did nearly all the talking. This must have been followed by screening interviews that I do not recall. David Caminer, then the manager of programming, reminds me that at lunch I explained my "unflattering degree." I had never been good at learning by rote, so I usually had a bad time with the "book learning," but I maintained that I could always look up the "book work." It was the application of book work to a new problem that was important and at which I excelled. However both were required for a good degree. Caminer recalls that he recommended hiring me. Later I returned to TRT and he told me that Lyons had recently hired a psychologist and I was to be reviewed by him. I remember taking some tests and then TRT told me they would offer me a job in spite of the psychologist's negative recommendation. The job offer carried a three-month probation period, but the salary was significantly higher than the conditional offer I had from the War Office. It was, as they say, no contest.

Before I began work, the results of the mathematics exams were published in *The Times*. I had only managed to scrape by with a pass degree. I shared his honor with no one.

The First 15 Months:
1953–1954

My first supervisor was Leo Fantl, who taught me many pragmatic and theoretical lessons. I owe him many thanks and he deserves more recognition for his style of program design at both the overall and the coding level. He was a very patient and skilled teacher. We sat at back-to-back desks so that we faced each other and could easily discuss anything that came up.

Fantl reported to Derek Hemy at that time, who reported to David Caminer. I think Frank Land and Mary Blood reported to John Grover, who reported to Hemy. Thus, including Caminer, there were just six of us in programming at that time. I believe I was promoted to report to Caminer about mid-1954. In 1953 we (Hemy and below) were all in one room with the data entry staff. We were in a room directly off the LEO I room. In the United States this would have been called operating in a "bull pen." It facilitated cooperative working and teamwork. I still miss that working environment.

As I remember it, on my first day Leo Fantl gave me the manual to study. It covered both hardware and circuits, and also the instruction set with some examples. Before lunch I told him I had finished. I think he then quizzed me on it. I was told months (or was it years?) later that this had caused some consternation. I think the study of the manual was supposed to take several days. I had turned out to be a very fast studier and programming came very easily to me. I think my next assignment was to understand the "initial orders." They constituted a very tricky and clever piece of coding that, when the computer was switched on, booted the computer into a state ready to start working.

The first 15 months now seem like the most productive time of my career. As the descriptions that I give below show, I started with commercial service bureau work for outside customers and two jobs for J. Lyons, but within six months I was heavily involved with mathematical jobs. I began with work on subroutines we received from Cambridge and went on to improve floating-point services to facilitate matrix arithmetic operations.

While I recall close supervision and guidance from Fantl at the start, I was soon given a lot of responsibility and implemented my ideas freely.

Office-Related Jobs

Throughout my whole career at LEO I was often pulled from other tasks to do consulting or service work for customers. I believe that this happened to all of us. As a result, LEO people were very flexible and it helped them stay in touch with users' needs. It was on two of these jobs that I first learned about rounding errors. I made mistakes in the one job and started to learn my trade in the other.

Legal and General: November-December 1953. The job was to compile the specifications and flow-chart an insurance group pension scheme for monthly renewals, and then bring the four programs to a successful UK first demonstration. I worked with an actuary from Legal and General called Jecks, who smoked a foul pipe with home-brewed tobacco. Frank Land "quite vividly remember[s] the halo of black smoke surrounding the corner in which [I] worked with Jecks." In today's jargon the job was a "defined contribution" group pension scheme. He gave me a hard time about testing the result and said he would prepare 300 cases. When he found out the amount of work needed, he reduced it to about 12 cases (I'm sure it was less than 20). Even on that small a sample the demonstration showed that they had significantly underpaid surrender values to two people. They did go back and refund the outstanding amounts. He made much of the fact that my rounding errors were often 1 or 2 pennies wrong, which I thought trivial compared to the underpayments. Today I am amazed that this was being done so soon after I started work. I must have had considerable coaching, and certainly had not yet learned about rounding techniques.

PAYE Tax Tables: November-December 1953. I received my first lesson on rounding techniques on these programs, which covered the full range of PAYE tables distributed to all British employers. They had been initially prepared on LEO in 1953, before I arrived. In 1954, when I was involved, we were ready to run, but the rates did not change and there was no run. The rates changed in 1955 and the tables were duly processed on budget night, immediately after the Chancellor of the Exchequer had made his statement, but I was not involved. I assisted Leo Fantl, who taught me a great deal about correcting rounding errors. That was very tricky arithmetic using short 17-bit numbers (approximately five decimal places) and replicating what had been done on desk calculators. Such precision is widely ignored today, or overcome (sometimes) with double-length arithmetic.

Market Analysis: January-March 1954. This was the first British general cross-tabulation program for market research. It was implemented for the Lyons Market Analysis group. The main analysis was a correlation of ice-cream sales with temperature. This was of great importance for Lyons. There was a limited period for which ice cream could be cold-stored, and a balance had to be struck between over-producing and failing to meet the market demand. These jobs had a resident kernel program and repeatedly passed data via punched cards. One aggressive user was a Mr. Lamberth, the market research expert at Lyons. He was in such a hurry that he joined me the evening I was doing my last test runs so he could do his operational run immediately. He also wanted to stay around to be able to choose his next analysis "online" as he saw the results. On one run I misoperated and fed one of the sets of data twice. He looked at it and told me to continue because the duplicated data on that run would not matter. Users could be very pragmatic when in a hurry for results. However, the program worked well and was still in use in 1963.

Teashop Statistics: January 1954. My role in the Lyons Teashops distribution suite was to plan and code the statistics section. As Caminer points out, this represented an effort by LEO programming to introduce "by exception" reporting to the Lyons management. It exploited the data used for distributing supplies to teashops to pick out the best and worst performers. Unfortunately, little use was made of the results. Managers at that time preferred, as so many have done since, to continue to scan the full set of summary statistics. I had the job of working out the probable rounding errors, as (using short 17-bit numbers) we started with hundredths of a penny per bun. To avoid having to use long words to hold data, we rounded at successive levels of aggregation to the nearest penny, eighth of a pound (half-crown), and finally to pounds. I was worried because the overall error due to rounding was about $14 a day. The Head of the Cost Accounting Department (another Cambridge mathematician) laughed. Other errors swamped such a low number.

Mathematical Service Jobs

This was the set of activities that really pushed my career. It was wonderful good fortune to be in the right place at the right time. How Lyons had the nerve to entrust this work to me is difficult to believe. However, as I learned from Caminer, it had been necessary to move Fantl to fill the gap left by Hemy's resignation, and it was the way of the organization to stretch young people to the full extent of their abilities. Before this time LEO had already done much mathematical work for customers, some of which included their own programmers, and I was fortunate to have good ideas that enabled the service bureau to earn plenty of income from such jobs.

Early in 1954 I was put in charge of receiving and converting Cambridge EDSAC subroutines (as issued) into LEO format. Many of these routines were mathematical: floating point, matrix inversion,

Runge-Kutta approximations, trigonometric functions, and so on. Most of these had already been converted and I had to deal with only a few new and improved ones. My job was to convert them to the LEO notation, a straightforward task, and then run them to ensure that they worked correctly. I never found errors in the Cambridge subroutines, and even when I thought I had found an error I ended up on the telephone getting a patient lesson in Chebyshev polynomials from David Wheeler and a referral to the appropriate numerical analysis textbook. As a research student, Wheeler had been one of the earliest members of the Wilkes team at the Cambridge Mathematical Laboratory. He was my contact at EDSAC. Many years later (about 1986), I ran into Wheeler at Heathrow airport and we sat beside each other on a flight to New York. I was able to thank him for his help so long ago and to reminisce about the early days. Dr. Wheeler became Professor of Computer Science at Cambridge University, where he spent most of his career.

Matrix Inversion: April-June 1954

Handley Page Aircraft wanted to compute flutter characteristics for different wing designs and this required matrix inversion. They had done some work with NPL (National Physical Laboratory) using their DEUCE computer. NPL was a Government Scientific establishment that was also a pioneer in early computers. This was my first big job, and I found it fascinating. It was also the area where I believe I did some pioneering work on matrix arithmetic that (as was typical at LEO) we were too busy to get published and/or recognized.

Ernest Roberts joined us from Oxford in mid-1954 and subsequently worked on all the mathematical jobs.

Significant-Digit Floating Point. Computers did not have built-in hardware for floating-point operations in those days. We used subroutines that, naturally, were painfully slow. I wanted to speed up the slow (programmed) floating point. We used or adapted subroutines that we got from the Mathematical Laboratory at Cambridge University. Many needed minor adjustments to put into our local notation. Fantl noticed a reference in a publication called *Computer Abstracts* to a paper (in German, later translated for me by Fantl) by Professors Bauer and Samuelson of Munich on a special form of floating point that discarded "pseudo accurate digits." This was later (I think in the late 1960s) rediscovered in the United States by N. Metropolis and called "significant-digit arithmetic." Its great property is that it directly shows how many significant digits have probably been lost as a calculation progresses. This loss usually happens when two nearly equal numbers are subtracted, and in the classic case for matrix inversion produces singular matrices, which is closely akin to dividing by zero. It also speeded up floating-point subroutines because it avoided the need to scale the resulting numbers to "normal form." I implemented the significant-digit scheme, and it was wonderful to see how the significant digits gradually grew fewer as the hours of calculation passed. I think it is a great loss that built-in floating point does not have this feature, at least as an option.

Pivotal Selection. I also used a pivotal selection method reported in the literature that avoided singularities. This process automatically selected the largest value in the next row to be the pivot (divider) for the next step. Since each row was input on cards in turn, I devised an automatic method to retain the next pivotal row. The difficult trick for me was to discover the way the answer's rows had to be reshuffled to correct for the pivotal selection. I deduced the rules empirically by working with small test matrices.

Checksums. In those days computers were subject to intermittent errors. Certainly a run of more than an hour needed to include ways to detect errors. One of the rules of run design at LEO was the convention that all the clerical applications would bring forward totals to be reconciled with the carry-forward totals at the end of each section of a job. The mathematical programs had no such existing conventions. With the prospect of runs lasting more than an hour, I sought a way to at least know when an error had occurred. I have no idea where this need arose or whether it was called to my attention by, most likely, Fantl, or else Caminer. My solution was to add a set of row sums to the matrix, and then compute these row sums independently for each "pivot" step and for the final inverse. Thus we verified each of the row totals after each step (pivot) in the inversion. For the added cost of processing an extra column, we had confirmation of whether there had been any miscalculation on each step of the inversion. This was a very powerful and economic technique that gave our customers confidence that the results were correct. A key feature is that it is more secure than repeating the calculation twice, since this technique compares the results from two mathematically equivalent but different calculations. This was a forerunner of the row and column totals used in the Matrix Arithmetic Language.

Verifying Results Like an Accountant. I had been given a matrix (I am not sure whether I requested it, or whether I was told to get it by the user or by Fantl or Caminer) that the National Physical Laboratory had inverted for Handley Page. It was about 8×8 elements in size. My small 3×3 test matrix agreed with my hand calculations, but my inverse of the

NPL matrix failed. My result was totally different from the result supplied by NPL. I spent a week at a hand calculator trying to find my error. Suddenly I realized that there is a simple test. If you multiply a matrix by its inverse, it produces a diagonal matrix. How could I have been so stupid as to have forgotten this? So I made the test. My result passed the test; NPL's did not. After this discovery I telephoned Jim Wilkinson, the top numerical analyst at NPL. I was told that NPL used to do the pivotal selection by hand and that the operator had misoperated. I suppose this is as good an example as any of the difference in attitude between the researchers who invented the early procedures and the more mundane clerical/accounting approach. The extra effort to verify an answer is not a large overhead. An $n \times n$ matrix inversion needs n^4 operations to be carried out and the multiplication to verify needs only n^3. I would be surprised if the places where such calculations were carried out on rows of manual machines had not devised and used such verification techniques. I was not grateful to NPL for the trouble they had caused me.

Higher-Level Matrix Arithmetic Language: July–December 1954

Calculating Row and Column Discrepancies: July–December 1954. Next, Handley Page wanted to do other matrix calculations, mostly long strings of multiplications and a few additions of matrices and vectors. I programmed their calculations using the significant-digit subroutines. At this time I extended the idea of row totals that were independently calculated and verified. I augmented each $n \times m$ matrix by an extra row and column to get an $(n + 1) \times (m + 1)$ matrix with negative row and column totals so that each row or column should sum to zero. This was also used to check the input of the initial data. It is obvious that if you add two such matrices element by element then the resultant matrix should also sum each column and row to zero, or, more precisely, sum to give a discrepancy caused by rounding errors. It turns out, as I discovered empirically, that if you multiply an $(n + 1) \times m$ matrix by an $m \times (p + 1)$ matrix, you get an $(n + 1) \times (p + 1)$ result with independently calculated row and column sums. These can then be summed to find the new discrepancies.

This job turned out to be a string of calculations that ran for eight hours. Somewhere in there I made a stupid error that wasted hours of computer time and jeopardized meeting the Monday-morning deadline that we had promised for the results. Caminer threatened to fire me and I was very nervous. According to recent behavioral theory, the resulting stress should have imprinted the details very clearly on my memory. It did.

The first production run produced a result matrix of about 8×8. On Monday morning the user met Caminer and myself in Caminer's office. The customer had hand-calculated one value. When that value agreed with the computed value, Caminer congratulated the user on being correct! The reaction was typical. The assumption was that, after all the checks had been built in, the LEO results *should* always be correct, while it had to be recognized that the outside world, whatever its expertise, was likely to be fallible.

This run also demonstrated nicely how, over the 8 hours it took to run, the original 8-decimal-digit numbers slowly reduced in significance to as few as 4 digits, and the rounding discrepancies in the row and column sums slowly grew from zero to one or two digits.

Matrix Arithmetic Language. The next set of calculations was different and needed a different program. I was upset at this. So I designed and programmed what today we would call a higher-level language that did matrix arithmetic, addition, subtraction, and multiplication of vectors and matrices. I do not know where I got the idea. I cannot recall having heard or read about any other model to imitate, nor getting a suggestion from a colleague. Many future jobs were run using these routines. It was easy to program and must have been far cheaper and more accurate than hand calculations. It was also used in jobs to compute eigenvectors and values. It turned out to produce lots of revenue in the otherwise quiet night shifts over the next few years.

This was all in my first 15 months at LEO.

Consulting in the Middle Period: 1954–1958

Between the intensive work on mathematical processes in 1954 and the intensive work for LEO III beginning in 1958, I worked on many customers' nonscientific applications. I did not recognize this change at the time, which was actually marked by my having the title "Senior Consultant" rather than "Senior Manager." Indeed, promotions were so rapid for some of us that it seemed that Lyons ran out of formally established grade levels.

During this period LEO was expanding rapidly and always hiring new people. The variety of the work was ever-changing, and the job sizes ran from the huge Railways Distancing job to the tiny Wage Ready Reckoner for truck drivers. I also joined my colleagues in helping to plan and give LEO I training courses that lasted five weeks, for both external users and LEO programming staff. We also had "computer appreciation" classes for executives, and a class we gave to the data preparation staff. I only remember enjoying teaching, especially the courses we gave to the data preparation people who later went on to become "junior operators."

Service Work. During this period my notes show that I was involved at one level or another with at least 20 applications, all but one of which were for LEO clients other than J. Lyons. This was being performed in parallel with the LEO I and II support, which continued until the increasing needs of LEO III took up most of my time. Other people were as busy as I. It was a period of rapid growth.

This was the period when I got my rapid and intensive education in clear and precise writing. I hope I learned it with good humor. I remember clearly an occasion when I had written a document of some length and it had a summary at the end. Caminer altered it to put an outline at the beginning, and then TRT decided to change that to a summary at the end. So I theorized that we needed to know how many reviewers there would be in order to be able to predict whether a summary at the end or an outline at the beginning would prevail.

Market Research: January–March 1955. A significant task in this period was to provide service for two external market research organizations.

One was Attwood Statistics, a leader in the field. I don't remember who programmed the market research applications (it may have been Arthur Payman). When I negotiated the specifications, we were told very emphatically that every percentage point was vital in market share of soap products, and also that they had to be "adjusted" to add up to 100. I asked how we would treat three equal shares. I produced several cases where the requirements were impossible to fill, including three equal shares. They called their client, who immediately understood and agreed that "33 + 33 + 33 = 99" was realistic. So we let the rounding fall where it would without adjustment. Again you can see that rounding is a perpetual and misunderstood problem, but in this case the user did understand what was happening. In the last decade we have started to see the annotation "Totals do not add up to 100 percent due to rounding" in newspapers and even corporate annual reports. Some education is taking place.

Railways Distancing: January 1955 until mid-1957. I prepared estimates and plans for the challenging job of computing and tabulating the shortest distance between all pairs of all 7000 British railway goods stations. It took over 18 months of the spare computer time at nights and weekends. Caminer directed me to find a way to break down the job into several thousand manageable, simple chunks. Thus we could have short runs of reconcilable batches of work, and the operators could see that they were not misoperating. This was an early lesson in the advantage of dividing work, or any large problem, into many small, more manageable parts. The program that I coded was not large, but the inside loop would be executed tens of millions of times. I think everyone had input to improve the algorithm we used. I recall that, over the whole job, each instruction in the inside loop required something impressive like one week of computer time.

Mr. Hankey, our customer, had an office at Euston station, where they had been grinding out distances by hand to meet legislative requirements to maintain and publish these distances, which were used for billing. New sidings opened up faster than the small staff could produce the mandated listings. Apparently it was easier (and cheaper?) to get us to recompute all the distances than to get the law changed. It was an excellent source of income for the service bureau and introduced the use of 24-hour running of service bureau computers, filling in with chunks of work that were not time-critical.

Various Designs and Estimates: 1956–1959. This was where I had some very rapid education in business practices. I had to produce many proposals and specifications, and I clearly remember having to write and rewrite documents over and over again to satisfy Caminer. The education stood me in good stead many years later when I worked at a large insurance company in New York. I had developed at LEO an understanding of how to organize clerical work of many types.

During 1956 I produced designs and estimates for about nine applications, including production breakdown, stores control, and dealer replenishment (Ford), mail order control (Freemans), shop replenishment (Littlewoods), and ice-cream retailer statistics (J. Lyons). These last four were implemented as planned and were still running in 1961.

In 1957 I produced job plans and estimates for central warehouse replenishment (Boots) and retailer invoicing (Rowntrees). However, LEO II was looking very aged by this time, with the onset of second-generation systems, and the orders went elsewhere. Later in the year I produced design specifications for Ford's parts control. For a time I worked with Frank Land on this job and then left it with him to complete. The design of LEO III was beginning to demand most of my time.

In 1958 I outlined a plan for production control (Ford) and prepared offers for two government statistics applications and one for salesman control. I also advised on a special program to plan ice-cream distribution on a day-to-day basis (J. Lyons). Around this time a new programmer worked for me on a tiny job to produce a truck drivers' wage ready reckoner, to be given away by the publishers of *Headlight*, a magazine for truck drivers. This was probably our smallest client in those years. We seemed to turn away nothing in those days. On a much larger scale, I prepared a proposal for a government pension scheme control in January of 1959.

Although I was not involved directly, we used the matrix routines to do a job related to pneumoconiosis for the National Coal Board (NCB). The user, named Ashworth, had been at Sidney Sussex College one year ahead of me. We also did some statistical analyses using what was known as "Monte Carlo" models to evaluate alternative evacuation plans related to accidents in mines. Jacob Bronowski was the head of the NCB then. He hired bright people and stimulated interesting work.

This applications work was carried out while my principal role was being responsible for the software support for the computers.

System Software and Utilities: 1955–1960

LEO I and II: 1955–57.　My major involvement with system software was triggered by the resignation of Hemy in mid-1955. I took over the software responsibilities for the future LEO II, though I recall little interaction with Hemy when he left LEO I did not require much support by now. The main work on test and maintenance programs, and also the modified Initial Orders from Cambridge, were very stable. There were only the new and/or improved subroutines from Cambridge to deal with. LEO II brought new challenges, including drum storage, magnetic tape facilities, and alphabetic facilities needed for the more advanced printers.

It was during 1957 that LEO II/1 was installed. We cleaned out the remaining logical faults, and then I directed the planning and production of standard test and utility programs. I was also responsible for the specification of alpha facilities that we expected would be added later. The diagnostic test routines were developed from the LEO I facilities. The major utility routines were for postmortem use after completing (or failing) the test run of a job. The "comparison" routines printed out only locations where contents had changed. The hardest task was to produce these routines using a minimal amount of memory (called *storage* at the time, because at LEO words like *brain* and *memory* were unacceptable). Space had to be found to read in the cards and prepare printed output. I inherited a library from LEO I that had already developed these techniques.

Fantl notes that because LEO II used a longer word length than LEO I, we needed to recalculate the coefficients for the subroutines using Chebyshev polynomials, which we formerly got from the Cambridge Mathematical Laboratory. He started a nontrivial project to compute them automatically, and finally completed it on a PC in the early 1990s as a hobby. My own notes show that in 1957 I was planning and directing the development of the LEO II drum store routines to perform two level dynamic assignments automatically. The drum facilities were strongly influenced by the work at Manchester University, who pioneered the use of drum storage, especially how to overcome the slow access times. They were clear leaders in developing the concept of "paging," and they described the phenomenon of "thrashing" at a very early stage. Also in 1957 I planned and directed the production of a complete set of input/output magnetic tape routines, including auto-checking, alignment, and restart control features. The magnetic tape facilities were relatively straightforward. We just extended the concepts developed for punched cards with the added advantage (complication) of "read after write" and parity checking. I do remember that the hardware designs of different makes of tape drives were varied. They attempted to avoid the overhead of gaps between blocks and do automatic error correction. Some were quite exotic and seemed to invite low reliability.

In the last half of 1958 I prepared standard procedures for the new LEO II service center. At this time I was promoted to Manager of Programming Techniques, reporting directly to the Managing Director (TRT). An important task was to prepare for LEO II/5, which was soon to be installed at Hartree House. This system was the first LEO to employ magnetic tape and was also equipped with a magnetic drum. The promotion also covered the work for LEO III. Thus there was plenty of continuity on the software side of the LEO computers.

LEO III: 1957–60.   I was responsible for most of the input into the LEO III design from the software and user's points of view. This involved working with John Pinkerton, who became a very good friend and mentor to me. It was a big advantage to work on a small team with a common experience of two prior generations of computers to draw upon.

My major objectives for LEO III were:

1. To find a good way to handle decimal and monetary values while not losing too much in speed.

2. To find ways to reduce the time and resources needed to sort large volumes of data on tape, because that had been a major limitation on earlier computers.

3. To use microcoding to handle efficiently complex transactions, making intensive use of the central processor unit (CPU).

4. To find a way of doing multiprogramming that did not generate too much overhead.

To form a background for this work I started a library of reports on all competitors' equipment and developments in programming languages. I remember going to very few computer meetings, but certainly collected literature, as encouraged by Fantl. I managed to get specifications of the latest UK and U.S. computers.

Someone (I suppose Fantl) encouraged me in this reading, and someone authorized a subscription to the expensive John Diebold computer catalog updating service from New York. I think I was the sole reader. The Diebold publication was poorly done, and in 1961 in the United States I became the designer and editor of *Auerbach Standard EDP Reports*, which I, at least, thought was a far superior product. I based it upon the data I would have liked to have had at LEO. It grew and profited, while the Diebold publication died.

I was (and still am) a voracious reader of technical literature. Many of the design features for LEO III probably came from such input. I tried to identify the really useful and straightforward ideas that were discussed. I first heard of multiprogramming at a seminar in Cambridge given by Stanley Gill when he returned from a sabbatical in the U.S. Later he published a paper in the *Computer Journal*. Gill was an early member of the EDSAC team at Cambridge and later joined Ferranti.

Microprogramming: May–December 1958

LEO III really started as far as I was concerned with my work on the microprogramming of the LEO III arithmetic unit and the design of the data structures and instruction code. I worked mainly with Pinkerton and John Sylvester, one of his senior engineers, who was very bright and quickly able to understand the programming needs. We got on very well together. Microcoding was a technique invented by Maurice Wilkes. It greatly simplified the implementation of complex functions and is similar to today's RISC technology. It enabled a designer to provide a simple, small, fast set of primitive operations that could then be programmed to provide the apparent instruction set. As implemented by the LEO engineers it was an array of cores on a board that could be taken out and replaced easily, especially compared with rewiring circuits. Microcoding also gave us the confidence to attempt complex instructions, because the design the engineers devised caused the penalty for mistakes to be far less than that for "hard-wiring." It was also possible to supply different sets of microcode to different users. I designed the microcode set and had a major input in the choices of interrupts, the logic of the interrupts, and error/fault indicators. In parallel I was outlining the major instructions for use by the programmers, and also outlining how we would use these interrupt features in the input/output control routines. Two important functions that we put into the instruction set were variable radix arithmetic and merging large sets of blocks of data. Ernest Roberts, who had previously worked with me on mathematical jobs, came over to join me on the LEO III software.

Mixed Radix Arithmetic.   At this time I was unhappy about the difficulties of using binary machines for clerical work, especially the need to convert both input and output and the need to match COBOL facilities to handle digits and characters individually. However, I was even more unhappy with the way decimal machines could not handle monetary values. As a result I conceived and designed the "radix register" scheme to allow mixed radix arithmetic. It used an extra register in the arithmetic unit that could specify a separate radix for each digit position. In this case the pence were one digit, with a radix of 12, and shillings were represented by two digits with radices 10 and 2. It turned out to be useful in other cases (e.g., units of time [hours, minutes], units of weight, and cases where there might be fractions of a penny). As I recall, it used one extra register, and for a typical "add" instruction just a few extra steps in the microcode. Thus it had little speed penalty. It was really a very simple scheme to implement. Fantl recently recalled it as "fiendishly cunning."

Merge Instructions.   A big handicap in making applications viable in terms of elapsed time and cost was the overhead of sorting large volumes of data. Several special "merge" instructions were created to reduce the CPU load for sorting. This was supplemented by the use of automatic buffering for input and output that was continued from the LEO I and II designs. This is a good example of having to integrate data design, input/output hardware, and system software. This also influenced the design of the Master Control, because at that time the main use of multiprogramming was seen to be one main application (typically CPU-limited) running in parallel with tape sorting and printing, which exploited the use of input/output buffers. Thus we wanted the sort routines to use very little of the CPU time. The special microcoded merge instructions turned out to be very successful and powerful in this respect.

CLEO: February 1959

I proposed the concept and did the first design of CLEO, a high-level language directed at using the special facilities of LEO III. It was something of a merger of ALGOL and COBOL features. I had been following the development of "automatic programming," as it was then called, and had met Grace Hopper at an NPL conference on this subject in 1958. She was a pioneer in this subject and we remained in touch until her retirement.

With respect to CLEO, I remember that we used far less complexity and scope than COBOL in order to make it easier to implement. While it still seems to me to have been a good decision not to embark on a full-scale compiler without more experience, I did not have to live through any of the negative consequences that LEO people may have experienced, which might have led me to a different conclusion.

Memory Sharing Control:
July–November 1959

One of the key topics for multiprogramming was how to stop parallel programs from interfering with each other. There were several ideas being described and discussed. I devised a simple scheme that tagged each word with the "ID" number of the program to which it was allocated. Naturally this was done in continuous blocks. The scheme used hardware to prevent access to any location outside the allocated area. It was not very flexible or elaborate but would do the job easily until we had more experience. A major advantage of this approach was that the testing for violations could be done with no time penalty and thus avoided extra microcode steps on each instruction that accessed memory. The overhead came only with the use of the microcode to set up the pattern of the tags. This was performed only when jobs were changing and used a very small fraction of the time.

Testing Microcode:
November–December 1959

Earlier in the year the engineers had created a primitive computer to test out their LEO III circuit designs. It used a short word length of 8 bits. I designed the small instruction set and we also provided a programmer, David Owen, and the necessary test programs. I think it was my idea to use the breadboard machine to test out the microcode design. We built a memory-resident interpreter that executed the microcode steps. Each instruction's set of microcode steps was put on a punched paper tape and formed into a long (7 to 15 foot) loop of paper tape. Each test required one circuit of the loop. We used a fast paper tape reader. This was an idea to save storage that I had seen used on EDSAC in 1953. A mathematics graduate, Colin Reeves, at my college had used it at that time, six years earlier, to study Schrödinger's equations. Owen virtually "lived" out at the factory on Minerva Road. This was a real time-saver and enabled us to check out the microcode well before building the first LEO III.

Master Routine and Utilities 1960

The prime task in 1960, my last year with LEO, was to complete the first definition of the structure of the master routine and the other system software needed for LEO III. This involved bringing together the work that had been done on interrupts and memory protection in the hardware and the ideas that had been forming on how precisely the software would make use of them to facilitate user-friendly applications program writing and efficient operation. An important contribution was a seminar at Cambridge, where Stanley Gill described the basic ideas of multiprogramming.

The basic master routine facilities and interconnections were documented in this period to form the basis of the detailed flowcharts that followed. Small implementation teams were set up under Roberts to implement the software. This included the master routine, with its multiprogramming controls, the sort routines exploiting the special merge micro-operations, a CLEO compiler, and a conventional lower-level assembler. The fact that Roberts was firmly in place by the time that I left for the United States made it possible for me to depart confident that the mass of work still to be done was in thoroughly competent hands.

Observations from 1994

My strongest impressions looking back are:

1. My main overall impression now of my colleagues at LEO, and others I met at J. Lyons, is that I have never worked since with as competent, bright, and stimulating a group of people. I have never since come across a group as well organized in management and systems. Later in my career I often came upon problems that were solved at LEO many years earlier.

2. The well-documented flowcharts that were reviewed and approved *before* coding; the checking of coding by a *second person*; the preparation of expected results *before* test runs: the *nonuse of programmers* to do the keypunching—all of which were violated by the practices that I saw in the United States in 1961 and later. The practice, at least by 1955, of having operators do the test runs.

3. Both Caminer and TRT taught me how to write well. Documents (whether memos, letters, reports, or specifications) were revised and rerevised. I am nowadays an expert on the half-page memo that is enough to get an OK annotation affixed. I think good, clear writing was one of the best and most useful lessons I learned.

4. In the same vein, the careful and consistent way that programs were documented (or annotated) stayed with me for years and is still in use. In the United States I was appalled at the casual documentation practices (if any), especially the scant use of carefully drawn flowcharts. I have become convinced that there are two kinds of programmers: those who see things graphically (using flowcharts) and those who see code with formulas and "procedures" like mathematical proofs. I still find it difficult to read or write the latter style, as required by modern programming (actually this began in the late 1950s with languages such as FORTRAN and ALGOL). Often, in difficult cases, I just sit back and draw a flowchart. I think that making a flowchart look neat helped good design. This is probably related to the fact that I was always much better at pure geometry than complex algebra (analytic geometry).

5. The careful analysis of such things as rounding errors that was typical of the thoroughness and professionalism of the LEO people. Rounding problems are still cropping up and are not understood. This is especially true in PC software, where using binary arithmetic produces some incorrect cash amounts. I think Fantl deserves more credit for his careful analysis of rounding errors and also for his use of other mathematical techniques such as Runge-Kutta and Chebyshev polynomials. I learned much from him and David Wheeler of the Cambridge Mathematical Laboratory (see also Fantl's notes in Chapter 14).

     As I am writing these notes, *The New York Times* is running a story of an error in the latest Pentium chip from Intel that has a rounding error that occurs in the fifth decimal place. There are also reports of significant errors in simple "four-function" programmed "calculators" provided in some PC operating system "shells." The process of using checksums (mentioned earlier) would have shown up the floating-point division errors that have been experienced in early releases. There are also other ways of checking mathematical calculations, but these are not practiced much nowadays. The general practice is to assume that PCs run correctly and I doubt whether error control techniques are still remembered by more than a few people.

6. On a more mundane but crucial level, LEO jobs always made thorough use of check totals and validity checks. It was a way of life that I

found in only a minority of places in the early days of computing. This may well be because in my first few years in the United States I was not involved with clerical applications.

7. I now realize that the early work done on system software was very thorough. I had almost no maintenance to do. The ideas used before I arrived carried forward easily to later machines. There seems to be a lot of discussion in Peter Bird's book of the engineers overcoming problems (and they do seem to have had their share), but surely there was a very low occurrence of software errors, due in large part to items 1 to 6 above. I also attribute success in matrix work to this way of behaving.

8. The LEO Service Bureau attracted and retained a very interesting set of customers. It competed well against all others in commercial work and held its own against scientific and technical competitors. It made it a wonderful place to work. We were constantly challenged and had very few failures.

9. At LEO the programming staff, represented first by Hemy, then by me, had a very large say in the design of the computers—about 100 percent of the instruction set and a lot in the input and output error checking, signals, and interrupts. This was not so true in the United States. There were odd designs there. I remember one computer whose index registers counted $-2, -1, -0, +0, +1 \ldots$ (!) because the engineers could not understand why we might want to count through zero. This machine tried to handle interrupts by saving the address of the "next" instruction. Unfortunately there were two instructions per word and they did not save the half-address.

10. I think (and other less involved people may disagree) that my implementations of (a) significant floating-point arithmetic, (b) the use of row and column checksums on matrices, and (c) the development of a general-purpose matrix arithmetic language were all inspired by work pioneered in clerical operations, and contributed to quicker results and greater confidence in the results of long runs.

11. As I reread this list it seems to me that I paid little attention to the history being made. I still do not know how we got so much done. At the time I had no experience to use as a comparison, and I was both busy and having fun. I am surprised at the lack of interest on the programming side to publish achievements. We were so busy and did not exist in a research or academic environment where such publication is ingrained. After getting to the United States I was encouraged to publish, and must have average around three or four papers or talks a year.

People

In addition to the remarks that occur above I remember the following.

LEO was a very social group. There was the music club (run by Caminer's secretary, Joan Hyam, who also drew the handsome flowcharts). It managed to get free tickets to BBC concerts and half-price tickets in the Grand Circle at the Convent Garden opera. That is where I learned to enjoy a wide range of opera. I remember the night we saw a young Joan Sutherland in *La Sonnambula* early in her career and not far from us in the front row of the Grand Tier was this gorgeous and sophisticated beauty . . . Callas. Another social event was the Lyons interdepartmental tennis league. We had two teams (six players playing doubles, round robin), but the teams from the bakeries, with players from the West Indies, always seemed to win. I was the organizer for LEO and captained a team with TRT as my partner! He wore long white trousers. We did quite well, as I recall. Events were played at the wonderful Lyons sports grounds in Sudbury, and we had group singalongs on the Underground.

At work TRT was as intimidating, but not as fierce, as Caminer. I mostly saw him in meetings. I think he needed more explanation and rationale than Fantl or Caminer. The latter was a fierce and intimidating figure to me, and razor sharp in his questions. I used to say that if I gave him a document to review, he would open it to any page at random and find at least one typo or some other error. Reading others' memoirs, and with the insight I have had as he critiqued my memoirs, has increased my respect and admiration for the way he ran the programming office. I learned much of my skill for producing applications under his tutelage. I hardly ever saw Simmons. I saw Mr. Anthony only a few times and had no interaction that I recall. He appeared interested and courteous.

Among my colleagues Fantl was even brighter than I realized at the time, a powerful analytic mind, every ready to solve a tricky problem; a patient teacher and a clear explainer. I have discussed him a little elsewhere. I owe him a lot and probably never thanked him properly. Frank Land and I had little work overlap that I remember, but we must have had considerable contact sitting next to each other. Also he got me into a London School of Economics (LSE) colloquium on Linear Programming that his wife Ailsa Land (then Professor and now Professor Emeritus at LSE) cochaired. At those meetings I saw some of the "big names" in British numerical computing, e.g., K. D. Tocher, Steven Vajda, Martin Beale, and Christopher Strachey. I remember Peter Hermon being one of the most bright, industrious, and argumentative (or should it be challenging?) of our recruits. He went on to a brilliant career and we stayed in touch from time to time. Others alongside whom I worked were Alan

Jacobs, Arthur Payman, Pat Cooper (who became Mrs. Fantl), Mary Blood, John Lewis, and John Grover, but we all had our own jobs to do and my contact with them was mainly social. In fact, the social contact included swapping rent-controlled flats and making up groups to go out to arts events and parties.

Nothing was more important or stimulating than this sense of fellowship and mutual esteem, which ran across all sections of the LEO team. It was a club as well as a workplace. We could rely on each other when the need arose at work, and we found each other good company when work was laid aside. It was a wonderful beginning to a career and set standards to which I have always tried to adhere in subsequent years.

17

A Reminiscence

PETER HERMON

The Raw Trainee

I joined LEO Computers in September of 1955 and straight away joined the five-week training course, along with half a dozen other new recruits and a handful of potential customers. As a model of clarity and professionalism, I have seen nothing since to rival it. We were introduced, in completely nontechnical language, to the four parts of the computer: store, input/output, arithmetic unit, and coordinator. We were given a thorough grounding in programming, and we were taught something of the practicalities involved in applying computers to commercial work: the need for data validation, reconciliation accounts and restart points, for example. All this in 1955! Many users—indeed some manufacturers—had barely grasped the need for such disciplines many years later.

The course culminated in our writing and implementing on LEO a model job centered around calculating sales representatives' commission and producing elementary sales statistics. Here we were additionally brought face to face with flow-charting, job planning, and debugging.

Model of clarity though it may have been, there was at least one instance where the course missed a trick. It was perhaps the second day of the course when they started to talk about Hollerith cards. Never having worked outside an academic environment in mathematics, I had no idea what these were. Not wishing to look foolish in front of the class I therefore started asking oblique questions in the coffee and tea breaks, searching for clues so that I could piece together what these mysterious objects were. Eventually I won through without my ignorance being discovered, but not before an early "theory" had to be ditched when it became clear that LEO had complicated the issue by extending the conventional use of cards punched in decimal notation to catering for binary numbers as well. I subsequently learned that I was not alone in my ignorance. I found out later that several of my fellow trainees had been similarly puzzled!

Even at this early stage in the history of computing the nonplaying "experts" had arrived. They were to manifest themselves forcibly in the early computer journals and provide an ongoing irritant to the "doers." I recall one occasion when one of the potential customer representatives (he was from one of Britain's most prestigious companies) repeatedly took issue with the senior LEO executive who was lecturing at the time. He knew it all. Eventually the lecturer (who subsequently became LEO's head of sales!) lost his patience and, in front of the class, advised his tormentor to "go and take a running jump at himself." Turnover in the company was presumably high because in spite of this an order duly followed a few years later.

Cutting Teeth on the Ford Payroll

The course over, I was told to report to Leo Fantl to work on the Ford payroll (the first really big commercial bureau job LEO had landed) along with Arthur Payman, a fellow trainee. Others were not so lucky. A Cambridge honors graduate who had been a bit of a plodder on the course was told his career with LEO was over. I remember hearing him argue that "this wasn't my fault, that wasn't my fault," etc., only to get the unarguable riposte from David Caminer (DTC): "I'm not sacking you because you're incompetent, but because you're unlucky!" No second chance. That was the way it was in those early years. Quality was everything. Either there was a spark or you were out.

Leo Fantl verbally explained what E1C, the code name for our program, was all about. There was no written specification: half an hour's quick talking with a few handwritten scribbled diagrams (and Leo's writing was pretty awful) and that was it. Subsequent supervision was minimal.

At the same time it needs to be stressed that such was the *esprit de corps* in those early days—indeed throughout the whole of my time at LEO—that everyone helped everyone. A problem had only to be raised at a coffee or tea break, for example, for virtually the whole programming office to pitch in with help and advice, whether it was related to their own job or not. Where supervision was minimal—and I was as much guilty of this as anyone—it was because we were all "doers," actively engaged in the day-to-day minutiae of detail as well as managing. We were all part of a concentration of talent that can rarely have been equaled in any programming office anywhere. Supervision therefore tended to be something that was sought rather than imposed.

I doubt whether either Arthur or I really understood what E1C was all about. This was mechanical computing *par excellence*, converting a series of inputs into a series of outputs with minimal comprehension of the transforming logic. But in the end we got there. E1C at last worked, albeit with a vast number of blisters. And this was the version that went into productive use, for when Leo told us to rewrite it, consolidating the blisters, we ended up with more blisters in the new version that we started with in the old and eventually the rewrite was aborted.

After E1C it was a relief to be given a program to develop from the beginning, even if it was only a simple one. E1T's role was to take details of new Ford employees on punched cards and consolidate them into the main brought-forward record pack. There was also a second program, E1T Prep, which had to be run first to transfer the joiner's details from the paper tape on which they were initially perforated.

It was all very exciting. Here were two jobs that by their very nature had to be got going quickly. And E1T Prep almost worked first time. Before long I was beginning to experience the famed LEO pressure. Testing time was at a premium and many was the time you would walk over to Cadby Hall from the Elms House glasshouse, complete with your box full of test data, only to be told "it's down."

All too often the only way to get time on the machine was to hang around in the evening. What time you were likely to get home was one of the big unknowns. No overtime was paid, but there was a consolation nonetheless. Anyone working after 7:30 p.m. was allowed to go to the manager's dining room for supper. Because of the round-the-clock nature of the Lyons's manufacturing and delivery routine, the Manager's Mess, as it was called, was open day and night. For us programmers, who, ranked as mere supervisors, were normally constrained to eat in a lesser place, this was riches indeed.

December that year brought a pay raise from $2300 to $2400 part of LEO's policy of "little often"—not a bad outcome considering that in those days $1500 was regarded as a good starting salary for an honors graduate. With Lyons also offering a discount on 40¢ worth of their cakes for the festive season, a merry Christmas was had by all.

Interlude

With the Ford payroll out of the way a variety of jobs came my way. One was a salary survey for the Office Management Association (O53), which worked the first time! Well, almost. It was all about calculating standard deviations, and I had used n in the denominator of the standard deviation formula for n parameters, unaware that there was an alternative formula that used $n-1$. The simple, one instruction change was soon made and honor restored. At least it was not a programming error. But this incident made a profound impression on me: accept nothing; check everything.

I was even given a customer inquiry to evaluate, from the Metropolitan Water Board. I remember studying it at the Green Line bus stop at the bottom of Brook Green and all the way home. Sensing the immense potential we had at our fingertips was far more gripping than the *Evening Standard*. By the time I arrived at the office the next day an outline proposal was already complete. Alas, the MWB never followed up.

One night there was a shortage of operators and a couple of colleagues and I were enlisted to take charge of an overnight run aimed at producing some medical statistics on punched cards. All seemed to be going well, and at about 3 a.m., surrounded by mountains of cards with the punch still crunching merrily away, we were proudly fondling some of the cards, thinking no doubt of the heroes we would be in the morning. Imagine our dismay, then, when the first card we looked at had no holes. Nor the second, nor the third—none of them! We had spent hours "punching" mountains of blank cards. A distraught phone call resulted in our being told to abandon the run. The following morning David Caminer, though naturally disappointed, took it remarkably philosophically. The explanation? We had forgotten to insert the plugboard in the punch.

One day I was told to help Personnel interview potential recruits. "Personnel" was actually one man, and we got on well. I remember being somewhat dazzled when he confided that the aim was for real achievers to earn $2800 by the time they were 30 (in the event, I was to beat this quite comfortably).

We started offering Saturday morning interviews to anyone interested in joining LEO: no need to apply, just drop in. This produced a great harvest, with one morning alone producing both Alan Jacobs and John Lewis. After his time at LEO Alan later became Head of Computer Services at both British Airways and Sainsbury's. John became a LEO payroll expert. Later on he also reached a senior position in British Airways, with particular strength in equipment configuration and software, where his attention to detail meant he rarely missed a trick.

A further surprise came when, after only several months, I was asked to run, and do most of the lecturing on, the next training course. This was a most enjoyable experience. Two of the students were A. O. Bell and E. W. Popham from the Imperial Tobacco Company (ICT), the holding company of the well-known Wills and Players tobacco empires and a potential customer for a LEO II. More on them later. Another student was Geoffrey Mills, a Lyons executive specializing in office methods and organization who had just been deputed to take charge of LEO sales.

After these challenges it was a disappointment and a chore to have to revert to checking Frank Land's L6 ice-cream sales programs. But the gods smiled on me yet again. John Grover, who had been expected to take charge of the E17 sales accounting suite for the now consummated sale to ITC, suddenly resigned and I was promoted in his place. My salary was adjusted to $2600.

Imperial Tobacco (E17)

Here was a real ground-floor opportunity. John had barely started on E17 when I took over. I had just the one young assistant, Bob Brett. Bob was one of the finest coders I've ever known—probably the finest—but though he would eventually lead the coding team on E17 he was heavily engaged on L5, the Lyons bakery sales job, for the time being and would remain so for some months. So, apart from the odd consultation to keep him in the picture, I was on my own.

This worried me at first. The ITC job was reputed to be the most complex LEO had so far handled and I had no commercial experience worth speaking of. "Don't worry," said David Caminer, "it's all common sense." I did not believe him and wished I had had some accounting knowledge. But how right he was, as I later came to realize time and time again.

I always remembered this advice when I came across O&M people painstakingly charting existing procedures in the minutest detail as a prelude to computerization. Whoever looked at the nice neat charts they produced, with their multiplicity of symbols, or even understood them? How much simpler, and quicker, to cut through the jungle of usually irrelevant detail by concentrating on what the system was trying to achieve and following through what outputs were required from what inputs.

My opposite numbers in ITC were the same Bell and Popham I had earlier taught on their programming course, together with an O&M man from Wills named Allen. I call them Bell, Popham, and Allen because (odd though it must seem today) I never did know their first names. Though we had a cordial enough relationship, it was a very formal one— befitting the times—with letters always starting off Dear Hermon or Dear Bell. Bell was acknowledged as the senior man. The others were never allowed to write in the company's name.

Bell reported to A. G. Wright, a man known to all concerned as "The Master." His title, Office Methods and Equipment Manager, disguised the commanding presence of a man who wielded an influence in the company out of all proportion to the rather junior status usually associated with his nominal job. He had reputedly married into the Wills family. To be invited into his office for a one-to-one talk was an honor indeed. He usually preferred group discussions in Bell's office on the infrequent occasions he involved himself at all. In his office the only thing I ever saw on his desk was an open copy of the *Financial Times*. Whether this was a studied pose or an indication of the way he really spent his time I still do not know to this day.

Even by the standards of the 1950s ITC was a very hierarchical and formal organization. Everyone knew his or her place. On one visit, when I accompanied John Simmons and David Caminer, we were split up and taken to three separate dining rooms for lunch, each according to The Master's evaluation of our stations in life. Uniquely in my business experience, ITC also celebrated tea in some style. Every afternoon at 3:45 managers retired to a special room where afternoon tea was served: silver teapot, sponge cakes, all the trimmings. The downside came in the evening. No one was supposed to go home while there was still a Main Board Director in the building. Many was the time, therefore, that I would leave to catch my train back to London, leaving Bell and Popham glumly playing out time.

I visited Bristol most weeks during the job requirements phase, usually for one or two days. The *modus operandi* was that, accompanied by Bell and Popham, and sometimes Allen, I would work my way around the various line managers whose work would be affected.

Any concerns I may have started out with about my lack of commercial background soon disappeared. It was not long before I realized that I knew as much as anyone about Wills' office methods and, before long, significantly more. Bell and his colleagues were continually dumbfounded at what came to light when the fine detail of Wills' systems was subjected to rigorous analysis and unearthed, as well as the seemingly rambling way in which it all came out and the apparent contradictions that emerged, which meant that we had to cross-check everything by asking the same or related questions on a subsequent occasion or of other people. Clearly nothing like this had been seen before. Later on, of course, as I worked on more and more companies, I realized that far from being unusual, this was par for the course. But at the time our opinion of Wills was mixed to say the least.

Bell was completely in awe of LEO. "How do you do that: by using some indicator?" became a recurring question. To be told what LEO could or could not do carried much the same force as "Thus saith the

Lord." This is not to be critical of Bell and his colleagues. They were men of their time, bemused by so powerful a new tool. And in all fairness it must be said that when the time came to write up the manual procedures to support E17, they produced a document to compete with the best.

It was soon apparent that, compared with anything LEO had so far encountered, E17 posed a number of new challenges. The relatively large number of accounts, the size of the product range, and the complexity of the programs demanded drum storage for the first time. The need for high-speed alphanumeric printing necessitated a new printer, the Powers Samastronic. Furthermore, since it was the company's policy to dispatch orders received by first post later the same day, there was a premium on speed and reliability. The need for speed also ruled out any possibility of presorting input and so necessitated a degree of random access to the customer master record. But it was not just in hardware and operational demands that E17's sting lay. The requirements themselves turned out to be surprisingly intricate.

This was most apparent in pricing and credit control. For example, every cigarette line in an order could be invoiced at one of four prices depending on the total size of the order. Moreover, if one order in an accounting period reached one of the break points for better terms, then every other order for cigarettes in the same period, whether placed earlier or later, also qualified. Tobaccos, snuffs, and cigars, each of them constituting a separate category, were treated similarly, except that now there were only two invoice prices.

Cigars posed further complications in that, once eligibility for best terms had been gained in a given period, it could be carried over to two other periods of the customer's choosing. Furthermore, any cigar order above a certain amount entitled the customer to extended credit. Each of these rules was cloaked in a welter of interlocking detail.

There was a host of other frills. Better terms could sometimes be anticipated. Orders that were a "near miss" for better terms received special consideration. There was a maze of rules governing what terms to apply when orders had to be split for various reasons. Multibranch organizations earned their terms on the total ordering pattern across all branches, even though the branches might order separately. A truly labyrinthine set of rules governed the method by which goods were dispatched and packing cases made up. And so on. This was quite a challenge considering it was LEO's first invoicing job outside Lyons, with its compact range of 80 bakery items, only one price per item, and simple credit control.

Even so, it would be wrong to make too much of this. Today E17 would be nothing out of the ordinary, and if it ever wore the crown as LEO's most challenging job it cannot have been for more than a few months.

It would be wrong, too, to imply that Wills always "dug in" and were reluctant to change and simplify. They were quick, for example, to take up our suggestion that LEO should print individualized order forms for representatives to take round on their next call, showing which brands the customer usually ordered and any other lines the Sales Management particularly wished to promote. Alongside the order form, the representative's copy also detailed the customer's ordering pattern over the past three periods.

Sometimes we must have been a bit of a trial to them, though it rarely showed. I remember going home one day, having just discovered that the Powers printer could manage only 17 alpha characters on each line, and boiling down the descriptions of Wills' entire product line until they conformed, ready for a meeting the following morning. There was no discussion with the warehouse staff who would pack from these description. But it was done sensibly and it worked.

In a few cases, however, they did dig in. Take book matches. Here was a product that was minuscule in relation to their main brands, yet which they insisted had to have its own routines and even its own invoices on specially distinctive stationery.

One day we came to discuss statistics. I had high hopes here. As a former mathematician I had visions of analyses that would really show LEO's mettle, involving trends, extrapolations, detection of significant variations, and so on, especially as Wills had a fully fledged statistics department.

For some reason our first meeting ended in clouds of cigarette smoke and near acrimony. Perhaps we pressed them too hard. At any rate, they had few ideas except to compare this year's sales with last year's sales. It was left that we would come back to them with suggestions. This we did a couple of weeks later, offering them last-year comparisons (because that is what they wanted) and comparisons against budget (because that is what they ought to have wanted). But they would not have it. "How can you set budgets for a business like ours?" was the cry. "How can you manage?" we mused. And so year-to-year comparisons was how it remained.

I wrote the functional specification for one of the two statistics programs, E17F, the evening my eldest son, David, was born, in between rushing upstairs to assist the midwife with cups of tea.

I always had the impression that the statistics people tried to get back at us when they insisted that LEO must be able to go back one or two complete years and recompile all the sale figures as they would have had new area groupings and sales territories been in operation (redissection). With large volumes, only punched-card storage, and their insistence on accurate cut-off points, this would have been a costly, time-consuming, and error-prone undertaking. Nevertheless we drew up a plan showing how it could be done. I doubt very much, though, that it was ever put to the test.

The requirements specification/job plan was finally published in November of 1956, and then it was relatively plain sailing, with Bell and Popham proving excellent implementers. Perhaps it was just as well that there were some complications in systems design. LEO II was delayed for a few months by technical problems with the higher-performance Mercury delay lines, and we were able to mask this and avoid customer concern by placing the blame for the ensuing delay on "unexpected systems complexities."

November of 1956 also saw my promotion to Assistant Manager, with a significant salary hike from $2600 to $3200. Not long after this, in a small waiting room at Paddington station, The Master invited me to join ITC as their computer guru. The bait was a raise to $3800 and the promise of a career for life with the giddy expectation of $5600 by the age of 40. TRT, at least, was keen for me to accept. It would be a good way to make sure all went well with such a prestigious customer. I remember feeling slightly miffed at being valued so lightly, but accepted nonetheless, lured by the money and the thought of running my own show.

In any event, I never moved to Bristol and within six months returned to LEO ($4600 and, quite soon, a company car). The staid predictability of ITC was no match for the vitality and camaraderie of LEO.

Wills were no luckier when they came to recruit programmers. The two we selected from their office staff turned out to be plodders (by LEO standards at least) and it was not long before we were telling them to take them back. This caused some considerable shock waves, even culminating in one of The Master's rare appearances. In retrospect we were probably a bit hasty. The tempo and demands in Wills were never likely to demand the excellence we looked for in LEO staff. As if to prove us wrong, one of the Wills rejects left the company shortly afterwards to enter the computer industry, where, to his credit, he later made quite a mark as a consultant.

Consultancy

As the LEO programmer Bob Brett got on with the coding and the Bell-Popham combination took up the challenge of implementation, my job gradually evolved into "consultancy." This meant carrying out appraisals and preparing proposals, including fairly detailed job plans, for prospective LEO II sales. To start with this involved working alongside so-called salesmen. As the salesmen had never before operated in office systems, let alone large-scale data processing, they were frequently out of their depth. When they also began to see themselves as virtual chaperones, real tension began to build up. Things came to a head during a visit to BOAC, when I had to follow an especially obtuse yet interventionist colleague out to the washroom so that we could decide how to get our act together. Shortly after this the sales role was clarified as being simply to gain initial openings and all was well.

There was no industry specialization in those days. We took on all comers. My portfolio included Dorman Long (a steel company), ICI, Tate & Lyle, Beechams, Esso, Dunlop, Renold Chains, and a whole raft of Gas and Electricity Boards. Keeping all the balls in the air left no time for boredom, and an essential skill was to be able to plan itineraries so as to put in personal appearances sufficiently frequently to prevent any customer feeling neglected.

There were some odd ideas around. Yorkshire Electricity had a very intelligent man leading their computer studies, but he never reconciled himself to LEO not having a table look-up instruction. "We must not waste the computer's time doing multiplication," he used to say. Far better, he maintained, to look up the extensions from a stored table.

But at least that was tolerable, even funny in its way. What was harder to take was working flat out on a proposal for Esso, 14 hours a day, seven days a week for three weeks, only to have TRT the next day, quite oblivious to all the sweat and toil, start pulling it to pieces over some trifling details. But that was TRT at his most cantankerous.

Then there was the sunny evening in Manchester when, in all innocence, I settled down after dinner to prepare a presentation on production planning, including machine loading, in readiness for a meeting the following morning. Small wonder that my confidence began to evaporate as the evening wore on! In any event, we managed to steer the meeting on to the safer shores of production control and so maintained our reputations intact. Such was our pioneering zeal that it never entered our heads that we were unlikely ever to be able to improve on the one man who, day in and day out, regarded machine loading as his personal fiefdom and solved it, in his own words, "much as you would a giant jigsaw puzzle."

One of my last tasks at LEO was to skeleton-code a job for Bertelsmann, a German publishing house, as a check on the timings. As a general rule we had always hitherto assumed that in business applications, with proper use of the buffers, processing time would be completely overlapped by input/output. This exercise showed how mistaken we must often have been. Though the Bertelsmann programs were by no means complex, processing times could not be contained within input/output and would add their own, not insignificant, contribution to run times. Fortunately, with the much faster LEO II now on the horizon, this revelation was less traumatic than it might otherwise have been.

Resume

I remember those days as if it were yesterday. Going to work was not simply a challenge but an adventure too, not simply a vehicle for the intellect but a field for the imagination to work on. It was almost, dare I say, a canvas for artistic expression.

Much of the excitement came from the thrill of handling a job in its entirety: definition, store layout, coding, testing, operating instructions, and user liaison. Not for us the drudgery of the assembly-line coder. In our enthusiasm (and sometimes naïvety) nothing was sacrosanct, nothing impossible. Defining the job with sufficient precision was the key, and if that could be done the rest would surely follow. Never more so than in LEO was necessity the mother of invention. Invited to tackle airline pro-rating, a job that finally succumbed to automation in the mid-70s on IBM 370-168s, we were undeterred. Asked for a bid to process the National Census we complied. Perhaps, occasionally, we were lucky in not being selected. But with the evidence of what we did achieve, who can say?

It is hard to believe today that reliability and capacity were not more important considerations to us than they were. But they were not. Cutting down a program to fit into the available store, speeding up a loop, packing more information on to a card, simplifying interjob links: these were the determinants of success. And the foundations of excitement.

When I try to isolate what were to me the chief characteristics of the LEO approach, the following come immediately to mind, not in any particular order. All the points seem obvious enough now, but 40 years ago they were little short of revolutionary.

- The strategic overview, i.e., the need to plan a job overall before tackling isolated parts in detail. Well into the 1960s (indeed even into the 1980s) this approach was not understood. IBM tried to persuade Dunlop to concentrate on depot stock control before even thinking of an integrated sales accounting suite. When I arrived at BOAC they were looking at reservations, passenger check-in, and message switching as three quite separate applications.

- The adversarial approach to clarifying requirements, i.e., asking the same question of different people, asking the same question of the same people in different ways, and actively seeking out inconsistencies like a lawyer cross-examining in court.

- Balance between computer and manual procedures, i.e., not trying to computerize everything just for the sake of it but rather recognizing that there were occasions when simple manual procedures could do better.

- The emphasis on quality people, i.e., on paying "little often," on delegating real responsibility very early on, on calling a spade a spade and weeding out nonperformers or those who were simply "unlucky."

- The need for budgetary control. So obvious, but who in those early days did it—or for many years after!

And then there were the remarkable people whose vision created and nurtured LEO. It is true that in Lyons they had a company of just the right size and complexity to make meaningful clerical work possible on the early LEO and one that was by then well versed in seeking office efficiency. But that was itself, to a large degree, a product of the work of the early pioneers. J. R. M. Simmons: austere, analytical, displaying an Olympian detachment from the daily cut and thrust. T. R. Thompson (TRT): the impatient, highly strung visionary, priding himself on always being open to suggestion (as indeed he often was) but sometimes curiously stubborn and opinionated (as in his opposition for so long to mass storage, magnetic tape, and alphanumeric printing). David Caminer: a perfectionist and driver; a man intensely loyal to his staff whom some could have taken, at times, as over-demanding had it not been for his integrity, ability, and dedication. John Pinkerton: the one who believed that technology was there to serve users (and acted on it!) and who had the gift, typical of so many first-class minds, of being able to explain the most obscure technicalities in everyday language.

Below them was an impressive team of assistant managers: Leo Fantl, John Gosden, John Grover, Jim Smith . . . .

Dunlop

In October of 1959 I left LEO to join Dunlop as head of computing for the UK Group. However, I had not left the LEO environment. Discussions for the sale of a LEO III to Dunlop had been going on for some time, and I had led for LEO on its proposal for a fully comprehensive sales accounting, stock control, and sales statistics suite. It was now my job to implement it. This duly happened, smoothly and on target.

Perhaps the greatest testimony I can pay to the LEO style is that at Dunlop, a large sprawling company with a rather leaden-footed management, there was never any real excitement and never any possibility of a rocky ride, much less failure. Demanding though the jobs were in size and scope, the LEO methodology and technology were by then, in the early 1960s, well able to cope and the main challenge was to rouse users from their lethargy.

As if to compensate for that my responsibilities soon began to take on an international dimension, and I was lucky in being able to make an almost immediate impact. Shortly after joining I was sent on a brief visit to Dunlop France in Paris. They were using an IBM punched-card calculator (a 604, I think) but a 650 computer was due in three months' time. "What are you going to do with it?" I asked. "Replace the 604," they replied. "What for?" I asked. "Because the 650 is more powerful" they replied. "Have you started any planning for it?" They had not. They were confused by technology. Their sole motivation was to keep up with technology for technology's sake, and when my final meeting with the Chairman took place later in the day, he announced with a flourish that "'le 650 est abandonné."

So in one day, deploying only LEO's dictum that systems planning is paramount, I won a credibility that was to stand me in good stead for the rest of my time in Dunlop, and saved them many times over the costs of my services for the five years I remained there.

Before long I was *de facto* head of computing for the group worldwide, in which role I was able to make similar (although not always so dramatic) contributions to the Dunlop companies in the United States, Canada, Eire, South Africa, Rhodesia, India, and Malaysia.

BOAC/British Airways

I am lucky in having had two highs in my working life. One was LEO: the other was being given virtual *carte blanche* in BOAC (and later British Airways) to create, almost from scratch, a global real-time network linking over 10,000 terminals based on a complex of computers sited in London and supporting, 24 hours a day, second by second, practically every aspect of the airline's activity. This was the well-known BOADICEA project. At its peak some 3000 staff members were involved in BA alone, quite apart from people working on the direct online links that were forged to other airlines, travel companies, and communications agencies.

I left Dunlop for BOAC in March of 1965. I was now in the big league with single jobs taking up to 300 person-years to develop; with worldwide real-time communications links; and where system breakdown could lead to grounded aircraft, with all that entailed for an organization marketing a totally perishable product and continually in the public eye. Yet over the course of the 18 years during which information systems reported to me, not once did we have a noticeably late cutover, a botched implementation, or a budget overrun. This is an extraordinary claim, but it is true, and a factor that was acknowledged in our winning two Queen's Awards.

The credit for all this goes back to the disciplines and controls that were forged at LEO all those years before. They may have been refined and extended but they came out of the original LEO stable for all of that. And lest anyone detect a note of immodesty, or question the relevance of my British Airways experience in a paper on LEO, let me say straight-away that the BOAC team that developed BOADICEA contained a solid nucleus of ex-LEO staff: at least nine managers with others down the line.

Later, during my 18 years with BOAC and British Airways, when I moved into General Management and joined the Board—leading the air-line's productivity campaigns—and became Managing Director of its European Services, though the scale and nature of the problems with which I contended far exceeded anything I had encountered at LEO, I know that much of my success was due to what I learned in my early years at LEO: the direct common-sense, no-nonsense, "call a spade a spade" questioning approach based on "why?"; eschewing jargon; getting to the heart of a problem by cutting through the unkempt scrubland of irrelevant detail; and never tolerating anything second rate. I may have left LEO the company in 1959 and LEO the computing environment in 1965, but the spirit of LEO lived on. After all, my training at LEO was the only training I ever had!

PART 3
Innovators

18

Lyons Teashops

RALPH LAND

Before World War II, the Lyons teashops were a prominent part of the national scene. They were the places where office workers went to lunch and shoppers had their tea. They appeared frequently in novels. A story based on contemporary London could scarcely avoid them. The first of the teashops had opened on a splendid site in Piccadilly a little before Queen Victoria's Diamond Jubilee. It was an immediate success, and within the year the newly established J. Lyons & Co. had opened eight more of them.

By the outbreak of the war in 1939 the number had increased to more than 250 in London and the provinces. Their popularity stemmed from the conscious effort of the Lyons founders to set entirely new catering standards for the ordinary man and woman of limited income. They were welcoming, with their elegant, gleaming white frontages and fascias adorned with golden art deco lettering. There was no mistaking them. Inside they provided comfortable surroundings and inexpensive food of a consistent high quality. Customers were served by rigorously selected and trained waitresses, clad in dresses made to measure by the company's own dressmaking department. The "nippies" as they were called, with their fashionable, starched white aprons, collars, and head-dresses, were familiar to everyone.

Customers were encouraged to make any comments on food or service that occurred to them on the back of their bills, and these were meticulously collated on a Daily Report that was immediately read and acted upon by the directors of the company. In targeting the teashops early in its life, LEO could be said to be invading a national institution.

World War II

The war brought many changes. Most visibly, it ceased to be possible to staff the shops with waitresses. The teashops turned to and pioneered self-service, intended for the duration of the war only, but it turned out no longer to be economic to bring back the nippies after the war had ended. A probable contributor to the continuation of this fundamental change was that the small army of employees needed to arrive at the reconciliation of bills issued by each waitress with records of the goods taken out of the servery was no longer required. A massive and costly clerical task had gone away.

Behind the scenes there was another major change. To overcome the severe shortage of skilled cooks. Lyons had innovated early in the war by preparing dishes centrally and freezing them for delivery. The dishes were then reheated in the teashops on equipment well ahead of its time. This all meant that quality could be maintained at the high uniform standards on which the company had built its reputation.

With this changed profile the teashops continued to be phenomenally successful in the early postwar years. It was not long, however, before they were running into profitability problems. Success depended on good locations, and most of the teashops were on prime sites with excellent values for alternative uses. Moreover, as property values increased it became correspondingly difficult to open new shops on good sites at affordable rents. The situation was exacerbated by the fact that 70 shops had been lost through enemy action during the war, so that the total number was now reduced to 180 in London and surrounding areas.

The Teashops Distribution Job

In these circumstances Lyons recognized the need for management changes in order to continue to develop the business in postwar conditions. An outcome was that the system for distributing goods daily to the teashops from the centralized kitchens and stores was one of the first to which the LEO applications staff gave their attention. By the time I joined the Teashops Division in 1953 to become their Management Accountant, the Teashops Distribution Job, L2, was already in full operation.

On the management side the Division was being thoroughly shaken up. Alec Kirby, a high-flying young manager from the Statistical office, who was familiar with both LEO and the Simmons management requirements, was brought in and promoted to become effectively chief executive of the Teashops Division. Bob Steel was imported to become Controller, to whom I then reported as Management Accountant.

This new management structure was superimposed on the existing old-style teashops management, which continued in place for a number of years. This was a strictly hierarchical system directed by a member of the owning family, Felix Salmon, and led by a team of highly authoritarian Teashops Supervisors under Mr. Jenkins and Miss Joerin. At the bottom of the structure each teashop was managed by a Teashop Manager who was responsible for the day-to-day running of each shop. Most of the senior Supervisors had served in the division before the war. Many had been selected for their physical presence—for example, on the basis of physical size. The teashops at that time employed some of the most formidable woman managers to be seen in Britain. These people were trained to follow the detailed rules established by top management meticulously. They were not, however, people used to dealing with or understanding financial information or management accounts.

The L2 application, which is described fully in the demonstration brief that forms Appendix C, could therefore be regarded as a good example of modern technology grafted on to a prewar, almost 19th-century, management structure. It is remarkable to note how the design of this system foreshadowed today's integrated management systems, with its ordering procedure giving rise to the organization of production, packing, dispatching, and accounting and leading to the generation of management information appropriate to each level of management.

At the time the technology available to provide an integrated system of this type was relatively primitive. For example, operators from the computer center telephoned each teashop every day, at a fixed time, so that order amendment information could be given by the manager over the telephone, to be punched by the telephone operator onto punched cards. However, some of the teashops had no telephones and had to use public telephone boxes, hoping that at the proper time the manager would have access to the telephone. A crash program to install telephones at all teashops was rapidly implemented.

I recall that, although the reduction in workload on the managers through the standard order procedure and other practical advantages were widely appreciated, the Divisional and Section Supervisors were ill-prepared by their background to utilize the management information supplied as a by-product of the system. This information aimed at piercing the global results and shedding light on what had given rise to them.

As the Demonstration Brief points out:

> If there was an increase or falling off in the sales of any item it was a major operation to trace it back to any particular group of shops . . . Using conventional methods it would have been formidable indeed.

The brief warns, though, that if every figure relevant to the teashops' results were to be printed out, they would fill a book each week. It stresses that the intention in the job was that only significant figures should be reported and that each level of management should be asked to consider only those figures within its immediate scope of executive responsibility.

Consequently, the additional information output by LEO was highly selective, with particular emphasis on the poorest performances at each level for each commodity group. However, those responsible for the systems design at LEO confess that what was produced was very much of their own devising rather than stemming from the wish list of the teashops management at the different levels. It was, it could be claimed, what the systems designers would have liked had they been running the teashops. But they were not, and those who were, were disinclined to change methods that had been successfully relied upon for more than 50 years. As a consequence, the innovative management information was poorly understood and largely ignored until Alec Kirby arrived on the scene, and even then it cannot be said that it became part of the natural culture of the teashops' organization.

Teashops' Wages

Following the successful introduction of the teashops distribution system it was agreed that the payroll should be transferred to LEO II from a punched-card system, which at that time was the only punched-card-based payroll system used by Lyons.

One of the main features of the payroll was the extraordinarily high turnover of staff. The payroll was designed to cope with some 11,000 staff members altogether, since annual staff turnover amounted, I believe, to over 100 percent. Many of the categories of staff, such as kitchen porters and wash-up staff, were virtually casual workers, many of them part-time. Since the food was centrally prepared, no skilled cooking staff were required. The other important feature, and perhaps the main reason for the payroll being on punched cards, was the high mobility of the staff. This meant that in any one week a large number of payments had to be made at the shop in which staff were temporarily working rather than in their "home" shop. The punched-card system could cope with this through a final sort on cards, enabling their paychecks, pay, and cash dissection to be sent to the right teashop. On LEO II this provided no major difficulty provided the right "pay at" information was notified in time. Punched cards continued to be used for the "pay ats."

Another valuable advantage provided by the LEO system was the ability to make two calculations for each person with a minimum loss of speed, one using the rates laid down by the Catering Wage Act and one for the Lyons rates. The greater rate was paid to ensure compliance with the Act, which had been introduced in an effort to prevent to widespread exploitation of catering staff by less responsible companies.

Brian Mills, from LEO, was given the task of preparing the payroll system for LEO II/1 and assigned John Aris to this task as his first major job following his basic training. As I recall, the transfer of the payroll was successfully accomplished on the basis of one section of teashops at a time with only minor transitional problems.

The efficient functioning of the teashops depended on the ability to cost-effectively manage the rapidly changing workforce. We decided, therefore, to use data derived from the teashops payroll to create a system of Time Analysis as a major management tool. John Aris and I devised an analysis of labor use at each teashop based on the raw data fed into the payroll. This was submitted to each manager weekly and summarized by section and division.

Alec Kirby managed the Teashops Division substantially via regular monthly meetings comprising the eight divisional supervisors and members of his staff groupings. The chief purpose of the meetings was to analyze sales and gross profit performance through the L2 statistics and cost performance through the Time Analysis statistics. The supervisors went through similar procedures with their section supervisors and they directly with their teashops managers.

Although Time Analysis was intended to be a key management tool, it became unpopular with the teashop managers, partly because of the amount of extra data they had to provide in addition to the data need for payroll, but also largely because it forced them to take action on staffing their shops, the need for which they tended to dispute. On investigating the problems we found that the system was error-prone; too much of the data contained errors, either errors of origination, errors of interpretation, or problems of data transcription.

While the concept behind Time Analysis was excellent, we found that, in practice, the system could not be used effectively and it gradually fell into abeyance as a management tool before it was abandoned altogether. The lesson was learned that, while staff can be persuaded to produce correctly data that is self-evidently necessary for operational purposes, they are less inclined to take very seriously extra paperwork that is required "only" for management information purposes.

Conclusion

The Distribution and Payroll applications were functionally unqualified successes, putting the teashops organization in the forefront of computer implementation in the whole world at the time, but the failure to make use of their "added value" potential meant that their effect on the fortunes of the company was only marginal. By themselves they were unable to arrest the decline of the teashops' popularity and therefore profitability as the market changed with the disappearance of the early postwar shortages. The top management was no longer as closely in touch with popular taste as it had been in the days of the original Joe Lyons.

Eventually the teashops were doomed to die, despite belated efforts at modernization and an unsuccessful experiment with the reintroduction of a prewar-style nippy service. For my own part I had realized through my personal experience with LEO and from what I had heard from my twin brother, Frank, who had been with LEO since 1953, that that was where my future lay, and in 1959 I joined him there.

19

Glyn Mills Bank and Army and Air Force Officers Payroll

JOHN LEWIS

In the late 1950s, Army and Royal Air Force officers could elect to be paid either directly by the War Office or Air Ministry or through what were known as "agents." The City bankers Glyn Mills & Co. were responsible for the pay of 9000 officers. Another old-established house, the Cox and King's branch of Lloyds Bank, handled the pay of the remainder of the officers who chose to be paid in this way.

When LEO Computers was awarded the contract for processing the Glyn Mills component, LEO was already well accustomed to working in this field. Payroll had been the earliest large-scale office application to be run on LEO, and over time the Lyons payrolls had been joined on LEO I and LEO II by those for the Ford Motor Company and then those for the Stewarts and Lloyds steelworks at Corby, the CAV vehicle accessories factories, Kodak, Tate & Lyle, British Railways Hotels, and a consortium of London boroughs. Despite being tailored to the special requirements of the particular organizations, all of these payrolls had many common characteristics.

Apart from the same requirements to calculate pay and allowances and make deductions, the officers payroll differed radically from those for most commercial, industrial, and administrative undertakings.

Current data, known for historic reasons as "casualties," came in randomly from Army and Air Force stations all around the world. If no casualty had been received since the last payroll run, an officer's pay was calculated according to the information already held on his record without further authorization. Where there were changes to be made to pay, allowances, or deductions, these were notified not on a form but on what where termed "Part III" orders issued by the officer's regiment or station. These authorized the change and the effective start and/or end dates. The monetary value was either included in the Part III order or was available from War Office or Air Ministry tables. Casualties were normally notified retrospectively and one casualty could later override another. Hence it was imperative that casualties were processed in chronological order of issue.

Officers' net pay consisted of a number of taxable and nontaxable allowances and deductions. Items were paid or deducted at daily, weekly (on a specific day of the week: child benefit on one day, National Insurance on another), monthly, or quarterly rates (for the regimental bands).

Another feature was that an officer's record had to contain a complete history of the effective date and rate for each item of pay, allowance, and deduction, so that when a change was notified, sometimes reaching back into the past, the net effect could be calculated and the payment or recovery made. Clearly, therefore, the history record was of indeterminate length, in contrast to the fixed-length permanent record maintained for the other payrolls processed on LEO. The paycheck, too, had to be more flexible. On average an officer might have seven items to be detailed, but there could be 20 or more.

By way of introduction to Services' payrolls, LEO had earlier been invited to submit proposals for a computer system to process the Army "other ranks" payroll (which was awarded to IBM for what subsequently became the Worthy Down installation). Having gained experience of army "other rank" payrolls while doing my National Service, I prepared this proposal. Having also experienced, firsthand, the vagaries of the officers payroll system, I was to use my knowledge in the summer of 1958 to prepare a proposal and the specification for this system for Glyn Mills.

The Glyn's payroll office was located at Lampton, off the Great West Road near Heathrow Airport, where Mr. Jordan, the Office Manager, was ably assisted by Miss Hanney, her deputy Miss McCrystall, and a dedicated staff.

Before the advent of LEO, the payroll was processed manually apart from an address plate system to print the officer's name and the bank branch code. The paychecks were direct deposit slip-sized and when completed were sorted by clearing bank and issued through the general bank clearing system to be credited to the officer's account at his or her branch; the branch would then forward the check with the next bank statement. Remember that at this time all check sorting, control totaling, and clearing was handled manually; bank account numbers had not been introduced and MICR character recognition had not yet been developed.

When a schedule of casualty events was received in the office, a sequence number was allocated for audit and a copy of each individual casualty was matched with the officer's personal file. A study was made to determine the ongoing consequence from the start of the next monthly payroll, and calculations were also made for any retrospective changes. The manual history record sheet was updated and appropriate entries entered on the next month's paycheck. At the end of the month, the check was completed by entering the other ongoing payments and deductions, and by calculating the income tax and net pay. The allocation of payments and deductions to vote heads (accounting categories) could then be assembled. All this was a totally manual procedure with intense peaks of activity at the end of each month.

The paycheck detailed the net payment period (unless it was a continuing item unchanged from the previous month) and the net payment or deduction for each item. A copy of the check was filed with the officer's records, which included a full pay history.

The Officers Computer Record

All officers had a unique service number, but their payroll records were identified only by their names. The records were consequently held in alphabetical order; copies of the payroll and casualty slips were filed together—all in alphabetical order. For the LEO payroll a pseudo-identity number was allocated to each officer and used throughout the system to simplify the identification of an officer. Initially, five-digit numbers were allocated at incremental intervals of five to allow new officers to be allocated a number in alphabetical sequence in the appropriate numerical gap. (While there was provision for a wholesale renumbering, I do not know whether it was ever necessary to use it.)

Officers were identified on the paycheck by their initials and full name—one family with a history of several generations of service in the army had a surname of 27 characters!

One of the major innovations required for processing this payroll was the ability to handle a record of variable, and in theory infinite, length in a computer with small (by today's standards, minute) memory. Each record was divided into three parts. The first part held static information, for example the identity number, name, and bank code.

The second part held data about each of the (theoretically 150) different payment and deduction item codes that the officer had at some time received or paid: first the current ongoing items, followed by historic items relating to changes that had occurred before the start of the current month.

Information held for each item code consisted of "date from" and "date to" values (if not current). A range of numbers were allocated to taxable (1–49), nontaxable (50–99), and deduction (100–150) item codes, and further tables identified the frequency of activity and the vote head associated with each item code. Item code numbers and their descriptions were preprinted on the reverse of the paycheck direct deposit slip. There was also provision for printing the description of new codes on the front of the paycheck. In this way the system was fully generalized and capable of handling existing and new codes of whatever nature. Nowhere within the system was the actual description of a code held, except for printing on allocation and control reports.

The third part was of fixed format and held running totals, for example, for tax to date, tax code, and basis, which were required only toward the end for the calculation of tax and net pay.

By ordering the record in this way it was possible to process the theoretically infinite record sequentially within a finite area of main store. Escape routines to use additional space on the magnetic drum were included.

The Paycheck

As mentioned, paychecks were direct deposit-sized and passed through the general bank clearing system. The clearing banks' format required the right-hand side to contain only the account-holder's name, the bank code, and the net amount.

Space on the paycheck was at a premium to contain all the information. The remaining space was divided into three columns, for taxable pay, nontaxable pay, and deductions. Each column contained the item code number, the "effective from" date (if not from the first of the month), the "effective to" date (if not the last day in the month), and the calculated amount. The totals for each column were also printed. Up to 10 items could be printed in each column, and provision was made to "overflow" to a second paycheck if necessary. Other items included tax code, tax basis, gross taxable pay to date, and tax paid to date.

A copy of the paycheck was filed with the officer's records and a further continuous copy was filed as the payroll.

The Computer System

Nothwithstanding the differences already referred to, the organization of the computer system followed what had become classic payroll lines. An outline chart of the main programs is shown in Figure 19.1. An amendment program, known as E41A, processed all casualty notifications in preparation for the next monthly payroll, prepared records for officers to be added to the payroll, and processed changes to the more permanent details, for example, bank or tax codes. A monthly payroll calculation program, E41B, calculated and printed the paychecks/payroll and updated the records. A reconciliation program, E41B2, read all the control total data accumulated during the E41B processing run and printed the totaled reconciliation accounts to prove the accuracy of the processing and the allocations to vote heads and clearing banks.

An outline flowchart

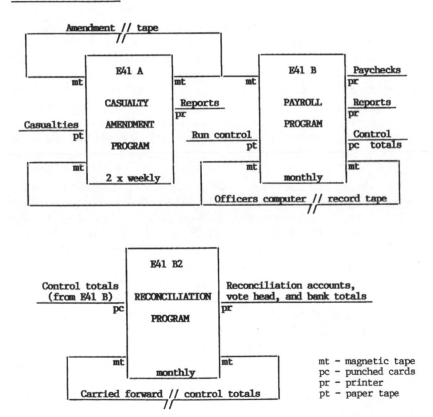

Figure 19.1.

Unusually for LEO payrolls, there was an input editing program. Most commercial programs controlled their input either by exception or by control totaling. However, on this payroll, input data—casualties—arrived at random; chronological sequence and validity checking was very desirable to reduce to a minimum the risk of failing to produce a valid paycheck. A further program was used initially to create the officers' data records, and another, at the end of each tax year, to print the P60 certificates of pay received and tax deducted, add the new tax codes, and clear the totals ready for the start of the new tax year. These programs are not included in Figure 19.1.

The payrolls for the Army and RAF officers used the same computer programs. The Army officers were processed in one run and the RAF officers in another to take account of the different vote head allocations.

Data Input

A casualty slip was prepared manually for each and every occurrence notified. It had to be assumed that a new casualty advice superseded the previous notification for the same item code. A number of different preprinted forms were available that covered every conceived situation. A simple case could be to notify an increase in pay from a specified date that would require a precoded form number, the officer's LEO identity number, the item code for pay, the "effective from" date, and the amount per day. A more complicated example could be to notify the payment of an allowance between two dates. Matters then became more complicated when two or more changes to pay, say, were received with the same casualty schedule covering different periods and then, before the next payroll run, a further set of casualties, again affecting pay, were received that could well cancel out some or all of the information notified earlier! Other casualty slips were available to notify changes to basic data—tax code, bank code, etc.— and a large form was used to submit all the details for a new officer. The form and item numbers were assigned so that all the forms for one officer when submitted in numerical order would be input in the correct order. To ensure that casualties were processed in chronological sequence, casualties were collected into batches and given a sequence number.

By today's practice all this manual sorting will appear old-fashioned but, at the time, sorting on the computer was a very slow and cumbersome operation, and the Glyn's staff were very experienced and efficient in this type of work.

The data on a batch of casualty slips were punched onto paper tape, the conventional LEO raw data input medium, and passed through the data vetting program to check for accuracy and report any errors. The input data were then ready for the amendment program.

The Amendment Program: E41A

This program was normally run about twice a week to spread the workload both in the Glyn's office and on LEO. The purpose was to prepare updated officers' personal details by recording the effect of the casualties received since the previous payroll run. The officers' computer records were held on magnetic tape, and being a sequential file every record had to be read for every run of the program. An amendment record tape was used to accumulate, throughout the month, the amended records of all officers who had been affected by a casualty notification. This amendment record tape was carried forward to either the next run of the amendment program or the monthly payroll program. The input data was submitted in the same order as the data on the record file, namely by casualty type/item type within officer number. A "blank" amendment record tape was used for the first run of the amendment program after a run of the payroll program.

Casualties dealing with new officers or changes to personal details were straightforward to process and required only creating or amending the record and carrying the updated record forward on the amendment record tape.

Casualties notifying changes to items of pay, allowances, or deductions were a different matter! For each of these casualties it was first necessary to pick out from the officer's computer record the "past" history: date from, date to (or "open" as an ongoing item), and the amount. The next step was to take the new casualties for this item and create a "net" updated history record. The "updated" history was then carried forward on the amendment record tape as a complete "updated" officer's computer record. Before the next run, further casualties might be received and require a reassembly of the already "updated" record—and this could happen more than once before the next payroll run!

In practice, of course, in any month the majority of the officers' records were not affected by any casualty notification.

The Payroll Program: E41B

This program was run a few days before the end of each month in time to get the paychecks passed through the bank clearing system and posted to officers' accounts by the first of the month. Its purpose was to calculate the pay, print a paycheck for each officer, and update the corresponding personal computer record. A copy of the paycheck was used as the payroll for the office and audit purposes. All the data required was held on last month's officers' computer record tape and the amendment tape produced from the last run of the amendment program E41A.

A preliminary step was to calculate the number of days in the month, the number of Tuesdays and Thursdays in the month, and to determine whether this was a month in which quarterly payments were made to the regimental bands.

The brought-forward officers' computer record tape and the amendment tape were inspected to determine the next officer, in numerical order, to be processed. If the only record for the officer was held on the brought-forward record tape, the details of items of pay and deductions were assembled ready for the payroll calculation; if a record for the next officer was held only on the amendment tape, then this record was used.

However, a record held on both tapes indicated that casualties had been notified since the last payroll run and retrospective adjustments might be necessary. If the history record had been updated, the "updated" history record was compared, change by change, with the "past" history record and, for those periods that differed, adjustment payment (or deduction) lines were calculated detailing the start and end dates and the total amount to be printed on the paycheck, and the "old" record on the brought-forward record tape was discarded.

The net total of taxable items was used together with other tax data to calculate this month's tax due. The paycheck was then printed and the updated officer's record carried forward. Charges were added to the vote head and clearing bank totals.

This was the first payroll that was processed on a monthly basis. The income tax routines had been written for payments to be made weekly, so it was necessary to make a copy of the tax routines from an existing payroll—plagiarism was practiced by all LEO programmers—and convert them to a monthly basis. At that time, the Inland Revenue insisted that computer tax calculation routines should reproduce, precisely, the same answer—rounding errors and all—as the printed tax tables they issued. Careful adjustment of the conversion constants was necessary. Although programmers normally worked with numerical data as scaled integral numbers, both LEO I and LEO II actually worked in pure binary, with numbers held as a fraction in the range 1 to −1. Binary/decimal and binary/monetary conversion and reconversion functions were built-in. LEO I did not have a division function; when necessary a subroutine was used, and in LEO II it was an "optional extra." To avoid the time used for division, "division by a constant" was effected by multiplying by its reciprocal, which was held as a program constant. The conversion constants used in the tax routines required very careful calculation and adjustment to avoid differences in rounding errors.

To put a perspective on the speed of the LEO II computer, each additional instruction in the innermost calculation loop added five minutes to the processing time for the monthly run! All programmers were very conscious of this, and time and ingenuity was used to save many "five minutes a month."

Calendar Dates

Anticipating the then unannounced international ISO standard, dates were held as "year-month-day," each field being in binary, so a whole date used "7-4-3" = 14 bits. Casualties could be directly compared for correct chronological sequence. Subroutines were written to determine the number of days, the number of Tuesdays (say), the number of months, or number of quarters between any two dates. We were confident that the system would last through to the end of the century, and only a moment's thought was given to what would happen after December 31, 1999. It was decided that it would not be our problem!

George McLeman spend many hours wrestling with the coding of these routines. The method used was chosen as it was necessary to print the "effective from" and/or "effective to" dates on the paycheck when not actually covering the whole month's period of the payment. It was also helpful during problem investigation to be able to quickly read a date from the dump of a record. With hindsight, an alternative method of using a base date and converting future dates to the number of days from the base date might have been easier in some respects. But remember that LEO II was a binary computer: negative numbers were held as a "complement," so that reconverting large binary numbers to decimal was not a fast exercise! The emphasis was on making the monthly run as streamlined as possible, even at the expense of additional computer time for processing casualties.

Accounting Controls

Individual allowances and deductions were accumulated under vote heads according to the item code for recharging the allowances to the Government and paying deductions, for example, for income tax to the Inland Revenue. The net totals were balanced with the total of the payroll. Net pay was analyzed by clearing bank code.

Reconciliation controls were maintained under a number of different headings. A comprehensive system had been developed and used extensively in all LEO payrolls; it had proved invaluable in ensuring the overall accuracy of the processing. Basically, totals for brought-forward, additions, deletions, and carried-forward values were accumulated at each stage of the processing and, normally in a separate consolidation operation, were balanced to prove the process.

For example, the "tax to date" account would be:

Tax brought forward
+ Tax from casualty amendments
+ Tax for joiners   − Tax for leavers
  (new officers)   (retiring officers)
+ Tax deducted this period   − Tax carried forward   = Discrepancy

The "discrepancy" on all account tabulations was printed in a separate right-hand column so that, when checking the reports for the accuracy and consistency of the processing, any value other than zero was clearly visible.

Restart Totals

A practice established from the start of LEO was to arrange the processing so that if (or, more commonly in the early days, when) a problem arose that caused the processing to be abandoned, it would be possible to restart the processing from a predetermined point. These points were at that time called *restart points*; now, hopefully more confidently and accurately, they are called *checkpoints*. Control totals accumulated during processing were "dumped," normally onto punched cards, to be subsequently summarized in a reconciliation program.

This practice was followed and the E41B2 program accumulated all the control totals dumped at each restart point and printed accounting control accounts.

Fallback

An emergency payroll system was devised to enable paychecks and a payroll to be produced should the computer, for some reason, be unable to process the payroll and it prove necessary to fall back to a manual procedure. A file of paychecks with only the name and bank code printed was maintained and, in the event of an emergency, the month's payroll could be produced by using this file and entering a cash amount estimated from last month's pay on each officer's blank paycheck. The cash amount would be regarded as an advance of pay to be recovered from the run that successfully processed the month's payroll. A blank paycheck form was produced initially for every new officer and whenever a change was made to the details held on this paycheck.

To my knowledge, it was never necessary to use the fallback procedure.

LEO II/5

The computer scheduled for the payroll was LEO II/5, the Service Bureau
computer eventually installed in Hartree House early in 1959. The Glyn's
officers payroll was to be the first application to be run on the computer.

LEO II/5, besides having Samastronic printers and magnetic drums,
was to be the first LEO II computer to be equipped with magnetic tape
(from Decca). It is very doubtful whether it would have been either possible or economic to process as much of the job as was done without the
use of magnetic tape for file handling or drums for additional storage.
Certainly with only the basic LEO II storage the applications would have
to have been broken down into a large number of discrete program runs
and would have required many different card decks to (mis)handle.

Pressure was on to use LEO II/5 as productively as possible as soon as
possible. Development work for the magnetic tape control routines (*software* was not a word in use at this time), program testing of the Glyn's
payroll, and engineer training, testing, and development time were
scheduled in fierce competition with each other throughout the day and
well into the evenings, particularly during the winter of 1958 at the
Minerva Road factory.

The winter of 1958 was a cold one, and the programmer's hut at the
back of the car park was cold, being mainly heated by the prototype core
store memory on test in the hut—a programmer's extra duty was to
phone the development engineer every time there was a check failure on
the store. The transport cafe at the end of Minerva Road served memorable meals late into the evening.

The LEO II/5 main store consisted of 2048 addressable short words,
equivalent to under 10,000 4-bit characters in today's parlance! (Even a
modest word processing computer has a memory of 512,000 alphanumeric characters.) This store consisted of 64 mercury delay line tubes,
which had to accommodate input and output areas for each peripheral
device and working locations for active programs, data, and control
totals. Instructions could be operated on only while held in this main
store, and data had to be accessed from and written into main store locations. One tube had to be allocated to each input and output area, each of
these payroll jobs required at least one area for data input, one for printed output, three for magnetic tape (in and out), and two for drums (in
and out). Thus at once 11 percent (7/64) of the main store had been allocated for input/output areas, leaving only some 1824 short words for
working locations.

There was a considerable amount of paging required to bring in sections of program stored on the magnetic drums. To reduce the access time for all input and output data, a system first established in the mid-1950s for calling data forward into the annex associated with each channel enabled the data, when actually required, to be transferred from the annex tube into main storage at electronic speed. The output operation transferred data to the annex at electronic speed and subsequently to the slower output device. This system was efficient for sequential devices, but not so quick for random access devices like drums, as it was not always known sufficiently in advance which data to read.

Considerable skill was required first in laying out the program into paging sizes and then organizing the transfer of data to optimize the efficiency of the program. Certainly when the programs were first coded there was always plenty of room for improvement!

The Samastronic Printer

The Samastronic printer on LEO II/5 was a 140-character 300-lines-per-minute alphanumeric printer—simple in concept but very difficult to maintain and achieve consistently good quality printed output. Every print position was fitted with a stylus attached through a flexible tube to a solenoid, and all the 140 styluses were attached in-line to a bar that oscillated across the width of a character. When instructed to print a line, the paper moved forward and the styluses all traced a sine curve across the area allotted to a character. At appropriate intervals each stylus was activated by its solenoid in a pattern that stabbed out the chosen character. (Today's dot-matrix printer equivalent has a grid, often of 5×7 styluses, which stabs out one character at a time as the print head moves across the platen.) The top copy was printed from the styluses by an inked print ribbon the width of the 140 print positions. Carbon paper, interleaved with other paper, was used when more than one copy was required.

A dual carriage feature was of questionable value. This feature enabled the computer to print out two separate independent streams of output from one printer. One use was for printing the paychecks on one side and reports at the other. The problem here was that if the paper used by one output was of significantly larger quantity than the other, then the smaller one (in this case the reports) suffered by having its surface smudged by the print ribbon being dragged across it as the ribbon was moved forward to satisfy the needs of the other paper (the paychecks).

Magnetic Tape

Magnetic tape data was written (and read) in fixed-sized blocks along the tape corresponding to a tube's worth of data from the main store—32 short words or 160 4-bit characters. The tape was premarked into blocks spaced to minimize the time delay and wasted tape caused by the need to be able to start and stop the tape movement between each block. The gap was subsequently used to write more data. When the tape had been written to the end in the first direction, the tape reversed and the data was written "round the bend," filling in the gaps on the way back. The whole tape could therefore be used for data, and a full tape did not need rewinding after use.

Magnetic "dropout" was a significant problem and adequate steps were necessary to ensure that data were accurately written onto tape.

The magnetic tape control routines enabled a programmer to use a write instruction and the control routines transferred a block of data to tape, adding a check total and block number. "Read-after-write" electronics checked that the data had been written correctly, and if not, "canceled" the data with a mark and rewrote the data repeatedly until successful. A read instruction obtained the next correctly written block in sequence and checked its correctness before transferring control back to the application program. The magnetic drums used for program routines, etc., were similarly checked. These precautions were essential!

The reliability of the Decca servo mechanisms left much to be desired. Initially there were many instances when the reel servos would both simultaneously unwind the tape, leaving a heap of loose tape in the deck reservoirs. What was worse was when the servos both simultaneously wound in their tape, and a long thin piece of stretched tape was left in the middle of the reel, requiring a new reel and a rerun of the previous job.

The LEO II/5 computer was the first unit to occupy the new Hartree House premises located over Whiteley's store in Queensway. When the computer was moved in, the site was occupied by builders, and although the computer room was almost finished the other accommodation was still primitive. The women had to use the Whiteley's restrooms except on Thursday afternoons (half-day closing), when a walk to the end of Queensway was necessary.

Glyn Mills personalities concerned with the project included John Glyn, the Chairman, who on one occasion at a splendid lunch hosted by Anthony Salmon in best Lyons Director style at Cadby Hall appeared anxious, at a suitable interval after lunch, to get away. It so happened that there was a cricket match at Lord's that afternoon that required his attention. On another occasion, David Caminer and John Lewis met Jeremy Morse in the Directors' Parlor at Glyn's Head Office in London. It was a magnificent room leading off the main banking hall, paneled from floor to ceiling, with four large desks positioned one in each corner. Such was the lifestyle of the merchant bankers.

Many programmers worked on the project from the autumn of 1958 through the summer of 1959. George McLeman, Diane Bray, Barry Fox, and Bernard Pierce were into the programming from the outset and Jenny Baker, Mary Coombs, Alan Jacobs, and Margaret James were deep in the project by cutover. Jack Warriner was the operations manager, with Charlie O'Brien and Jim Scattergood the leading operators, while George Manley and Frank Walker led the engineers who built the computer and maintained it.

One of the satisfactory outcomes of the Glyns' payroll project was that three pairs of programmers found they had more than work on the E41 project in common and got married. More than 30 years later all are still flourishing together, which is more than can be said for LEO II, the project, and even Glyn Mills!

20

Stewarts and Lloyds Steelworks

HAMISH ARCHIBALD

> Bliss was it in that dawn to be alive,
> But to be young was very heaven!

Wordsworth's lines exactly described my emotions as I walked through Kensington in the early morning sunshine with two colleagues, Bob Caldwell and Ron Bailey, on our way to Cadby Hall. It was the spring of 1957, and we, too, were engaged in a revolution—one which, over the period of my career then just beginning, was to change dramatically the ways by which businesses were managed.

I had graduated in 1956 and, seeking a career in business consultancy, had been recruited as a trainee by Stewarts and Lloyds Ltd. with a view to entering the Organization and Methods department after a period of experience in the steelworks. Nothing had been mentioned, either at the interview or afterwards, about the company's interest in obtaining a computer for business applications. As a student I had heard of LEO I and was vaguely aware of the type of projects being pioneered by J. Lyons. But it never occurred to me that I might become involved in such an activity, let alone devote a working lifetime to it. It came as a considerable surprise, therefore, when I was summoned one day in late November of 1956 by the personnel department, to be confronted with the question of whether I would consider presenting myself for selection as a "computer programmer." The personnel manager clearly had little knowledge of what was involved or of the qualities required, but presented me with copies of a couple of articles that, he said, "would explain it all." The only recollection I have of their content is a heading describing the programmer as "the high priest of the electronic age." Perhaps that is what caught my imagination, because I took the job, which led to me sacrificing my working life to the computer!

The company had, apparently, been recruiting through its not inconsiderable personnel resources for likely candidates, with varying degrees of success. There was, of course, no supply of trained programmers on the labor market at that time. It was generally held in those days that a company embarking on the application of a computer to its business activities required three programmers. Two had already been found: Bob Caldwell, a statistician by profession employed in the company's Scottish works, and Ron Bailey, a senior clerk in the Central Calculating Department at Corby, Northamptonshire. A crucial step was success in the aptitude test devised by Lyons.

Consequently, off I went to London, where, at Cadby Hall, in the company of several others from my firm and elsewhere, I took the test. Following a general introduction, two short lectures were given on "arithmetic orders" and on "sequence change." Test papers explored one's understanding of these novel concepts and the ability to use them to solve simple problems. While we recovered from this exacting experience, the papers were marked. My first indication of possible success was being singled out for an individual, as opposed to a collective, tour of the LEO I installation. This also gave me the opportunity to ply my guide, John Lewis, with questions about the world of programming. Within a few weeks, in early January of 1957, I met my new colleagues for the first time at a small hotel in Kensington, and we braced ourselves for the LEO II "Training Course for Programmers and Operators, " which was to commence the following day.

The roots of Stewards and Lloyds, subsequently embraced within British Steel, lay back in the mid-19th century. The company was a tube-maker—primarily based on steel, but also using iron, concrete, and later plastics. Its works were grouped in the east Glasgow area, in the Midlands, and in South Wales. There were numerous associated companies overseas and a widespread distribution network in the UK. An interest in the possibilities of the computer was not surprising. The company had long been innovators—in production technology, in staff training, and in methods of administration including mechanization, to give but a few examples. Its courage in breaking new ground was unsurpassed which is illustrated most vividly by the development of the major production facility of Corby Works during the depths of the depression in the 1930s. Thus the concept of introducing one of the business world's first computers was likely to fall on receptive, although demanding, ears.

The initiator was Neil Pollock, then manager of Organization and Methods and later British Steel's first director of Management Services.

Neil had been with the company since the 1930s and after the war had returned to take up a management position. He more than anyone, knew the advantages of obtaining the prior support of "key players." Consequently, such company heavyweights as L.M.T. Castle, J. Carson, and G.H.T. Macleod would be "on board" before the decision-seeking presentation to the full directorate was made at the company's annual Gleneagles Conference in 1956.

Because of the novelty of the project, the sanction was a conditional one—after all, LEO II was still a paper computer. Agreement to acquire LEO II would be given provided it could be demonstrated to Stewarts and Lloyds' satisfaction that the computer could process part of the steelworks payroll with absolute accuracy and in repeated adherence to a demanding weekly time-scale. Given that that test could be met, the wider objectives were to make savings through increased staff productivity to improve the speed, accuracy, and uniformity of methods across the company and to explore the potential for production planning.

The three of us, led by Bob Caldwell, presented ourselves at Cadby Hall for the programming course. For five weeks LEO Computers Ltd. taught a motley collection of students about the workings and, as foreseen in those days, the potential of the computer. New recruits to LEO, staff like us from prospective users, and others perhaps on a break from firms of accountants, consultants, and banks, were subjected to formal lectures on such diverse topics as binary arithmetic, simple circuit elements, programming for decimal cards, multiply and shift, and programmed precautions. The culmination came with the model job, when what had been taught—and hopefully learned—was put into practice by syndicates planning, designing, programming, and testing a limited application. The testing stages remained a paper exercise because LEO II remained—as far as we were concerned—a paper computer.

The diligence and care with which LEO personnel monitored their student charges was awesome. Homework was obligatory, each evening I wrote up my lecture notes so that the following day they could be checked out by my supervisor with appropriate corrections and explanations being made. I have my notes here as I write—almost 40 years later—with each page initialed by the supervisor. Exercises had to be completed, and I well remember the comforting flash of insight one evening as everything fell into place! The quality and methods of supervision pointed up an attribute that we soon recognized to be a key element of programming. Checking and rechecking of code and taking meticulous care when examining results proved to be essential components of effective computing work.

Our company had arranged for us to stay on after the course. This was both to assist with the programming of our works payroll—which was by that time well advanced—and to gather experience of "real" programming. We joined the "payroll" team led by Leo Fantl and including John

Lewis, Geoff Pye, and Mary Blood. The programming office at Elms House, Cadby Hall, was impressive only for the intellect and industry of its occupants. Physically it was a drab place, with desks drawn up in formal rows: we programmers three deep along the room facing the windows, and the seniors, Bob included, overlooking us with their backs to the light. Whether this was for their comfort, to ensure that our noses were kept to the grindstone, or merely to offer prestige I never did discover. Certainly the work was highly motivating; its intrinsic interest, together with the knowledge that we were at the forefront of great events, rendered any managerial pressure quite superfluous. Through a glass partition behind us, in its own room, grew LEO II/1, labored over by engineers with their white coats and oscilloscopes. Everyone in the programming office followed progress avidly. The great day arrived. An engineer inquired whether anyone had a program that used only half the store. We all had—or could fix it that we had! How exhilarating to get hands on!

As the machine became more available, hours of work became of no consequence. Testing went on at all hours—refreshed by the excellent Cadby Hall midnight suppers—until both the computer and programs were judged ready for the agreed payroll trials. It hadn't all been work, however. We found LEO staff to be friendly people and I recall with pleasure evenings at the homes of the Caminer and Fantl families, ice-skating sessions with Mary Blood (or was it Coombs?) and her husband, and, of course, Lyons' cricket league matches with Ron Bailey erasing smiles from the faces of the Ice-Cream Department team!

Back at our Corby base, where it was intended to install LEO II/3, there was much supporting activity. The staff was being trained, forms designed and printed, data collected, and logistic plans made for the trial runs. In these matters the O&M department was active. Heavily involved were Alex Mackie, an Australian, on transfer to the parent company, and Tony Morris, a recent graduate recruit and the first of a succession of people taken on to do systems work. So too was the Central Calculating Department (CCD), which would be responsible for data preparation and controls on data and results. Perhaps an important factor in the easy acceptance of LEO was that computing was grafted into an existing department rather than being set up as an entirely new venture. A leading light here was Jimmy Clark, soon to become Computer Manager, an astute Scot who, like many others of our nationality, had emigrated to Corby from Clydeside. Among staff and management generally there was an absence of acrimony about the LEO development—although this didn't prevent one department head being labeled by Neil Pollock as "the abominable no man"! My conception at that time was that the company had invested much effort on staff administration and had found it rewarding.

The parallel runs began. They involved a tight time schedule made more demanding by the need to complete the unaccustomed additional tasks of form-filling ("wages authorities" replacing clock cards to initiate the calculation process), data preparation, and transfer of the paper tapes and documents to London by car. Moreover, after the return of LEO-produced paychecks and accounts to Corby, detailed comparison of computer and clerical results had to be made, and appropriate amendments raised. In the main this went smoothly, although I recall one crisis following a late-in-the-day discovery at Corby of an error affecting the whole payroll. In early evening Jimmy Clark set off for London with data and results to initiate a "midnight oil" session involving the entire payroll team, closely monitored by David Caminer. Daylight had broken before the revisions reached Corby, but without any real disturbance to the timetable. Confidence in LEO grew quickly and the traditional clerical process gave way to the electronic. The workforce began to receive computer-prepared paychecks. The efficacy of LEO had been demonstrated.

One interesting innovation was "the ten bob scheme" which ultimately saved many hours of work in the wages departments. Coin handling and counting were largely abolished by LEO rounding wages up, with overpayments being deducted the following week. Of course, the idea raised objections—mainly from management—some suggesting it might be contrary to the Truck Acts and others that the employees would not have change in their pockets to get their Friday bus home!

The order for LEO II/3 having been confirmed, we turned our attention to enlarging the application portfolio. We left the LEO programming office with regrets, but with many happy and enduring memories installing ourselves at Corby in temporary accommodation comprising a windowless and often airless room at the rear of an exhibition building. Fact-finding and the bulk of management liaison for future work were to be done by O&M, headed by Neil Pollock. Job design, including programming, was the role of the programming team, which became part of the CCD (now the Computer and Calculating Department) under Jimmy Clark and within the Corby Works organization.

In retrospect this was not an ideal setup, although such tensions as became apparent were largely related to personalities—a common feature whatever the organization—and to the frustrations of O&M staff, who not having received computer training, would often have difficulty in understanding the need for key elements in the design of jobs. Eventually these difficulties evaporated as computer training became more pervasive, as mutual respect developed, and, finally, as programming was absorbed into the O&M Department. The new CCD was a remarkable social phenomenon, with people from a wide variety of backgrounds, ages, and experience working together on the whole harmoniously—again fired by the realization that we were in at the beginning of fundamental change.

Bob Kiteley and Frank Irving from O&M's Birmingham office became involved with the programming team on new developments in the fields of works stores accounting and sales invoicing for the regional warehouse network. Sometimes the limitations of LEO—small memory size, lack of alphabetical printing, and 80-column cards—called for ingenious solutions, such as the methods developed to produce invoices, via punched cards, on IBM Hectowriters. These were often team efforts engaging the skills and enthusiasm of programmers, engineers, and operational staff. Meanwhile the computer payroll was extended to further sections of the workforce, projects were begun in various aspects of cost accounting, and a start was made to evaluating designs of pipework structures. More limited progress was achieved in a production planning application that sought to develop daily digging programs for local ore quarries supplying the Corby blast furnaces. This system had largely been developed at Elms House from information supplied by the minerals planners. Later, its initial failure—often highlighted by operators abandoning excessively long runs on the forgivable assumption that a program was looping—could be seen to be due to overambitious specification and complexity. A lesson learned! Subsequently, severe curtailment of objectives enabled attention to be concentrated on the kernel of the problem and success to be achieved.

In the midst of this development activity, LEO II/3 arrived with an additional bonus. Notwithstanding its suffix, and our expectations, we had taken delivery of the first LEO to be installed outside the Lyons organization. It was housed in a special building erected on stilts above an old canteen block. Once the replacement canteen was ready, the old was demolished by the effective, although rather inelegant, method of bashing its walls with an ingot suspended on a crane. This however, had worrying although fortunately only temporary side effects. Not only did the ingot's impacts cause earthquake-like tremors to run across the floor, but they also appeared to create ripples within the mercury delay lines! Horrified, standing in front of the oscilloscopes, we watched binary digits fall out of the store!

The workload built up: dayshift, extended dayshift, two shifts, then three. For the next 13 years LEO dutifully served the company—laying a foundation of confidence in the future of business computing not only for Stewarts and Lloyds, but also helping to do so for the wider steel industry and, indeed, industry at large. (For a time, the Corby LEO almost seemed to be the focus of world attention as phalanxes of visitors from home and overseas trooped through Jimmy Clark's office!) On June 23, 1971, after—as someone calculated—consuming 2600 miles of paper tape and 124 million punched cards, LEO closed down. Fittingly, the pioneers—Raymond Thompson, David Caminer, and Neil Pollock—together with the initial programming, engineering, and operating teams, gathered for that historic and memorable event.

In a particularly personal way, LEO's impact remains. Almost 40 years ago, on that January evening in London, two Scots, Bob Caldwell and Hamish Archibald, met for the first time. Countless happy family gatherings later and after collaboration on these notes, we are still going strong.

21

The General Post Office (I)

NINIAN EADIE

The way in which a tiny band of engineers developed the first computers captures the imagination of industrial historians. However, the story of how the technology was put to work on commercial problems also deserves to be told. The dedication and skill shown by the early systems engineers and programmers was at least as remarkable as that of their engineering counterparts.

J. Lyons, the parent of LEO Computers Ltd., was a pioneer in the field of organization and methods, and developed LEO I not as an exercise in technical innovation but to improve management control in its own business. T. R. Thompson believed passionately in measuring performance against budget, and was a missionary for management by exception. When he was made responsible for LEO, he carried this business ethos into his new company.

Today, customers take it for granted that computers can be used in commerce, but in the early years LEO consultants (for there were no salesmen at that time) spent immense efforts in analyzing business processes and persuading customers that they could be handled by a computer. The business benefits were paramount in the sale, and the technology had to be overcome to achieve a successful outcome. In many ways LEO did then what IT companies would like customers to believe they do now—it sold business solutions.

The imagination of the engineers and business consultants in LEO was more than matched by the courage of the early customers who were persuaded to automate their businesses using this as yet unproven technology. One such was the General Post Office.

In the 1960s the Post Office was an organization of 400,000 employees, more than 100,000 of them postal carriers working from 23,000 post offices. In addition to the mail and telephone services, the Post Office was responsible for the Department of National Savings, which ran the Post Office Savings Bank and the Premium Bonds Office, forerunner of today's National Lottery. The Post Office also established its own bureau, the National Data Processing Service (NDPS), which was responsible, among other contracts, for the London Airport Cargo Handling System (LACES). The Post Office was one of the largest organizations anywhere in the world, and its computer projects, while not different in kind from those successfully implemented in the 1950s, were of a scale not so far attempted.

On December 16, 1964, the Post Office placed a contract for five LEO 326 computers with a total value of $7 million. The contract was announced by the then Postmaster General, Anthony Wedgwood Benn, at the Post Office headquarters in St. Martins Le Grand in the city of London. The Minister said, "The current order for delivery in 1965/66 and 1966/67 is the largest order for computers for general purpose commercial data processing so far announced in Europe." He went on to say, "This order is only an installment . . . to satisfy the Post Office's needs for computer capacity, a great deal more equipment remains to be bought."

The order was a massive vote of confidence for LEO and reflected the experience that had been gained through the use of two LEO III machines ordered in 1963 and installed in Charles House in West London and Lytham St. Annes near Blackpool in the Department of National Savings (DNS). These machines were used for Premium Bond records, the Stock Department, and GPO maintenance stores control, and for program development.

LEO III, announced in 1960, was one of the first transistor machines. LEO Computers manufactured all the electronic units and attached the best third-party peripherals it could find. LEO III made use of Ampex magnetic tape units and Anelex drum printers, and input was by means of Elliott paper tape readers. Immediate access memory was 13 μs core store with a capacity of 8192 words. The LEO 326 was a "stretched" version of LEO III with either a 2.5 or 6 μs core store, or a combination of both. The Post Office eventually installed 11 LEO 326s, each with 16,384 words of the faster 2.5 μs stores, 15 Ampex tape decks, and two Anelex printers. The price of each of these machines was more than $1.4 million. Later the Post Office also installed a number of System 4 machines.

At this time programming was done in a powerful autocode, called Intercode, a vast improvement on the machine code that had been used on earlier machines, but still labor-intensive. High-level languages had not yet gained universal acceptance, especially from users with large programs that made heavy demands on memory and performance. With the Post Office applications, where the main loops had to be traversed many thousands of times on each run, the savings to be gained by experienced programmers from working in Intercode made its choice almost automatic.

From the outset Telephone Billing was envisaged as the centerpiece of a wholly integrated complex, embracing all aspects of the telephone service from installation and maintenance to accounting. Indeed, when he made his announcement at GPO headquarters, the Postmaster General had by his side a diagram referred to as "the sky at night," which showed the master plan for computerizing all aspects of the telephone service. Telephone billing was carried out on a regional basis, eventually with two LEOs in each center. These were additionally equipped with 2000-card-per-minute Uptime readers to process the 40-column cards carrying the details of operator-connected calls. Large regions required 400,000 of these cards to be read each day.

The Post Office was by far our largest customer and commanded appropriate attention. The staffing consisted of a Senior Consultant, a Chief Programmer for each main application, a large number of systems and programming staff—as many as 80 at any one time—and, eventually, a Contracts Engineer to look after the paperwork. Programming was usually carried out by mixed teams of Post Office and LEO staff members under the direction of the LEO Chief Programmer, but some contracts, like that for the National Giro, were carried out entirely by LEO staff. Progress was reviewed monthly by David Caminer, LEO's Sales Director, and C. R. Smith, the Director of the Post Office Organization and Methods Department (later Department of Computer and Office Services, or DOCOS). At these meetings the reliability and availability of each machine was discussed, together with progress in implementing the various projects. Since IT projects did not go smoothly even in those days, these meetings were often stormy. The most common issues were slippage in development time-scales and hardware reliability problems. Briefing David Caminer for these meetings was a perilous experience, particularly so when it was in the car on the way to Post Office headquarters. On one occasion he became so incensed that he deliberately drove the wrong way up a one-way street.

The Post Office tendering procedure made use of an evaluation method of their own invention that was used to establish cost/performance curves for each competitor's equipment. The approach was based on the "Post Office work unit," a carefully constructed mix of instructions based on representative workloads. However, cost/performance did not just cover CPU performance; it also included the time taken to transfer data from magnetic tape into main store, giving a far more realistic evaluation of the machine's ability to handle the very large files required by the Post Office.

The LEO III instruction set was implemented in microcode, physically magnetic cores arranged in a matrix. This made it possible to implement powerful input/output functions and to add new instructions simply. This facility was used to develop a special "compare" instruction for the Post Office, enabling the machine to decide, in a single cycle, whether or not a record was active. This enabled the magnetic tape to be driven at the optimum speed, giving LEO a significant performance advantage in the cost/performance calculations.

Before delivery, each machine had to undergo an extensive set of trials conducted by the Post Office Engineering Department. They measured the speed of each instruction, certified the machine for electrical safety, and stress-tested the machine for two weeks using real programs.

In operation, multiprogramming was used extensively to achieve the necessary throughput, and typically three or four programs were scheduled simultaneously. This required skillful operation to ensure that the machine was kept fully loaded. Typically there would be two operators on the console and three or four loaders whose job was to service the magnetic tapes and printers. A separate job assembly area outside the computer room was set aside for batching the input and for distributing the output. In addition there were data preparation operators beyond count whose job was to punch the paper tape with additions and deletions to the master file details.

The operating system that controlled all this work was known as The Master, and was restricted to the first 4096 words of store. This was because instructions in subsequent store blocks attracted an indirect addressing overhead. The benefit of this arrangement was that you could add new facilities only by pruning unwanted undergrowth. Despite its restricted size, it seemed to deal with everything that today occupies many megabytes of main store and disk space.

Although I was not aware of it at the time, there was very little experience anywhere in the world of projects as large as those at the Post Office. As a result, the customer and the manufacturer were often learning together. In our first attempts at an application with very large files, Telephone Billing, a small programming team brought the system to readiness in a remarkably short time, but Premium Bonds proved to be far more difficult. Although it was superficially simple, it was strewn with complications, which exposed inexperience on both sides. It must also be said that the system was not improved by the intervention of the responsible government minister, who insisted that customers should be able to buy or sell bonds with numbers that were not consecutive, not an easy thing to handle on magnetic tape.

These projects were extremely large, even by today's standards, and showed up any lack of discipline in either the contractor or the user management. During the 1950s, LEO Computers had developed a well-proven implementation methodology, but even this customer did not always see the importance of sticking to it.

The methodology first required the production of a detailed Systems Specification, setting out the requirements of the application in end-user terms. This was developed by the customer in conjunction with representatives of the end-user departments. This was followed by the Program Specification, which translated the Systems Specification into the computer runs required of a batch system. This was signed off by the user department to ensure that the requirements had been fully understood. Next the Test Plan was established. Test packs were developed in parallel with design and coding. Programmers conducted module tests using their own test data, but once they were satisfied that the programs were working the whole suite was put into linked trials. During this period the program suites were run repeatedly, first against the test packs used so far, and then against large-scale data extracted from past live running for which the live output results were available. C. R. Smith was determined that no error would ever reach a customer, and as a consequence Systems Trials sometimes continued for many months before the programs were able to successfully process all the tests that had been devised. Finally, the system was run in parallel with the manual operation for a period before being cut over to live use. It typically took two calendar years and 150 person years of effort to bring such projects to large-volume live running.

The key to the success of this methodology was effective change control, and it was not until the Premium Bond and Telephone Billing Applications had been completed that the Post Office could be said to have fully put this into effect. Later projects, like the Post Office Savings Bank and the National Giro, benefited greatly from this understanding. The methodology provided a firm foundation on the basis of which the Post Office was to undertake the successful LACES project, which required, among other things, writing a new real-time operating system to handle the demands of a fully online system.

Today these projects may not appear unusual, but in the mid-1960s automating the Savings Bank, which had 22 million live accounts, to which each year 100 million deposits or withdrawals had to be applied, or Telephone Billing, with its 6 million subscribers and 26 million telephone bills a year, were remarkable feats of software engineering, bearing in mind the tools available and the lack of any professional body of experience to draw on. It also required an unusual degree of trust and commitment between customer and supplier.

A few anecdotes may help to capture the spirit of the age.

The mutual dependence of customer and supplier was tested to the limit by the project to automate the Premium Bonds Office, with its 15 million bond-holders. On the assurance of the LEO Programming Manager, based on the specification he had been given that the project would be ready on schedule, the Post Office decided to risk beginning the take-on of the large data files before the programs had been tested to completion. Accordingly, 200 members of the data preparation staff set to work on the immense data files. Unfortunately, when the programs entered linked trials, the transactions were unable to get much beyond the sixth program, and the project was postponed month by month with increasing acrimony. It became increasingly apparent that the employees engaged in punching the paper tape were losing ground to the growing pile of amendments. Eventually a difficult meeting took place in which we had to advise C. R. Smith that it would be quicker to throw away all the punching done to date and start again from scratch. Thus a very large amount of clerical effort was written off to experience.

Many of the departments that were being computerized were jumping straight from quill pen to high-tech. The Savings Bank, which happened to be a neighbor of J. Lyons in Blythe Road, Hammersmith, was certainly a case in point. It consisted of huge halls, decorated with white glazed tiles, and resembled nothing so much as an oversized public lavatory. Each hall contained hundreds of clerks whose job was to update, by hand, the index cards containing details of the customer accounts. The Premium Bond Office in Lytham St. Annes had much the same ambience. It was housed in wartime Nissen huts, each bearing the letters of the accounts for which it was responsible, such as "Ta to Tg." There were clerks whose entire life was encompassed by a single letter of the alphabet.

From time to time C. R. Smith came up with experimental projects. One such was the project to read postal orders. The assistance of John Pinkerton was procured and a machine was constructed by Crosfield Electronics to provide output signals that could be read by the computer. The serial number on each postal order was encoded in magnetic ink using CMC7, and these numbers were read by wrapping the postal order around a vacuum drum. Unfortunately, the postal orders, which were printed on flimsy security paper, were inclined to fly off the drum, requiring excellent fielding skills of the operators. Subsequently it was decided to install the readers in Chesterfield, in the English Midlands, where used postal orders were stored after encashment, and to transmit the data to Charles House using a data transmission link. This must have been one of the earliest commercial uses of data transmission.

One project that never fulfilled its promise was C. R. Smith's plans for Post Office Counter Automation. He approached LEO with a requirement for a machine to be fitted to each counter position that would be capable of processing roughly 70 different transaction types. Designs were produced by Elliott Automation and English Numbering Machines but failed to achieve the target price of $2100. Had he succeeded he would have invented the personal computer, but he was a little ahead of his time.

Printing telephone bills was extremely time-consuming using the Anelex printers, and early experiments were made using a Xeronic Printer. This printed both the variable and standing information at the same time. A machine was installed in Charles House but was never sufficiently successful to be implemented in the other regions.

More successful was the experimental work in scheduling the Post Office vans using linear programming. In addition to the mathematical aspects of the work, the programs had to embrace the full body of union rules and regulations, such as how long a driver could work without a coffee break. The programs written by the LEO Operations Research Consultant demonstrated that significant savings could be made, but the project foundered on the problems of gaining union acceptance.

Having established a considerable competence in data processing, the GPO decided that it would go into the bureau business. To achieve this, a bill had to be introduced to Parliament authorizing the change to the GPO's charter. C. R. Smith was in his element during the drafting stage, and personally shepherded it through the house. The Act was duly passed, and subsequently contracts were obtained for the Trustee Savings Banks and for the Heathrow Customs and Excise system.

At about the same time Harold Wilson, the then Prime Minister, decided that the UK should have a National Giro, which he saw as a bank for the poorer members of society. The Post Office, with its Savings Bank experience, was selected to establish the new organization from the ground up. A new building was built in Bootle, a depressed area near Liverpool, and four System 4 computers were installed. The computer implementation was subcontracted to English Electric LEO as a turnkey project and we marshalled all the experience gathered over the previous five years to tackle the project. We fought hard on the system design and on change control, insisting that one team be assigned to the project as originally specified and another to deal with changes and amendments. By the time the project went live, the second team was as big as the first, and there were more than 80 systems and programming employees in total. The charge for the whole project, as I recall, was $500,000.

The National Giro project demonstrated that systems engineering and programming had come of age. Even very large jobs could be accurately estimated and implemented on time and within budget. The disciplines developed at the Post Office for offer evaluation, acceptance testing, and systems specification and programming had been adopted right across the government; indeed, they had become the professional practice of the industry at large. As we moved on to the big real-time systems, such as LACES, we were able to draw on these professional skills and apply them successfully to radically new technologies.

Looking back, the Post Office was the best kind of customer: it set stretching goals, made intolerable demands, and insisted on value for money—but it was tolerant when despite our very best efforts, things did not always turn out for the best. Perhaps we learned at the customer's expense, but how else do you start a new industry?

C. R. Smith was an unusual man for a civil servant. He liked to see himself as a thorn in the flesh of his superiors. However, he was also a man of vision and one who took considerable risks to achieve his objectives. He gave us a hard time when projects ran late or machines fell over, but he also defended us to his masters. We didn't see these political battles, but in retrospect he must have needed a lot of skill to retain the continued support of the users and of the Post Office Board when things went badly. David Caminer was a man of equal determination, who fiercely believed in meeting his commitments to the customer and expected his staff to show an equal dedication. Both fought strongly for their principles during the monthly progress meetings, but they were seldom unable to agree on a common plan when they lunched afterward at the Prospect of Whitby on the Thames riverside at Wapping. Neither was properly appreciated by their less imaginative superiors, for they did not suffer fools gladly—no knighthood for C. R. Smith, and no ICL Board Directorship for David Caminer. However, together they may be said to have laid the foundation of commercial computing in the UK.

22

The General Post Office (II)

MURRAY LAVER

In 1956 I moved from the Organization & Efficiency Branch of the Post Office Engineering Department to replace Jim Merriman, who had been assigned to the Treasury. The Post Office administration was then evaluating offers for computing equipment to process the payroll of London postal carriers, and it was suddenly assailed by doubts about whether any of the new-fangled machines available actually worked. As an electronic engineer at headquarters, I was given a week to assess the six machines under consideration. I hastened to visit each company, including LEO Computers at Cadby Hall.

I remember being impressed with the fact that, although LEO was derived from Cambridge University's EDSAC, it had been modified to adapt it to commercial work—for instance, to do mixed-radix arithmetic—and that its construction had been somewhat (though not completely) tidied up. I watched, and admired, its quasi-online input as a group of telephone operators listened to managers of Lyons teashops in London who rang at prearranged time to report only what variations each required from the standard seasonally adjusted daily order. The keyboard operators entered the information as they listened, recording the data directly on punched cards for input to the computer.

LEO Computers had planned to use magnetic tape for file storage, but had been let down by its subcontractor (STC), which had mistakenly expected the recording of binary digits to be easy compared with high-fidelity music. The problem lay not there but in the need to start, stop, and back up the tape precisely in a few milliseconds, and to continue to do so frequently and reliably over long periods. The Post Office was keen to gain experience in magnetic tape, which it correctly saw as the way ahead, and the contract was reluctantly awarded elsewhere.

In 1963 I took the place that Merriman had held at the Treasury, and in 1965 moved to the fledgling Ministry of Technology to head its Computer Division. Mintech's aim was twofold: firstly, to promote the use of computers in education, business, and industry, and secondly to press for the use of British-made machines wherever possible. Computers were then seen as the high-tech end of electronic engineering, and LEO Computers suffered the disadvantage of being outside the accepted group of suppliers of electronic equipment for defense systems and for scientific use.

That particular disadvantage had operated against LEO as early as the 1950s, when the government's National Research Development Corporation (NRDC) was channeling support to Ferranti, Elliott, and EMI—but not to LEO. In Britain, generally, we were slow to realize that the computer market for commercial work would outgrow and greatly exceed the markets for science and engineering, and also that winning that market would depend much more on understanding and supporting business users' needs than on electronic wizardry. LEO Computers did so understand, having grown directly out of a business user's needs.

In the early days, government was a trendsetter in the use of computers, but unfortunately most government users believed that computers were highly complex electronic machines and were obstinately reluctant to trust any but the established electrical engineering companies they knew. They were especially skeptical that a machine produced by a catering company could meet their needs.

The Post Office, however, had moved on from payroll and, under Nick Smith, its dynamic Director of Computing and Office Services (DOCOS), had begun to install the much improved LEO 326 to handle telephone billing—a massive and crucial operation.

In 1968 Nick Smith retired and I returned from Mintech to take his place in what had become the National Data Processing Service (NDPS). The telephone system was expanding rapidly, and the corresponding billing load was growing beyond the capacity of the five LEO 326s then installed. By that date, also, LEO Computers had been absorbed into ICL after a series of mergers.

ICL was developing its new (2900) series to rationalize the somewhat diverse product line it had inherited from its constituent bodies. NDPS was busy designing a new telephone billing system with the 2900 series in mind. However, the continuing rapid growth of billings required urgent action to hold the fort until the new system could become operational in 1979. Several local authorities were then replacing their LEO 326 machines and NDPS bought some of these second-hand, but overload still threatened. Almost my first act on arriving in NDPS was to ask ICL to manufacture two more LEO 326s; they were understandably horrified, but there was no way in which we could complete the programming and acceptance of a 2900-based system in time. Reluctantly ICL agreed, and we agreed not to advertise the fact that they were producing an obsolete model, or to imply that NDPS preferred this "bird in the hand" to the promise of a future new model.

At the peak of their use, in 1976, NDPS was operating 11 LEO 326s in six centers carrying heavy loads of billing work:

Center	Machines	Load(hrs/week)
Bristol	2	87
Cardiff	1	79
Derby	2	212
Edinburgh	1	116
Kensington	4	190
Portsmouth	1	92
Totals	11	776

In 1969 I remember taking an American visitor to our Kensington center, which then had only two very busy LEO 326s installed in distinctly workday accommodation. He told me proudly that "in the States" they now had computers that could run more than one program at a time. I led him across to the Shift Leader of one of the LEOs and asked what was being processed. She replied, apologetically, that only three programs were running together at present—two independent billing files and an error-checked input to a data-file online from Chesterfield. She was annoyed that the data to run the fourth program scheduled had been held up.

Lessons

Three morals can be drawn from the LEO story:
1. Do not judge a horse by its stable; look at its parentage. A good thing can come out of a teashop! But in the shop's back room you need people like T. R. Thompson, David Caminer, John Pinkerton, and Maurice Wilkes. Government money for R&D should be put behind good people, rather than poured into long-established organizations.

2. LEO Computers suffered by having no previously established customer base on which to build, unlike BTM and Powers Samas in accounting and Ferranti, Elliott, and others in defense electronics.
3. The initial, obvious, application area for a new technique may well not prove to be its principal use; thus for computers it was not science or engineering, but commercial data processing.

Coda

LEO was the first computer to be designed specifically for office use; that was its strength in application, but a weakness in securing a wider acceptance. LEO was an excellent workhorse, and served the Post Office well. It was a pity that LEO's distinctive contribution to the development of computing in Britain was diminished when LEO Computers was absorbed into a larger conglomerate.

23
Freemans Mail Order

MIKE JACKSON

Introduction

This chapter describes that first "complete" application of a computer to a very large agency catalog mail-order business. This all took place between 1964 and 1969. I think it to be an extraordinary success story by any standard worldwide, and especially so in light of later experiences of large companies' and public bodies' difficulties in achieving major benefits to their operations, right up to the present day.

Looking back, the success was possible only as a result of a probably unique combination of circumstances. At the time, our heads were down working very hard on achieving the objectives, and we did not realize how privileged we were to have such possibilities.

The relevant factors were:

- The "ethos" of a private business, although Freemans had just been "floated" in 1963.

- The direct hands-on management style of the directors.

- The lack of a senior management level initially. In 1964, over 60 of the staff thought they reported directly to David Jones, the MD.

- The directors giving their absolute backing to the computer team, and in particular, bringing me in at a level effectively above all except the directors.

- My natural identification with the early J. Lyons concepts of applying computer methods to a business as a whole.

- My own training in, and admiration of, LEO-designed methods and disciplines for systems design and implementation.

- The LEO 326 computer, which had at the time a large competitive lead in sheer computing power, magnified by its special microprogrammed facilities.

- Peter Smith, recruited initially as Chief Programmer, who proved to be for me the perfect partner.

- The weekly management meeting, at which every matter of importance to company operations was raised. It ensured excellent coordination across departments.

- My own determination to achieve the objectives, and my orientation to customer service.

Readers will be aware of the substantial inflation since the 1960's. Present equivalents of the monetary amounts quoted in this account would be about roughly 15 times greater.

Agency Mail Order

This had grown greatly in the 1950s, with GUS, Littlewoods, Grattan's, and Freemans being the largest operators. It depended on a social phenomenon that was curiously British. Other countries had well-developed catalog mail order, especially the United States, with Sears, but these were straightforward operations from which the customer ordered and paid directly for items selected. In the UK, literally millions of women were running businesses from their homes, selling to family and friends on credit, being responsible for collection, and forwarding of installments weekly. They produced proper paperwork accounting showing the amount collected from each customer.

Agents ordered goods to be sent on approval, and no payment for goods was due until the customer had seen and accepted them. The agent was responsible for accounting all goods ordered by reporting sales or returning unsold items. For this work the agent retained 10 percent of cash collected as commission, together with the postage cost of goods she returned. This she accounted for on the weekly payment slip.

It seems almost extraordinary that such large businesses were not just viable but expanding greatly. By far the biggest balance sheet item of the companies was the customer debt being paid by weekly installments. The recovery was totally dependent on the diligence of millions of women throughout the country.

Just after the war, Freemans annual turnover was about $2.8 million. In 1964 Freemans had sales of $84 million, $8.4 million in pretax profit, over 200,000 agents, and about 5 percent of the total market. Large, expensive color catalogs were sent to all agents twice a year, containing about 50,000 different items for sale. Each shoe or dress size was a different item for customer ordering, stock management, and dispatch. The average was about seven customers for each agent.

In general, items were sold on 20 weeks revolving credit to each customer. That is, each customer paid one-twentieth of the total outstanding balance each week. The agent accounted for cash received from each customer each week and kept a record of the outstanding balance.

Freemans Operation

In 1964, around 100,000 order forms with an average of three items were received each week. Freemans were changing over to biweekly payments by agents, which meant about 100,000 payment slips were received each week. In addition, because of the goods on approval basis, each item sent had to be recorded subsequently on a sales or returns slip.

The precomputer methods in force were state of the art. Business success obviously depended on efficiency and accuracy on:

1. Handling and dispatching orders for goods.

2. Monitoring agency debt and stock on approval.

3. Stock control to minimize losses from both stock-outs and leftovers.

4. Early recognition of bad debt liabilities, to stop further dispatches.

5. Recognition of uneconomic agents, to avoid cost of expensive catalogs.

In addition, the overall service, and catalog range and pricing, had to be attractive to agents and their customers in a most competitive marketplace.

Clearly, large numbers of well-organized staff were needed to handle the volume. About 4500 were employed at the South London site (the Christmas party was held in the Royal Albert Hall). Of these, 350 were required just to open the mail, some starting at 5:30 a.m., and that department had the responsibility of handling the cash.

Many of the staff were part-time and most were women. In the Agency Administration Department, one full-time clerk with a full-time assistant administered about 500 agents. The assistant's responsibility was to keep all paperwork relating to each agent properly filed. The clerk had the task of going through the files continuously to review each agent each month to:

1. Check that correct cash had been received.
2. Check that all goods sent on approval had been accounted for in a reasonable time.
3. Issue "stop" notices to the order handling department if bad debt was indicated.
4. Deal with all correspondence from the agents in her section.
5. Appraise each agent each half year to decide whether an inadequate volume of business and/or bad debt should remove the agent from the list for dispatch of the next catalog.

The Computer Project

By 1962 most major mail-order companies were considering the possibility of using computers in their work. Goods invoicing was generally being handled by punched-card tabulators, and it seemed a natural progression to move to computer systems in this area, which could be readily extended to stock records and accounts. Freemans invited offers from the major suppliers, of which there were many at the time. They engaged the consultants Urwick Diebold to advise them on this.

In 1963 they placed the order for a LEO 326 system, at a cost of about $1.4 million, with a budget of $700,000 for systems development.

I had been with LEO Computers since 1957, initially as a programmer. I had been involved in a very wide range of projects, and from 1962–63 had managed, successfully, the LEO tender and subsequent contract negotiations for the initial GPO order for two LEO 326 machines to a total value of $3.5 million. Despite this success, I had for some time realized that the creation of really successful systems can be achieved only from within an organization. As a result of my representing this to my boss, David Caminer, Sales Director at LEO, he recommended me to Freemans. I joined them as Computer Manager in May of 1964, a few months before delivery of the equipment.

While the original Freemans request was for a system powerful enough to handle both the agent ordering/stock control work and the agents' accounts operations, it was made clear almost as soon as I joined that they had no confidence that agents' accounts could be computerized. There was considerable nervousness about this among directors (and sheer disbelief in some) and in all senior agency administration staff.

In any event, the immediate need was to get the order handling, dispatch note/invoicing, and stock records work under way. The core operation of this was at the time done with a bank of 35 punched-card tabulators, many in a worn-out state. The dispatch notes had the agents' names and addresses printed by a large bank of Addressograph machines, each agent having a plate for this purpose, which carried a "stop" tag if the agency clerk considered that payments and/or clearances of items on approval were overdue.

Goods Orders/Invoices and Stock Records

In objectives and structure, this work was straightforward. In practical terms, the sheer volume of stock items, agents for name and address details, and order lines to handle each day meant that we could not make any significant implementation step without the most careful appraisal of all design assumptions, proving them not just by system tests but also by pilot running. Everything had to be done in manageable steps, as the volumes prevented any possibility of large-scale parallel running.

The LEO equipment was installed in mid-1965, and in September that year we started handling the first pilot merchandise section for invoicing. Addressing continued to be by plates, because we would never have tried file setup for both merchandise and agents' details for the same development step. Quite apart from tailoring the job, large numbers of staff had to be reoriented to new methods with each step.

By mid-November we were invoicing about 20 percent of the volume, and held it there for the large pre-Christmas demand, when staff would be under great pressure. Full transfer to the system was completed section by section during the early months of 1966.

We were ready by then to take on the agents' name and address records from the plates.

At the time, there was no technology available for direct data entry into computer records. Raw data entry had to be by some intermediate medium, generally punched cards or paper tape. Almost universal use was made at the time of a two-step punch/verify process, to keep entry errors at an acceptable level. While at Freemans we did this for file setup and amendment, and a major cost benefit was achieved by avoiding this two-step verification process for the volume transactions.

We added a check letter to all goods' item numbers and agents' numbers. Data entry was by Olivetti accounting machines, which could check the numbers at key-in time. They could also check batch totals and number of documents in batch. Nearly all orders were for single items. We proved that, with these checks made by the entry machines, punch/

verify duplication was unnecessary. This was to prove even more valuable later, when we processed agents' cash, as the machines were able to
total the cash slips to prove that cash amounts had been correctly entered.

These days, it may be difficult to contemplate major computer applications without some form of direct access to records. It needed the next generation of the 1970s for this to be possible. We did install two Autolectors, a
form of mark-sensing document reader, to enable agency office staff to
request printouts of agent records, set or remove stops on dispatches, etc.,
giving an overnight service.

Approval Stock Management

The whole rationale of the business was based on the agent's ability to
order goods for customers on a sale or return basis, with no cash liability
until a sale was confirmed. As noted above, the agent claimed the costs
of sending unwanted goods back.

At any one time, in 1965 volumes, total uncleared approval at cost price
was over $2.8 million. Business success obviously depended on monitor-
ing the age and amounts of uncleared approval held by each agent to
send reminders and, where appropriate, stop further dispatches. The
200,000 agents were split up among seven offices, not all at the headquarters site, and then to sections handling 250 to 750 agents, according to the
clerks' experience and skill and whether they were part- or full-time.

It was clearly a major task in paper handling and filing to route a copy
of each dispatch note, sales note, and return note to the appropriate
agent's file, quite apart from the soul-destroying clerical task of marking
off each item from the dispatch note when sold or returned. Only when
that had been done could the routing checking of each agent's approval
holding be done. Inevitably, there was a significant level of document
loss and filing error.

It was an elementary task for the new computer system to keep records
by agent of goods when printing dispatch notes. As soon as we had completed the entry agents' details of name and address, credit-worthiness,
etc., we started to process the sales and return slips and keep up-to-date
records of uncleared approval for each agent. In system development
terms this was elementary, but in impact, especially psychological impact,
it was enormous.

As always, we introduced the operational change by first pilot-run-
ning a small section in parallel. Then, after applying any lessons learned
to the systems and procedures, we went to full live-running the small
section under close management monitoring, and then extended the job
stage by stage across the business.

Having started to keep approval stock records on the system, we took a couple of agency sections, that is about 1000 agents, with the office supervisor's close monitoring, and simply withheld the dispatch, sales, and return notes, and made available to them computer report of excessive or overaged approval and an overnight enquiry service to enable them to deal with queries.

Since this removed 70 percent of the paperwork handling and filing in the sections involved, as well as alleviating the tedious routine scanning, it was immediately sought after by all who were shown it. We came nearest to overreaching ourselves on this one, by succumbing to pressure to stop filing sales notes on a company-wide basis before we had established proper trained capacity in data entry. We built up a big backlog of unprocessed sales, causing some nervousness among some directors—but we made it.

Suddenly, agency staff could handle double the number of agents! The company had good management figures on age and distribution of over $2.8 million of assets and on returns and sales rates. Because the routine scanning was now impartial and automatic, approval stock as a percentage of sales started reducing.

In no more than about three months from the first pilot tests, literally thousands of staff came to have direct experience with the way a well-designed system can change, for the better, their whole working environment.

Yet it was conceptually, only a simple step on the back of the large job of a goods dispatching system. While that initial job had halved the staff for order processing, this had been an expected benefit from installing the equipment and had little impact otherwise.

Agency Accounting

There were serious doubts, indicated above, of the potential value of a computer system to agency administration. These did not just stem from the wariness of computers and fears of inadequacy in staff at all levels, though they continue to plague businesses today.

There was also a justified respect, which I shared, for the efficiency of the existing agents' payment slip system. The form design, coupled with the method of stapling them in the files partially overlapped, enabled a rapid eye-scanning appraisal of the history of payments made by each customer. I do not think that there was any serious doubt about our ability to set up a system to record agents' cash payments and keep records of outstanding debt. But since clerks did not do any transcription of the information on the slip as submitted by the agent, how could it be economic to employ staff to transcribe the information into computer records?

More fundamentally, the success of the whole business depended absolutely on the individual appraisal of agents at the time of catalog issue. The business would quickly be ruined if it acquired too much bad debt, or bore the costs of sending catalogs to too many uneconomic agents. It would just as quickly fail if, on the other hand, it arbitrarily shut too many off, thereby cutting its volume of business and writing off agents. They were very expensive to recruit.

At the time I joined, the consultants had been asked to prepare a pilot scheme to assess the possibility of processing agents' accounts. The job in course of preparation was no more than an accounts recording system, and no serious addressing of the above points had been made. That work was abandoned.

After being shown around all departments on joining, it was my custom, once a week or so, to go into an agency office just to "sniff the air" to be aware of their pressures, to look at what one or two clerks were actually doing. In my mind a real breakthrough was developing. There was no way that I could convey in words my mental picture, and I certainly could not convince anyone. All this was in the background while the initial developments were monopolizing everyone's attention.

Peter Smith, as always, supported me, and following the success of the approval stock system the relationship with both directors and senior agency staff was excellent. I simply requested and immediately received approval to use a section of 500 agents to experiment on, for the full-time release of an excellent agents' office supervisor, Mrs. Thompson, and my wife, Helen, to write the agency accounts computer program. The response to that last request was, "We are a family company, aren't we?"

Helen had also been at LEO Computers, where we had met, and had been responsible for all service bureau programming and over 50 professional programmers. At the time, she was at home looking after our first child.

This job, agents' accounts, was the big one, all or nothing. It was an opportunity to show how computer systems really could serve a business.

We used a weighted average system, known as "exponential smoothing" to appraise the performance of individual customers and agents against expectations. There were separate factors for payments, return rate, and bad debt.

When the pilot scheme was working, it was easy to show that the cost of entering payment slip details into the computer records was significantly less than distributing and clipping the slips into the correct agents' files. It was also evident that the methods I had designed for systematic checking by the computer of agents' work was certainly no less effective than those of the clerks in identifying agents requiring reminders or other action. By automatically sending first- and second-stage reminders, agency office work was further reduced.

This, in conjuction with the ever-increasing difficulty of recruiting a sufficient number of staff at an economic rate in the London area in the 1960s (all our competitors were based in the north, where clerical and office costs were significantly lower), gained the approval to transfer all agents' accounts records to the system.

The direct clerical outcome of the method changes was dramatic. A full-time agency clerk could now handle over 2000 agents, and had a much more interesting job. She had to deal only with correspondence and exception reports, and had little of the routine slog.

Impact on Business Management

Just as the acquisition of necessary information for handling orders and dispatches gave us the basis for the dramatic benefit for extending into approval stock management, so the recording of agents' payment details completed the records needed on which to base quite a different order of contribution to the management of the business.

As an example, the need to appraise each agent each half-year to determine who justified the issue of the next catalog had been thought of as essentially a human judgment task. However, the changing criteria had to be explained to office supervisors and then to the hundreds of clerks who had to apply them. These in turn were inevitably of varied quality and were under pressure of work from many directions.

We developed the *v factor*, which was a figure representing the annual value of each agent. The machine put into a simple formula the sales, bad debt, returns, and length of service. Each time the catalog was issued, the formula was reappraised and a schedule printed analyzing the number of agents above each value of the factor. Two values, v1 and v2, were decided by a group of just three people. Agents below v1 would not receive a catalog. Those between v1 and v2 would receive a catalog with a letter of special promotion. Those above v2, the great majority would be sent the new catalog normally. The exact number of catalogs required would be known.

All that was required to implement this was for one person in the computer department to be told the decided values for v1 and v2, who would ensure that the appropriate two sets of address labels were printed. These labels were then sent direct to the catalog dispatching section of the warehouse. Literally, a few working hours of top management had replaced many thousands of clerks' hours in the agency office. Even more important, the computer was a most obedient implementor of policy. This operation alone was regarded as a significant contributor to operating profit by its impartial filtering out of uneconomic agents.

Who were the three people mentioned above? They were Ralph Aldred, Finance Director; Peter Smith, who by that time was directly responsible to me for all Agency Administration; and me.

Similarly, rules for sending out reminder letters for late payments or approval clearance and for putting stops on further orders were decided by a small top management group. Implementation of their decisions required only one programmer to spend an hour or two making the necessary changes to the system, and from the next day on, the hundreds of such actions taken each day would be in accordance with the new policy. By 1968, just three years after the LEO had been delivered, we had turned around the whole orientation of thousands of people's work. During a period in which absolute volumes of transactions and number of agents increased by 50 percent, we had:

1. Reduced the actual staff numbers by 20 percent, i.e., almost halved the staff requirement per transaction.

2. Given the staff much better working conditions and more interesting work.

3. Given top management the information and the tools to enable direct control of the major factors affecting profitability.

In that year, 1968, I was appointed a Director.

Warehousing and Goods Dispatch

During the developments in office procedures described above, there had been little effect on the warehouse operation. Its methods were comparable with the office methods of 1964, that is, heavily labor-intensive. The continued expansion of volume had caused separate premises to be opened, with a consequent increase in carriage costs from the inevitable split of agents' orders into more than one parcel. Further pressure in the mid-1960s resulted in taking a disused tram depot in Charlton in 1966 for a large section of merchandise, which inevitably further encroached on operating margins and management coordination.

However, in the early 1960s just as the directors had been very forward-looking in addressing the future needs of office operation, there had been parallel studies on warehouse rationalization and mechanization. In 1966 they appointed a warehouse manager from Ford to take responsibility for both ongoing warehouse operations and the plans for modernization.

His style did not fit the company very well, and he was replaced in 1968. He was, by then, well underway with detailed methods and equipment planning. He left at about the time contracts were placed for a completely new $8.4 million center and its mechanized equipment to be built on a green field site at Peterborough.

It doesn't take much imagination to see the task. Quite apart from the need to provide for future expansion, we had to cope with the volume arising from the 50,000 stock lines in a current catalog, plus another 100,000 lines of items arriving for the next catalog and left over from the last, and the seasonal lines carried over the intervening catalog.

Stock items were of almost every conceivable shape, size, and weight to occupy racking. A typical agent's order would require just three items to be collected from anywhere in a warehouse 350 yards across and put into one parcel. About 30,000 such parcels were to be assembled, packed, labeled, and dispatched each day, with serious marketing and customer relation problems in the event of errors or delays.

The newly designed operation depended absolutely on each day's orders from agents being analyzed and scheduled by the computer. The complete day's dispatches were split up into batches of 20 minutes work for one packer. For the particular day, the computer would then decide how many packing stations needed to be staffed for the work to be done in the scheduled number of hours. This was typically about 30 stations. Each 20-minute batch would then be allotted to a particular packing station. Goods for the first 20-minute batch for all stations were then re-sorted to the particular racking area where they were stored, and "picking lists" printed for each area. These enabled goods to be picked and routed to the appropriate packer. The picking lists were in the form of self-adhesive labels to be stuck onto the items, which were placed on the conveyor system to the packing area. The conveyors from the picking areas merged the goods into four streams, at which an operator read the label for each item and keyed in the required packing station, which routed it correctly.

The computer printed the dispatch note/address label sets in packing batch order, so each packer had just the documents and labels for the 20 minutes work in order to select from the delivered items the correct ones to pack for each parcel.

The warehouse manager received a full analysis of the next day's work each afternoon and was notified of the number of batches, the number of packing stations to be staffed, and the workload on each picking area. The total warehouse staff was reduced from 3000 to 1500.

Other Departments

Of course, the more normal expected benefits were received by other areas in the company.

Merchandise departments were responsible for selection, ordering, and stock levels of catalog items. They had been maintaining their own stock records for stock control purposes, independently from those used by the order processing department for dispatch availability. They came to accept the computer stock records for their needs, and in addition received proper analysis of demand and returns rates, low and excessive stock warnings, item group profitability, etc.

The marketing department was responsible for advertising and agent recruitment. It had been accustomed to receiving analyses of response from advertisements. We were able to expand this greatly by further analyzing agent quality. Information on sales volumes, longevity, returns rates, and bad debts from agents recruited from different journals or newspapers, at different times of year, or from different geographical areas, etc., were made available by computer analysis. This much improved the average economics of agent recruitment.

Management accounts were transformed. From all the detailed records of agency debt, warehouse and approval stock, and cost and selling prices for each item, together with all the normal company accounting transaction records, we could run off a profit and loss accounts and balance sheets for the company at any time.

Overall

Looking back now, in comparison with the scene today, it continues to awe me that such a large organization was completely turned around in almost every respect in just five years. In particular, there were no difficult people relationships. The reorganization was done without disturbance to staff morale, and we were able to avoid significant compulsory redundancy, except in the London warehouse staff when that operation was moved to Peterborough.

Yet at the start, I was the only person of thousands who had any vision of what they were going to get. You could say that their trust was naïve! The fact was that we did everything in small steps, enabling a fully justified confidence to develop. In the early days there was no strong company middle management, which so often these days stands in the way of the kinds of computer application we all believed in at LEO.

I visited Grattan's in both 1964 and 1970. Though competitors, the directors of the two companies had a good personal relationship. On the first visit, Grattan's were ahead in using a computer system of invoicing. At the second visit, they still had not implemented any form of agents' accounting, and there was still great skepticism on this among management. They were studying computer requirements to support mechanized warehousing. But the most staggering thing to me was that they were employing a staff of 60 systems developers! We had never had more than 15, and had achieved how much? Perhaps 100 times more real contribution?

The facts show that Freemans were able in the 1970s to be the most profitable and fastest growing in the sector. Quality and speed of service and operating cost efficiency all fed through to the marketplace. But how would you value the most exceptional factor of all? That was the capability the system gave for three or four people not only to be informed sufficiently, but to provide the tool to effect decisions on all major business management controls without conveying the requirements to sometimes hundred of others for action.

Two little snippets of fact:

1. The impartial, systematic appraisal of agents, and the action automatically taken, caused a reduction in average debt and approval stock that more than covered the whole capital cost of the equipment and systems development. The very large benefits to operating costs, service level to agents, management control, etc., cost nothing.

2. Quite apart from actually doing more than all the work that was possibly expected when the LEO was ordered in 1963, we also used the same machine in 1970 to perform all the scheduling work for the new warehouse on a very tight daily schedule on much larger volumes.

These may qualify for world records!

24
The Royal Dockyards

REG CANN

The cost accounting department of the four Royal Dockyards has a long history in the mechanized manipulation of data. There were punched-card installations at Chatham and Portsmouth as far back as the early 1930s. Their tasks covered payroll, including the calculation of various types of payment by results and the costing of labor, material, and services (cranes, docks, motor transport, electric current, and so on). The volume of the tasks was large by any standards, since the payroll at each of the two larger yards was over 20,000 and the material transactions covered all issues to and returns from the many centers of activity in the Dockyards, the Fleet, and Fleet Establishments resulted in around 30,000 transactions per week at each yard. Devonport embraced punched-card processing in the early 1950s and Rosyth in the late 1950s. The punched-card installation at each yard employed about 60 people, known as *machine grades:* 30 on data preparation, punching and verifying cards and 30 on the operation of the machines manipulating the cards. There were sorters, collators, interpolators, tabulators, and cross-adding punches. For visitors, the installations were most impressive, with much physical activity. The machines, supplied by Powers Samas, used the more attractive round and oval holes in cards instead of the more commonly used square ones.

In the mid-1950s, Powers Samas, later merged into ICT, produced the PCC, the Program Controlled Computer, and the three Dockyards, Portsmouth, Devonport, and Chatham, took these on board. The PCC used punched-card input and output. It did not have a printer, but it could hold a program of 160 instructions held in the form of rivets in boards. The program was written in machine language and converted to binary. This was then expressed on the program boards by the presence or absence of a rivet. Information was stored on a magnetic drum containing four tracks, each with 40 words. The PCC was a valve-based machine, generating a great deal of heat that had to be ducted away, and was extremely temperamental, so much so that before each operational run we ran a test pack and checked the results physically to ascertain what sort of a mood the machine was in that day. However, it could calculate income tax of all types in one run, a task that had previously taken about 30 operations through the various punched-card machines. It was marvelous, but it was temperamental and its rivets sometimes needed to be cleaned with erasers.

Choosing the Computer

That was the position when visits to the Business Efficiency Exhibitions of 1960 and 1961 made us realize that rapid progress was being made in computing technology, and if we wanted to remain in the forefront then we had to replace our equipment. Top management was convinced, and a small team of four people was set up in Portsmouth in 1962. The task was formulated, which was made easier by the fact that we had a long experience in the use of sequential card files. In 1963 the team moved to London for 18 months for negotiation with the various computer manufacturers. We had discussions with 11 manufacturers: English Electric, EMI, ICT, Honeywell, NCR, Burroughs, Remington Rand, De La Rue Bull, AEI, IBM, and LEO Computers Ltd.

As we got into these discussions, it became clear to us that, while they were trying to sell us hardware of which they well knew the technical capabilities, not all of them were knowledgeable in the ways in which the machines could be used to process business data, or indeed had the software to do so. LEO Computers were well equipped here. They had the practical experience of business processing, proven software, a high-level language (CLEO), a proven compiler, and a proven operating system. None of the other manufacturers could match this.

There was one particular area of difficulty to which we needed to apply ourselves—data preparation. The working week in the Dockyards ended on Friday afternoon, but work cards, showing for each worker the tasks, suitably coded, on which they been employed, were not completed and physically collected together until Friday evening. Consequently, with the time necessary to capture those data on punching machines, costing information was not available to the Dockyard Management until the middle of the following week. We had to improve on that.

It was our good fortune that we came across the Autolector. We had looked at some bar-making devices and we had practical experience with mark-sensed punch cards. Woolworths and football betting companies were experimenting and Lyons had the Lector, which read bar marks on forms fed to the reader by hand. Lector was offline but Lyons were working on an automatic paper feed and intended to put the machine online. This interested us very much, and it turned out to be the solution to our problem.

The 11 manufacturers were reduced to a short list of four: NCR, Honeywell, ICT, and LEO. We entered into more detailed discussions to determine what configuration would be required to carry out our tasks, timings, availability of hardware and software, prices, maintenance and serviceability, and the many other factors we needed to take into consideration.

As was to be expected, we had to convince the Treasury that what we intended to do was economically sound. We were required to produce a detailed costing over a projected 10-year period. Unless the costing showed profit over the existing system, then our chances of getting the money for the hardware were pretty remote. The costing had to include the capital cost of the equipment, of air conditioning which was considerable, of systems and programming work, of data preparation and operating, of clerical staff using the system, of depreciation of equipment, and so on. In addition, a Treasury official was assigned to the team to satisfy himself that the costings were comprehensive and reasonable, thereby safeguarding public funds.

LEO emerged as the winner, an important factor being the Autolector, which would produce a significant reduction in the cost of data preparation. In addition to this, we were impressed with the quality of the LEO systems advisers and their practical experience in commercial processing work. Two machines were ordered for the Portsmouth and Devonport Dockyards. They were LEO IIIs, and each configuration contained one Autolector, six tape decks, two printers, two card readers, one card punch, and 12K long words of core. The total cost of the two machines was around $1.25 million, quite a bit of money in those days.

Preparing the System

The systems and programming team was increased from 4 to 12, all of them specially selected. After a programming course at Portsmouth and

London in July of 1964, the team set up shop at Cambridge Barracks, Portsmouth, and carried out more detailed work. We had the services for a year or so of an experienced LEO programmer, on hire from LEO Computers. It was a well-knit team, young keen, exuberant, and extremely capable. They were recruited from staff who were already experienced in running the work to be computerized (payroll and costing), but had no previous systems or programming experience. The team later contained two blind programmers, also trained by LEO, who had devised compilation and training facilities in Braille. The investment was worthwhile. The guide dog, Rustler, became a full member of the team, the most relaxed member.

It was recognized that the interface between the computer operations and the customer, in this case the Finance Manager of the Dockyard, was crucial to the success of the venture. A small Clerical Procedures Team was therefore set up to ensure that the customer's requirements were met and to instruct and train the customer in the effective use of the system. The relationship tended to be confrontational, but it did contribute considerably to the smoothness of the operation.

There followed a period of intense systems and programming activity. The first LEO III machine was delivered to Portsmouth in November 1965, and the second to Devonport in mid-1966. Up to then, we had been using the LEO Company's machine in London for compiling and trials. The delivery of our machine improved remarkably the turn-around time and accelerated our progress.

Autolector

We had taken one calculated risk. When we placed the order early in 1964, the Autolector was not fully operational, and as far as I can remember was still being developed from the Lector. However, from all the information we could gather and taking into account the experience, reputation, and ability of the people developing it, we formed the opinion that it was a risk worth taking, since the benefits to be gained were so great. Our faith was justified. We did have a great deal to learn on its operational use. We had very good professional advice and help from the Stationery Office in selecting the most suitable (and economical) type of paper to be used in the printing. Different types of paper and thicknesses were examined for luminosity, static content, and toughness.

The registration of printing was crucial, and only a handful of firms claimed to be capable of printing to the accuracy required. Even so, there ensued a considerable period of trial and error in the production of early prototypes before both the firms finally involved and the team were satisfied that the very precise standards of print could be consistently maintained. This was because the control marks the on side of the form that triggered the optical reading needed to be printed to an accuracy of ten thousandths of an inch, as did the squareness of the printing across the form.

Forms were first drawn up by hand at four times normal size and after checking were photographed down to the required size. In this way the necessary accuracy was more readily achieved. Not only the proofs, but also a sample of every new batch of forms, had to be checked with an optical micrometer. It was time-consuming and tedious, but absolutely necessary.

Recording Work and Time

I should mention here the Recording Sections in the Dockyards. The Finance Managers employed Recorders of Work who supervised the Dockyards' attendance recording procedure, and recorded on work cards the times that each worker spent on each task—refits of RFA and RN ships, maintenance, storekeeping, repayment, etc.—and the measurement of work completed leading to payment by results bonuses. It was the Recorders responsibility to convert this information into bar marks on Work Card and Times & Absence documents to be read by the Autolector. The documents were produced for each worker each week by the computer, showing name, Yard number, center of activity, and so on, both in plain language and in bar-marked form for subsequent reading on the Autolector. It was called a turn-around document.

After printing, the documents were dispatched to the Recorders of Work throughout the Yard. A separate Time & Absence turn-around document was also produced for each employee for payroll purposes, with name and pay number premarked and providing for input of time payable at various enhancements plus various categories of nonattendance. There were 38 types of Autolector forms altogether. Specimens of three original forms are shown as Figures 24.1 to 24.3. Each worker had one attendance form but could have any number of Work Card forms.

With the week finishing on Friday afternoon, the completed forms arrived back in the computer installation on the Friday evening and there was then much furious activity in feeding Autolector and sorting the two files of data. The records on each file for each employee were reconciled and discrepancies printed out for investigation and correction, the benefit being that we were able to produce a Labor Force Distribution Statement by Monday morning and commence payroll processing that day. Any reconciliation errors that affected pay were input as corrections to Time & Absence details.

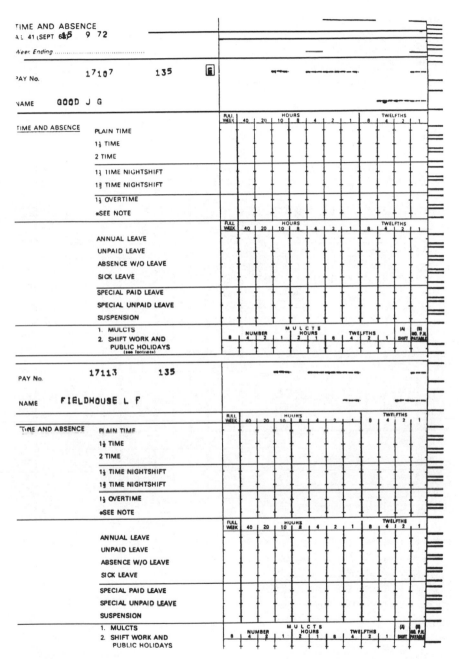

Figure 24.1.

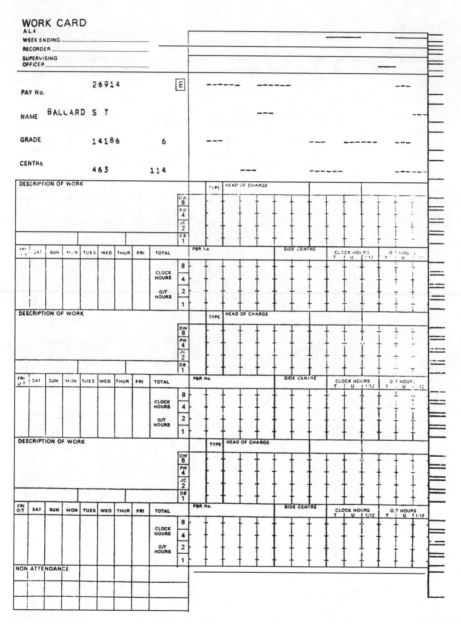

Figure 24.2.

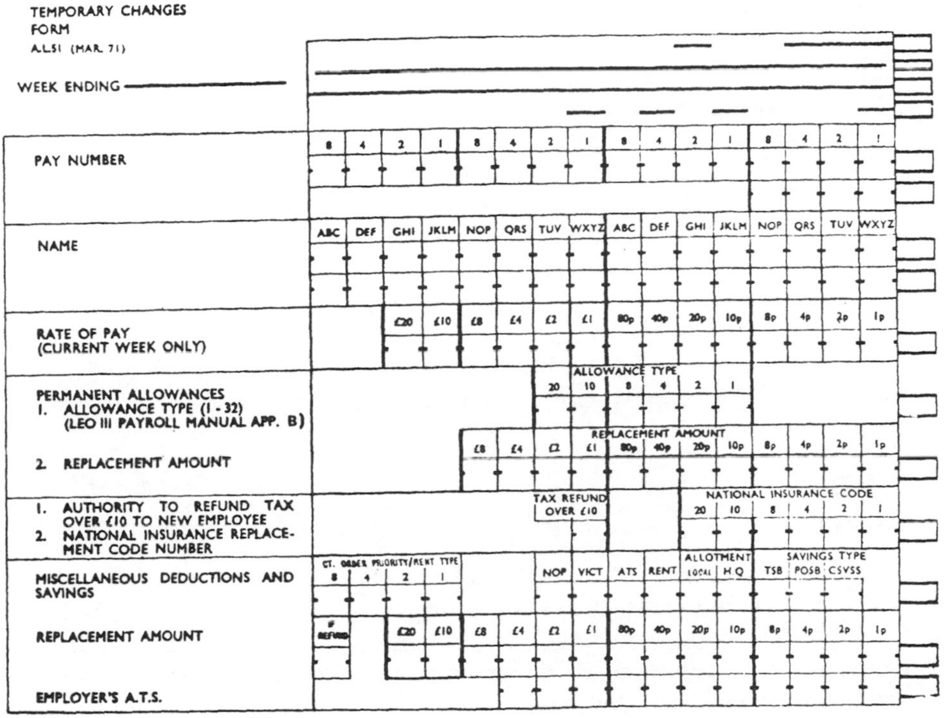

TEMPORARY CHANGES
FORM
A.L.51 (MAR. 71)

WEEK ENDING ————————

PAY NUMBER	8	4	2	1	8	4	2	1	8	4	2	1	8	4	2	1
NAME	ABC	DEF	GHI	JKLM	NOP	QRS	TUV	WXYZ	ABC	DEF	GHI	JKLM	NOP	QRS	TUV	WXYZ
RATE OF PAY (CURRENT WEEK ONLY)	£20	£10	£8	£4	£2	£1	80p	40p	20p	10p	8p	4p	2p	1p		

PERMANENT ALLOWANCES
1. ALLOWANCE TYPE (1 - 32)
   (LEO III PAYROLL MANUAL APP. B)

ALLOWANCE TYPE: 20 10 8 4 2 1

2. REPLACEMENT AMOUNT

REPLACEMENT AMOUNT: £8 £4 £2 £1 80p 40p 20p 10p 8p 4p 2p 1p

1. AUTHORITY TO REFUND TAX OVER £10 TO NEW EMPLOYEE
2. NATIONAL INSURANCE REPLACEMENT CODE NUMBER

TAX REFUND OVER £10

NATIONAL INSURANCE CODE: 20 10 8 4 2 1

MISCELLANEOUS DEDUCTIONS AND SAVINGS

CT. ORDER PRIORITY/RENT TYPE: 8 4 2 1

NOP VICT ATS RENT

ALLOTMENT: LOCAL HQ

SAVINGS TYPE: TSB POSB CSVSS

REPLACEMENT AMOUNT

REFUND £20 £10 £8 £4 £2 £1 80p 40p 20p 10p 8p 4p 2p 1p

EMPLOYER'S A.T.S.

Figure 24.3.

Loading the System

The first task to go live was payroll at Portsmouth in mid-1966. It was taken on in small batches to start with and run in parallel with the existing system for a minimum of three weeks. The results from the parallel systems for a minimum of three weeks. The results from the parallel systems were checked and, when clear, the existing system was dropped and the next batch taken on. The checking revealed not only clear errors but also unanticipated differences. The old method relied on an aggregate method of calculating from hours and rates of pay, whereas the computer calculated more accurately to several decimal places and then rounded up or down. This resulted in numerous differences of one or two pennies. The program was, therefore, modified to simulate the old method for the parallel period only and to revert to precise calculation thereafter. It was time-consuming and required a considerable clerical commitment, but it was safe and instilled confidence in the customer.

It was around this time that the possibility of extending the purchase to cover Chatham and Rosyth Dockyards was examined. The systems and programming did not require a great deal of alteration to cope with all four yards instead of two, and it made sense. This is in fact what happened, and two LEO 360s were ordered. They were faster machines, having a 6.0 µs cycle time as against the 13.5 µs of the LEO IIIs.

It did not seem sensible to have the faster machine at Rosyth, the smallest yard, and in 1967 the LEO III was transferred to Rosyth from Portsmouth and the LEO 360 delivered to Portsmouth and the LEO 360 delivered to Portsmouth. By this time we were live at Portsmouth and it took a great deal of organization from the technical and operating staff to effect the transfer without a break in operational running. The GPO's LEO 326 at Portsmouth came to our assistance, but we had to use Chatham's Autolector.

Control

The operational take-over of tasks started at Portsmouth in 1966 was followed by Devonport and then Rosyth, and was completed at Chatham in 1968. It was a long haul, involving a huge training exercise covering recording staff, computer operating staff, and clerical staff. Systems and programs were controlled centrally by the team, which remained at Portsmouth. Amendments to programs could be authorized only by the Central Team, which was increased to just over 20 and remained at this figure throughout the life of the machines. One trained and experienced programmer was sent to each of the three other yards to be a liaison with the Central Team and to deal with local emergencies. It was a system that worked well. Communications in the 1960s were not what they are now, but we were linked by teleprinters. Programs were amended centrally and copies, on tape, were sent to the three yards by post; it was cumbersome but it resulted in effective control.

Results

An outcome of the new system was that the pay envelope could now be produced on Tuesday, allowing time for the money to be inserted for payment at noon on Thursday instead of on Friday.

The value of the Labor Force Distribution Statement was considerably enchanced because it too was now produced earlier than before, on Monday morning. It provided, for management, the total labor deployment in person weeks by trades over projects, ships, and overheads in the previous week. It also showed, by trade and project, overtime worked, work within and outside incentive schemes, and waiting time.

A separate analysis of waiting time showed the reasons for waiting—lack of material, transport or cranes, waiting for other trades, and so on.

The Dockyard activities were also fully costed. All labor, material, and service costs were assigned to Heads of Charge, which could be in as much detail as the management required. Cumulative costs were gathered under each Head of Charge through the financial year and over longer periods for projects, such as new construction or large refits that overran the financial year. Information was fed to appropriate levels of management, highlighting significant levels of over- and underspending against budget. Altogether there were about 60 different kinds of costing returns tabulated for management.

Impact

The impact on the Finance Managers' clerical staff was considerable, even apart from reducing their number and changing the work pattern for those who remained.

On the costing side, members of the clerical staff were used to having huge printouts by their desks of labor, material, and service cumulative costs from which they could extract information as required. With LEO, routine returns were produced on the computer and inquiry runs made on the magnetic tape files several times a week. The staff merely completed bar-marked documents showing the scope and depth of their inquiry. The result was on their desks in a day or so. But they had lost the feeling of security that came with their printouts, and Finance Managers took a lot of convincing that this was a much more efficient use of resources. It all required a lot of training, understanding, and confidence, but it worked.

Nevertheless, we were concerned about the transfer of knowledge from a large number of people to a very small number of systems designers, programmers, and programs. As work was transferred from the clerical staff to the computer, the former inevitably became less aware of what the processing involved and more concerned with the detailed, specific requirement of feeding the system. It is, I suppose, the inevitable result of automation. The only answer that we could see was to ensure that documentation was as good as we could make it and that it was kept up to date. It was exercise not very popular with programmers, who much preferred writing programs to the task of getting the documentation or operating instructions up to date.

We were also aware of our vulnerability to changes in systems and programming staff. Nobody knows a program as well as the programmer who wrote it—especially a large program—but we could not keep our team together indefinitely. Civil Service pay did not match salaries in the private sector, so some people left for other jobs; in addition, promotions did happen and people did get sick, and we had to ensure that we had the capacity and ability to maintain and amend programs and systems. We attempted to insure ourselves a little by spreading the knowledge in the team. It was always a worry, though.

Other Danger Areas

Three other danger areas were the serviceability of the computer and its peripheral equipment, its air conditioning, and the electricity supply. The serviceability of the LEOs, as far as I can remember, was very good, with a percentage in the high 90s, but the possibility of failure of the mainframe or peripherals at a crucial time had to be faced. The possibility of 20,000 inhabitants in the Portsmouth or Plymouth areas not being paid could not be contemplated. Each yard was assigned a standby installation and exercises were carried out periodically to ensure that the standby arrangements worked. It involved the transfer at short notice of operating staff, magnetic tapes (the correct ones), documents, stationery, etc., to the standby installation. The Dockyard transport system was always most obliging. Each yard too had its standby electric current generator, which would be switched on automatically in the event of a mains failure or the quality of the electricity supply falling outside the tolerances required by the mainframe.

Decommissioning

The LEOs continued to work until 1977. A decommissioning ceremony was held at Portsmouth in March of that year, presided over by the Port Admiral, Rear Admiral W.J. Graham, who had won fame as the captain of the British aircraft carrier, the Ark Royal. It was held in the presence of many of those who had been responsible for the LEO being there and for its operation. Its last printout wished its successor, an ICL 1904S with a Longine OMR reader manufactured by Kendata, every success.

It was pointed out at the ceremony that the project had been successful on three counts:

1. It performed its task with the hardware ordered in the first instance.

2. It was economically viable—it made a profit.

3. It took on its tasks within the original time-scale.

Not many projects have achieved all three, and it did not miss a payment in 11 years.

One final point—I think that everybody who took part in the venture experienced great job satisfaction. It was exciting, demanding, exacting (as we made the rules as we went along), sometimes nerve-wracking, and sometimes frightening, but at the end we felt a great sense of achievement. There was a great camaraderie in the team; in fact, 30 years later we still have a reunion every other year.

PART 4

Innovating Abroad and an Evaluation

25
Into South Africa
LEO FANTL

Introduction to South Africa

Rand Mines

In the late 1950s, Rand Mines, the oldest surviving mining house in South Africa, investigated the possibility of employing computers for their administrative functions and certain technical projects such as the estimation of ore reserves and the valuation of mines.

Various proposals were received from British and American companies, all of which seemed to Rand Mines to offer underpowered equipment. The director in charge of the investigation, F.E. Hay, decided at that stage to call on the several companies in person. In the course of his visits in 1959, he "came across" LEO Computers and established contact. Later that year he obtained board approval to ask us what was required.

There were at that time some 15 gold mines, collieries, and chrome mines directly under Rand Mines' administrative control, as well as extensive industrial interests in cement, lime, and steel. The need for powerful computing facilities seemed intuitively obvious, but no systematic analysis had yet been done. At that time only six gold mines in the group employed computing equipment of any sort, and that was very small.

Hay's view was that, while it would be difficult to justify a machine of LEO III power for the Rand Mines group alone, a viable operation could be run if it were also made available to others in the industry and to trade and commerce at large. LEO Computers was prepared to support such an activity with know-how and this became the determining factor. An agreement to set up a joint venture was signed in Johannesburg in

June of 1960. Having prepared the offer it fell to me to launch the South African company. I arrived in Johannesburg at the beginning of July, 1960. John Gosden had seen me off at Heathrow in his Armstrong Siddeley Sapphire and it seemed like a bad start when we got stuck in traffic. David Caminer had been in Johannesburg for two or three weeks finalizing the agreement and making contacts in leading South African enterprises. He and Jackie, his wife, who had been setting up the office, met me at Jan Smuts airport.

Commencing the following week David and I called on senior figures in many of the following :

- Fergusson, Johannesburg Stock Exchange
- Neethling, CSIR, Pretoria (the Government scientific and industrial research organization)
- Smith, Anglo-American Corporation (the most powerful of the mining groups)
- Hamilton, Manager, City Deep gold mine (one of the Rand Mines group)
- Vanderbijl Patk, SASOL (the synthetic coal and oil plant)
- Latham, Stewarts and Lloyds, Vereeniging (the steel company associates of S&L in Britain)
- Duncan, Cement Producers Association
- Careen, Johannesburg Municipality
- Biebar, Old Mutual, one of South Africa's leading insurance companies.

On the weekend we lunched with another senior manager of the Rand Mines group, Chris Watermeyer, and his wife and then went to the Inanda Club and Crystal Waters in the Magaliesberg to take stock. We stayed in a thatch rondavel and I wrote up all the profundities of native pay that we had absorbed that week.

Following our visits we were offered a contract by the Cement Producers Association, but, at this stage, by none of the others. The wily ones dug as much out of us as they could without payment and filed their notes until they were ready. Others didn't care or didn't catch on. But it was a good introduction for me; the fundamental facts of life about South Africa and our new partner were uncovered in those few hectic days.

The Next Six Months

The first priority clearly was to get staff and have them trained in the UK. We also needed to set up an organization able to comprehend and program the mines' needs, to sell applications to the head office and the mines, to prepare for the computer and running the jobs, and of course to get the programs ready. We also had to deal with data capture, get the other groups interested and committed, and help Rand Mines sell all of this to the mines' administrative staff. They were about to be relieved of the tedium of repetitive administrative work, but, sadly, for all the good intentions, many were also to lose jobs they had thought secure for life, as well as their self-respect. All of this took years, of course, but the groundwork had to be laid.

Rand Mines looked after me well. I was quartered on the management floor, in an office overlooking Simmonds Street, in the Corner House, built at the turn of the century when Rand Mines was beginning to be the power in the land. I had no staff apart from a brilliant secretary. I still remember vividly saying that I needed a street map of Johannesburg. The next thing I knew, there was a driver calling for me to take me to the CNA to buy a map. It must have been at least 120 yards away. My boss was F.E. Hay DSO, I think, FiFi for short, who as a manager of Rand Mines was one of the inner circle. Managers had responsibility for companies and large areas of concern. FiFi was chairman of many companies and the EDP project. He was a Chartered Accountant. I got a lot of help and support from him.

The Main Areas

Staff Recruitment

In the first few years we hardly had any competition. A bureau was running a Stantec Zebra, doing jobs for free. I can't remember who ran it. The Old Mutual in Cape Town were running a Ferranti Perseus, and Later Orion and SANLAM ran a Burroughs. But there was an awareness. Strangely, there always is in this country. So when we let it be known that we were recruiting, there was no dearth of candidates, and good ones at that. In those first few months I recruited Bob Day, Liza Waymouth, Faith van Rooyen, and Barbara MacIver. They all did splendid, crucially important work, and the latter two are still employed as far as I know. Bob was at the helm nearly half the company's life. They went to London at the end of that year to be trained. In fact, those first years were easy as far as staff recruiting went. Our reputation was good, there was an abundance of excellent candidates and no competition, and our job was exciting. It was just hard work.

How to Sell It to the Mines?

The message was to be, "Anyone who wants to can join LEO." (The company adopted various names over the years, but I shall stick to LEO.) In that way there need be no redundancies. Anybody whose job was going to be eliminated would be considered for a job at LEO, in the interests of which appreciation courses would be held to explain what computers were all about and everybody could attend. This meant visiting maybe 20 establishments, some several times over a radius of 300 miles, giving the full LEO staff selection course, marking papers, and interviewing promising candidates (and ones that were not-so-promising). Since we did not relax our acceptance test standard of 80 to 100 percent, we had as I recall not a single successful applicant from the mines from the 1000 plus I interviewed. Faith van Rooyen and Barbara MacIver were from the head office. Faith had been with a research scientist at Corner House.

The vast majority of applicants had no idea what it was all about and seemed relieved not to be offered a job by me. Those who lost their jobs, and there were many, did so over several years. There was no general staff reaction, so the purpose was met. But there were some who took it very badly. Len White at Pilgrims Rest, where I think he was chief of native time, "ignored me" for years—even once at the Royal Hotel, where I was having a lonely breakfast. Ken Lendrum at ERPM, who was to become LEO Company Secretary, also comes to mind. We were to become good friends but it took many years.

Organizational

Lofty Moore had been Assistant Mine Secretary at Crown Mines, but had been attached to the head office for some time, where he was responsible for EDP exploration. He had favored ICT and secretly resented us. He was now assigned to me and stayed with LEO until he retired shortly before I did. His knowledge of mine systems was encyclopedic and he had a very sound appreciation of methods. He was a great friend, loyal and true. He passed on recently, but had to live through the murder of his wife Viv in particularly harrowing circumstances. Without Lofty we would not have achieved what we did so quickly.

Computer Officers

In this period the thought of appointing computer officers on each mine also arose—another absolutely vital move. Their task was to communicate with mine secretaries and heads of departments being computerized and to set up and run data capture. In the initial stages they acted as vital links between Lofty and the mines in fine-tuning systems points and ensuring that the mines' voices were heard. Later they helped with the preparation of trial data for all jobs. This became so big a task that one of their number, Brian Muir, was transferred to the head office doing this work full-time.

The computer officers were of senior status, having been at least heads of departments. One was Jack Taylor at the ERPM gold mine. I can hear him still calling in a timekeeper during initial running and bellowing, "The computer wants to know why you didn't blah, blah, blah. . . ." A side benefit that did not dawn on me until later was that by virtue of their seniority and ability these men could easily have become the focus of resistance to us. But by being actively involved at all stages, they in fact became staunch allies, fiercely loyal to LEO and the projects.

This approach was to stand us in good stead at Virginia, Anglo-Vaal's Free State mine, where on our first visit we encountered a chief time-keeper, Mr. Marais, I think, who was clearly hostile. He was thoroughly prepared to shoot us down at every point. As we drove home that night in deep despair, the thought came to me that here was our perfect computer officer. The head office wasn't convinced but agreed to give it a try. It turned out to be highly successful.

Premises

As soon as we grew in numbers we had to move out of Corner House, which was crammed full (the new Corner House was already being planned). So we moved across the road on Commissioner Street into some crummy building that served as our home until our new building was completed at 36 Anderson Street. This was specially built for us, with a whole floor for the computer, first floor for management, and then space for programmers and data preparation. The building was meant as a testing ground for ideas that were going to be applied in the new Corner House, and as a consequence we gained the benefit of nice modern paneling, carpets, etc. The computer room was excellent, all laid out for overall logistical convenience. Tony Barnes came out at some point to help us with the layouts and general planning. He, Arthur Payman, and I went off to the Kruger Park and Swaziland for a weekend.

Progress at the Head Office

Soon after David left, I arranged a meeting at the head office with the aim of getting the project moving ahead and decisions made and promulgated. It didn't go as well as I expected measured against the way things were being done back home. But at least it was something. A few weeks later I came down to earth with a bump—nothing was being done by anybody, because the meeting had not been "properly constituted" and therefore had no mandate to decide anything. That was my last effort of that kind in Corner House. After that I worked through the appropriate individuals, leaving them to go through the channels.

"Race Relations"

Over time the full measure of the racial problem slowly dawned on me. I decided to do what I could to run LEO as I would have done anywhere else. Clearly that had to be done with the knowledge and support of Rand Mines (and later Sage Holdings), which was readily given. So we introduced common wage scales, which of course did not take effect until blacks became operators and, much later, programmers. But later on, we put Elliot, the manager of the loaders, on the executive committee. Lack of education was a hindrance.

Alexander Elliot was something of a radical. He was fond of saying there was nothing wrong with apartheid, provided it was applied the other way around. He left in the early 1970s to join Anglo-American's personnel division. In his farewell speech he recalled the manner of his recruitment to LEO. It must have been around 1962, when blacks were customarily recruited off the pavement on a daily basis, depending on whether they appeared to be strong enough. When he heard of vacancies for loaders at LEO, he came along to apply. "Loaders" was an internal code name for junior operator, an occupation officially reserved for whites. He was shown into my office, where he recalled my offering him a seat and my secretary bringing in his tea on a silver tray. Apparently it made an impression on him.

But relations at LEO between the races were always excellent, even though the laws of the land had to be observed.

Progress with Jobs

Share Transfers

While we were marking time running appreciation courses and such in the first six months, the Rand Mines Share Transfer Department asked me to look at their operations. This was new to me. It was to become a major application, not only for Rand Mines but also Union Corporation and Anglo-Vaal. The companies were very profitable in their own right, but required routine work. Major clients took it as a favor to be relieved of this chore. This job was commissioned long before the mining jobs were authorized.

Not surprisingly Anglo-American got wind of the project somehow and Smith invited me to investigate their Transfer Office. Naturally I was elated—here was our entrée into Anglo! Like a fool I went into ever more detail, and when Arthur came out he helped me with the project. We finished up actually writing a spec. Then they turned us down on some ground or other. That was a bitter lesson, and I thought I had learned it well. But the next time I became involved with Anglo-American it was to cost us even more! The bitterest lessons are the ones you learn again and again and again.

Cape Asbestos

Another first was Cape Asbestos. They were somehow connected to Rand Mines, but it wasn't a direct management relation, probably a cross-holding arrangement. They were mining high-grade asbestos, which was soon to be banned worldwide. They weren't as critical as Rand Mines and the systems we devised for others were always good enough for them—until they started running.

Their main mine was at Penge, in Lebowa, pretty rough country about 250 miles northeast of Johannesburg. The scenery was breathtaking, but it was a prohibited area. Whites were allowed only on the road and within the confines of the mine. The mine had a splendid butcher's shop. Whenever anyone went there, they had to bring back incredible fillets of steak.

Cape Asbestos also signed up before Rand Mines.

Union Corporation

David had established contact with Partridge, a head office secretary. Certainly Partridge came back to me some time after that to find out more about our plans. A rough diamond, Partridge wasn't all that interested in specs and technicalities. He needed to believe in the people he was dealing with. This was a bit unnerving at first, but okay once I saw what was happening. I also saw a lot of Mr. Munroe the Chief Consulting Engineer. He was a different kettle of fish entirely. He needed to understand. But I never really knew how things were getting on until one day Partridge phoned and in his gruff, inconsequential delivery said, "Well you see, we've decided to put Evander on first, so will you fix it up?" or words to that effect. They also beat Rand Mines to it, though after that Corner House could hardly say no.

I have a vivid memory of Bill Marshall, their liaison man with LEO, driving Bob Day around the bend making opening statements of all past sins at our regular progress meetings.

The Copper Belt

I think Arthur Payman came with me to the Copper Belt once or twice. He was the first consultant to join me from London. Then I went alone until Joe Crouch arrived and he helped a lot. We went to Ndola, Kitwe and the surrounds, to Anglo and Rhodesian Selection Trust companies.

The idea was to indoctrinate mines with the potential for computers and to explain what we were doing for mines on the reef. Response was good, but once again it was expensive, and it was not our practice to ask for a consultancy fee.

The Main Applications

African Pay

The workforce was drawn from the main ethnic groups of subequatorial Africa. The Chamber of Mines (an association of all groups, providing a wide range of administrative, research, and negotiating facilities) used to run recruiting stations dealing also with transport and initial funding. In the territories, going to work on the mines had become a tradition. Conditions may have been hard, even inhuman by Western standards, but in relation to conditions at home they were acceptable. The pay was good, and since part of earnings had to be remitted directly home, local governments regarded the activity as valuble and therefore supported it.

However, the workers had their own firm stake in their homes and took it for granted that when the rains came, for example, they were off home to do the planting or whatever. They worked on the ticket system. A little book containing 30 tickets constituted the current contract. Each day of work meant another ticket. At the end of the book, pay was due. If an individual had planned to go home that day, he would not take kindly to being told that the computer was down and to come back next week for his money.

The pay provisions generally were straightforward, nothing out of the ordinary. The conditions were common to members of the Chamber. There were local variations, but these could usually be accommodated without difficulty in our programs.

White Pay

This was on pretty conventional lines, with common paydays and the type of attendance and pay documentation one finds in any Western payroll. Where the difficulties arose was in the incredible complexity of the special remuneration schemes in force. Conditions of work, grades of skill, and experience required for certain types of job, and actual qualifications all added to the diversity of the pay calculations. It was generally accepted on the mines that the Chief White Timekeeper was the closest thing to Einstein on the mine. Everybody expressed doubts about LEO's ability to deal with the payroll. They hadn't reckoned with Bob Day's tenacity, the brilliance of Faith and Liza, and of course Lofty's insight and social mine contacts. He knew everyone and knew exactly who to go and see about a specific problem. In general, by the time he had resolved how to deal with a problem and drawn up data forms and result layouts, we could take it for granted that everybody would be happy. Ultimately our programmers came to know as much about non-native pay as the mine staff did, and often they would be involved in dealing with the mines, who relied completely on their expertise and judgment.

Stores

The mines were very careful about observing the approved order procedures, and our system was geared to support this. Reordering consumables was routine and straightforward, but nonconsumables were difficult. We went to much trouble with our forecasting methods and in time even I became quite expert in exponential smoothing, much in vogue at that time. As I recall, we got help from London, and Mike Josephs in particular was helpful. A big feature was supporting mine stocktaking. Literacy was not all that high, and the diversity of spares stocked for certain types of equipment, spanning many years of operation, made it vital to give the stocktakers as much information and in as helpful a manner as possible.

Ore Reserves

I refer later to the relatively limited choices before management in optimizing mining performance. This made it all the more important to know as accurately as possible just where the gold was, in what concentration, how deep, the composition of rock, etc. Much work was put into this aspect by the Chamber of Mines. Peter Pirow of Rand Mines was loaned to LEO in the early years and did much original work in this field, and was the driving force behind our service application here.

Optimization

I have referred to David's attempts early on to gain fall out benefits from the clerical jobs we were to mount. Right from the outset he had begun to probe the possibility of establishing stope (work-site) profitability; hence our visit in the week after I arrived to Hamiliton, the Manager of the City Deep gold mine. The most promising suggestion was to establish stope costing in order to determine what should be mined and what should not. Indeed, Lofty was keen on the concept. Although, as we were soon to learn, stope rationalization was not acceptable, he felt that the next higher organizational level, the area, was amenable to the approach. Nor was he alone in this; Prince, a mine manager, was a powerful ally. Sadly he died in a rockfall at Blyvoor. But to the best of my recollection, we didn't really get area costing off the ground.

The reason for rejecting stope costing was that a stope had to be part of a much bigger activity. A stope generally was the workplace at a strip of rockface. It had to be served by the convey or rail transport system and ventilation had to be provided as well as water, at the least. All of this cost money and could be justified only if the infrastructure could serve as large an area as possible. So could an individual, low-grade stope be simply ignored and work be concentrated on neighboring, high-grade stopes? The answer was no. The mines were already operating at great depths, many thousands of feet in places, and the danger of the dreaded rockburst was ever-present. To contain it, drilling had to take place not in accordance with the quality of the grade, but of safety. So once a decision had been made to mine a certain area, the whole of that area had to be mined, so-called longwall mining. All one could hope to achieve in those conditions was to omit unnecessary operations, such as crushing rock that did not contain ore. It could be used instead to pack empty spaces below.

An item of considerable value in mining is machine spares. The mining and transportation machinery invariably comes in for heavy use and spares are expensive, so cost of stores is a very significant item in the overall cost structure. Tight control of stores administration then seemed a promising line of attack in an exercise such as we were engaged in. But here, too, other factors came into play. The workforce or drilling machinery or whatever was invariably far removed from the main store and if spare replacement was dependent on a time-consuming process of requisition, collecting, and transporting from store, many hours could be lost, at significant cost due to lost production. Therefore mines operated substores near the stopes, stocked to cope with the more common emergencies at minimum dislocation to production.

A mine captain or underground manager might have been responsible for a number of such stores, and would not hesitate to move stock around to where it was most urgently needed, regardless of stope-costing demarcations. The first casualty in the hectic schedule of underground staff was the paperwork, so that the substore in effect became a bottomless pit. It is not surprising then that when a manager began to reach his monthly cost limit, he didn't bother with pep talks and threats —he simply had the store locked.

Expecting a rigorously controlled store administration system to result in significant cost rationalization was thus not realistic. Things may be different now, but this was the situation as we found it.

The Logistics of the Operational Runs

The Daily Schedule

Native pay had to run daily, because every day was payday for one-thirtieth of the payroll. Ideally we should have had one machine per mine (the Anglo-American/IBM approach) or data transmission. The first approach was not possible because LEO was too big and expensive. The second approach was not at that time feasible on technical grounds. So we had to do it the old-fashioned way: collect data and deliver results by bicycle, car, bus, or airplane, depending on distance and facilities. This meant clockwork precision in controlling and executing our daily load. Twenty-four-hour shift working was an obvious necessity.

Less obvious were the actual disciplines needed to run an operation like that successfully. It is impossible to imagine all the things that can go wrong in ensuring that for any particular mine on any particular night certain reports are run on the appropriate stationery, in the correct number of copies, cut up, collated, put in the correct boxes, stacked in the correct pigeonhole, collected on time, and delivered at the correct stage for onward transmission, like the bus terminal and not Rand Airport. Many is the time that some of us had to dash off somewhere at 6:30 a.m. or thereabouts because a box had been left off. It was in those early days that I developed the habit of getting in before the boxes left in the morning. That way I could be sure of finding out what happened on the shift.

Management Style

We had in fact to develop an entirely different management style. It took years to find what would work and what wouldn't. Basically there were two techniques:

Software

We found that we needed to know far more about what was actually going on than the operating software was able to tell us, things like the impact of job mix on throughput; precise details of operator actions when and for what reason; and dynamic state of play reports on sensitive jobs to enable us to reschedule in time to get the vital things off to the plane. Bob Kaye, then already our senior operator, played the leading role here. He developed all the ideas and wrote the software patches with only gentle nudging from me. He was one of the best operators I have come across. He was an artist. He could smell how the jobs were running. He seemed clairvoyant. All of this needed to be instilled into the operators and disassembly clerks.

Management

In a regime like this, because it was impossible to predict all calamities and guard against them sitting at a desk and thinking about them, we finished up with a mechanism we called the Production Meeting. This was chaired by the most senior manager available, as soon as possible after the event, with everyone present who might contribute. Anyone could call it but had to monitor implementation and report back to the chairman. It worked well. We never stopped the practice, long after we had stopped running the mines. I suppose it was nothing but glorified crisis management, but I believe the approach had these tangible benefits:

- It taught individuals that no problem was acceptable. Everything had to be put right.
- It showed the thought process:
  –What is the *real* problem here?
  –What is the truly effective solution?
  –Must we monitor the corrective action?
- It made individuals feel responsible by showing them that everyone, from the top down, was ready to fix problems.
- Occasionally we would submit the (obligatory) minutes to clients to explain what had gone wrong and what we were doing about it.

People and Projects
I Remember

The role of consultants was of crucial importance. Most of our prospects were novices in data processing and needed hand-holding. That is when a detached, impartial approach is most needed. I and those of us responsible for bureau results generally took a blindfold approach, much as we would have denied this at the time. Naturally, there had to be experience, not only in data processing applications, but also in systems and business administration, and there had to be a gift for innovation. These were rare qualities indeed, and not surprisingly it took years before we were able to grow an indigenous team. In the meanwhile, we had to rely entirely on support from the UK.

I have already mentioned Arthur Payman. He was a philosopher by training and he had been on the tail end of the Ford payroll project in London. It was a tremendous help to be able to rely on him with non-mining projects and to bounce ideas off him. He had a tremendous, wry sense of humor and was an excellent lecturer. Alas, after six months or so he had had enough. He said he missed his science fiction books, but I suspect he found much more wrong than that.

Brian Mills, I think, came out next. We had been working on the British Railways Hotels and Catering Services and Greenwich Borough payrolls together and very quickly got on the same wavelength again. The first priority at that time was the design of the days' pay suite, which Brian took responsibility for. As usual, he took his time getting on top of a complex system, and as usual I can't have been the ideal boss to work for. Time was pressing. But in the end, he was proved absolutely right. The job was extremely well designed, and as I recall it was mounted with remarkable ease. Brian was then able to devote his time and efforts to a wide spread of other applications.

After two years Brian returned home and Ninian Eadie joined us. I had not met Ninian before; he had been with LEO for only two years, but his impact was immediate and dramatic. He had done his National Service in the Royal Navy, been educated at Winchester, rowed at Oxford, spent his spare time sailing, and was clearly a gentleman. Up to that time some of our associates in Rand Mines (FiFi, I gather) had regarded the LEO crowd as socially somewhat below par—ballpoint pens in breast pockets and such. Ninian changed all that with his self-effacing style, good looks, and devastating smile. He immediately broke down everyone's reserve and became an instant success at the Corner House. But this was deceptive. He worked tremendously hard at the somewhat daunting task he had been set: to sell LEO III computers to organizations outside the mining houses. He never gave up, and eventually succeeded in selling one to Consolidated Glass.

Other consultants from the UK who gave valuable help were Mike Josephs and Mick Mears.

At Corner House, as I have already indicated, liaison with the principal users was complicated by the need to observe house rules, etiquette, and office hierarchies. Board meetings, relations with outside shareholders, and legal matters all required detailed knowledge of procedures, intergroup relations, and often legalities. It was a veritable minefield, in which I would have been lost without help. This was of course a common problem, since mining houses like Rand Mines acted primarily as administrators. The method of dealing with a problem was to employ head-office secretaries, who each assumed responsibility for a group of companies. Our own guiding spirits, Derek Harraway, Miles Dunderdale, and Tony Barron, will forever be remembered with fond and grateful memories.

Implementation of the days' payroll (at that stage known as African pay), white pay, and stores was of course what it was all about. The initial definitions and design were done by Brian Mills and Lofty Moore, but as I recall Bob Day started work on the specification of African pay, Liza Waymouth on white, and Faith van Rooyen on stores. All three were busy on all three jobs at various times, but ultimately, when they became senior programmers, assumed full responsibility. In retrospect I still find it difficult to credit their incredible achievement in such a short time.

Bob Day was a typical South African. With an outstanding secondary education record, he joined the Post Office as a technical apprentice and completed his training as the top performer for the whole country. Bob is mainly Afrikaner, but was totally bilingual. When he took our appreciation course, he had never done any programming, but I still remember his hostile stare during my lectures—and how I leaned over him while he was writing his test, to see if he was actually making sense. He got 100 percent.

Liza Waymouth was experienced when she joined us. She had been with one of our aircraft company clients in London and remembered me. Vivacious and full of life and fun, she was probably the brightest of our programmers.

Faith van Rooyen had been involved with practical computing but not on computers. She left and joined us again and is perhaps the most dependable, hard-working tower of strength I have ever come across. At the time of writing this, Faith is still active with what remains of LEO, although I believe she is getting ready to hang up her gloves and sail around the world with her husband.

Barbara MacIver, now Barbara Chelius, was the baby of the group—not really, of course, but she seemed young and innocent and angelically friendly to all. Over the years I have come to realize that under that innocent smile lay a razor-sharp, merciless mind. No one ever pulled the wool over Barbara's eyes. She is still a part-timer.

A key area of course was production, which covered our operating, data preparation, and local mine data capture. Joe Crouch took the lead here. Joe had not worked with me in the UK, but had been involved with Doug Comish, I believe. In many ways Joe was another Derek Hemy, incredibly quick to grasp a new point, clear-thinking, and a good writer. His direction of the preparations and subsequent management of operations was outstanding. I had chosen Joe to succeed me, but this turned out not to be to his liking. Later he did much difficult design work for the Sage group, notably Sage Life, the group's insurance company.

Then and later, right up to the last few years, some of the men who joined LEO from the mines played a pivotal role in the company's development. I have already mentioned Lofty Moore, an all-arounder who knew the mine system like no one did. He would work all hours, day and night, weekends and Christmas, provided he could come in late in the morning.

And then there was Ken Lendrum, who was I think assistant secretary at Rose Deep and became our company secretary and chief accountant. The number of times he got me out of trouble was legion. When his wife died, he was devastated, but after a while he carried on with a difficult job as if nothing had happened.

Later Years

End of Phase One in South Africa

For me, 1965 marked the end of the first phase in South Africa. I returned to the UK as planned and took up the management of Product Planning in English Electric LEO Marconi, as LEO computers had become while I had been away.

In the barely three years that had elapsed since LEO III had been delivered by air to Johannesburg, a firm foundation had been laid for Rand Mines' own employment of the system and for its use by the wider industrial community on a service basis. A strong team had been recruited and trained, with South Africans working alongside the small group of LEO staff from the UK who had decided to stay behind and make their homes there. It was in many ways a considerable success story, but not all our ambitions had been realized.

It was time to ask myself again what Rand Mines had been looking for when I first arrived. Primarily, the system had to deliver well-working administrative procedures. People had to be paid correctly and on time. Stores control of the conventional kind had to be performed: reordering, back orders, creditor accounting, and allocation of costs— these were the things that mattered to them. Staff economies were important and these were achieved with a consequent reduction in administrative costs. But there was also some expectation that the computer would assist in the intricate annual wage negotiations. Pay awards were never straightforward, but I am not aware that the computer ever assisted significantly in this area.

As to our own ambitions, the hope that we built up of contributing materially to the efficiency and profitability of the practical mining operations also went largely unrealized. The constraining factor was that most of the mines were government-leased, and this meant that within rather close limits mining had to aim at winning the maximum quantity of gold-bearing ore, almost regardless of cost. This was a highly effective way of prolonging the life of a mine and optimizing reserves, but clearly not helpful to the computer optimization of short-term returns.

On the more conventional side, LEO certainly made life easier for Rand Mines in terms of administrative efficiency and in coping with fluctuations in labor supply and production levels. In the end I was astonished at how close we came to my original estimates. Early on, my chief operator had warned me that the machine would not cope with more than native pay, never mind non-native pay and stores or indeed the loads of the other mining groups. That was the real battle. In any event, the same LEO III processed, at its peak, the administrative procedures of 56 mines, including payroll and stores, together with a wide variety of technical functions.

The Final Phase

LEO South Africa continued to prosper in the second half of the 1960s. Excellent progress was made in fine-tuning the mining jobs and in signing up other mining groups, notably Anglo-Vaal, who took a part of the equity and a seat on the LEO Board, Johannesburg Consolidated Investments (JCI) also placed its work on the Service Bureau.

By this time, Rand Mines, faced with a decline in the profitability of its mining interests, had decided to diversify, and the LEO activity was seen as one of the vehicles for growth by investment. SBSA (Service Bureaus of South Africa) was taken over and when I came back to South Africa in 1970 small bureaus were operating in Cape Town, Port Elizabeth, and Pretoria, as well as the main center in Johannesburg. Each was running its own small machine, initially a Burroughs 500. I rejoined as Chairman of the organization.

The emphasis remained on applications know-how rather than on the particular system being used. Nonetheless, there was a fundamental cleavage between the centralized large-scale operation running for the mines and the local small systems. The software was quite different. It took some effort to live up to our claim to be national in coverage because of this diversity.

Things deteriorated further in the Rand Mines core businesses, and in 1972 the group merged with Barlows, the principal South African industrial conglomerate. Barlows already had a strong internal EDP activity and did not wish to become more deeply involved. Although they were extremely helpful and supportive, it was clear from the outset that there was no place for LEO in the new group. We were offloaded to the Sage Group, which was primarily a financial services organization. Its Chairman, Louis Shill, had been one of the cofounders of the unit trust movement.

Adjusting to our new home was difficult. The ethos of the group was essentially sales-orientated. I should describe the group role as that of the successful "macho insurance salesman." We never really meshed, much as we tried. Louis Shill still gave us his unstinting support and encouragement, yet we remained outside the mainstream of activity. In the end, LEO South Africa disintegrated, and, as is so often the case, that part of the story is not pretty.

Standing back now, at a distance way beyond my reach at an earlier time, I should say that the story of LEO SA was a microcosm of the story of LEO as a whole. Just as LEO at home was absorbed first into English Electric and then into ICL, LEO SA became first part of Barlows and eventually of Sage. One reflects that diverging too far from the core business might be a failing, particularly when special circumstances arise, such as new people, new corporate alignment, or just plain hard times. If this is accompanied by a lapse in vision or uncertainty about the main thrust, disaster seems almost inevitable. Perhaps this was the case at Rand Mines, which pioneered the use of computers for integrated office work in South Africa but was powerless to save its own long-established business, mining, from decline.

It may be argued that Lyons, too, were straying too far when they went beyond innovating with computers in their offices and also took on their design, manufacture, and marketing. They might have done more for themselves by waiting and stimulating others to produce what was needed. Meanwhile they might have thought up Kentucky Fried Chicken or McDonald's fast food. In the same way, Rand Mines might have profited from standing back for a while and making do with a small, unadventurous system in every mine. Notwithstanding their computer pioneering, Rand Mines was bought out by the conglomerate Barlows, while the industry leader, Anglo-American, for all its early computer caution, went on from strength to strength.

Fortune does not always favor the brave. Nonetheless, to many who were involved, LEO South Africa was a chapter of our lives of tremendous significance, excitement, achievement, and comradeship not known since the war. To outsiders, indeed to the national scene, we acted as a stimulant and a catalyst. For years, to be anybody in EDP in South Africa you had to have been with LEO at some point in your career.

26
Behind the Iron Curtain

RALPH LAND

Introduction

Late in 1964, T.R. Thompson summoned me to his office to inform me that I had been appointed as Export Manager, and early in 1965 I moved to the new EELM marketing headquarters at Portland House. My new responsibilities theoretically included that part of the world where there were no EELM operating companies, thus excluding South Africa and Australia. In practice, other than some small activity in Holland, I became effectively responsible for the East European market. This meant the Communist countries that were part of the Soviet Union-dominated COMECON, plus Yugoslavia. Thompson described this market to me as the "soft underbelly of Europe."

The particular reason for choosing me to spearhead the entry of the LEO innovation into Europe seems to be that I spoke fluent German. In any event, that was to prove of limited value in some of the territories we tackled. However, I also took with me valuable experience to supplement what I had gained as a user of computer services during my period as a Management Accountant in the Teashops Office. These experiences proved to be invaluable in the new environment of the Iron Curtain, where hard selling was looked at with suspicion but professional expertise was much respected. Additionally, the LEO approach to innovation and problem-solving enabled us find new and innovative methods of marketing our products in countries looked upon by many as too difficult even to attempt.

Experience

During my period with LEO I had been through a programming course, and after a short apprenticeship as a shift operator had gained experience in bureau management. I had chaired innumerable meetings to establish the operating regimes for the LEO III systems that we were planning to export. This gave me confidence that the systems would meet the needs of our users and that with the clear and practical operating manuals that we had devised they would be able to make efficient use of them.

Also from my period in bureau management I had learned a great deal about the need to curb over-enthusiasm on the part of users. An extreme case was Richards Shops, a prominent retail fashion clothing chain, where the chief accountant was so convinced by the potential LEO application that he refused to accept that the system should be introduced only after pilot running in parallel and then taken on section by section. He insisted on dropping his old system and putting every shop on the new system on the first computer run. Our major mistake was to accept his instructions. It was disaster, and to save the day we had to provide staff to reestablish their manual systems until the problems were solved. In the end, the bureau served Richards Shops with excellent results for many years, but it was an experience I was determined not to repeat. The Richards Shops job, too, provided a benchmark for future jobs in the retail trade, using simple input information from sales tags to provide a multiplicity of accounting and management information.

As my final assignment before Thompson summoned me to his office and presented me with "the world with a few exceptions," I gained experience in the mechanics of marketing as Manager of the London office. This was shortly after the merger in 1963 between LEO and the computer division of English Electric to form EELM. The special character of the London office, which had responsibility for banks, insurance, building societies, and the finance markets, was that English Electric had had the greater successes in these markets, so the London office was largely staffed with people from that background.

As my brother has described in Chapter 15, the English Electric culture was vastly different from that of LEO. In LEO, sales were achieved by consultants, who were computer application experts and who, through their understanding of industry in general and the techniques of systems analysis, could develop computer solutions for their potential customers for virtually any requirement. The English Electric sales force had only a rudimentary understanding of computers, but fronted all sales activity, supported by systems analysts, frequently recruited from the industries they were advising, such as banking and insurance.

At that time I was, as I now realize, somewhat arrogantly convinced that the LEO approach was the only correct approach, despite the relative success in London of the English Electric approach. Consequently, as a first step, I arranged for the sales force to be given more intensive computer training. As it happens, some of those who had been most successful in selling performed poorly on their computer courses. Secondly, over a period, the supporting systems analysts were promoted over the salespeople as consultants, not, as it proved, always successfully.

With hindsight it became clear that this approach undervalued the contribution that the English Electric salespeople had made or could make in the future. I took this lesson to my new assignment abroad, where it was equally unlikely that all-round consultants, at home in both systems analysis and marketing, would be encountered.

But I also took with me the almost overwhelming sense of pioneering achievement that I had encountered when I first joined LEO. Within LEO motivation was incredible. T.R. Thompson and David Caminer, in particular, were simply not prepared to accept that the impossible could not be achieved. In consequence, the seemingly impossible was achieved more often than not. Everyone was under stress, but it was a productive stress unique in my experience.

Managing Exports

By the time I arrived on the scene, LEO had already achieved its first major successes in Czechoslovakia, in addition to establishing a reputation in the Soviet Union, Poland, Yugoslavia, and, to a lesser extent, other East European countries. This way wholly the result of the indefatigable efforts of Dan Broido. Born in Russia and a fluent Russian speaker, he was convinced that East Europe provided significant market opportunities, I remember well, soon after I took over, walking with him through the streets of Moscow as he recited page after page of Pushkin's poetry from memory.

Although Russians had been advanced in the development of game theory and theoretical cybernetics, Stalin had decreed that computers were a tool of bourgeois exploitation. In consequence, computer developments in the 1950s lagged substantially behind those of the West. By the early 1960s this was becoming evident to the planners. Hence Broido found a ready audience when he started to visit this area and very soon the East European markets became his sole activity in LEO.

EELM in Czechoslovakia

Czechoslovakia was at that time the most sophisticated computer market in the whole region. In addition to a computer design institute, there were institutes for automation and for systems design. There was talk of a Czech engineer, trained at the Institute, who had emigrated to the U.S. and become successful at IBM. Although there were dozens of Russian computers in use, they were mainly primitive first-generation Urals, which were extremely unreliable and almost without peripherals, used mainly for mathematical work. The early Minsk computers were better, but still well behind typical Western equipment of that time. The main Western computers installed were British Elliott 803s and Zuse computers from Germany, which were also mainly used for mathematical and engineering applications. No equipment comparable to a LEO III had yet been seen. The Authorities were ready to invest scarce foreign currency to acquire state-of-the-art Western technology and application know-how, almost certainly with the specific approval of the Russians.

Following many visits to Prague and Ostrava, and a number of return visits by Czechs to London, Broido had negotiated the sale of three major systems by the time I arrived. A LEO 360 was sold to VLD, which was the computing laboratory of the Czech Railways, managed by a tough and, I believe, completely honest, convinced Communist named Sebek. Another was sold to NHKG, a major steelworks in Ostrava. In addition, as a result of English Electric expertise in industrial applications, a KDF6 was supplied to control part of the rolling mill. A LEO 326 was sold to the Czech department of social security, partly on the basis of LEO's experience with the Department of Health and Social Security in Britain. The total order, valued in excess of $3.5 million was up to that time the largest export order achieved by EELM.

All three systems were to be installed in 1966. Our first need was to set up an office in Prague under Fred Lamond, an experienced and brilliant computer analyst and polyglot recruited from Univac. This was one of the first British offices in Czechoslovakia, Lamond was supported by a team of service engineers, programmers, and systems analysts attached to each customer and to support new sales activity. Altogether, the team comprised some nine expatriates, supplemented frequently by short-term visitors from the UK. At the same time, a continuous stream of Czechs came to the UK for training: service engineers, who would maintain the equipment, and programmers and systems analysts, most of whom were academically highly qualified and of high caliber.

One of the conditions our staff had to cope with was the oppressive security arrangements. Normal access to their Czech colleagues was almost impossible. Much of the detail of the work was withheld from us. When, for example, we required data to size equipment needs or store requirements, it was often either withheld or blatantly incorrect. Allowing "economic data" to fall into the hands of Westerners was a serious crime throughout the region.

Another issue we had to learn to cope with was the natural consequence of having to negotiate with the monopoly Foreign Trade Organizations as purchasers of equipment on behalf of end users. Their personnel were professionally trained as negotiators. We were amateurs. They deployed a wide variety of stratagems to put us at a disadvantage, such as seating us so that the light fell into our eyes, using time pressures against us, alternating tough unyielding negotiators with friendly compliant people, using commercial threats (including possible threats against our personnel) and holding out excellent future prospects in return for concessions now. For us, success depended on becoming even more skilled negotiators. It also became a rule never to enter a negotiating session without a colleague.

However, despite all the problems of working in a tightly controlled Communist country, many enduring friendships were formed. We respected the ability of our Czech counterparts. The opening ceremonies for the installations were notable events that were well publicized in the country, and it was usual for a director from EELM to attend. David Caminer joined us for the opening of the computer center at NHKG. The three installations performed well on a multishift basis and remained active until 1979 or 1980.

In 1966 the Czech government decided to raise the visibility of computers in the Republic by mounting a major international computer exhibition in Prague, called Incomex, over three weeks. We agreed to ship and exhibit a complete LEO 360 installation. We shared a large exhibition hall, as a British pavilion, with ICT and Elliott Automation. IBM, Univac, Honeywell, NCR, and most of the world's major computer companies also participated.

Visitors came from all of Eastern Europe, but especially from the Soviet Union. They were usually top people, from design engineers to systems designers, who required precise and detailed technical information. Our local team was heavily stretched, but was supported by LEO managers and consultants, including David Caminer, Frank Land, Doug Comish, Alan Jacobs, and John Aris. Because of its success, the Czech organizers pressed the exhibitors to extend the exhibition by a further two weeks. Most agreed. In some respects this exhibition was a turning point. It marked the official opening of the East European computer market to the West.

While the market had been, at least to some extent, competitive, it now became intensely so. IBM set up an East Europe headquarters ROECE, in Vienna, which was allowed rather more operational freedom than a normal IBM operation and employed at its peak about 2500 staff members at headquarters and in the various countries. The other major competitors were ICT and Elliot Automation.

Following Incomex and the successful commissioning of the three LEO computers, sales activity increased considerably, by now, though, for System 4 computers. Our last LEO III sale to VZKG, a major steel and engineering combine in Ostrava, was converted at their insistence, during final negotiations with KOVO, to be a System 4 computer.

Later in 1967, EELM had acquired Elliott Automation. One of their more successful operations had been their East European one. They had preceded LEO into Eastern Europe and had been especially successful in Czechoslovakia, with a good number of 803 computers and one 503 bureau. The equipment was mainly used for technical work. I inherited the majority of Elliott's East Europe team at Borehamwood and in the individual countries, and proceeded to integrate them into the EELM team, where they mostly fitted in well, adding considerable weight to our efforts.

It soon became apparent that Czechoslovakia would be unable to fund the convertible currency required to pay for all the projected computer imports. We realized that the only way to move forward was to accept counter trade, or barter, as a means of financing new business. In general, this depended on helping our end users to export more. Clearly, products that had a ready market and were competitively priced were not made available for counter trade. Consequently, we were usually offered products that were close to unsellable. For example, we were offered, at a later time, such curiosities as racing camels, untrained wild falcons, moose skins, and, on one occasion, goat horns to be sold in the Far East as aphrodisiacs. These never became deals. We were, however, able to create markets for a wide range of products at a cost that was acceptable or could be factored into the price of our equipment.

We decided to become more proactive in this area. I had recently recruited a Romanian-born Israeli engineer, Moshe Peled, as country manager for our office in Bucharest. We decided to turn him into our first counter-trade expert and manager. He continued in this role well into the ICL era, completing numerous counter-trade transactions that amounted to many million dollars value. He developed our first ventures into film financing. Czechoslovakia had an excellent and, by Western standards, inexpensive film industry. A number of Western film producers were anxious to use these facilities. We provided prefinancing to enable a number of films to be shot at the Prague studios. This money was repaid after the film was made, but the value was credited to EELM for the purchase of a System 4 computer by the Prague City Council and later for other installations.

One of the by-products of this film activity was that most of our staff living in Prague, including Vic Carter, who had succeeded Lamond as our country manager, participated in one of the films as extras or in minor parts. Carter had been recruited to join the export department following a successful career as an army officer. After initial training he was assigned to a British project to gain practical experience and then rapidly promoted to become country manager.

In 1968, Prague became the center of the world's focus as the Czechs sought to throw off Stalinist rule. The Prague Spring was an extraordinary experience. The spirit of enthusiasm and joy among the people in the streets, their eyes literally shining, remains unforgettable. At the same time you could foresee the disaster to come. The accelerating dismantling of the Communist system was inevitably going to be too much for the Soviets to accept. When the invasion came, the population resisted passively. Our foreign trade partner sent us a telex on the day of the invasion, August 22, 1968, that, translated into English, read: "Our country has been occupied by the Soviet Army against our will. We are momentarily unable to deal with your business matters. We are doing everything possible to ensure that the truth will win—VERITAS VINCIT."

At that time Carter escaped arrest by the Russians as they invaded by a mixture of bluster and luck. While many Western companies left Czechoslovakia, EELM stayed on. This loyalty was much appreciated then and later.

Despite the growth of competition, EELM remained market leader for Western computers throughout this period, continuing to outsell IBM, who had vastly greater resources devoted to this market at their disposal. The reasons were partly due to pro-British feeling, combined with politically inspired anti-American attitudes, but were mostly due to the LEO approach to support and advice, which was based on a real attempt to understand the customer's requirements as well as the power of the equipment and, not least, our approach to counter trade.

EELM in the Soviet Union

While our business and organization was being developed in Czechoslovakia and Poland, Broido continued his activities in the Soviet Union. He had been working on this market since 1961, holding seminars and lecturing in Moscow, Minsk, and Novosibirsk. At that time there was very little competitive activity. Consequently, a more serious effort from EELM was welcomed and we agreed to participate in a major exhibition in Sokolniki Park on the ourskirts of Moscow in 1967.

The exhibition, like Incomex, was supported by many of the senior consultants and managers from London. There were, as always large numbers of visitors thirsting for information. We could hardly cope with the incessant demands for literature. Most of our documentation had been translated by Dan Broido and printed in Russian, which, at that time, was hardly the norm for British exporters. In fact, because so much of the computer terminology had no agreed Russian equivalents, Broido virtually established the *de facto* standards for English-Russian computer terminology.

Another event was a visit to our exhibition stand by the then UK Minister of Technology, Tony Benn, together with Russian Deputy Prime Minister Kirillin. Benn sat at the operator's console discussing the computer performance details with some knowledge. The Russians were immensely impressed by this young, self-assured minister, who already had experience of LEO through his previous position as Postmaster General.

The exhibition was important for our future in the Soviet Union. Neverthless, we failed in our main objective to sell the computer off the stand to our main and long-standing prospect, Gosnab, the State Committee for Supplies. The LEO 360 had to be shipped back to Britain and, as elsewhere, we had to switch our offer to a System 4/50. It proved impossible to sell either used equipment or technology, other than the latest, to any of the East European markets.

At that time in the Soviet Union, the awareness of Western progress with computer technology, compared with their own backwardness, was causing increasing concern to the Soviet establishment. Russian theoretical work continued to be good and they managed, on the whole, to present themselves well at international conferences. Their practical achievements, however, were poor. The structure of the decision-making process was complex. The main participants were Gosplan, the State Planning committee, the State Committee for Science and Technology under Deputy Prime Minister Kirillin, the Academy of Science, and major research, and development institutes in Novosibirsk and Minsk, which provided support. The key organizations in Moscow were the Institute of Automation and Telemechanics under Academician Trapeznikov and an institute developing industrial computers under Professor Naumov. The production side was covered by the Ministry of Instrumentation, headed by an old-time Bolshevisk, Deputy Prime Minister Rudnev. Foreign trade issues were the responsibility of the FTO Mashpriborintorg and later, spun out of it, the FTO Electronorgtechnica, which was to become in due course one of the largest FTO's. During the next few years, we were to establish good relations with all of these organizations, from ministers to officials and specialists.

Broido's main contacts at that time worked for Academician Trapeznikov at the Institute of Automation and Telemechanics, which became our main partner in developing the market. Our particular friends were Professor Alexander Lerner, deputy director of the Institute, who had an

international reputation in cybernetics, his colleague Professor Mamikonov, and the General Secretary of the Institute and probably the most
influential man, Oleg Aven. Gosnab, which was the key organization
implementing Gosplan's national plan directives, was chosen to be the
first organization to have a large Western computer installation. The
Institute was made responsible for advising them.

Following the exhibition and after considerable discussions in Moscow
and in London, negotiations for a System 4/50 were started, where upon
we received permission to open a technical support office in Moscow. At
that time few foreign companies were allowed to set up offices of any
kind in the Soviet Union. Don Riley, a tough and resilient New Zealander
who had been working as an Operations Research consultant for EELM in
London, agreed to head our new support office in Moscow with responsibility for the Gosnab project. He was not, of course, allowed to support
any sales activity. The first office was one room in the Peking Hotel, in
central Moscow, which also became his home for the next few years.

In parallel with the Gosnab discussions, we started detailed evaluations of possible computer projects with the Institute of Automation for a
computer and with another of their clients, Morflot, the State Merchant
Marine. While the negotiations with Gosnab seemed interminable, our
proposals of a 4/70 for the institute and a large 4/50 for Morflot made
rapid progress.

Late in December 1967 I received a telex in London urging me to come
to Moscow over Christmas and up to the New Year. Mashpriborintorg
had been allocated money for the three computers under negotiation,
which needed to be committed by December 31. Accordingly, I decided to
fly to Moscow with my wife on Christmas Eve. Dan Broido was to join me
in Moscow on Christmas Day. Unfortunately, a blizzard over Moscow
caused the plane, with Broido on board, to be diverted first to Tehran and
then to Karachi, where he spent the next 48 hours in his thermal underwear, heavy suit, fur coat, and fur hat before flying back to London.

I was, therefore, left alone in Moscow to negotiate three contracts
against all of our rules on negotiating methods. After three days of continuous negotiation the contracts, worth more than $7 million, were
signed. On December 30 I hired the whole foreign currency bar at the
National Hotel for a celebration and reception for all our partners and
friends in Moscow.

Despite the premature death of the Gosnab computer manager and
problems with the preparation of the computer premises, the 4/50 was
commissioned. Most of the work was connected with scheduling supplies to industry in accordance with the plan. A wide range of additional
work for other State organizations was also carried out. At one time computer reliability began to decline rapidly because no financial provision

had been made for the purchase of spare parts after the exhaustion of the initial two-year spares kit. It took the FTO over a year to sort this problem out a typical example of the kind of problems that beset the Russian economy.

Both the Morflot and the Institute machines were successfully installed in 1968. It became necessary to increase the size of our Moscow team with more service engineers, programmers, systems analysts, and instructors. We also employed more Russian personnel. At one time, there were 30 expatriate families in the Soviet Union, mainly in Moscow, living in the Ostankino Hotel and other similar second-grade hotels. They faced similar but even more acute problems than their colleagues in other East European countries. Harry Armitage, who went to Moscow as a programming instructor, lived there with his wife and two young children in a two-room suite, cooking for the family on a single electric ring stove hidden during the day in a trunk. It is astonishing that so many of our people and their families put up with such difficulties so cheerfully.

Our Russian staff had to report regularly on our activities. They could not form close or even friendly relations, and if they were permitted to form relations we automatically assumed they were members of the KGB. Some of our people found this atmosphere too claustrophobic to stay, but the majority were determined to get the most out of their lives in Moscow. One of our engineers, was a good rugby player and managed to play incognito for the Russian Air Force team. In the winter, cross-country skiing was popular. In the summer they went to the Bay of Joys or the diplomatic beach for swimming and water sports.

In the meantime, the Russian programming team at the institute was able to optimize the J operating system on the 4/70 to an extraordinarily high level of efficiency. This was an impressive demonstration of their capability. However, when they advised Morflot and to a lesser extent Gosnab, the results were disappointing, They found the discipline that was required to implement routine clerical tasks, such as writing data vetting or editing programs, uninteresting. On the other hand, discussion of a control algorithm would kindle their immediate interest. Similarly, the service engineers were mostly highly qualified and performed brilliantly on training courses, but became, on the whole, poor service engineers. They preferred to use their newly learned skills to redesign the computer or, more important still, to write papers leading to higher qualifications and thereby to better pay.

Although we had been able to sell and install the 4/70 at the institute, the deteriorating East-West relations, combined with increasing Western concern about the leaking of potentially sensitive military information, led to a progressive tightening of the COCOM restrictions on computer exports. The computer in which the Soviets had the greatest interest, the

4/70, was now ruled out by COCOM. In order to sell the most powerful equipment permitted by COCOM, we specified a computer that was less powerful than the 4/70 but more powerful than the 4/60, called the 4/62. On the basis of my forecast that we could sell over 50 of these, EELM agreed to modify the 4/70 to this specification and offer it as an additional product in the range. In practice, the slowing down of the 4/70 did not involve significant design resources. However, once available, we sold two 4/62 computers, both to our next major customer, the Ministry of Foreign Trade.

During 1968 the number of potential customers increased rapidly. In addition to the Ministry of Foreign Trade, we studied the requirements of Aeroflot for a reservation system (in conjunction with Peter Hermon and Alan Jacobs of BOAC). We also studied the requirements of Gosplan to replace a number of Elliott 803 computers that had been installed in the early 1960s.

Perhaps the most striking success of the "LEO approach" was achieved in obtaining the contract for Azulcar, the manufacturer of the Moskvich motor car, in Moscow. Despite the almost paranoid fear of disclosing economic data to Westerners, we were requested to study the requirement for a production control system for the plant, and eventually Dataskill obtained a turnkey contract to design and write the complete software suite for production control, worth in excess of $2.8 million, implemented by a considerable team of systems analysts and programmers mainly located in Moscow. This breakthrough was probably the result of the disappointing performance by the Institute of Automation in Developing the application for the Morflot installation.

Another prospective customer was the Soviet Port Authority. They sent a top delegation and we visited the Port of London Authority. We were being entertained for dinner by the PLA when a message was brought in that the British Government had just expelled some 110 Soviet diplomats resident in the UK for espionage activities. The atmosphere froze in the room. On the next day the delegation returned to Moscow and never resumed discussions with us. For a time relations were difficult and contacts constrained. More seriously, our staff in Moscow was harassed. Demonstrators outside the Anglo-American School in Moscow forced mothers to hand their children out through side windows to avoid abuse from the demonstrators. Although we gave serious consideration to evacuating our families, most of our people preferred to stay until the crisis had passed.

Nevertheless, the deterioration of the political position created a number of problems. Our good friend Professor Lerner felt himself affected by growing anti-Semitism, despite the fact he had an exceedingly privileged position compared with most Russians, and he applied to emigrate to Israel. He was not granted permission and was dismissed from his position. His son, who worked for us, was withdrawn by the authorities. Lerner became a leading "refusenik" but survived with the support of a group of leading British and American academics. After more than a decade he was allowed to leave for Israel, where he was appointed to a position as a professor emeritus.

In the growing atmosphere of international tension, the expectations of the 1960s were never fulfilled. At that time it had seemed realistic that each of the installations in key areas of the Soviet economy would be multiplied many times. Good business levels were achieved, but the Cold War and the embargo on technology trade prevented the breakthrough that had at one time seemed possible.

Expansion in Eastern Europe

In the five years from 1963 the successes in Czechoslovakia and the Soviet Union were built upon to open up operations in all the other countries of the region except Albania. Broido had made an early inroad in Poland, shortly followed by Yugoslavia and then Hungary, Romania, and Bulgaria. The pattern became first a sales success and then the establishment of a support office, responsible for the installation of equipment, the training and supervision of programmers and service engineers, and the provision of guidance on the specification of requirements and the systems design. This office would be staffed mainly by expatriates drawn from experienced British staff. Eventually a fully representative office would be opened.

The development of this expansion coincided with the changes in name and ownership that took LEO Computers, at the start, through English Electric LEO and English Electric LEO Marconi to English Electric Computers in 1967, when the Lyons interest was relinquished. There was, however, little reflection of this in the overseas mode of operation, other than that, where appropriate, the additional practical knowhow of English Electric in steel mill operations was brought into play. The approach remained one of offering not just equipment but also the solid experience that had been gained at home in bringing large-scale, integrated applications to successful fruition. The offer to help achieve similar success made an appeal in those countries that felt left behind in the introduction of all but small computers. While this was often of compelling interest, there was the constraint that acceptance of help conflicted with official dogma, which feared contamination by Western thought. The very fact that despite these problems we were often able to make contributions to the effective use of their computer systems and to establish personal relations must have played some part in the ultimate opening out to the West and the collapse of the command economy system.

The readiness of the Czech industrial and government installations to show off their achievements and to speak of the stimulus and cooperation that they had received from us was a potent factor. The evident closeness of the London management to what was happening in Eastern Europe also played its part and was made manifest whenever a visit was organized for senior personnel and when staff were sent to the UK for training. The prospective purchasers were made to feel wanted as people, and this was attractive to them in the chilly atmosphere of the times.

A feature of all the countries, though, was the desire to be self-sufficient in all respects, so that while the promise of experienced support staff was always seen as a major advantage, we were seldom able to penetrate deeply enough to advise as much on the systems analysis as we would have wished.

After Prague, the next office to be opened was in Warsaw. This followed the signing of a number of System 4 orders, culminating in a large system for the State Statistical Office, GUS. Placed in charge of the office was Roger Landau, who had previously been a project manager in Prague and before that had worked for me as a systems consultant on the LEO III/1 Bureau in Hartee House.

A general feature of business in Eastern Europe at this time was the high level of contact needed in order to achieve ultimate success. Our operating methods required us to keep excellent relations not only with the end users, but also with the Foreign Trade Organization, which controlled hard currency availability, and the several ministries and institutes in the decision-making process. Typically, high-level personalities would include the minister of Foreign Trade, the minister of Technology, and the minister responsible for the end-user industry. In one extreme case I identified 15 organizations or individuals who needed to give their approval before formal contract negotiations could start. The final signature was that of the deputy prime minister.

In Hungary a strong EELM team enabled us to sell our top-of-the-line 4/70 to the Hungarian equivalent of the Soviet Gosplan. Other orders soon followed. The Hungarian Ministry of Technology played a part in deciding which manufacturer to favor. I remember taking the responsible deputy minister to Kidsgrove, where in the computer hall I commented that there was more computing power there than in the whole of Hungary. He was deeply offended. It took time to repair that breach of good relations.

The scene in Yugoslavia was different. Having opted out of the Soviet bloc, the country had created a modified system of Communism based on considerable decentralization of decision-making. The total market for computers became relatively larger and more Western-inclined than any of the other Eastern European markets. IBM and DEC recognized the opportunity and became well installed, dominating the market. EELM established a useful foothold again because of the excellent relationship Broido established with the Yugoslav Federal Army authorities. Our breakthrough came with an order from them for a large 4/50 configuration for their supplies headquarters in Belgrade. There was little evidence in this period that Yugoslavia would later dissolve into a group of warring states.

After EELM

At the time of the ICL formation in 1968, both ICT and EELM had well-established positions in Eastern Europe, although ours was a somewhat larger business. The first decision to rationalize our future activity on the basis of the majority of customers in each country soon failed. Hungary made it clear that they were not prepared to give business to ICL if the opportunity to consider System 4 was denied them. The Solomonic decision was then made to split the combined operation into two, with the previous ICT head of their Eastern Europe operation taking charge of all except the Soviet Union, which fell to me. Theoretically the full range of equipment was available in both parts of the operation.

After a year this too was changed after Sandy Walker, the ex-ICT manager, requested a transfer, and I was asked to take responsibility for a reconstituted ICL East Europe and Soviet Union Division. Although there had to be compromises on country managers, the LEO and EEC personnel in these territories came through much less affected than had inevitably been the case at home.

Business continued to grow, despite increasing competition from domestically produced systems and from U.S. companies, such as IBM and Univac. ICL remained ahead of IBM for a number of years, but business later stagnated for a time as the general atmosphere deteriorated. Over this period it was not a natural market for ICL, preoccupied as it had to be with more immediately calculable overseas markets, particularly those in Western Europe and the old Dominions. Because of the protracted negotiations, many conflicting authorities, and still tightening currency problems, it was near to impossible to forecast when cash would eventually flow. This was not easy for a company based on and indeed depending on firm annual targets and the rewards derived from achieving them.

Nonetheless, ICL continued to trade successfully and profitably, especially in Poland and Czechoslovakia, but also in the Soviet Union and other territories. ICL continued to build the reputation for care and cooperation that dated right back to the first LEO installations in Czechoslovakia in 1965. This reputation remains today. The ICL *Corporate Review 1994* commented, "Our successful track record in Central and Eastern Europe led to us being chosen by McDonald's for its strategic IT partner for expansion into this region, and we are supplying a range of services including training, project management, installation, and maintenance. " We had not generally been permitted to do all of this in the earlier security-conscious days!

27

The LEO
Approach—An
Evaluation

JOHN ARIS

These recollections, which I hope are accurate but are not guaranteed to be so, cover not the "heroic age" but the period from 1958 to the first delivery of System 4 in 1966. They mainly concern system design then and now, and more personal anecdotes are presented as end notes. It is astonishing how far the art of system design and programming had already come by 1958, in the 10 years since the heroic age began.

I joined LEO on September 1, 1958:[1] the main action at the time was on LEO II/1, a machine with cards, paper tape, and printer but no magnetic tape and no backing store. During the following eight years there were two and a half revolutions in system design, brought about successively by magnetic tape, multiprogramming, and random-access devices. Programming was equally revolutionized by high-level languages and operating systems. This chapter attempts to record the effects of these revolutions and to compare present practice.

It will immediately be objected that the above paragraph is grossly technology-dependent, whereas system design is a wider discipline and technology dependencies are low-order details within it. True—but that is largely how it felt at the time.

Nevertheless, let me start from the wider discipline.

Principles

Early on, as a programmer, I was not much involved in system design: that was done by my betters. It was not taught in training courses and was very much the product of experience. How it was tackled, I now realize, derived essentially from Lyon's pre-LEO experience, "user pull" not "technology push"; this was unique in the computing world at the time and still scarce today. There were six articles of faith, which one somehow came to know and to practice:

1. The computer system should be thorough and radical. Getting anything into a computer is a major effort so make the most of it. Understand the system in its entirety. Plan it as a whole. Rethink, rather than automate what is there. Maximize the savings in clerical effort, stock holdings. response time to customers, or whatever. Make the data sweat, by producing management information as well as transactions. Don't leave what could be done effectively by computer to be done by hand. Do a proper job.

2. Check everything. The data will be full of errors. Make provision to amend absolutely anything. The computer will break down frequently, so make sure everybody knows when this has happened. Reconcile everything, as a precaution against misoperation and program errors as well as machine faults. Program errors are a deadly sin, to be eliminated come what may.

3. Design of input and output documents is crucial. They govern the efficiency both of the computer system and of the human system surrounding it. Both careful thought and practical experiment are necessary to get them right.

4. Detailed system specifications must be written, agreed, and frozen before programming can begin.

5. Computer time is expensive, and programmer time cheap. Using a lot of human effort and ingenuity to minimize run times is an excellent bargain.

6. Before a computer can be configured (sized was a later term), even in a presale situation, enough work must be done both on the specification and on the detailed system design to ensure that the configuration will be powerful enough. This may result in a bigger (and more expensive) proposed machine than the competition, but the intelligent customer will believe us and be grateful.

These principles served LEO and its customers nobly; many of the early LEO jobs still look sophisticated today. They held, more or less, throughout the period 1958 to 66. Before I plunge into the technology-dependent revolutions, let me outline how they look today. I will enlarge on some of these comparisons in the section *System Design Today*, which looks at them from the perspective of the system design issues of 1995; what follows is still geared to the principles of 1958.

Perhaps the most important difference between the systems worlds then and now lies in the senior management understanding of the potential of computing. This may not be wonderful today, but it was virtually zero then. Such computing knowledge as there was lay with suppliers, not users, so technology push was hard to avoid, even by a supplier as user-oriented as LEO. The purchase of a computer was often more a matter of indulgence than a true piece of decision-making. A few visionary individuals at top- and middle-management levels stood out; where LEO worked with one of these, results were usually excellent. LEO also sometimes managed to carry through the appropriate vision in the absence of such a sponsor, refusing to be bogged down in partial or misconceived applications, but this was a risky strategy.

It was in this primitive world that the six principles were applied. How do they look today?

The first, that systems should be both thorough and radical, looks good, but it must be admitted that it was and is a counsel of perfection. Lyons, and so LEO, were good at it, and we sometimes credited our customers with more ability to do the same than they actually possessed. It was the enterprising customers who came to LEO, rather than to the competition, but even so many of them were less enterprising than LEO recommended. To this day, process reengineering is a daunting challenge. If LEO was at fault, it was a heroic direction.

The second principle, to check everything, has become less of an issue with reliable hardware and modern programming tools, but as a principle (particularly in relation to rigorous checking of input data) it remains utterly sound.

The third, that document design is crucial, is as true as ever. It is enshrined in the discipline, now recognized as vital, of human-computer interface design.

The fourth, specify and freeze, has had a long innings and opinions still differ over it, often with real passion. In my opinion a perfect, detailed, and frozen specification was and is an unattainable dream. Prototyping, one step at a time, and even trial-and-error approaches are for most systems the sensible way to meet client expectations. These, however, were unthinkable in the days before programming tools. A frozen specification in those early days was essential.

The fifth, spend effort to optimize run time, has of course been exploded by spectacular falls in hardware costs (despite the gluttonous demands operating systems now make on hardware) and almost equally spectacular rises in labor costs. This was already starting to happen in the early 1960s.

The sixth, configure with great care, has gone. Prospective customers were seldom as grateful as they should have been—do we always give the job to the plumber who sucks his teeth and says "This is going to be difficult"— and virtue as its own reward was unsatisfying. Of course, one can now enhance configurations more or less out of petty cash.

One further comment. If followed from our set of principles that every systems problem inevitably required a unique solution. The whole idea of packaged software, constraining both the user's desires and opportunities, ran counter to them. Nonetheless, packages began to appear in the early 1960s, and LEO could have been quicker to recognize that they had merit.

Computer Systems

Let me now turn from principles to system design in the narrower sense: the process of responding to an identified requirement with an efficient computer solution. Of all LEO's achievements, its skill at this was perhaps outstanding.

In the days of LEO II/1, the problem seemed relatively straightforward. There would always be one or more main files, on tightly packed binary punched cards; the requirement was to pass through these as few times as possible, attempting to carry out all necessary calculations in the time taken to read/punch the cards and print the results. This was sometimes feasible, because both card punch and printer were slow (100 cycles/minute). On the other hand, fitting the program for all the calculations into the limited LEO II/1 memory (2048×19 bit words), leaving a mandatory contingency free for future program changes, was quite a challenge.

Of course this apparently simple system design strategy had its complications. It was not always obvious what the main files should be, or in what sequence they should be arranged. A payroll file ordered by cost centers or by individuals' identity numbers? Stock control based on a bin file or a supplier file, or both? Should tables such as price lists be held in memory or run through as a file? Transaction data and file amendments, and intermediate results passed between programs, had to be coaxed into the right sequence to match the appropriate main file, which often required considerable operator effort. Printouts might be required in a different sequence again. A strategic choice was necessary between paper tape input (variable-length data) and punched cards (fixed size, but could be sorted). Main file design could be crucial, again involving questions of fixed- and variable-length fields. What runs were needed: daily? weekly? monthly? yearly?

The scope for creativity, particularly when it came to applications like parts explosion, was satisfying. Flowcharts showing the programs that made up a system were drawn and redrawn many times. So were flowcharts of the logic within individual programs.

There was a lot of housekeeping too. Restart points, in case of breakdown when well into a long run, had to be provided.[2] Halts with displayed identity numbers and operator options had to be built in.[3] Reconciliations of the computer's calculations were made, by my time, I suspect more to reassure customers than because they were actually useful.[4] My recollection is that they were quietly dropped when LEO III came in.

Coding was another enjoyable intellectual challenge (except for the boring easy bits). LEO II programs were written in machine code with relative as opposed to absolute addressing.[5] The repertoire of instructions was rich,[6] and minimizing the number of instructions taken could absorb many delightful hours. The complex result was supposed to be carefully annotated so somebody else could pick up the code later, to correct or update it, without having to spend as many hours again trying to understand it.

Documentation in general had to be meticulous. Specifications and flowcharts were to be kept strictly in step with changes in the program code. Operating instructions, in considerable detail, were required. So were user manuals. Most of us were less than perfect at achieving all this. . . .

Great emphasis was laid on checking the correctness of programs. They were carefully checked through by another programmer before being allowed near the machine. Test data, supposedly exercising every route through the program (on reflection, I doubt this was possible), had to be prepared. Rather surprisingly, you were then allowed to operate your own program trials. Later on, the customer had to provide volumes of real data, and pilot and parallel runs took place. My impression is that these measures were remarkably successful, even though an occasional bug got through.

Revolutions

The first revolution in system design arose from the introduction of magnetic tape as the medium for main files and for intermediate results between programs. This was revolutionary for no fewer than four reasons: firstly because file design was no longer constrained by punched-card formats; secondly because it was now unrealistic to hope for all calculation to take place during input/output time; thirdly because it became much less burdensome to pass through a file several times; and fourthly because files could no longer be sorted or otherwise accessed offline. Though the wider principles were not changed, system flowcharts started to look different, with fewer but more elaborate files and more runs. A sort utility program soon appeared and was featured as almost every second run. And bigger jobs could be tackled.

The second revolution was multiprogramming, which arrived, together with significantly larger memories, with LEO III. In theory multiprogramming meant anything could be run concurrently with anything else. In practice, at least where clerical jobs involving input/output devices (as distinct from mathematical work) were concerned, this was unrealistic and a disciplined plan for sharing was needed. This typically took the form of a machine divided into three "streams": a data capture stream, with an input device, one tape deck, and a chunk of memory, which vetted all the data and produced a "clean" data tape; a print stream, driven by another tape deck; and a main stream, with most of the memory and four tape decks (one input, one output, and two for reading/rewriting the master file), to do the bulk of the computation (and also the sorts, which on LEO III used a powerful hardware merge/sort instruction). There were considerable savings in time and also in convenience as a consequence, such as being able to submit data (and any necessary corrections) in any sequence. And again bigger and more complex jobs became feasible.

The half-revolution—it never fully happened, certainly in the LEO era—was the use of random-access devices. In theory these allow far more flexibility and efficiency to the system designer, instead of having to flog all the way through long magnetic tape files. In practice the indexing problem (finding what you want) is so formidable that most early systems using random-access devices actually still processed their files sequentially.[7] Also the early devices (drums on LEO II and III) were small and slow, so their influence on system design was minor (at least you could get tables, and a lot of extra program routines, onto them).

Much of the LEO II thinking—optimize use of memory space, pack files as tightly as possible with data to minimize file passing time, flow-chart everything, check everything, document everything—survived these revolutions. However, programming became a significantly different occupation as LEO III matured. From the first days of LEO III, the master routine handled the input/output devices, the operator interface, the restart procedures, and other standardizable functions. This both made the operators' task less complex and saved the programmers a good deal of time and errors, but at the cost of what seemed at the time a lot of memory (4K words!) and of some loss of independence, flexibility, and professional pride.

CLEO, which was COBOL-like in its scope, came along rather later and repeated the process, making programming easier and more bug-free at a further cost in memory occupancy, run time, file packing capability, and professional pride. Programming as such was now perceptibly on the road to being deskilled. Not everybody in LEO was enthusiastic, although most but not all of the customers adopted CLEO.

These two developments were perhaps rather ahead of their time, like so many LEO innovations. In retrospect it is clear that they were eminently right, but computers were still slow, small, and very expensive.[8] The LEO compromise between machine and labor cost optimization in the early 1960s was perhaps as well-judged as anybody's.

Another development at this time was that some customers began to want to do their own thing in systems and programming terms, without the benefit of LEO's help. Lyons were a prime example. This was healthy but frustrating; LEO's best capabilities were not being deployed, and we found ourselves in reactive rather than proactive mode. There was no longer room or time to study in depth. With hindsight the market was eventually bound to move massively that way. LEO's niche, based on systems and programming expertise, could only shrink—as indeed it did. It is intriguing that now, with the rise of outsourcing, the pendulum seems to have started to swing the other way.

Some Projects

To add some real-life experience to some of the points made above, let me briefly describe three of the projects in which I was involved. I have not picked the typical success stories (Lyons Teashops payroll, Ilford, Inland Revenue, Customs and Excise, and so on), but jobs with unusual, thought-provoking features.

British Oxygen (LEO II/7) was a bit of a disaster. It was an ambitious project, covering parts explosion, production scheduling, and stock control, plus costing, management information, and all the trimmings. Designing the system, using magnetic tape and a drum, was difficult but successful. The six principles were all faithfully observed. Implementation looked as if it was going to be a long haul but perfectly feasible. But during the long haul it started to go sour. The detailed work had all been done by LEO people, in close consultation with our customer. The problem was that the customer had less knowledge of the detailed requirements and of changing company strategies, and less political clout, than we (or he) had realized. We were implementing a simplified model, not the reality. In the end we had to withdraw. The moral being that the six principles were vital, but they were not enough.

Shell Mex and BP (SMBP), LEO's second-largest customer, was far from a disaster, but it was a rough ride. The application, on LEO IIIs, was pricing, invoicing, sales ledger, customer statements, and sales statistics, plus a separate application to explore statistically a collection already made (on Ferranti Pegasus magnetic tapes) of marketing data. A combined LEO/SMBP[9] team did the specification, system design, and implementation. Relationships were excellent. The rough ride had two elements, technical and commercial. Technically, the price structure turned out to be far more complex than had been realized; it is only half an exaggeration to say that there was a special price for every customer and for every product. We cracked it, but it was, I believe, by far the most complex computer pricing system of its day. The commercial problem stemmed from having ignored the sixth principle: unusually, LEO had not been involved in application design or sizing presale. It was a novel experience to find a customer confident enough to tackle these for them- selves, and insistent on doing so. They did not appear troubled by the complexity—perhaps at the senior level at which we were having most contact, they were not aware of it. Their many discussions with LEO had always been on what services could be provided rather than about how in detail our equipment would perform any specific job. Nonetheless, because of the competitive pressures we had undertaken to ensure the job was done, and indeed that SMBP need pay only when implementa- tion was complete, so it was a decided setback when it turned out that the complexity called for about twice as much computer as anticipated. This was an interesting challenge to negotiating skill! But goodwill all around fortunately triumphed, and the savings realized by SMBP turned out better than their original estimate. The moral for this one is that you neglect any of the six principles at your peril, but you may get away with it (LEO's competitors had this moral well on board).[10]

The job for the Government Dockyards (LEO III) was an unqualified success. It was a payroll and labor costing application using Autolector for its input, and eventually expanded to cover all four Navy Dockyards. After LEO had outlined the system strategy and trained the team, this small, keen, rather junior but very competent group of civil servants did most of the detailed design and programming with comparatively little help from LEO. They mastered CLEO, and the eccentricities of Autolector form design and operation, with impressively little fuss. The project ran to time, to budget, and with no nasty surprises in the sizing. This moral is if sound principles have been established and are observed, it doesn't take a host of high-powered computer experts to succeed. A first-hand account of this project is given in Chapter 24.[11]

Let me also, for the record, quote two of my most abject failures of the period. I failed to persuade the *Financial Times* that they should use a computer to produce their daily ration of share prices and financial sta- tistics. And I utterly failed to convince the Ordnance Survey that com- puters could do anything useful for them at all.

New Devices

Another theme that runs through the period is revolutions in input/out- put technology. I've mentioned tape and drums, but the time period also saw the introduction of alphanumeric printers, xerographic printers, docu- ment readers (manually or automatically fed), Kimball tag readers, mag- netic and optical character recognition, disk files, magnetic card memory devices, online data transmission, faster everything. . . . Whatever it was, some competitor had it, LEO didn't, and some customer wanted it (the exception was the Lector document readers, which LEO pioneered). LEO was short of development effort and was reluctant to expand the product line, but quite often we found the commercial pressure too great to resist.

Sometimes we could ingeniously pervert existing product line items. We read 65-column cards through an 80-column reader with some fancy work on the plugboard. We printed graph plots on large blank expanses of paper, for the lines joining them to be drawn in by hand. We printed Braille (sideways!) using the full stops on a standard printer. More ambitiously, an electronic-cum-program rig-up was used to read the Pegasus magnetic tapes. Special fast 21-column card readers (2000 cards per minute!) were found and attached for Post Office telephone billing without having to change the interface or the software.

Some devices needed a form of system design in their own right, effectively a specification for their electronic logic. Autolector needed quite elaborate internal precautions against document misalignments and misreads. The Xeronic printer's ambitious facilities and its inability to stop (a fire risk) required a lot of logic, much of which Rank Xerox hadn't thought of.[12]

The most challenging device design problem was online data transmission, manifested as analog pseudo-digital, telegraph-type signaling, which had to be multiplexed in and out on a collection of concurrent lines. The customer was the Ministry of Pensions and National Insurance (MPNI), with its sickness/unemployment benefit project, and we put forward the totally novel (at that time) solution of a Marconi Myriad as a front-end processor. It was expensive, but clearly the right way to do the job. Alas, we didn't get the order and so didn't implement what would have been another important world first. I suspect, however, that the development engineers may not have been totally sorry!

I handled some of the bigger customers in the latter part of the period (Lyons, Shell Mex, and the government), so I got more than my share of these situations. The biggest drama, again initiated by MPNI, was a quest for large-scale (100 megabytes!) random-access devices. We hoped the RCA RACE magnetic card file would cope. An agonizing series of full-day trials of the device's reliability was held for the Treasury engineers; it failed about once an hour, which was not acceptable. We tried Data Products's big disk file. It worked, but cost a fortune. Life doesn't contain such excitements nowadays. . . .

System Design Today

It may be interesting, after all this thinking back into the mind frame of 30 years ago, to return to the present and look at LEO's systems work from today's perspective.

My view nowadays of systems is that there are rather few universal truths about them; they vary considerably from one another along a number of dimensions. A few, for example, require and get enormously detailed specifications (e.g., for safety reasons, aircraft control systems), whereas others start not so much with specifications as objectives (my chairman once said to me, "Build me a system to help me run the Group!"). Most lie between these poles. Some are hugely complex and demand careful sizing, even today; most do not. Some are so complex that the only sensible approach is to split them up. Some have to be tailor-made; others can be bought in the form of a package. Some cannot carry out their vital functions without collecting and structuring a vast multimedia database; others can afford to take the line that 10 percent of the data will yield 90 percent of the system benefit. Some demand not just functional but structural and cultural change in the organizations that implement them; others are painless.

In this confusing situation, two current conflicting trends can be distinguished. On the one hand, the world has noticed the advantages of simplicity and is trying to achieve it, through modularizing systems, through applying the Pareto 80:20 principle,[13] and through using preexisting standardized software where possible. On the other hand, better and cheaper hardware and gradual improvement in programming tools are encouraging ever more ambitious projects. It would be nice to think that nothing as impossibly complex as the U. S. Star Wars project, or as impossibly all-things-to-all-people as the UK Stock Exchange's Taurus, will be attempted again . . . . But I am pessimistic! I would at least strongly advocate not giving the full treatment to systems that do not need it. Where mountains are not absolutely essential, build molehills.

Senior management sponsors of computer systems with vision do not yet grow on trees. It is still not unknown to find limited, small-vision technical people being fielded to speak for users, or too-busy, frightened-of-the-computer senior management deputing one of their tired or bypassed colleagues to be the organization's "leader" in this area.

In the light of these views, let me look at some of today's system design issues for organizations of the kind that were LEO's customers, and relate them back to the LEO era. The issues to be discussed are business process reengineering, business ownership of systems, "hard" and "soft" specifications, management information, databases, sizing, project justification, and outsourcing.

Business Process Reengineering

I will start with business process reengineering: the radical and continuing redesign of the processes that constitute a business's operations. This is so fashionable today that almost any new system is described as BPR, but properly the operative word is *radical*. The concept is close to LEO's first principle, but now as then it is proving difficult to achieve. The problem is not one of computing but of change management. Radical redesign is hugely demanding on leadership and management competence and intensely painful to all concerned; its computing aspects are by comparison easy.

LEO did not fully realize this—nor do most MIS suppliers, nor a good many in-house MIS departments, even today. In practice in the LEO period, computing projects were not usually managed, or even visible, at a high enough level for truly radical redesign to have any chance of success. The management skills hardly existed. Even Lyons, who, with a truly visionary sponsor on the Board in the person of John Simmons, with an impressive track record and with a master plan, were better placed to attempt it than most, tripped over the politics and the leadership demands it entailed. Actually, the success of most LEO implementations suggests that the balance we struck between radicalism and timidity was usually well-judged. The advocates of business reengineering are still feeling for a similar balance in today's higher-profile circumstances.

Ownership

A feature of these circumstances is the still open question of the "ownership" of systems: who, in a user organization, is the sponsor of a system? Who is the budget-holder? How can the necessary relationship of trust and empathy be built between the line function and the MIS people? The significance of these questions was not fully apparent in the LEO period. We thought we could battle our way through despite the disinclination of top people to involve themselves (though the British Oxygen disaster was a pointer). But it is now clear that this issue is crucial to big systems design, particularly where it is radical. Best practice is slowly emerging.

Frozen Specifications

How about the frozen specification? Nowadays there is a spectrum of good practice. For systems where the requirements can be tightly defined, or "hard," perhaps in an engineering context, the best practice is to freeze and implement one module at a time, then proceed to the next. Tight change control, and ease of making changes, must be integral parts of both specification and implementation (easier said than done). At the other extreme, where the requirements are "soft", probably in a knowledge-based or aesthetic context, the best practice is to proceed through a series of prototyping iterations. Needless to say, most real systems do not fall neatly into either of these categories[14] and compromises have to be found—another art not well developed today. There are fewer hard (and nearly hard) jobs awaiting their first implementation today than there used to be, but it is probably still true that erring in the direction of making specifications too hard carries less risk than making them too soft.

LEO practice tended toward the hard end of this spectrum. This was fine as a discipline, and succeeded in hardish applications such as payroll or pricing and invoicing. It perhaps constrained flexibility in such contexts as stock and production control, but that is wisdom after the event. A less successful area for LEO was the softer area of management information. We could see that this was potentially of great value, but were seldom able to make it so in practice. Specifications were ingeniously devised, duly agreed and implemented, but the trial-and-error interplay needed to hone facts into real management usefulness was too difficult, both for the managers (who lacked both the patience and the faith for the process) and for the implementors. Again the management skills were not there. Nor perhaps did we fully appreciate that information about the outside world is often more important for management than that produced from internal systems.

Databases

Where is the world now on databases? The term has unhelpfully developed two distinct meanings: a collection of reference material, or a comprehensive set of data for a set of applications. As far as reference databases are concerned, number and word collections are today well implemented, though there is still a distance to go on pictures, sound, and other media. In application databases we are still struggling. Integrating all relevant data into a big system now looks, if anything, less feasible in the light of experience than it did 20 years ago. Collecting, verifying, structuring, and maintaining data are all expensive games, and the benefits of massive integration have proved elusive. Prudent practice today is to build must-have databases rather than nice-to-have ones, building in the capability to expand easily.

This could be seen as a cycling back to LEO practice, which certainly did not favor undue proliferation of data, though the reason for this was more to do with shortage of memory space and the desire to keep files, and hence running times, short than with any database philosophy. I cannot imagine LEO encouraging the building up of large-scale data just in case it might be useful, nor would I encourage anybody to do that today.

Sizing and Project Justification

Is sizing important in these days of massive, cheap computing power and memories? Only sometimes, in demanding applications where the volume is large and/or response times are crucial. For these, as David Caminer has put it, the sizing task has not gone away; it has simply become more difficult, requiring the ministrations of a new class of expert. Elsewhere the need for this onerous discipline has mercifully receded.

LEO was rightly hot on sizing. Punched-card capacity, magnetic tape capacity, memory capacity, calculation time and overall run time were all treated as crucial (and usually underestimated by the competition). It was another tough challenge that was pleasing to tackle and get right[15]—but it was also an intellectual overhead of which the world is now well relieved.

Project justification is another fine art that has changed, but in this case toward more challenge, demand, and satisfaction, not less. Today relatively few projects start in green fields, most obvious clerical savings have been made, and any new computing investment is not easily isolated for analysis. Justification is largely about intangible benefits and costs, and should (but often does not!) include sophisticated project scoping and careful examination of risks. Again, the best practice is slowly emerging. That said, connoisseurs of human frailty will be pleased that justification by management hunch has not gone away.

That phenomenon was not unknown in the LEO era, but more often we were concerned with quantifiable direct savings. We and our customers were reasonably skilled at estimating these. Life, in this respect at least, was simpler then.

Outsourcing

My last issue for discussion is outsourcing: another strong current computing fashion. The jury is still out, but it seems likely that good practice occupies a spectrum from outsourcing only occasionally used skills (e.g., hardware maintenance) to outsourcing all computing and telecommunications activity up to but not including requirement specification. The right position on this spectrum will of course depend on the circumstances of the organization. Detailed system design, implementation, and operations can all undoubtedly be successfully outsourced, though best practice in managing the outsourced situation is not yet clear and the economics can be questionable.

Comparing LEO practice in this area is thought-provoking. LEO in the early days normally produced, or took a major part in producing, its customers' system specifications, detailed system designs, and project plans. We often did the lion's share of the programming, but expected customers to do their own operating (except, of course, for bureau customers). Sometimes they even did their own hardware maintenance. This *modus operandi* then largely dropped out for some 25 years,[16] but is now back with us! Outsourcer suppliers today claim, just as LEO did, that they have the specialist skills that it is not sensible for customers to develop in-house. They even claim, as LEO did, to be able to specify customers' requirements for them, but today's customers are doubtful: can outsiders ever fully grasp the intimate business issues involved in doing so? One must ask whether LEO did it well either. The probable answer is that we were far from perfect, but at the time the customers would have done it worse. Customers have gained a lot of skills since.

If outsourcing was a good idea in the LEO period and is a good idea now, why the 25-year gap? Did LEO miss a niche? The gap arose, I suppose, because the individuals skilled in what is now called outsourcing were few and expensive in the early 1960s, and their number could not possibly have been expanded fast enough to meet the exploding needs of the market over that period. Customers recognized the need to stand on their own two feet and react quickly to the opportunities of computing. Experience was the requirement, and in the absence of a substantial force of people with more general experience, they settled for lesser, local experience, often based on nonintegrated punched-card jobs, created in-house.[17] But perhaps there could have been a niche, and perhaps LEO could have filled it. It would have been tough to market the service, especially with many large industrial concerns still reluctant to learn from "the teashops company," but it is difficult not to think that the opportunity was there.

Satisfaction

One of the great attractions of working at LEO was the variety: programmers also designed systems, managed projects, taught,[18] sold (in a gentlemanly sort of way), negotiated contracts, staffed exhibitions, and invented (see *New Devices*, above). I was even taken on a five-week trip to the United States as a computer advisor to John Simmons(!).[19] I spent about a day a week for a year with the engineers specifying the details of System 4. We even once got a business course, on balance sheets and so forth, from Lyons management.[20] It was all fun, most of the time. The other great attraction was the colleagues. LEO's selection procedures obviously had something. Everybody was congenial to know and a pleasure to work with. I have never again found this to the same degree.

Notes

1. Papers on LEO were sent to me by the University Appointments Board as an afterthought—like all the best classicists I had no clear idea what I wanted to do—and the initial attraction was that LEO alumni seemed to have no trouble in finding jobs elsewhere if they wanted them! The interview and aptitude test process was a huge encouragement to join. I gather I caused consternation by sticking out for an extra $140 a year. I got it, but was put firmly in my place a

year or so later by being kindly told that I was doing very well but should not expect ever to get more than $5600 a year.

2. Ilford had a system whereby a single standard punched card, put at the head of a card pack, would restart any program—the world's first, vestigial operating system?

3. 63/31, a row of eleven 1s in binary, always signaled run end; 42/21 was an expected intermediate stop, e.g., to allow a change of stationery; and so forth.

4. Only twice in five years did I personally encounter a genuine but nonobvious machine error (and by then it was very hard to convince the engineers that such a thing could happen), and in neither case did a reconciliation detect it. The Treasury Support Unit thought well of LEO central processor reliability.

5. Perhaps it should be called a quasi-assembler.

6. A Letchworth Institute course in which I lectured ran a competition between machine codes for the neatest extraction of a square root by Newton's method. LEO II won without having to invoke its square root single instruction.

7. It has taken modern, highly complex software and modern calculation speeds to solve this problem. The benefits of random access turn out to be about real-time response speed, where this matters, and hands-off operation (no tapes to change), rather than about system design flexibility.

8. LEO III/7 had to be invoiced to Lyons, over a weekend, on Lyons' own invoice stationery. It overflowed the monetary column by three orders of magnitude!

9. At one stage the SMBP manager was Stanley Day, who had for some years in his spare time been producing a definitive catalog for the *Gramophone* magazine of all long-playing disks available in the UK. This made him an honorary computer expert at least—how he did it without a computer I cannot in retrospect imagine.

10. The Pegasus tapes were successfully converted, but no striking conclusions were ever reached from the marketing data so far as I know. This is a pity: the thinking behind such data exploration was very advanced for the time.

11. I was touched many years later to be hunted down (I had left ICL by then) and invited to the closing ceremony of the last Dockyards LEO.

12. My report on it to Lyons listed, as I recall, some 40 logical shortcomings. Rank Xerox, to my amazement, said they would put them all right, and did. (They also offered me a job!)

13. This can be a temptation to laziness rather than efficiency.

14. Frank Land developed this concept by distinguishing four archetypal situations:
    a) the situation in which requirements are known and specifications can be frozen. The design problem is then to provide as accurate and efficient translation of the specification into a set of programs, data bases, and procedures as possible.
    b) the situation in which the requirements change rapidly because the environment in which the system has to operate changes rapidly and unpredictably. The design problem is now how to make the system rapidly adjustable and flexible.
    c) the situation where the requirements are uncertain or emergent, as in an EIS or many DSS. The design problem is how to make the system a learning system. Techniques such as prototyping fit this category.
    d) the situation where the operation of the system itself changes the environment and hence the requirements next time around are different. The design problem then becomes for the system to be adaptive.

    Of course, very few systems map into just one of these categories.

15. RACE, with its random magnetic card selection times interacting with a fixed read/write cycle, was a particularly beautiful example.

16. LACES, the Heathrow imports handling system, was one notable exception.

17. It could be argued that what they got was outsourcing by another name: computer teams that were never fully integrated into the organization and were always regarded as something of an alien implant.

18. I was surprised to find myself supervising a trainee in the course that started a week after my own finished, and lecturing in the course after that.

19. At one stage in the visit we were kindly put up by NCR in their VIP guesthouse in Dayton, Ohio, which turned out to be the former stately home of no less a person than Orville Wright. We "oohed" and "aahed" to find that he had lived to see jet flight—but it is no less remarkable that John Simmons in his turn lived to see personal computers everywhere.

20. As a result of pressure from, I think, Mike Gifford, who later became Finance Director of Cadbury Schweppes and then Chief Executive of the Rank Organization.

A

Extracts from the Report of T. R. Thompson and O. W. Standingford on their visit to the United States: May/June 1947

(With acknowledgments to J. Lyons & Co. Ltd.)

Section D. Electronic Machines in the Office

I. Introduction

An electronic machine or computer is, in essence, a machine that counts and records by means of electrons. Electrons move at very high speeds, and the speed at which electronic machines work is correspondingly high.

The electronic computer was developed as a result of wartime research, and when its existence was made public by the press, it was the subject of some sensational journalism. The original Electronic Numerical Integrator and Computer (ENIAC) was called The Electronic Brain, and it was credited with powers of reasoning and judgment that it does not in fact possess and that as far as can be seen at the moment, it never will possess. It is nonetheless a remarkable invention and one that will have far-reaching effects.

Interest has so far been focused on two possible uses: carrying out involved ballistic calculations and carrying out other involved calculations for scientific and purely mathematical purposes. Our object in inquiring into the nature and possibilities of this machine was to find out whether it, or any adaptation of it, was capable of being put to use in commercial offices, and, if this was not the case, to try to stimulate the development of such a machine.

This report sets out the results of the inquiry and seeks to show some of the possibilities of the machine by indicating what is already known to be technically possible and what has, in fact, already been achieved in the laboratory. Most components, if not all, are already in operation in one form or another. Further research is, however, necessary before these various components can be made to work together satisfactorily as a machine for everyday use in the commercial world. Research with the object of building such a machine has already been started in a number of places and progress seems to be rapid. It would nevertheless be unwise to attempt to predict how long it will be before such a satisfactory machine can be marketed. It will certainly not be less than two years and some of those engaged in research would prefer to estimate it at 10 years.

The functions that are technically possible and that a commercial machine could, as far as we can see, be designed to carry out are listed below. They are functions of the type performed by punched-card equipment, but whereas the punched-card machine operates at mechanical speeds, the electronic machine operates at electronic speeds and requires less intervention by clerks (or machine minders) in its processes.

1. The machine will receive and store information. This information may be in terms of either figures or words, both of which will necessarily be in code. It is this "memory" function of the machine that offers the greatest possibilities. The term *memory* is used by the scientists, for lack of a better term, to refer to that part of the machine in which facts are recorded and from which they can be made available to the computing and writing devices. It serves the same purpose as the punched card on which information is recorded in terms of holes punched in certain positions. The card is used to pass this information to the calculating or tabulating machines as required for various processes.

2. The machine will receive and store in its memory operational instructions, again in code. These instructions may consist of an involved series of orders. They are instrumental in making the machine work in a certain way so that once a process has been started no further intervention is necessary until the finished product is ready.

3. According to the orders placed in its memory, the machine will select any item of information from its memory and either record it in some predetermined manner or use it in further operations.

4. According to the orders placed in its memory the machine will select from its memory and bring together associated words or figures.

5. The machine will compare words or figures and react, according to the orders given to it, to any differences it may find. It will thus carry out automatically a predetermined checking process.

6. The machine will, in accordance with the orders given to it, select figures from its memory and add, subtract, multiply, or divide them. It will store the results of these calculations so that they can be used as a basis of further calculations or else record them as a final result.

7. The information contained in the memory of the machine can at any time be extracted and made available in written form, and in any order that may be required.

It is something of an achievement to have produced a machine that is capable of carrying out these functions. But the real achievement is to have produced a machine that will carry out these functions at electronic speed. The machine performs its calculations at speeds that can be expressed only in terms of hundreds of thousands of movements per second. It is obviously wasteful to have a machine that is capable of working at these superhuman speeds unless the information it is to work upon can be made available to it at relatively comparable speeds. The feeding clearly cannot be directly by clerks but mechanical and electrical means have been devised that are satisfactory.

The sections of the report that follow set out in general terms how such functions as have been mentioned can be carried out by a machine and the kind of machines we have seen that can do them.

II. Coding for Electronic Machines

Electronic computation is carried out by means of electrical impulses. Any material that is fed into the computer must therefore first be expressed or coded in terms of pulses. The impulse code is not new; it is used to transmit messages by teleprinter. When a teleprinter key is depressed the appropriate letter, figure, or symbol is coded as a series of electrical impulses that pass along the wires to the receiving machine, where they cause the selection and operation of the corresponding type. A teleprinter is, in fact, an impulse-coding machine.

The type of impulse code used in electronic machines is known as the Binary System, since it contains only two symbols usually represented by the two digits *1* and *0*. It is also called the "Yes-No" system as *1* can represent *Yes* a positive impulse) and *0* can represent *No* (a negative impulse). The example below shows one way in which the numbers 1 to 15 can be expressed in terms of combinations of *Yes* (1) and *No* (0).

0 = 0000	1 = 0001	2 = 0010	3 = 0011
4 = 0100	5 = 0101	6 = 0110	7 = 0111
8 = 1000	9 = 1001	10 = 1010	11 = 1011
12 = 1100	13 = 1101	14 = 1110	15 = 1111

Anything expressed in this Binary System can easily be expressed either mechanically, electrically, or magnetically. For instance, *Yes* can be signaled by electric current being switched on, and *No* by its being switched off. Or *Yes* can be represented by a positive electrical charge and *No* by a negative charge.

Note: Besides the Binary System it is possible to express numbers according to a coded decimal system. Such a system is used in the Bell Telephone Relaying Machines.

Punched cards have been used as a means of feeding electronic machines, but in the later models a device used for high-speed telegraphy has been successfully introduced. For the latter, teletypists operate machines that punch holes in a paper tape to correspond with the Binary System code (Figure A.1).

Each *1* (or *Yes*) is represented by a hole punched in the appropriate position on the tape; each *0* (or *No*) is represented by the appropriate position being left untouched.

For visual checking, the information can be printed on the tape as well as punched, but the simplest way of ensuring accuracy is probably to

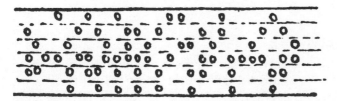

Figure A.1. Paper tape.

prepare a second tape on a special comparing machine. A second typist prepares a tape independently, with the original tape running through the machine simultaneously. Whenever the second typing differs from the first, the typist is unable to operate the key, and investigates. If the typists are typing incorrectly, they can proceed by touching the correct key; if the first tape is wrong, they touch a lever that enables them to punch one character different from that on the first tape. The second tape is thus almost certainly accurate. Both operators may, however (as in any checking system), make the same mistake. This comparing machine is merely an adaptation of equipment already on the market.

The verified tape can be converted into electrical impulses at high speed. Wherever there is a hole punched in the paper, positive electric current will pass for an infinitesimal period of time. Where there is no hole punched, the machine will register this fact as a negative current.

Material for electronic computation, expressed in this form, may be of three kinds:

    (a) descriptive information, e.g., names of materials or employees.

    (b) numbers for calculations, e.g., prices of materials or rates of pay.

    (c) instructions ("orders") as to the calculations needed, e.g., multiply or take a subtotal.

In all cases the problem of expression in terms of impulses is one of setting up a suitable code. We have seen examples of such complete codes and are well satisfied that there would be no difficulty in setting up a code suitable for commercial purposes.

III. Feeding Impulses to the Machines

If full advantage of the electronic computer's speed is to be taken, it must be fed at speeds comparable with electronic speed. How best to achieve this is one of the problems that the research laboratories are tackling. Whichever method is used the process must, of course, start with human speeds. Means have to be devised, therefore, whereby as many teleprinter operators as required prepare teleprinter tapes or other media for feeding sufficient material to keep the computer working.

There are a number of methods in operation whereby material can be made available to the computer, the first two having been mentioned briefly already.

    (a) Punched cards. These were the means of feeding all the original computers such as ENIAC and the Harvard Mark I. They are also used to feed the standard computer made by International Business Machines, which we saw working at the Office Machinery Exhibition at Cincinnati. They are, however, slow, the limiting factor being the speed at which cards can be fed mechanically. This system is fairly satisfactory for involved mathematical calculations when the computer has to carry out a sequence of operations that may take a considerable time (even hours) after the initial information has been inserted. The Harvard Mark I, although slow by comparison with later models, does work that would require some 200 to 300 clerks if done by means of ordinary calculating machines. But the same advantages would not be obtained in the commercial office where the problem is to carry out a large number of simple calculations.

(b) Punched tape. The teleprinter-punched paper tape (see specimen on page 340) can be fed into the machine faster than punched cards, but there is again a mechanical limitation. If the tape is run too quickly, it is liable to break when starting and stopping. It is used for feeding orders to the Harvard Mark I and may be a cheap and satisfactory method of doing this in commercial machines.

(c) Magnetic wire. Impulses can be recorded magnetically on a steel wire. This system is widely used for recording sound, particularly by radio broadcasting stations (the BBC has used it for many years). While ordinary steel wire is suitable for recording sound, a stronger wire is needed to stand the strain of rapid starting and stopping. Princeton University laboratory is therefore experimenting with a very fine steel-coated phosphor-bronze wire on which they hope to stack 100 to 200 impulses to the inch. "Yes" impulses are expressed by a tiny longitudinal magnetic field; "No" impulses are expressed by leaving a segment of the wire unmagnetized (see section B.1). This wire can be wound from one spool to another, starting and stopping quickly without breaking, at a speed of 50 feet per second, which at 150 impulses to the inch means 90,000 impulses per second. If this means is perfected it provides a means of feeding at speeds which will keep the computer reasonably busy. There are, however, technical problems yet to be solved before such speeds can be satisfactorily used in a working model.

(d) Magnetic tape. As a cheaper alternative to magnetic wire, Harvard has used successfully in its Mark II machine a paper tape coated with a magnetic substance (see section B.2). They are further experimenting with a treated plastic tape that they expect to be able to run at much higher speeds than paper.

While the methods outlined above may be excellent for some purposes, there is one facility, important in commercial work, that they do not offer: rapid reference by the computer to any part of the memory. If, for instance, income tax tables are fed into the machine on a wire tape, the whole length may need to be scanned before the code required is located.

The restriction on the speed of scanning is a mechanical one, and therefore speeds comparable with electronic working cannot be approached.

There are, however, other forms of memory in use or in the experimental stage which are either electronic or which work at super-mechanical speeds.

(e) Acoustic delay line. An electronic device described in section B.4.

(f) Selectron. A cathode ray tube capable of storing some 4,000 impulses that can be referred to by photo-electrical means (see section B.5). *[Not included in this extract]*

(g) Magnetic drum. A magnetic memory capable of being scanned rapidly, which is being built for the Harvard Mark III. This device, which is described in section B.3, is a steel cylinder magnetized in rings (in much the same way as magnetic wire). The information from any of 260,000 stored impulses can be located within ½ second, the average time required being ¼ second. As technical improvements are made, this speed may be improved upon 10 to even 20 times.

(h) Soundtrack recording. This is a system involving the mechanical removal of a black film from a transparent base. It is considered to be more suitable where the data is likely to be more permanent as it is less easily erased or altered.

Memories can be classified as either long-term or short-term. Long-term memories are those that can be stored away from the machine, i.e., punched cards and tapes or magnetic wires, tapes, and drums. Short-term memories are the acoustic delay line and the Selectron, which release all stored information as soon as the electric power is cut off. If a short-term memory device is used, therefore, it is essential that it be duplicated in long-term form, which may be the wire or tape used to feed the memory in the first place. Otherwise a breakdown of power supply would result in the loss of the information stored. Any information required to be fed to the computer over and over again, e.g., price lists, tax tables or rates of pay, will in any case need to be stored in long-term memories, however they are eventually fed to the computer. If magnetic devices are used for such long-term memories it will be possible to alter them quite easily; it is merely necessary to superimpose the new impulses when they will automatically replace the impulses already there. The auditing of long-term memories can also be effected quite simply by linking the memory to a teleprinter that will produce a written copy of the information coded in them.

When information stored magnetically is only of passing importance, e.g., orders received or hours worked in a particular week, the tapes, wires, or drums can easily be cleared of the magnetic fields by subjecting them to high-frequency currents. They can then be used again.

IV. The Carrying Out
of Computations

We have seen electronic machines and various components of them designed to be included in future machines. There is little point in attempting to describe their operation—we do not possess the technical knowledge—but the diagram in Figure A.2 may serve to give some idea of the processes that the various components of the machine carry out.

The machine is fed at mechanical speed through the input devices, producing a series of electrical impulses in the low-speed circuits. These impulses pass to the input synchronizer, which collects them in a storage device and then, by an ingenious and highly technical method, releases them at electronic speeds into the high-speed circuits. These electronic impulses pass to the memory, where they are stored until required. The memory contains both coded information and coded orders, which are

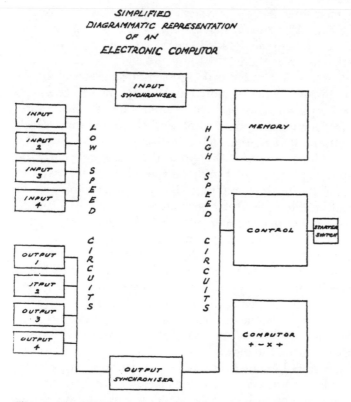

Figure A.2. Diagrammatic representation of an electronic computor.

now available to be drawn upon for use in the computer. The orders represent the clerical procedures to be followed (e.g., to read from the memory, to compute, to store in the memory, or to record through the output mechanism) and the information represents the words and figures to be used in that procedure.

Let us assume, for example, that the machine is required to carry out a series of simple multiplications, printing the product of each with a total for the series. The memory contains the coded multipliers and multiplicands, and the coded orders necessary to carry out the processes (i.e., to select, to multiply, to add, and to print).

When the machine is switched on certain complicated preliminaries take place, and the control operates to bring the first order from the memory. This order in turn causes the control to read the first multiplicand in the memory and record it temporarily in the computer. The control then continues to bring out the remaining orders in their sequence; the first multiplier is read from the memory and put into the computer, the multiplication is carried out, and the product is stored in the memory. When this sequence of orders has been carried out, the next order brought to the control will cause the sequence to be repeated for the second multiplicand and multiplier and so on, until the series is complete. When the last multiplication has been made, the control will cause another sequence of orders to be read from the memory and acted upon. All the products will be read from the memory, taken to the computer, totaled, and the result recorded in the memory. The memory now contains not only the information and orders originally fed to it, but also the products of the multiplications and the total of them.

The final order read by the control will cause the products and their total to be read from the memory and passed to the output synchronizer. Here the code impulses are reduced from electronic to mechanical speed and passed on to the output devices, which record them on magnetic wire or other medium. The magnetic wire is then taken from the machine and fed into a teleprinter, which automatically decodes and types the information in the desired form.

Some information should be given as to how the computer works, since this does all the calculations. In some respects it is the simplest part of the machine. Impulses pass into it and light up small valves. A row of valves, some lit and some not, shows a series of yes-no impulses representing a number in binary form. Another set of impulses representing another number can be superimposed into the first set so it adds and carries forward just as in ordinary addition. The resultant series of yes-nos expresses, in binary form, the sum of the two numbers. Similarly, the multiplication of two numbers is carried out by the repeated addition of two sets of impulses, so the result is the product of the two.

V. Outlines of Possible
Applications of the Machine to
Office Work

In order to illustrate the functions that the electronic computer will be capable of performing, outlines of some possible applications are given below.

It is not intended to present the outlines of perfect systems, but merely to show in practical terms what the machine will be capable of doing if all those functions that are now technically possible are incorporated into a commercial machine.

1. Sales Invoicing. In carrying out the job of invoicing, the office requires certain information that remains static, such as is normally contained in addressing plates and catalogs, and also information that varies from order to order, such as the quantities of goods to be sent to a customer. The static information can be recorded on magnetic wire so it can be fed readily into the memory of the machine when required for invoicing work.

This magnetic wire for permanent information would need to record the following:

    (a) Each customer's code, together with the full name and address and any shipping instructions.

    (b) The codes of the different lines of goods, together with their descriptions, selling prices, and such standard cost prices as may be involved.

When the machine was required to carry out an invoicing process, this magnetic wire would be fed into the memory and the information would remain available there as long as required.

There would also be a permanent magnetic wire carrying the series of instructions necessary for the process of invoicing. It would be a very detailed operating instruction in code form.

The variable information would need to be put on to a magnetic wire for each batch of orders received.

On receipt of a customer's order, it would be scrutinized generally and as to authority for credit. In particular it would be ascertained that the customer's code number was properly entered. The order would then be passed to a teletypist, who would type the following information:

    (a) The customer's code number.

    (b) The quantities and codes of the goods ordered.

    (c) Any discount rates.

The information on the teleprinter tape, after checking, would be transferred on to a magnetic wire.

When all the magnetic wires for a batch of orders were ready and the machine was free, the permanent information wire, the wires carrying the orders and the instruction wire for invoicing would all be fed into the memory, and by the turn of a switch the machine would then automatically perform the following operations at high speed:

(a) Read from the memory and record on the output wire the customer's name, address, and any shipping instructions, and the quantities, descriptions, and selling prices of the goods ordered.

(b) Calculate and record on the output wire the extensions at selling prices of the goods ordered.

(c) Total the invoice and record the total on the output wire.

(d) Calculate any discount and subtract this from the total, recording the discount and net total on the output wire.

(e) Accumulate in the memory running totals of the quantities of goods involved and of the totals of invoices and discounts.

(f) At the end of a run of invoices, record on the output wire the total quantity of each item and its extensions at the standard selling and cost rates.

The output wires would then be fed into a teleprinter, which would automatically type the invoices and labels and, at the end of the run, produce a written record of the total quantities of each item and its value at selling and standard cost rates.

2. Letter Writing. The electronic machine could also be used as a means of typing letters where large numbers of similar letters are to be written, as, for example, in a sales office. It is assumed that a number of standard salutations and closures of letters would be employed, that the persons to whom the letters are addressed would in the main be accepted customers, and that a number of standard paragraphs could be employed.

The correspondence clerk would dictate to the teletypist the following information:

(a) The customer's code number. If the letter was not to an established customer, then the name and address would be given.

(b) The code representing the standard salutation.

(c) The code numbers of any standard paragraphs to be employed.

(d) The text of any nonstandard paragraphs to be included.

(e) The code number of the standard closure to be used.

The teletypist would record this information on to a magnetic tape.

The codes, names and addresses of customers, and the standard salutations, paragraphs, and closures would be recorded on permanent magnetic wires that could be fed into the memory of the machine when required.

Given the two sets of magnetic wires, the machine would then prepare an output wire giving the full text of the letter. The output wire, when passed through a teleprinter, would then type the entire letter and address the envelope automatically.

3. Payroll. It is not proposed to elaborate a system whereby payroll could be dealt with electronically. The necessary processes, however, lend themselves admirably to adaptation. In preparing a payroll, recourse is necessary to certain static information, such as the key number and name of the employee, the basic rate, tax code, and various deductions to be made for national insurance, loan repayments, etc., All this information can be stored permanently on magnetic wire and put into the memory of the machine whenever required. The appropriate portions of the income tax tables can also be recorded on magnetic wires. (Alternatively the tax might be dealt with by means of a formula. It can deal with the variation in rates of tax when the taxable income is above different levels.)

Each week it will then remain to prepare a wire on which is recorded the employee's key number, the number of hours worked at various rates, the amount of any bonus earned, etc., after which the machine will carry out all the necessary calculations and provide on the output wire all the information necessary to print the payroll and to prepare information to be included in the employee's pay envelope.

The calculation of premium bonus, however involved, could also be carried out on the machine at a very high speed.

The illustrations given above have been selected in order to show that the electronic machine is capable of carrying out office processes that involve writing in words or figures, memorizing in words or figures, and calculating, whether the calculation be simple or complex.

VI. Contacts made in the United States

This report would not be complete without some statement about the contacts that were made in the United States and subsequently in England with people working on the Electronic Machines.

1. Dr. H. H. Goldstine of the Electronic Computer Project at the Institute for Advanced Study, Princeton University. Dr. Goldstine, a mathematical physicist, was originally in charge of the research for building ENIAC (Electronic Brain) at the Moore School of Electrical Engineering, University of Pennsylvania, in Philadelphia. He was our first contact in writing, made before we visited the U.S. He gave us the names of most of the other people engaged on official research.

We visited him first. Prior to our meeting him, he had not realized the scope for the use of electronic machinery in a commerical office, but when we outlined the problem to him, he at once became interested and proceeded immediately to outline lucidly how the problem could be tackled and what apparatus has already been developed that could be used in a general-purpose machine. He was very enthusiastic and asked us to come back again after we had seen other people in the States so that he could help us further.

Apparently he also wrote at once to Professor Hartree of Cambridge University, for within a week there was a letter at Cadby Hall asking us to come and see him and Dr. Wilkes, who is in charge of the laboratory at Cambridge that deals with electronic machines. (For notes of our visit to Cambridge, see section VII.)

When we revisited Dr. Goldstine toward the end of our trip, he outlined the construction of the machine we should need, and his engineers showed us actual components that would form part of the machine, as follows:

(a) an adaptation of the teleprinter for producing teleprinter code tape, the material being typed on the tape at the same time so that it could be visually checked if necessary.

(b) the apparatus for producing magnetic wire from the teleprinter code tape.

(c) apparatus for spinning magnetic wire from one reel to another at high speed.

(d) a piece of apparatus for automatic correction of any inaccuracies in the timing of electrical impulses, and also for eliminating any unwanted electrical impulses (such as coded instructions) before transferring the result to magnetic wire.

(e) a partly completed electronic computer taking up only a few cubic feet and much simpler in operation than the one included in ENIAC.

(f) a demonstration of the form taken by code impulses. This was done by throwing their shape on to the screen of a cathode ray oscilloscope.

2. The Moore School of Electrical Engineering, University of Pennsylvania, Philadelphia. This is where ENIAC was built by the original team of mathematical physicists, electrical engineers, etc., which has now been disbanded. A new group is carrying on with the research. They showed us a new machine that is being built for experimental purposes. It was working with all the essential components, including a set of acoustic delay line tubes of different sizes. The calculator was also working. At the time we visited the school, the only means of feeding the machine was by hand, but this, according to the engineers, was merely because they were testing it. The machine stood about six feet high, six feet across, and at the maximum was not more than two feet deep.

We discussed the commercial problem with the researchers. They showed interest but no enthusiasm for doing anything about it. There seemed a general air of apathy. It is clear that the spirit had gone out of the place when the original team was disbanded.

3. Mr. J. C. Eckert Jnr. of Electronic Control Company, Philadelphia.

Mr. Eckert is the electronic engineer who designed the parts and was in charge of the building of the ENIAC. He was well spoken of by Goldstine and others who had known him as being a first-class electrical engineer. He had broken with the Moore School over a question of patents and because the school would not contemplate the question of commercial development. He has, therefore, formed his own business to build commercial machines. He has applied for patents and has a contract with the U.S. Government for building a machine for census work. He has been subsidized by the government to build this machine. He described in detail his plans for building the machine, which, in his opinion, would be of general commercial use. It is very much in line with what Goldstine described and with what has been outlined in this report.

The Prudential Insurance Company of America is in discussion with him with the idea of having a machine built to do routine premium billing and actuarial calculations. The problem has been analyzed in electronic terms to show that the machine will be economic in practice. A contract is also being negotiated with A. C. Nielson, Management Consultants and Market Research Specialists of Chicago, with a view to their putting up money for research in return for certain rights to the machine.

4. Radio Corporation of America Laboratories, Penn's Neck, N.J.

The RCA Laboratories, although mainly concerned with electronics for radio work, have realized the possibilities of it in calculating machines and have therefore set up a special laboratory for research in this field. They have realized also the special importance of the memory aspect of the machine and are therefore concentrating on that. It is they who have developed the Selectron (*referred to earlier in Section III*).

They have built a number of experimental models, which were shown to us. They were not perfect in their working, as we were able to see for ourselves. The green fluorescent light that shows when a compartment of the memory is stimulated was leaking to compartments that had not been stimulated. The research engineers consider that it is only a question of time before they will have overcome these snags and built a perfect machine. The research men, Drs. Zworykin and Rajchman, had not realized the commercial aspect of electronic calculating machines, but saw the possibilities when we described our ideas. They were interested but showed no desire to take part in this development.

5. International Business Machine Co., New York. This company has already put an electronic multiplier on the market and we were able to see it in operation in the Office Machine Exhibition at Cincinnati. This machine, however, is made to replace their previously existing multiplier and is purely to be used in conjunction with their punched-card equipment. Continual research is going on, but as far as we were able to see the aim of this company is to use electronic calculation purely as an adjunct to punched cards.

The hiring cost of the electronic multiplier is $375 per month.

6. National Cash Register Co. at Dayton.

7. Burroughs Adding Machine Co. at Detroit. Both these companies have formed electronic research sections, but we were unable to learn what direction this research is taking. They treat the matter as highly secret.

8. U.S. Army at Aberdeen Proving Grounds. The ENIAC machine, which was originally built for ballistic purposes, is now being rebuilt at the Aberdeen Proving Grounds, which is concerned with testing new weapons. We obtained special permission to see the machine through the British Embassy, but at the last moment the permit was withdrawn without explanation except to say that the machine was now confidential. Dr. Goldstine, on hearing this, felt sure that the desire for secrecy arose because engineers must be having difficulty in getting the machine working again.

9. Prudential Insurance Company of America, Newark. This company has a large Methods Division for research into office systems, and within this division has set up a small section to deal with the development of electronic machines. In charge is Dr. Berkeley, who had experience with wartime research undertakings.

Their project is to build a machine that will carry out the premium billing of their millions of policy holders, a job that at present occupies a staff of some 300 clerks. They anticipate that this work can be done with less than 20 percent of the staff in about two days per month. The remainder of the machine's time will be given up to actuarial calculations. They are proceeding with detailed plans, and Dr. Berkeley is confident that they will have a machine installed within about two years. When they have established the premium billing, they propose to continue their investigations with a view to putting other routine work on the machine, including the writing of contracts for which they have some 2000 standard clauses from which to select. We were shown a number of the reports of their research that show the detailed examination of the problem. We were allowed to bring away copies of two or three of these, which include one that shows detailed times for the electronic set-up. Dr. Berkeley arranged for us to visit the Computation laboratory at Harvard University.

We understand that Prudential is the only commercial concern actively interested in the application of electronic machinery in its offices.

10. The Computation Laboratory at Harvard University, Cambridge, Mass. The computation laboratory under Professor Howard Aiken not only carries out research into electronic computation, but has two machines working and a third under construction. Here was found a very realistic approach. Professor Aiken is not only a mathematician but also an engineer, and in the course of three years work appears to have achieved far more than the Moore School at Philadelphia.

During the war Harvard was working for the U.S. Navy while Moore School worked for the U.S. Army. While Professor Aiken was aware of the possibilities of electronic calculation and was carrying out research, he took his main wartime object as the building of a machine that would work and keep working.

The Harvard Mark I is not therefore strictly an electronic calculator. It operates by high-speed magnetic relays. Compared with ENIAC it is slow, but it is more reliable. ENIAC was working satisfactorily for only 20 percent of the time (among other things it has 18,000 valves to go wrong); Mark I works well 80 percent of the time. It was seen working on mathematical tables, doing work that would require 300 clerks using ordinary calculating machinery. It is so reliable that the pages typed by the output teleprinter are sent straight to the printers for photographic plates to be made, and the volumes printed and published. No errors in the published tables have yet been located. Much was learned from Mark I, and 67 improvements have been made in three years of operation.

Mark II still uses relays for calculation and memory and is therefore massive, requiring a large room to house it. But it works at 12 times the speed of Mark I.

Mark III is in the course of construction, and some of the components were seen. It will be much smaller, about $6' \times 3' \times 10'$, and will consist of a high-speed magnetic drum memory (see section B.3) and a much improved electronic computer using less than 1000 valves. It will work 20 times as fast as Mark II. The cost of Mark III is expected to be under $75,000. The memory drums, capable of recording 260,000 impulses, will cost $20,000. (Selection tubes to give the same memory capacity would, Aiken estimated, cost $65,000.)

Professor Aiken's own faith, enthusiasm, and drive are reflected in everyone in the laboratory, and it is easy to see how they have achieved so much in so short a time. Aiken is intensely practical. For instance, while at Princeton they are endeavoring to pack 100 to 200 impulses to an inch of magnetic wire, at Harvard they use 10 to the inch, which they know will work satisfactorily now. When they see their way to increase the number without endangering the machine's accuracy, they will do so.

Aiken was enthusiastic about the commercial possibilities and would co-operate in any research in this direction. He is of the opinion that Professor Hartree of Cambridge would be the right man to work in this field, and also recommends Dr. Comrie of 23 Bedford Sq., London, as a collaborator in a consultative capacity.

Aiken has already thought beyond the field of pure office work and has been considering "electronic control," whereby a factory could be controlled automatically, all the processes being coordinated and made to work in accordance with a predetermined policy. He is of the opinion that we are on the threshold of a second industrial revolution, his only fear being that the world will not be able to produce a sufficient number of educated people to control its processes.

In his opinion, there are less than ten true experts in electronic computation and control in the world. Because of this, Harvard is going to start a special postgraduate course this year to provide people to intensify the inquiries in this field. They also intend to pursue research into electrochemical computation as soon as they can find a suitable person to do the work.

VII. Visit to the Mathematical Laboratory, Cambridge

On our return to England, we visited the Mathematical Laboratory, which is the department concerned with Electronic Computers. This department is headed by Dr. Wilkes, who went to America and studied Electronic Computers after Professor Hartree himself had been there and studied them.

Professor Hartree is a mathematical physicist: his work will be much facilitated by the use of electronic computers. On his return, he proposed to the University that a committee should be formed to consider the possibility of building an electronic computer in Cambridge. This committee was formed, and a sum of money was voted for the necessary research. Dr. Wilkes, who was already director of the Mathematical Laboratory, was given the job. Professor Hartree, although he is not concerned in the building of the machine, is very interested in it, and has written several booklets and given lectures, so as to stimulate interest in electronic computers.

We met both Professor Hartree and Dr. Wilkes and found them both keenly interested in our proposals for a commercial machine and prepared to make their knowledge and advice available. They had not previously realized the commercial possibilities of the machine, being preoccupied with its use in scientific research.

They are at present engaged in building a pilot machine with an acoustic delay line memory. The idea is that the pilot machine should be the simplest possible that will demonstrate what can be done. Thus the memory will be fed slowly by teleprinter and not at high speed. Once the pilot machine is working, they feel it will be easier to convince people of the immense value of the machine, so that funds will be forthcoming both to build the machine and finance further research.

Although Cambridge has been working on the machine only since late last year, as far as we can gather from our limited technical knowledge, they are already far in advance of the Moore School at Philadelphia, where the research is on similar lines. Whereas the Moore School is experimenting with 10-foot tubes at Cambridge they are building a machine incorporating tubes 4 to 5 feet in length. The definition of impulses as shown on the oscilloscope is excellent and far better than anything we saw in the United States. they have taken particular care to ensure that the face of the quartz crystals are parallel—a point that was not emphasized to us elsewhere.

Progress with the machine is slow and they talk of 12 to 18 months before completion. They have all their plans drawn and the hold-up is purely due to lack of money. Dr. Wilkes and one draftsman assistant alone are handling the job, assisted at the moment by two students. We told them that unless they can proceed more rapidly they may find machines for sale in the United States before they complete their first model. We were told that given £2000 ($5600) they could complete much more rapidly.

Both Professor Hartree and Dr. Wilkes were willing and ready to cooperate with us: in particular, they are interested in applying their machine to any clerical job we may suggest, and they are ready to assist in translating clerical procedure into terms of coded instructions.

VIII. Steps that might be taken by Lyons to advance the development of electronic machines

Our first concern is, of course, the advantages that Lyons may gain from the commercial development of electronic machines, but there is a wider aspect which cannot be overlooked. This machine may well be a prime factor in relieving the present economic distress of the country. In this latter respect we cannot help but feel that Lyons occupies a key position; no one else here, as far as we can learn, has realized the far-reaching possibilities of electronic machines.

We assume that Lyons will want to take full advantage of these machines for their own offices. It is possible for us to play a passive role by merely keeping in touch with developments, and in due course buying machines as they become available, probably from American sources. But such a role would not enable us to have any influence on the kind of machines built, and without commercial influence they may well be built in a form more suited to handling mathematical and census calculations owing to the influence of the large governmental concerns (*).

* The National Physical Laboratory (Dr. Turing and Dr. Wormersley) as we understand are working on projects of the Services and Board of Trade, but do not expect to show results for some years. There has been some reluctance to discuss the project with people outside, partly perhaps as a result of unfortunate advance publicity in the U.S.

If we are to play an active part in developing electronic machines there are a number of alternative ways in which we could act:

(a) We could encourage Professor Hartree to carry his research in directions which will produce machines of high memory capacity suitable for commercial purposes, working with him by providing him with clerical procedures for his experiments. Further, we might support his work financially, or endeavor to influence other bodies such as the Nuffield Trust to support him.

(b) We could put our ideas in the hands of a large electrical concern such as E.M.I. or G.E.C. and leave them to exploit the machine.

(c) We could work with Electronic Controls Inc., of Philadelphia, who would probably want some assistance in financing their project.

(d) We could approach the British Government, placing the matter in their hands to coordinate research in this country and make all resources available to make Britain first in the field.

(e) We could build a machine in our own workshops, drawing on information and advice from Harvard Universities.

Appendix B.1

Magnetic Wire

For many years sound has been recorded on steel wires by representing the speed and strength of vibrations as magnetic fields.

This method has been adapted for the recording of "Yes" and "No" impulses used in electronic machines. *Yes* can be represented by a longitudinal inal magnetic field and *No* by leaving a portion of the wire unmagnetized. The length of the magnetic field on the wire can be very tiny, and the depth of the fields into the wire is in terms of thousandths of an inch. Experiments have already shown that 100 to 200 separate impulses can be stored to the inch of wire without interfering with each other. The magnetic fields on the surface of the wire would appear as shown in Figure A.3.

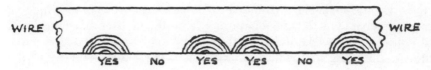

Figure A.3. Magnetic wire (1).

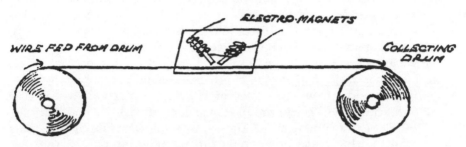

Figure A.4. Magnetic wire (2).

The plain steel wire that is adequate for sound recording is not suitable for feeding electronic machines at high speed, since it is liable to stretch or even break under the strain of starting and stopping. Experiments are therefore being carried out with phosphor-bronze wire coated either with steel or nickel to a thickness of about 1/1000 of an inch. It is in this thin coating that the magnetic fields are situated.

To magnetize the wire, it is fed rapidly past the poles of an electromagnet, which is being energized by electrical impulses representing the *Yes* and *No* code (Figure A.4).

It is essential that the wire should travel at a constant speed in relation to the electrical impulses, so the distance occupied by any impulse is standard. Synchronizing apparatus has been developed to ensure this.

Selected sections of a wire record can be altered without difficulty by imposing new impulses over those already existing. The whole of the fields on the wire can be erased by subjecting it to high-frequency currents so the same wire can, if required, be used over and over again for new sets of information.

Appendix B.2

Magnetized Tape

As an alternative to magnetized wire, a paper tape, coated with a magnetic layer, has been developed. It is less expensive than the wire and can be run at 1/10 the speed to give the same output. Whereas the wire can contain one string of impulses only, the tape can have a number of strings in parallel lines. The tape in use at Harvard is 1 inch wide and carries ten lines of impulses on its surface.

In spite of the lower running speed, there is always the possibility that the paper may break, and experiments are therefore being carried out with a magnetizeable plastic tape that may well prove more satisfactory than the wire.

Appendix B.3

The Magnetized Drum Memory

The magnetized drum has been developed to overcome the difficulty of scanning and rescanning a length of wire or tape.

The drum in use experimentally at Harvard is 10 inches in circumference and its surface is coated with nickel. Electromagnetic heads are staggered around the surface of the drum so there is one to each $\frac{1}{10}$ inch along its length. By means of these heads, Yes-No messages can be recorded magnetically in rings around the surface of the cylinder (see Figure A.5).

Any desired pocket in the memory is selected by first switching to the appropriate head and then, as the drum rotates on its axis, locating the points on the ring corresponding to the pocket.

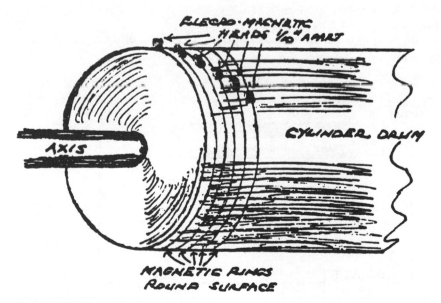

Figure A.5. Magnetic drum memory.

While the computer is in operation, the memory drums are kept revolving at 720 revolutions per minute. With each revolution the entire surface of the drum is scanned, that is, the entire memory is searched through twelve times in every second.

The memory for the Harvard Mark III computer will consist of eight drums all geared to one synchronized motor. The capacity will be 260,000 impulses, and the cost of the first model about $20,000

Appendix B.4

The Acoustic Delay Line

The acoustic delay line or mercury tank consists of a tube with a quartz crystal at each end and mercury between. The tube forms part of an electrical circuit, with a terminal on each quartz crystal. Electrical impulses traveling around the circuit arrive at one quartz crystal and have the effect of expanding the quartz, which sends a sound wave along the mercury, to strike the other quartz crystal, which, when struck, sets up an electrical impulse that continues around the circuit (Figure A.6).

The acoustic delay line consists, in effect, of a circuit in which a series of impulses travels around and around continually and at high speed. Impulses are fed into the circuit through a gate valve. The number of impulses in the series will depend upon the length of the tube. A 10-inch tube will accommodate a series of some 4000 impulses traveling around and around at the speed of sound in mercury. The series has a beginning and an end, and an individual impulse is recognized by its number in the sequence.

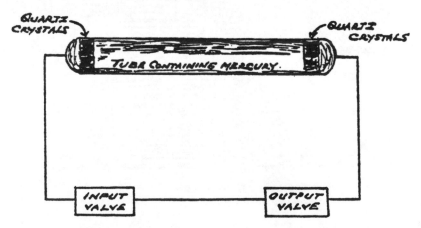

Figure A.6. Acoustic delay line.

For the purpose of the electronic machine the series of impulses is divided into memory "pockets," each of which can contain a predetermined number of "Yes" or "No" impulses. The size of the memory pocket for any machine would vary according to the purposes for which it is to be used, but it would probably consist of some 15 to 20 impulses in the case of a commercial model. Thus a 10-inch tube might contain 200 pockets of 20 impulses.

On receiving the appropriate order, the machine will extract through an outlet valve the contents of any one of the memory pockets and transfer it to the computer. To enable the machine to select any one of the memory pockets as they travel at high speed around the delay line circuit, an electronic clock counts the impulses as they pass. Not only has an efficient timing device been developed, but there is also a means of synchronizing the flow with the controlling clock so the starting and finishing points in the impulse stream can be recognized for counting purposes. A mechanism has also been devised that automatically checks the timing after each series of pockets has passed around the circuit, and, if necessary, corrects any faults.

The moment the current is switched off the impulses cease, and a new set of impulses can be fed in at high speed. If a change needs to be made to just a few impulses in the circuit, they can be put in at the appropriate point by means of the synchronizing clock, the new impulses replacing whatever was there before.

(Diagrams from the original report by R. J. Mumford, 1947)

B

Interview Between J.R.M. Simmons, Director and Chief Comptroller of J. Lyons & Co., and the Science Museum, London, Circa 1970s[1]

Interviewer (Chris Evans)

I'd like to start by thinking back to the period well before 1947 and just look at the background, the kind of company that Lyons itself was, and also your role in it. Did you in fact regard yourselves as a very progressive company in terms of office management methods?

JRMS

Lyons as a company was generally regarded as a very progressive company when I first joined it in 1923; in fact long before your time, in 1924—I think that was the date of the British Empire Exhibition at Wembley—Lyons was asked to undertake the catering because no

---

[1] Copyright © 1980 Trustees of the Science Museum, London. With acknowledgments to the Trustees of the Science Museum, London.

This is an edited transcript of the taped interview.

other organization could possibly have catered with the problem. They were a very progressive company and enjoyed a very considerable reputation, but when I joined it in 1923 from Cambridge the clerks in the office that I was put to work in were still working at big mahogany desks standing up writing or, if they wanted to sit down, sitting on high stools. It really was a Dickensian atmosphere. The management information that was produced for the managers of the business came straight out of the books of account of the company, the financial accounts, or they didn't exist at all. In fact I was engaged to try to build up a system of information for the management of the company that would be superior, more sensible, than just depending upon the profit and loss account and such. So, if you like, the office was rather distinct from the company in that respect. The company was already go ahead.

The production methods were advanced then?
Advanced for their time, yes.

I believe you and some of your fellow managers did come to be leading lights in what would now be called the organization and methods fraternity of this country. You set up an organization, didn't you?
I think by 1935 we were beginning to be recognized as enjoying something of the same reputation in the office world as the company did in the business world. There was the Office Management Association, as it was then known, which had been set up under a different name as early as 1918, but I didn't become aware of this until about 1932. I joined it then. I say by 1935 because it was in 1935 that we were able to introduce the first real development in our office practices that had been made up to that time.

What was this development?
The wholesale bakery side of the business, that is to say the bakery business not concerned with supplying our own teashops and restaurants, but concerned with supplying other shops up and down the country, had progressed to such an extent that the paperwork being conducted still by the accounts department, that is to say the department responsible for the books of account of the company, the paperwork was almost drowning the business. I was asked to look at the system to see if we could produce something that was better than what was going on at the present time. We introduced a system in which the customer's order was photographed by a brand-new machine called a Recordak and the order itself was returned to the customer as an invoice and all we had was the

photographic reproduction of the order. So all the paperwork disappeared.

So you were among the very early users of photocopying?

Indeed yes! So far as this country was concerned I would say that it was probably the first use of it. It wasn't photocopying as I understand the term quite precisely because it was a copy on miniature film.

So if we move forward to the late 1940s and look at the situation in Lyons then, had you then achieved a slim, efficient management organization or were there still tensions and difficulties that you needed some new technology to resolve?

Yes. Round about 1947 we had achieved the kind of office organization that we felt could be an efficient tool in giving the management of the business the information it required. During the latter part of the war, when it was obvious that we would presently be involved with dealing with the postwar situation, we had been giving a lot of thought to it, and round about 1947—I think possibly I'd put it a year or two later at 1949 or 1950—we had achieved this.

When did you personally first become aware of computers?

It was after the war in 1947, when two of my colleagues were going over to America in order to see what had happened in the office machinery world during the war period, and electronic computers had just come into the news. The papers were talking about the electronic brains over in America and they suggested that while they were over there that they should see how the electronic brains operated and whether there was any possibility of being able to use them in the office. I confess that I was very lukewarm about spending the time on this because I knew that if they found any equipment that they could use there was no hope at all of our being able to buy it, because we should not have been able then to get hold of the dollars to do so; but anyway it was information that we ought to have. They found a great deal of information about electronic computers, as they were at the time, but far and away the most important bit of information that they gathered was that Cambridge University mathematical laboratory was just about to embark on building its own computer. This of course dramatically changed the whole situation because that meant that we could collaborate, so we hoped, with people on the spot, and as they built their own mathematical machine there was at least the possibility that we might learn how to build a machine for our own purposes. It seemed a perfectly natural thing to do; there was no question of being able to buy a computer off the peg, but if Cambridge could build a machine, why couldn't we?

This famous visit to America by Thompson and Standingford—I've looked at the report of it and obviously they put a lot of work into seeing what work was being done in computing in the United States. Was it one of them, maybe Oliver Standingford, who had actually been the first to see the commercial possibilities of this electronic brain, as it was called?

It was the two of them together. I think probably Thompson took the lead rather than Standingford, but they put in a report as soon as they returned saying that they thought it would be of great benefit. They put a match to a bonfire that was already burning. The suggestion only had to be made to be one of those exciting things that are obvious when it is made.

What were the needs that you were aware of in the organization that you and your colleagues obviously felt could be met by this new and rather untried technology?

Well, now you have to go back again a bit. When I said, a little while back, that the offices in 1923 when I joined the company were almost Dickensian in character, that is not strictly true because another office, not mine, which we called the checking department, was already employing adding machines and had been almost since the inception of the company. They were employing quite a large number of adding machines, totaling up the waitresses' bills. At that time there were a lot of teashops, and all the service in the teashops was done by waitresses. There were millions of bills and these had to be added up to control the cash takings. It was a dead and alive job. There were some 300 women eventually doing nothing else but adding up and checking the adding up of waitresses' bills. It cried out for some kind of automatic machine to take over this work, which was not fit for human beings to undertake, and yet they had to because there was no other way of conducting the business. We dreamed of some wonderful machine where all you would need to do would be to feed in paper and press buttons and get all the answers that you wanted; it was all very naïve. That was really, if you like, the one single mainspring: the existence of the checking department, which by the time the war came was under my control. Paradoxically, by the end of the war, in 1947 we are talking about now, all the waitresses had disappeared, so the real need for the computer for that kind of job had also disappeared; but it was in our blood. We still employed large numbers of clerks doing a dreary kind of job. You see the difference between a routine office job and a routine factory job is that the routine factory job is doing the same thing, literally the same thing, time and time again. In the office you are doing the same kind of thing, but you're feeding in different figures to the machine all the time, you have got to concentrate, you can't even daydream. We had plenty of work, and that was really the reason why it was obvious to us that an automatic computer was what we wanted.

Did you have a real fear that you might not be able to employ clerks to do this dreary work? Did you think that the supply of people willing to do it would dry up?

Indeed we did. After the war, because everything was turned upside down and it seemed more than likely that with improved education of the youngsters they would not come forward to do this kind of work, it was very much in our minds.

To go back to the time of the visit by Thompson and Standingford, you presumably knew that they were going to look at computing in the United States. What did you expect would come of their investigations?

Initially I expected no more would come of it than that we should be forced to file this information against the time when it would be possible to get dollars from the Bank of England in order to buy some machine. Even that was almost a remote possibility because we knew these computers were mathematical computers, and a mathematical computer *per se* was not of the slightest use to us at all because we were dealing with a mass of information, not a complication of calculation. Do you understand what I mean by the difference between these two things?

This is the difference between, if you like, scientific computing and business computing?

I would prefer to use the term mathematical, simply because that is how we thought of it at the time. With a mathematical computer the mathematician has a very complicated problem to solve with a great deal of calculations to be made, but the original data is not voluminous—not particularly voluminous—and certainly the results are not particularly voluminous, but most important of all the time factor is not important, because if there wasn't a mathematical computer he wouldn't be able to make the calculation anyhow, because it would take more than a lifetime to perform all the calculations, so there is no problem of the volume of feeding data in and no problem of the volume of results produced. With the business computer the calculations are not very complicated, because if they were it would not be possible for the business to be carried on, but the volume of input and the volume of output is prodigious, and therefore what was necessary was to find some method of enabling the input mechanism to keep pace with the extraordinary speed of the computer itself and for the recording systems to do likewise at the end of the calculation. This was our problem.

We'll come in a minute to how you set about solving that problem, but a thing I would like to ask you is about the impact of that report when Thompson and Standingford returned. Were you, for example, surprised to find out that there were people like IBM who were looking in the United States at electronic methods of calculation to help with business problems?

I wasn't surprised because they weren't doing this. No one else seemed to be in the least interested. You see, you've got to remember that IBM and the other big punch-card machine manufacturers had enormous investment in punch-card machinery. They were not likely to want to switch over to something else that, if it were successful, would put the whole of their punch-card machines out of business.

Initially, then, there was no one in the United States or in Britain doing precisely what you were intending to do in terms of commercial computing, but as your work got under way, did you become worried about possible competition?

Yes indeed, because, you see, the visit to the United States was in 1947 and we didn't get permission to start building the computer until 1949, which was two years later, and by the end of 1949 we were beginning to put in a considerable investment; we were worried stiff all the time that we would be overtaken by one of the big boys and all our work just go down the drain, but we learned to live with it because the information that came our way was always to the effect that in about six months' time someone was going to produce a business computer and this six months in a very real sense became a constant. That is, as the years went on, while we were trying to solve our problems, it was always in six months that something was going to be produced, and indeed I remember that in early 1954, when LEO was working, there was the same six-month period being threatened. We had long ago given up worrying about it at all.

Dare I ask how long you expected it would take you when you first embarked on the construction of the computer?

I think probably we thought that once we had started it would take around two years.

In the report that Thompson and Standingford made when they returned from the United States I think they outlined five possible choices that would face Lyons if Lyons decided to take up computing, and these were, if I can recall this, to get the Cambridge group to develop something for you, to get one of the British electrical firms to develop something, to go to Electronic Controls Inc., which was Eckert's outfit in the States, to bring in the Government, or to do it yourselves.

I agree that the five were quite logical, but I think after the first discussions on their report that the choices really all disappeared, with the exception of the one that we should build it ourselves. We couldn't buy it from America because of the dollar situation; we knew perfectly well that no office machinery company in this country was contemplating it because we were in close touch with them. Cambridge certainly wouldn't be able to do it; we also had experience of Government in this kind of thing and this we didn't think was likely. That only left the possibility we should do it ourselves or just wait.

Cambridge couldn't do it, you felt, though you relied very heavily on them for technical assistance. Was it because you felt they weren't sufficiently aware of business problems?

Well, I don't know if you saw the covering note that I sent to the Board with Thompson and Standingford's report, but if I remember right, there I felt not because there was a lack of possibility of other people doing something, but because, inherently in this altogether radical change in the possibilities of business machinery, unless the user was prepared to take a hand in the building of the machine, the machine would never get built. Now Cambridge was clearly not a business user; it was not possible that they could do it.

Does this mean that the Lyons Board on discussing this report decided right away that the do-it-yourself solution would be the one if it was done at all?

It was a most extraordinary decision by the Board, there is no question about that, a very courageous one; at least I thought it was very courageous. Other people might have thought it was foolhardy, but no, they saw the force of the argument. Here we had this big office organization, which by definition was a gross extravagance on the back of the company, and the only way in which economies could be made (because at that stage we were really only thinking of making economies in existing routines, we had not reached the point where we began to see the possibilities in all sorts of other directions), the only way in which economies could be made on the scale that we thought could be made was if we did go ahead and build the computer. The only reservation they made was that before they would agree to our attempting to do this, Cambridge must prove that at least they knew how to build a computer themselves. That was really the only condition that was put: that nothing should be done until Cambridge had proved that their computer was capable of doing a mathematical job.

Was that the entire reason for the delay from 1947 when the idea was first raised to 1949 when the decision to build LEO was made?

Oh, yes. That condition was relaxed to the extent (I think I am right) that at the end of 1948 we did propose that we should engage a graduate electronics engineer so that he could fit himself into our organization before any attempt to start building began, and it was agreed that we might engage such a person because the possibility was that even if we didn't build a computer he might prove useful in some other direction. So we were given permission to do this, and again I think I am right in saying that John Pinkerton joined us right at the beginning of January 1949. But it was not until May of that year that Cambridge did its mathematical problem. What they had done was to compile a table of prime numbers, and they knew of course what the condition was that had been laid upon us and they telephoned us to tell us that this job had been accomplished satisfactorily. It was on a Thursday in May and it so happened that the Board of Lyons was having one of its biweekly Board Meetings, and I (I wasn't on the Board at the time) sent a message in to the chairman, Harry Salmon, to say that Cambridge had done this job and please could we go ahead with the building of the computer, and in about five or ten minutes out came the answer: yes!

To go back to January 1949, then, when you recruited Dr. Pinkerton. How did you actually recruit him?

We put an advertisement in *Nature,* I think it was, got a reply from Pinkerton, and I wrote to Dr. Wilkes—we knew that Pinkerton came from Cambridge, and was a graduate of Cambridge. I asked Dr. Wilkes whether he would be prepared to give Pinkerton a preliminary interview. To my astonishment Wilkes wrote back to say that he knew Pinkerton very well and there was no need for him to interview him. He couldn't recommend anybody better.

So what happened then?

I had already written to Pinkerton at the same time as I had written to Wilkes to ask him if he would be prepared to attend an interview with Wilkes, and I got a letter back saying that he certainly would: he already knew Wilkes very well, so there was no difficulty about that. So I simply had to say to Pinkerton, "Don't worry, come along and see us." When we'd offered him the job he said that he would like to have it, but he thought that it was only fair to tell us that he wasn't thinking of taking on the job as a life's work and that he would probably only stay with us for two or three years and then would want to move on to something else. But in fact, of course, he stayed with us right to the end. It was a very fortunate engagement. There was an extraordinary family atmosphere at Lyons at that time, and even though people left the company they never lost their affection for it. And Pinkerton, coming as a stranger, simply fitted in: marvelous!

He was very impressed by what he saw when he came for his interview. Had you put a lot of preparation into what you showed him and told him when he came?

I don't think so. If we were engaging anybody of his standing—well, I don't think we had actually engaged anyone of his standing before, but we had engaged other university graduates—we would spend a lot of time with them because we felt perhaps it was more important that they should understand us and like us than that we should understand them and like them. No, I don't think we gave any special treatment to him.

What was the nature of your collaboration with Cambridge?

Well, when Thompson and Standingford came back from the States with their report, they went almost immediately to make some kind of contact with Hartree and Wilkes at Cambridge, and they reported that they had been received very courteously and favorably. And presently about six of us went to make a rather more formal visit to Cambridge to try to cement the contact that had been already started by the first two. As a result of this, the Board agreed to do two things: first of all to make a donation to the university to help them in building their own computer, and, more to the point, to lend them a member of our own staff to work with them, to help them and to gain experience. Now this was a man called Lenaerts, who had been a clerk in the office before the war. During the war he had begun to learn something about electricity, if not electronics, and when he came out of the army he said he didn't want to return as a clerk; he would prefer to be in the electricians' department. So he was really admirably placed, having a foot in both camps, and he did good work for Cambridge, but from our point of view what was really important was that he gained real practical experience. And it wasn't simply just as a competent electrician; he was able to make suggestions to Wilkes to improve the building of their machine and he came away from them with very definite ideas on what ought to be done in our machine.

Now the impression I have of Wilkes is that he took a very academic view of research and information and felt that what he did was for the world to know and was really prepared to tell anyone about what he was doing. Did this attitude of his ever conflict with your commercial approach to the research?

His attitude certainly didn't conflict. I don't really understand why there should be any possibility that it should conflict.

Well, did you feel no need for secrecy about what you were doing?

Well, we had no secrets about the central computer because this was based quite definitely on the Cambridge EDSAC. If they had no secrets, we had no secrets. We were only happy to be able to learn from them. So far as the input and the output equipment was concerned, there of course our attitude was different. We were a business, Cambridge was not involved, and we had hopes of having patents that would be of value. Not that they came to anything in the end, for various reasons that are probably too long to go into at this point. So there was no conflict with Cambridge on that at all.

So after the 1949 go-ahead from the Board, you had this small team who were actually building the computer. Were you at the same time investigating the way that a computer would be used in the organization and the kind of programs it would run?

Yes. If we hadn't started before we got the go-ahead, we certainly started in earnest afterwards because it seemed obvious to us that, since we were equally ignorant on this matter, if we didn't begin right away we would end up with having a computer and not knowing how to use it. So almost immediately, within a month or two, it was agreed that we make a general study not only of the technical way in which the computer could be used, that is to say programming, but also what kind of changes were likely for us to make in the office organization to make it possible for the office to use the computer. On the programming side, David Caminer was brought to LEO with the task of learning from Cambridge how a program should be drawn in order to use the computer, and to develop programming in whatever way was necessary to make it possible to use it in an office organization, in a business environment. He had come from what we called the Systems Research Office, later known as O&M, so he was quite capable of doing his new task and at the same time working in collaboration with his old colleagues in the Systems Research Office, who would be responsible for the systems analysis.

How did you set about defining the problems that the computer could help, and the actual detailed way in which the computer could help—what we would now call systems analysis?

Well, first of all it was "What problem should we tackle?" Right from the beginning it was obvious that payroll was one of the jobs, if not the principal job, that would be suitable to be put onto the computer. I think that doesn't need explanation. It was a job that employed a great many clerks in the wages office. And apart from that, it was really a matter of looking around to see some kind of job that would bring the office into the business, not as a mere recorder of historical information, but as an organization capable of supplying vital information to the business in a way that they couldn't have had by orthodox methods. I really don't know what prompted the Teashop Orders, as we called it, except that I think it was a fairly obvious choice, because of the multiplicity of teashops we had at the time and the problem that we were dealing with perishable food-stuffs, and the necessity of trying as far as possible to coordinate the sales in the teashops with the manufacture in the factories. This was something that had always given trouble in the business and, if we could do anything to help solve it, this would be a real help. I think one had only to think of the job to realize that this was an exciting possibility.

So, it was at quite an early stage then that you began to think of the computer not merely as a super-clerical assistant, but as a source of management information?

I can't remember now when we first started to think of the computer in that way. But of course, from 1947 to 1949, when we were waiting for the word to go, we were thinking about it all the time, and I think very early on we realized that there was a whole new world to be opened up if only we could do it, and this was a way of selling the machine to the management of the company, because they weren't really interested in just what went on inside the office. Payroll, if there was any money to be saved, was well and good, but if we could induce them to make use of the computer in the business, this would be much more likely to produce a favorable decision when the time came. So, I think, long before 1949 we had got around to this.

Now coming to this from your background in office management, you obviously did a thorough job in that you redesigned procedures and you put a lot of work into forms, didn't you?

Well, yes, because, you see, as part of the problem of the input there was the problem that the mere transcribing of orthodox records into a form that was suitable for the computer would take up a very large part of the time that was going to be saved in the actual computing, and we did think a lot about automatic document reading, a problem that really hasn't been properly solved yet, of course. And at that time I thought the sensible thing to do was to consider whether, internally to the company, it was possible that forms should be arranged in really a binary system, let's say ticking or not ticking in a particular space, and that this would be a relatively simple way of using a photocell in order to detect whether there was a mark or whether there was not a mark.

Did you ever pursue that idea in practical terms?

Oh, yes. This was much later on, of course. We did have a document reader that was capable of reading a mark or no mark. We did use it: very much so.

The original report of Thompson and Standingford suggests that they were not very impressed with punched-card technology. Did you have a particular reason for disliking punched cards?

When you say they were not very impressed by it, wouldn't it be truer to say that they recognized pretty clearly the limitations of the punch-card technology? You see, here again so much had to be done in order to get the data on to the punched card that most of the potential savings would be swallowed up, and the card itself was expensive; I would have thought it was that rather than anything else.

You haven't asked me about our solution to the input and output mechanisms; may I go on to that?

Yes, indeed, you obviously looked at many alternatives and made your choice.

At the time when we started work on this, tape was just being used. I don't know now, I can't remember how extensively it was being used, but it was being used. But there was nothing, no kind of tape machine, that was capable of working at the kind of speed we wanted.

You mean magnetic tape?

Yes, magnetic tape. We thought this was a highly technological problem and that the sensible thing was to bring in some company that had experience in this kind of thing and collaborate with them on producing magnetic tape machines—storage machines—that were capable of working at the kind of speeds that we wanted. And the same thing with the output—that the output of the computer should be recorded on tape. It was a decision that was to produce more headaches so far as we were concerned than the whole of the rest of the project put together. I suppose it was before its time, the notion of using tape in this kind of way, and after a couple of years of frustration on all sides we just had to abandon this idea altogether. We then fell back, as we ought to have done at the beginning, being wise after the fact, to use punch-card machines as a means of feeding in information, when it was appropriate. We tried to do too much—we made the mistake that is commonly made, we made it many times ourselves, in embarking on a new project: instead of confining yourself as far as possible to the central problem, trying to put everything else right at the same time. No, if we had been content to use already existing systems for providing input and had simply confined ourselves to the problem of how they were to be linked up to the computer and the same thing with the output, we would have saved at least a couple of years' time and a great many headaches.

So you fell back on punched cards in the end.
Punch cards and punch tape.

What was actually the first real business job that LEO I did?
Oh, the payroll. As I think I've already said, because we'd embarked on the problem of systems analysis and programming before the computer was finished we had complete programs ready for three jobs: the payroll (if they were not completely ready they were nearly ready), the Teashops Orders, and another one concerned with the tea business. The computer was finished literally on Christmas Eve in 1953 and certainly by the first week in January a payroll program was being operated, to start off with simply in parallel with the conventional method, but I think it was early in February for the first time LEO did the job for about 1700 people in the bakeries on its own. And from then onwards we kind of lived on tenterhooks, afraid that the machine might break down and that the bakeries staff wouldn't get their money, but in fact it never did break down, and before the end of the year we had got about 10,000 people on the payroll and the Teashops Orders job was starting. It was all keyed in: the job was advanced as a whole, not only on the hardware, but the software at the same time. It was a curious situation to be in, a curious feeling: we were quite prepared, ready to do a computer job, and yet there was not a computer anywhere in the world able to do it.

You mention in your book a job called Bakery Sales Evaluation. Did you not try this out, at least, some time before 1954?
Oh yes, it was about the time when we were almost at the limits of frustration because of the new input and output equipment not coming to hand that it was proposed, and very sensibly too, that we ought to be doing a small job on what perhaps I might call the mathematical computer, which was what we were building at the time, all that we were capable of building at the time, so as to get some operating experience, to get a flavor of it. Oh, yes, this job was started in something like February or March of 1951 and was done week after week until eventually it was just slipped in without anyone noticing into LEO I when it was in operation.

So that it in a sense was the first bit of real commercial data processing?

Some people would say so; some people did say so. But I think not, because it could have been done on the Cambridge machine; for all I know perhaps it was done on the Cambridge machine—tried out—because they were in advance of us anyhow. This was not anything new, nobody would dream of using a computer in practice for a job like that, it wasn't really the kind of thing that we were aiming for.

During this period, if I am to believe what I have here, the Sunday Chronicle published an article in 1952 that said "scientists and accountants have been secretly working for eighteen months on a machine with which Britain may shake the world of big business." Was it as secret as all that, what you were doing?

I am not conscious of it being a secret; it wasn't being kept a secret deliberately, and indeed a great many people knew that we were trying it. No, it wasn't a secret; it was simply that people didn't believe in it, didn't believe anything could come of it.

Were you surprised when you saw the machine that you had had built actually doing this real job and succeeding?

I don't think so, because we had lived with the whole thing too long. We were relieved, but when you see somebody you know at the time when you are expecting to see that person, you are not surprised. All we felt was "thank goodness everything seems to be falling into place."

Did you ever have problems with programs? The thing that is a constant problem in programming these days is the inadvertent error or program bug. Did you have to do a lot of work on your programs to get them to work right?

Yes, a great deal of work on that. I would suppose, I would hope, far more problems than are encountered today, because if they are encountered today they have no business to be encountered today. We were working in an unknown field. Oh no, we had a lot of trouble, we knew we would have a lot of trouble, and that is one of the chief reasons why we had to start early.

After you had begun doing the payroll and these other jobs, you were clearly extending the number of jobs in the organization that were being done by the computer. What were the main problems, or the main things that you had to keep in mind at that stage?

I would say that the main problem, the intractable problem, was getting the management to appreciate that they themselves would have to change their attitude to their business problems if they were going to be able to make use of the computer. It was a problem that wasn't really solved in my day at all; I don't think it is solved now.

Did you try to train your managers in the use of the computer?

Oh, yes. But then, that was simply another problem, how to do the training. I can only say that, judging by results, I never really discovered how to do that.

What about the clerical staff? What was their reaction to the introduction of the computer?

Ah, now that was interesting, because we were frightened from the beginning that there might be trouble, and we came to the conclusion that the only thing to do was to take them into our confidence right from the beginning. Long before we ever got permission to go ahead with the computer we had meetings, first of all with all the other office managers, and then with the supervisors, and finally with the staff representatives, because we had an active staff committee, to tell them what was in the wind. But by the time we were really beginning, getting to the kind of 1949 period, it was obvious that it was going to take a very long time to program a big office job so as to be able to put it on the computer, and I was able, without any great difficulty, to persuade the Board that I might state that the company undertook that nobody would be fired as a result of the computer. They might be asked to change their job, but a job was guaranteed. Now there was nothing very clever about this, because we knew perfectly well that the ordinary erosion would be quite sufficient to take care of anything of this kind. So I think that without any doubt we had the goodwill of the rank-and-file members of the staff right from the beginning, and, long before there was anything tangible to show them, they were as excited as we were that something would come of it all. If there was any attitude that was different from ours it was a certain healthy skepticism that this interesting experiment would ever come to anything.

C

Demonstration Script (1955) for the Teashops Distribution Job (L2)

Parties of Lyons staff, or of visitors, frequently visited Cadby Hall to see LEO I in operation. Such visits were regarded as important exercises in employee relations and publicity and were conducted by senior members of the LEO team—often by T. R. Thompson himself. They were highly organized, using charts and specimen exhibits, and scripted. For the system description of the job L2 it is impossible to improve on the demonstration script, a long extract from which now follows.

C.T.
(With acknowledgments to J. Lyons & Co., Ltd.)

By way of demonstrating what LEO can do, we are going to show you how we handle the orders for the goods that are going to be used in 150 London teashops tomorrow. The goods are for the most part being produced now and some will be assembled and packed tonight and taken out by van at 6 o'clock tomorrow morning.

Before you actually see the job on LEO I, I ought to give you something of the background so you may have a practical picture of the way in which the teashops place their orders and how Dispatch organizes its deliveries. Each of the teashops is supplied each day from Cadby Hall with about 250 items that either appear on its menus or are sold in its front shop for the customer to take away.

The Old System

In the past, the ordering of the items was dealt with in a thoroughly straightforward manner. The managers of each teashop were provided with an order book containing a number of sheets for each day of the week and they duly wrote down their requirements and sent the forms into Cadby Hall a couple of days before required delivery. . . . There are different notes corresponding with different types of supplies, different packing sites, different deliveries. You can easily imagine how massive a chore the compiling of this great heap of paper must have seemed to the managers each day.

Nonetheless the system, though straightforward and orthodox in general approach, was not altogether conventional and was certainly not inefficient. The managers kept one carbon copy for their own reference, but the original order note was used for all other purposes. At different stages of its existence that single note served as the means of calculating total requirements, as the packing note, as the delivery note against which the goods were booked in and, eventually, when returned by the managers, as the means of charging the teashop with the goods that had been supplied.

The Pattern of Ordering

Under the impact of LEO and the formidable mass of data preparation represented by 250 items ordered each day by more than 150 teashops, we had to reconsider the system of ordering as a whole. In doing this we tried to follow the mental process of the teashop managers when they originated their order each day. We realized that the tendency was not to consider each line of the order book fresh each day as if they were dealing with a completely new situation, but to turn back to their orders for the same day of the previous week and unless there were some particular change in circumstances, to base their new orders very closely upon the old ones.

The Use of Estimates

We found that the variation in orders tended to occur not as between one week and the next so much as between one day and another day of any single week. And so the plan was conceived of asking the managers, under the guidance of their immediate supervision, to make an estimate of their sales for each day of the week. Then, as we saw it, that estimate could be used to avoid having the managers fill in all their orders each day; equally, it would avoid all that data having to be recorded on perforated tape before it could be used by LEO.

Keeping the Estimates up to Date

In place of the order book we are therefore using a set of Sales Estimate Sheets. . . . The quantities entered on these sheets remain in force as the estimates until the time comes for them to be reconsidered. The seasons pass, new items have to be put on the menu, or a trend in trade can develop for other reasons; so changes do have to be made from time to time. The arrangement we have come to is that all items are considered in a four-week rotation. It is convenient to divide the items, for dispatch and general control purposes, into eight batches; consequently, each week the managers are asked to reconsider their estimates for two of the batches. In practice, even these reconsiderations leave the estimates for a considerable number of the items unchanged from one period to the next.

The managers make their revisions on a copy of the Sales Estimate specially provided to them for the purpose. . . . They send the sheet to Cadby Hall and the changes are then used to amend a photographic master of the estimates. The old figure is rubbed out and the new one is penciled in. The master is photographed and one copy is returned to the managers to provide them with a record of the estimates they have set up.

Day-by-Day Amendments

What has so far been created in Cadby Hall is a comparatively long-term estimate of sales. But that isn't quite sufficient. The weather changes and a warm spell in the middle of winter will mean that customers will want more of one line and less of another. A rainy spell may have a generally depressive effect on trade. The road might be up outside the shop. The Lord Mayor's Procession might be passing. The goods for which the managers are responsible are in the main expected to be sold within 24 hours of receiving them. Consequently, it is quite impossible for them to stand by their estimates in all circumstances. And so it is arranged that each manager should be telephoned at a set time each afternoon to be given the opportunity of making changes deemed necessary to orders for delivery the following day. . . . They are taken down over the telephone and, to avoid transcription, we have arranged that the revisions should be punched straight into punched cards by the operator. In a moment I will take you downstairs to the Telephone Order Office, where today's revisions are now being recorded.

The Packing Notes

On the basis of the estimates for the day and the revisions received over the telephone, packing notes have to be prepared showing the revised quantity for each item for each teashop in the most convenient arrangement to suit the physical division of labor in dispatch. If I might mention LEO almost for the first time in this description of the job, I would like to show you the packing note just as LEO produces it. This sheet represents ten packing notes. As soon as it is produced it is guillotined into its ten separate parts.

On each note:
  there is the teashop number at the head
then in the first column
  there are the item numbers
and in the second column
  there are the quantities ordered.

At the foot of the first column of each packing note, there is the code number of the dispatch task of which the note is part; that is, the team that will handle the job.

Substitutions

In preparing the packing notes, we have started with the original estimates made by the managers for a particular day of the week for a month at a time; we have gone over the monthly revision of that estimate and we have heard, too, about the daily amendments made by the managers in the light of the different factors that occur to them.

But there is another factor that is outside the manager's control. That is the possibility that, owing to the breakdown in a factory or a sudden curtailment of supplies or a last-minute decision at Teashops Headquarters to make a change, substitutions will have to be made for some of the items that the managers have ordered. The packing notes produced by the calculator must obviously take account of alterations of that type too. . . .

The General Organization of the Job

The job that we are going to see is actually done in three phases, each of 50 shops. It is divided in order to avoid delaying the whole job until revisions have been received from all managers. The shops are telephoned in a definite sequence and, as soon as the first 50 have been called, their revision cards are taken to the Calculator Room and the packing notes for those shops produced. By the time the revisions for the next 50 shops are received, the calculator will have finished with the previous 50. And so on until the whole job is complete. . . .

There are two other matters I should mention before we show you behind the scenes.

As I mentioned at the outset, many of the items for which packing notes are being prepared are actually being manufactured at this moment. Consequently, the productive departments concerned want to know, as soon as possible, the overall extent to which teashops have been making alterations to the estimated requirements of different items. As it handles each revision, LEO works out the extent of the change and keeps a running total for the item. At the end of its phase of fifty shops, it prints off those totals. . . .

Perhaps a more obvious point is that dispatch wants not only the packing notes; they need also to be supplied with the total quantity of each item shown on these notes. Consequently, LEO has all the time been adding up the grand totals of each item. It prints them when it has finished all the teashops for each batch. . . .

Now you have seen the job being done, but I am afraid that there is a great deal more to it than can be realized just by looking at it. . . .

The Printing of the Packing Note

First there are one or two points regarding the packing notes. You may think that the calculator has merely to take estimated quantities for each item number, making any revision and printing the revised quantity on the packing note. This is not the case, however, for the item on the packing note is not the same as that on the teashop estimate sheet. Dispatch naturally wants to have the packing note made in an order convenient for sending the goods, and in general this is not a convenient order for the managers to consider what they want to order. Dispatch wants to have the code numbers to suit their convenience and the teashop managers want to have the items in numerical order as they appear on the estimate sheet. . . .

When the job is done by LEO there is no difficulty in having different sets of code numbers for two purposes. The orders are fed in with teashop code numbers and LEO translates them to those that suit dispatch printing the packing notes accordingly.

Another advantage is that, when either the teashop management or the dispatch management want to change their arrangements for certain items, involving a change in code numbers, each can make their own arrangements without having to have prolonged negotiations with the other. . . .

Some items are available in more than one size; for instance, potato salad is packed in 1 lb. and 4 lb. jars. The managers prefer to order in just one unit—so many lbs. of a single code number—but it is easier for dispatch to pack as many as possible in the larger unit, the 4 lb. jar, with the balance in 1 lb. jars, each size having its own code number.

Then again, when there is a composite dish on the menu, such as boiled beef, carrots and dumplings, the managers simply want to order so many portions of the composite dish with a single code number, but dispatch has to pack quite separately so many pounds of boiled beef, so many pounds of carrots and so many dumplings, each with its own code number, since the different items are packed from different assembly bins.

Accounting Figures

Next you may be interested in the accounting figures. The managers are held responsible for the goods supplied to them and the value of the goods to be sold. For each shop LEO values each item supplied at its selling price and keeps a running total of the total value of the goods supplied. The values accumulate only for a complete month, when the running total is printed to compare with the cash takings. Naturally, account has to be taken of any stocks held at the beginning and end of the month. It is not convenient to take stocks for all shops on the same day. Sometimes it is convenient on a Tuesday, sometimes on a Wednesday, and sometimes Thursday, according to which is the shop's half day. This means that LEO has to print out the running total for different shops on different days. There is, however, no difficulty in doing this as the information as to what is the week-ending day for a given teashop is supplied to LEO and LEO automatically prints the value of the total supplies to the shop for the month when this day is reached. When a shop shows up badly in a given month it may be decided that the check against the takings should be done weekly instead of monthly. Again, there is no difficulty in LEO giving the totals for such shops weekly.

Forecast Statistics

We have also mentioned that a lot of statistics are prepared. It has often been said that the value of statistics depends on the rapidity with which they are available. Figures which are prepared long after the event are seldom used productively. If they can be produced soon after the event they are more useful, but with LEO we have tried to go one better by preparing them before the event. We can do this because we have the estimated requirements of the teashop in advance and, subject to the effect of revisions, we can produce statistics showing the likely business each shop will do in the coming month. Each week, when the revised estimates are received for a batch of goods, the statistics are produced so that the management know what to expect.

To provide a numerical picture of the trade of 150 teashops, each handling 250 items and with a different pattern of sales from day to day, is not easy. In the past we were content to know the total sales of each item and the total value charged to each shop. If there was an increase or falling off in the sales of any item it was a major operation to trace it to any particular group of shops. To be prepared in advance for dealing with problems of that sort would have involved maintaining tens of thousands of running totals and using conventional methods it would have been a very formidable task indeed. Again, that is the kind of task for which LEO is particularly well prepared. But it is not sufficient to be able to aggregate great masses of totals and to perform calculations of percentages and relationships upon them and to print all the figures in neatly set-out tables. The figures that could be printed about the teashops each week could fill a book. It is imperative that, if the figures are to be acted upon in a tempo comparable with that in which they are produced, they should be selective; that only significant figures should be reported and that each level of management should be asked to consider only those figures within its immediate scope of executive responsibility.

We have a chart to show you how the teashops department is organized. The main administration is responsible for the whole, with a divisional superintendent in charge of each of the 8 divisions, each of which consists of 5 or 6 sections with a section supervisor in charge. Each section comprises 6 or 7 teashops with a manager in charge. Each teashop has a code number which indicates to which section or division it belongs. The plan we have adopted is to give the Teashops Administration only the statistics for the teashops as a whole and for each division. Similarly, each divisional superintendent is given the figures for his division and any significant figures for the different sections of the division. Likewise, the section supervisor is given the figures for his or her section and the significant figures for the different teashops in the section. Thus the director in charge, when querying the divisional superintendent, knows that the latter has information to enable him or her to give an answer to the query, and the same thing exists right down the line to the individual teashop. To illustrate the kind of statistics we give, I will draw your attention to specimen 12 *[not included]*. This provides information about the different kinds of goods which are sold in the front shop and sold and served in the teashops. You will see that there are a series of groups and information is given about each. This specimen is for the teashops as a whole, but there are similar statements for each division and each section for their respective branches of management.

For each commodity, e.g., small cakes in the front shop, is shown the division with the poorest result as compared with its own estimates of the previous week.

For that division it gives the quantity estimated in portions and the percentage it represents. As a comparison, it gives the overall percentage for all divisions. Then, having pinpointed for the commodity group the division that is the weakest link, the statement proceeds to indicate those days on which the estimates made by this division fell even below its own percentage for the week as a whole. As a result of this statement, it is possible for the Teashops Administration to take immediate action to remedy the weak points. The divisional superintendent can be asked what is the reason for the low estimate of small cakes on certain days, and this goes right down to the managers, who may be persuaded to take upward corrections when the time comes for their daily amendments.

Before leaving this statement, I must mention a useful facility that the management has at its disposal; that is, if it knows in advance that for some reason beyond its control a division or a section is bound to be low on a particular commodity group, it can send instructions that LEO is not to report that division or section, but the next lowest one instead.

Daily Statistics

If you are not already drowned in the whirlpool of even the comparatively limited selective statistics that LEO is called upon to produce, you will by now be at the point of asking whether it is not the easiest thing in the world for a manager to hoodwink the senior management by consistently and progressively estimating high and then returning to reality by phoning in alterations on the day before delivery. That has been taken care of by arranging for LEO to produce a statement each week showing all excessive upward and downward amendments telephoned in each day. The statement is produced at each level. Here is the statement *[not included]* at section supervisor level.

It shows for the section for each day of the week the total number of upward revisions, the value of those revisions and the percentage that that value represents of the total estimated value of the day. It shows similar figures for downward revisions.

Then, for each shop which had more than the average value of upward or downward revisions for each day, it prints particulars for that day.

Summing Up

You have now heard a great deal about this job that LEO does, but you may well be considering what does Lyons really get out of having LEO do this job.

1. We save the teashops managers a lot of writing.

2. Dispatch has a lot less paper to handle and the packing instructions are in simpler form.

3. Delivery notes are cut out and the sending of them to the teashops and back.

4. The job can be organized so that less office and dispatch work are done at inconvenient times of the evening and night, Saturdays, holidays, etc.

5. The Teashops management is more easily able to promote sales, to be aware of lines that do not pay, and of teashops, sections, or divisions that lag behind the remainder and to prevent teashop managers making trivial changes in what they order.

6. Last but not least, there is a net saving in clerical cost of the order of $560 per week.

Index

accounting and valuation applications, 10-11, 15, 25, 30, 32, 35, 94, 192-193, 267-269
ACE computer, 100
acoustic delay lines (*see* magnetic delay lines)
actuarial and insurance-related applications, 34, 52, 66, 116-117, 126, 161, 189, 350, 351-352
addresses, 44
Addressograph machines, 265
AEI, 275
Aiken, Howard, 18, 352-353
Aldred, Ralph, 270
ALGOL language, 200, 203
alignment routines, 198
Allen, Ivor, 211-215
Allied Breweries, 141
Allied Lyons, 141
Allied Suppliers, 126
alphanumerical data, 62
American Machine and Foundry Co., 16
Ampex magnetic tape drive, 91, 250
Anelex printers, 91, 120, 250, 255
Anglo-American Corporation, 290, 294
apprenticeship programs, 69-70
Archibald, Hamish, x, 62, 163, 243-248
Aris, John, ix, xxiii, 71, 95, 105, 119, 124, 134, 143-144, 227, 310, 321-336
arithmetic logic unit, 44, 82, 87, 207
arithmetic operations (*see also* scientific applications), 158-159
Armitage, Harry, 315
Armstrong Whitworth, 160
Army, U.S., 351
Army/Air Force Officers payroll application, 79-80, 229-242, **233**
assembler, 202
Atomic Energy Authority, U.K., 130
Attwood Statistics, 195
auto-checking routines, 198
Autolector (*see also* optical character recognition), 3, 105, 119, 120, 127, 131, 276, 277-278, 328
automation at J. Lyons & Co., 15, 40
Aven, Oleg, 314
Avery company, 120

Baby, the, early computer, 23
Bailey, Ron, 243, 244, 246
Baker, Jenny, 242
Bakery Sales Evaluation application, 1, 7, 10–11, 15, 24, 29–32, 372-373
ballistic calculations (*see also* missile trajectory), 34, 351
Bank of America, California, 52, 75
banking (*see* financial/banking applications)

Barclays Bank, 138
BARIC, 138
Barnes, Anthony B.(Tony), 2, 25, 39, 48, 51, 52, 54, 65, 95, 98, 99, 134, 187, 293
Barron, Tony, 301
Bauer, 191
Beale, Martin, 205
Beechams, 216
Bell, A.O., 210, 211-215
Benn, Anthony W., 118, 133, 250, 313
Bennett, John, 80
Benstead, Peter, 135
Berkeley, 351-352
Bertelsman Publishing, 216
billing (*see* invoicing applications)
binary data, 27, 29, 78, 159, 170, 203, 236, 257-258, 275, 324, 339-341
Bird, Peter, xxiii, 97-98, 137-138, 204
BIZMAC computer, 75, 76
Blackwell, Denis, 114
Blood, Mary, xxiv, 35, 50, 55, 71, 158, 162, 163, 188, 206, 242, 246
BOAC (*see* British Airways)
BOADICEA project, 219
Board of Trade, U.K., 106-107
Booth, G.W., 14, 17, 22, 68
Boots pharmaceutical company, 64-65, 196
bootstrapping, 25
Bowden, Brian, 104
Bowthorpe, John, 128
Bradley, xvii, 54-56
Bray, Diane, xxiv, 241
Brett, Bob, 62, 211, 215
British Airways, 143, 216, 217, 219-220
British Institute of Mangement, 65
British Insulated Callendar Cables, 126
British Oxygen, 81-82, 116, 327, 331
British Railways Hotels, 229
British Tabulating Machine Co. (BTM), 29, 52, 74, 82-83, 84, 260
British Telephone (BT), 108, 118–119, 123, 251–253
Broido, Dan, 95, 117, 119-120, 126, 139, 308, 309, 312-314, 317
Bronowski, Jacob, 197
Brown, 160
BTM 1201 computer, 52, 74
BTM 542 multiplier, 52
buffering, 86-87
Bulgaria (*see also* Soviet Union/Eastern Europe), 317-319
Burroughs, 18, 127, 275, 291, 351
Burroughs 500 computer, 304
Busby, 160
Butler, R.A., 66

Illustrations are in **boldface.**

Cadby Hall facilities, 1, 7, 9-10, 13-14, 23, 30, 36, 38, 39, 42, 64, 71, 77, 78, 79, 104, 131, 141, 157–158, 173, 187, 209, 246, 375
calculators, electronic, 45, 203
Caldwell, Bob, 62, 163, 243, 244, 245, 248
Cambridge University, 7, 11, 18, 19, 20, 21, 22, 25, 27, 33, 100, 159, 186, 191, 197, 257, 349, 353-354, 362-363, 366-367, 368-369, 373
Caminer, David T., ix, xvi, 2, 5, 25, 39, 48, 73–76, 101, 109, 114, 134, 136, 145, 158, 166, 167, 171, 178, 187, 188, 190, 192-196, 203, 205, 208, 210, 211, 212, 218, 241, 246, 247, 248, 251, 256, 259, 264, 290, 293, 297, 308, 310, 332–333, 369
Caminer, Jackie, 290
Campbell-Kelly, Martin, xxiii
Cann, Reg, xi, 127, 274-285
Cape Asbestos, South Africa, 295
Carson, J., 245
Carter, Vic, 312
Castle, L.M.T., (Bill), 62, 245
catalog (see Freemans; mail order)
catering business, 13-14
cathode ray tube, 23
CAV electrical car components co., 103, 108, 161-162, 164-165, 229
Cement Producers Assoc., South Africa, 290
Census Bureau, U.S., 52, 74-75
Cerebos Salt, 116
Charles House, London, 3, 117
Chebyshev polynomials, 162, 191, 197-198, 203
checkpoint restarts, 164-165, 238
checksums, 192, 193, 203-204
China, 117
chronology of LEO development, 1-4
Clark, Helen, see Jackson, Helen
Clark, Jimmy, 246-247, 248
Clements, Arthur, 92
CLEO language, 87-88, 200-201, 202, 275, 326, 328
clerical applications, 8, 26-27, 44-45, 103-104, 166, 374
COBOL, 88-89, 200, 201, 326
Cockfield, Arthur, 65
COCOM trade regulations (see also Soviet Union/Eastern Europe), 117, 139, 315-316
coding (see binary data; input/output; languages)
Coleman, Roger, 71, 81
Coles, Marjorie, 38
Colonial Mutual Life, 116-117
column/row discrepancies, 193-194
Colvilles, 126
Comish, Doug, 68, 71, 72, 95, 127, 116, 126, 134-135, 144, 302, 310
compilers, 88, 202

Computer Journal, 178
Computer Merger Project, 133
computer, diagram, **344**
Comrie, L. J., 353
configuration (sizing), 322, 323-324, 332-333
consoles, 11
Consolidated Glass, South Africa, 131
Consolidation project, 28-29
consultant services, 70-72, 94-95, 102, 178, 181, 194-197, 215-216
control-type computers, 100
cooling systems, 11, 76, 78-79
Coombs, John, 71
Coombs, Mary (see Blood, Mary)
Cooper, Pat, 163, 164, 206
counter trade, 311
Cousins, Frank, 122
Coventry Gauge and Tool, 11
Crawford, Ian, 71, 144, 164
Crouch, Joe, 81, 144, 295, 302
crystallography applications, 160
CSIR, Pretoria, 290
customer base, 136-137
Customs Service, U.K., 2, 106-107, 108
Czechoslovakia (see also Soviet Union/Eastern Europe), 117, 125, 309-312

databases, 186, 332
date calculations, 237
Davis, Colin, 68, 69, 72
Day, Bob, 291, 295, 301, 302
de Havilland, 160, 161
De La Rue Bull, 275
debugging, 165, 170, 172, 185
Decca, 239, 241
decimal data, 54, 78
decimal point/monetary values, 198, 236
Defense Department, U.S., 89-90
Delahunty, Matt, 100
DEUCE computer, 100, 191
Diebold, John, 74, 199
digital logic, 158
disk files, 328
Dixon, Paul, 67, 71, 144
Dockyards (see Royal Dockyards)
documentation, 203, 325
Dorman Long, 216
Draft Report on the EDVAC, 22
Drucker, Peter, xx-xxi
drum (see magnetic drum)
Dunderdale, Miles, 301
Dunlop Tire Co., xvi, 3, 93-94, 124, 143, 216, 218-219
Durlachers, see Wedd Durlacher
Dutton, Wally, 24, 60

Eadie, Ninian, xi, 108-109, 119, 124, 144, 179-180, 249-256, 301
Eastern Europe (*see* Soviet Union/Eastern Europe)
Eckert, J. Presper Jnr, 19, 22, 250, 366
Eckert-Mauchly Corp., 22, 23
Economist article, The Electronic Abacus, 65-66
Edinburgh, Duke of, 78
EDSAC computer, 1, 7-8, 11, 19-20, 22-23, 25, 26-27, 43, 44, 50, 86, 100, 159, 186, 187, 190-191, 201, 257, 369
EDSAC II computer, 86
EDVAC, 19
Edwards, Brian, 68, 70, 72, 82
eigenvalues, 160
electric relay computers, 18
Electronic Abacus, The, article, 65-66
Electronic Brain, earliest computers, xx, xxi, 17, 338, 363
electronic computers, 18
Electronic Controls Inc., 21, 350, 366
Elizabeth II, demonstration of LEO, 1, 40
Elliott 405 computer, 52
Elliott 503 computer, 311
Elliott 803 computer, 309, 311
Elliott Automation, 3, 74, 132, 255, 258, 260, 310, 311
Elliott paper tape readers, 250
Elliott, Alexander, 294
Elms House, 17, 71, 132, 142, 174, 246
EMI, 49-50, 61, 84, 127, 258, 275
EMIDEC 1100 computer, 84
English Electric, 70, 74, 132, 133, 137, 141, 142, 180, 275, 307-308
  merger, 97-109, 113-115, 182
English Electric Computers, 132, 317
English Electric LEO (EEL), 3, 97-109, 112, 113-115, 143, 255, 317
  Lyons disengagement, 120-121
English Electric LEO Marconi Computers (EELM), 3, 121, 127, 132, 142, 167, 303, 306, 317
English Numbering Machines Co., 255
ENIAC computer, xvi, 17, 18, 19, 22, 23, 338, 341, 349-350, 351, 352
ERMA computer, 52
error checking routines, 165, 193, 199, 203, 204, 322, 323, 325
Esso, 216
Ever Ready Battery Co., 64, 126
Exchequer, U.K., 66, 189
Excise Office, U.K., 2, 106-107, 108, 117, 125
executive course, 49
exponential smoothing, 268, 297

Fantl, Leo, xi, xxiv, 25, 29, 33, 35, 55, 62, 64, 71, 79, 92, 103, 106, 131, 144, 157-167, 173, 188, 190, 192, 197, 199, 203, 205, 208-209, 218, 245, 246, 289-305
Ferranti, 23, 29, 34, 52, 74, 127, 258, 260, 291, 327

Ferranti Packard FP 6000, 111
financial/banking applications (*see also* payroll applications), 52, 75, 79-80, 108-109, 126, 130, 131, 138, 166, 229-242, 254-255
fire damage to LEO 326/LEO III, 132
floating point calculations, 60, 185, 190-192, 204
flow charting, 165-166, 202, 203, 324, 325
Forbes, John, 88, 144
Ford Motor Co. U.K. , xvii, 1, 2, 54-55, 63-64, 68, 73-76, 81, 82, 162-163, 173, 175, 196, 208-209, 229
Ford Motor Co., U.S., 74-75
form letters, 347-348
FORTRAN language, 88-89, 203
Fox, Barry, 241
FP 6000 computer, 111
Freemans Mail Order Co., 3, 124-125, 196, 261-273
Fujitsu, 141

Galbraith, xxiii
GEC Research laboratories, 24, 141, 355
General Electric, U.S., 52
General Post Office (GPO), U.K., 107-109, 117-119, 123-124, 130, 132, 138-139, 249-260
Gibbs, Gordon, 24, 60
Gibson, Bob, 96
Gifford, Mike, 102, 135, 143
Gill, Stanley, 86, 161, 159, 199, 202
GIRO Bank (*see* General Post Office)
Global Business Books Awards, xvii
Gluckstein, Isadore, 44, 59
Gluckstein, Monte, Major, 14
Glyn Mills Bank (*see also* Army/Air Force Officers payroll), 79-80, 229-242
Glyn, John, 241
Goldstine, Herman H., 1, 18, 19, 348-349, 351
Gosden, John, xvi, xxiv, 35, 50, 63, 71, 72, 86, 87, 144, 159, 160, 162, 165, 173, 175, 185-206, 218, 290
Gosnab project,U.S.S.R., 314-315
Goverment Dockyards (*see* Royal Dockyards)
government applications, 2, 66, 80-81, 89-90, 106-107, 121-122, 166, 327, 329, 355, 366
Graham, W.J., 284
Greensmith, Dennis, 65
Greenwich/London Borough Council, 2, 106, 164
Grover, John, xxii, xxiv, 25, 30, 37, 50, 57, 61, 144, 158, 173, 188, 206, 211, 218
Gyngell, Peter, 64, 106, 117, 144, 175-176

H 200 computer, 111
Hackney consortium, 131
Haley, Colin, 98, 114
Handley Page Aircraft, 191, 193
Hankey, 196
Hanney, 230

hardware development, 142
Hargreaves, John, 103
Harraway, Derek, 301
Hartree House, 2, 78, 91, 101, 104, 138, 198, 239, 241
Hartree, Douglas, 18-21, 349, 353-354, 368
Harvard Mark I computer, 18, 341-342, 352
Harvard Mark II computer, 18, 54, 342, 352
Harvard Mark III computer, 343, 352, 358
Harvard University, 18, 21, 54, 341-342, 352-353
Hawker Siddeley, 160
Hay, F.E., 289, 291
Hay, Mike, 91, 166
Hayter, George, 143
Heinz, 116
Hemy, Derek, 24-25, 29, 33, 39, 49-50, 61, 145, 158, 160-162, 173, 188, 190, 204, 302
Hendry, John, 4, 29, 140
Hermon, Peter, x, xvi, xxiii, 55, 61-62, 71, 94, 124, 126, 143, 163, 205, 207-220, 316
heuristic logic, 63
Higbee's Department Stores, 76
history of J. Lyons & Co., 11-15
HM Dockyards (see Royal Dockyards)
Hollerith cards (see also punched card systems), 207-208
Hollerith, Herman, 82-83
Holley, Tim, 143
Holwill, Stan, 77
Honeywell, 111, 275, 276, 310
Honeywell H 200 (see H 200 computer)
Hopewell, Arthur, 92
Hopper, Grace, 201
Hudson Bay Co., 80
Humphreys, Arthur, 134, 135-136
Hungary (see also Soviet Union/Eastern Europe), 317-319
Hyam, Joan, 30, 158, 205

IBM, 18-19, 40, 52, 53, 61, 72, 83, 84-85, 89-90, 108, 110-112, 114, 115, 127, 130, 134, 179, 180, 217, 275, 309, 310, 311, 319, 341, 351, 365
IBM 1401 computer, 84-85, 111
IBM 1410 computer, 111, 112
IBM 360 computers, 3, 89, 110-112, 114, 115, 123, 130
IBM 604 computer, 219
IBM 650 computer, 52, 53, 74, 84, 219
IBM 700 series computers, 110-112
IBM 702 computer, 52-54
IBM 704 computer, 53
IBM 705 computer, 53-54, 74, 75
IBM Hectowriters, 248
ICL, 3, 132-139, 141, 144, 167, 216, 319-320
ICL 1904A computer, 138
ICL 1904S computer, 284
ICL 2900 computer, 258-259
ICL 2960 computer, 139
ICL, a Business and Technical History, xxiii

ICT, 3, 82-83, 111-113, 115, 127, 130-139, 179, 180, 274, 275, 276, 310, 311, 319
ICT 1201 computer, 84
ICT 1301 computer, 111-112
ICT 1900 computer, 112
Ilford Co., 81, 327
Imperial Metal Industries (IMI), 176
Imperial Tobacco Co. (ITC), 2, 61-62, 68, 76, 143, 210-215
incorporation of LEO Computers Ltd., 47-48
Industrial Expansion Act, 1968, 133
information technology, xv-xvi
Inland Revenue, 80-81, 160, 173-174, 189, 237-238
input/output (I/O) systems and techniques, 11, 26-30, 45, 51, 54, 78, 86-87, 120 170, 198-200, 207, 234, 239-240, 250, 252, 322, 323, 324, 325, 326, 328, 339-343, 371
installing LEO systems, 76-77
Institute of Chartered Accountants, 65
insurance actuarial applications, 34, 52, 66, 116-117, 126, 161, 189, 350, 351-352
integrated data processing, 118-119
Intercode language, 251
Intercode language, 87-88, 251
International Business Machines (see IBM)
International Computers and Tabulators (see ICT), 82-83
International Computing Services Ltd., 138
interrupts, 199, 204, 324
inventory applications, 8, 10-11, 32, 46-47, 57-58, 61-62, 76, 81, 94, 105, 171-172, 174, 176, 196, 211-215, 261-273
invoicing applications, 2, 8, 16-17, 19, 20, 49, 56-58, 75, 103-104, 123-124, 196, 251-254, 258-259, 261-273, 346-347, 375-383
Iron Curtain (see Soviet Union/Eastern Europe)
Irving, Frank, 247-248
Isaacs, Jeremy, 67

J operating systems, 315
J. Lyons & Co., xix, xv-xvi, 7, 137-138, 186-187, 196, 223-228, 243, 249, 360-362
J.D. Francis clockmaker, 174
Jackson, Helen, 71, 90-91, 95, 268
Jackson, Mike, xii, 71, 108-109, 119, 124-126, 143, 261-273
Jacobs, Alan, 67, 71, 95, 105, 143, 164, 205-206, 210, 242, 310, 316
James, Margaret, 242
Jecks, 189
Jenkins, 225
Jenkinson, Sid, 38
Joerin, 225
Johannesburg Consolidated Investments (JCI), 304
Johannesburg Stock Exchange, 290
Jones, David, 261
Jordan, 230
Josephs, Mike, 71, 95, 113, 118, 144, 297, 301

Kavanagh, Eric, 162
Kay, John, 168
Kaye, Bob, 299
Kaye, Ernest, 24, 60
Kayser Bondor, 116
KDF 6 computer, 100-102, 117, 309
KDF 9 computer, 100, 113, 128, 133
KDN 2 computer, 100
KDP 10 computer, 101, 102
Kendata, 284
keypunch systems, 27, 29
Kilby, Don, 98
Kimball tag readers, 78, 328
Kirby, Alec, 169, 224, 226, 227
Kirillin, Deputy Prime Minister U.S.S.R., 313
Kiteley, Bob, 247-248
KLX computer, 113
Knight, Eric, 161
Kodak, 64, 74-75, 163-164, 229
KPMG Peat Markwick, xvi

Lamberth, 190
Lamming, Neil, 102, 117, 144
Lamond, Fred, 309, 312
Land, Ailsa, 205
Land, Frank, x, xvi, xxiii, 35, 50, 57, 64, 71, 80, 95, 102, 126, 129, 142, 158, 160, 168-184, 188, 189, 196, 205, 211, 228, 310
Land, Ralph, xii-xiii, 47, 90-91, 126, 138, 139, 144, 223-228, 306-320
Landau, Roger, 318
languages, computer programming, 87-89, 115, 185, 186, 194, 200-201, 203, 251, 275, 321, 325, 326, 328
Laver, Murray, xiii, 139, 257-260
Lazards Banking, 101
Lector document reader, 3, 95, 105, 119, 120, 276, 328
Lenaerts, E.R., 24, 29, 39, 43-44, 60, 62, 145, 162, 368
Lendrum, Ken, 292, 302-303
LEO:The First Business Computer, xxiii, 97, 137–138
LEO 326, 3, 109, 117, 118, 123, 132, 138, 139, 140, 250, 258-259, 264, 282
LEO 360, 282, 309, 310
LEO and the Managers, 56, 104, 131
LEO Chronicle, xxiii
LEO Computers Ltd., xxii, 1, 3, 43-58, 134, 275, 276
    formation/incorporation, 47-48
    London headquarters, 78
    regrouping/reorganization, 49-51
    sales force, 48-49
LEO I, 1, 2, 27, 29, 33-42, 73, 80, 84, 100, 103, 170, 185, 195, 197-198, 200, 229, 236, 243, 249, 307
    payroll application, 36-39, 40

scientific service work, 33-35
workload increases, 41-42
LEO II, 1, 2, 43-72, 73, 74, 75, 78, 80, 81, 82, 84, 81, 85, 87, 93, 99, 100, 103, 131, 136-137, 162, 177, 181, 195-198, 200, 211, 215, 216, 226, 227, 229, 236, 239-242, 244, 245, 246, 321, 324, 326, 327
    applications, 61-64
    apprenticeship programs, 69-70
    consultant services, 70-72
    deadlines and delays, 60-61
    design and construction, 44-45, 50, 59-61
    Ford Motor Co., U.K., 54-56, 63-64
    Imperial Tobacco Co., 61-62
    invoicing application, 56-58
    last built, 81
    patent for, 45
    programming personnel recruitment efforts, 66-68
    prospective clients, 64-66
    Stewards and Lloyds, 62-63
    Teashops Distribution application, 45-47
    training for programmers, 68-69
LEO III, 2, 3, 76, 86-96, 97, 99, 100-105, 109, 111, 113, 117, 118, 119, 123, 126, 127, 128, 131, 132, 133, 138, 139, 140, 142, 162, 177, 181, 182, 195, 196, 198-200, 218, 250, 276-285, 303-304, 307, 309, 311, 318, 325, 326-328
    CAV electrical car components co., 103
    compilers, 88
    domestic installations, 93-94
    Dunlop Tire Co., 93-94
    General Post Office (GPO), U.K., 107-109
    government applications, 106-107
    government support lacking, 89-90
    language for programming, 87-89
    launching, 90-91
    LEO 326, 109
    Lyons installation, 104-105
    microprogramming techniques, 86, 88, 118, 199-200, 252
    multiprogramming techniques, 86-87, 89, 107, 185, 201, 252, 259, 325–326
    operating system development, 88
    overseas installation, 91-93
    processing speed, 87
    research and development efforts, 89-90
    semiconductor technology, 86
    Shell Mex and BP, 103-104
    Smith and Nephew health and sanitary products, 103
    software development, 87, 88
    Tubemakers Steel, Sydney, 105-106
LEO Reunion Society, xxiv
Lerner, Alexander, 313, 316-317
letter writing (*see* word processing)
Levy, Hank, 49
Lewis, John, xiii, xxiv, 67, 71, 79, 90, 95, 143, 163, 164, 206, 210, 229-242, 244-246
Liberator software, 111

Lightning Fasteners ICI, 176
Lightstone, Lyon, 134
linear programming, 255
Littlewoods, 196
London Boroughs consortium, 3, 106, 164, 229
London Bureau, 77-79, 90, 95
London Business School, 29
long-term memory, 343
Longtime OMR reader, 284
Lyons Computing Services Ltd., 9-15, 137
Lyons Electronic Office (LEO), xv, xvii, xx-xxiv, 7, 23
Lyons, J Lyons & Co. Ltd., xix, 137, 228
Lyons, Joseph, xx, 13, 137, 228

Macdonald, Hugh, 134
machine code (*see* languages)
Machines Bull, Paris, 62
MacIver, Barbara, 291, 292, 302
Mackie, Alex, 246
Macleod, G.H.T., 245
magnetic core storage systems, 2, 82
magnetic drum storage, 44, 61, 78, 86, 185, 197, 198, 239, 326, 328, 343, 352, 357-358
magnetic tape storage, 2, 23, 28, 31-32, 44, 78, 86, 91, 92, 107, 170, 185, 197, 198, 239, 240-242, 250, 252, 257-258, 321, 325, 328, 333, 342, 356-357, 371-372
magnetic wire storage, 28, 342 355-356, **356**
mail order applications (*see* Freemans), 196, 261-273
maintenance routines, 51, 115-116, 197, 204
Mamikonov, 314
Manchester Corporation, 106
Manchester University, 23, 198
Manley, George, 78-79, 242
Marais, 293
Marconi, 98, 113, 114, 121, 128, 329
market analysis application, 189-190, 195
marketing the LEO systems, 49, 70-72, 94-95, 102, 178, 181, 194-197, 215-216
mark-sensing (*see* optical character recognition)
Marshall, Bill, 295
Master, The (*see* operating systems; Wright, A.J.)
Masters, John, 49
mathematical applications, 190-191
matrix algebra, 160-161, 190, 191, 193-194, 204
Mauchly, John, 19, 22
McCrystall, 230
McLeman, George, 71, 95, 143, 237, 241
McPherson, 40
Mears, Mick, 301
Memoirs of a Computer Pioneer, xxiii
memory (*see* storage and memory)
memory-sharing control, 201

mercury (acoustic) delay lines, 23, 43-44, 77, 82, 215, 239, 248, 343, 358-359, **358**
merge operations, 87, 200, 326
Merriman, Jim, 257, 258
Meteorological Office, U.K., 1, 34, 160
Metropolitan Life Insurance Co., 52
microcoding, 198, 199-200
microprogramming, 86, 199-200
Mills, Brian, 71, 95, 144, 227, 301
Mills, Geoffrey, 48-49, 56, 211
Minerva Road facilities, 2, 73-74, 78, 79, 93, 98, 104, 239
Ministry of Pensions, U.K., 2, 80-81, 106-107, 166, 329
Ministry of Technology, 132, 133, 138, 258, 313
missile trajectory applications, 34, 160, 161, 165
Monte Carlo modeling, 197
Moore School of Electrical Engineering, 18, 19, 348, 349-350, 354
Moore, Donald, 47, 104
Moore, Lofty, 292, 297, 301, 302
Moore, Viv, 292
Morflot project, U.S.S.R., 314-315
Morgan, Tony, xxiv, 78-79, 92
Morris, Tony, 246
Morse, Jeremy, 241
Motherwell Steel mills, 126
Muir, Brian, 292
multiprograming, 86-87, 107, 128, 185, 198, 201, 202, 252, 321, 325-326
Munroe, 295
Myriad computers, 113, 114, 329

National Coal Board (NCB), 197
National Data Processing Service (NDPS), 108, 132, 138, 250, 258-259,
National Giro Bank (*see* General Post Office)
National Physical Laboratory, xxii, 34, 100, 191, 192-193, 355
National Research and Development Corp. (NRDC), 89-90, 258
National Savings Department , 3, 108, 124
Naumov, 313
NCR, 18, 127, 178, 275, 276, 310, 351
Nelson, Lord, 100
New Range Organization, 134
Newman, Betty, 58, 163, 164, 174
NHKG steelworks, 130, 309, 310
Nielson, A.C., 350
Nolan, Norton & Co., xvi
Nolan, Richard L., xv-xvi
Normand Co., 38
North Thames Gas Board, 176-177
Northampton Polytechnic (City University), 65

O'Brien, Charlie, 242
office applications, 17, 26-27, 30-32, 54
Office Management Association Conference, May 1955, 51-52, 59, 209-210

Officers payroll (*see* Army/Air Force Officers payroll)
Old Mutual, South Africa, 290, 291
operating systems, 88, 185, 186, 203, 252, 315, 321
optical mark recognition, 75-76, 95, 105, 119, 126, 127, 131, 254-255, 276-278, 284, 328
Ordnance Board application, 1, 33-34, 81
organization and methods (O&M)
   operations, 15, 36, 47, 48, 61, 62, 64, 96, 107, 108, 112, 113, 131, 211, 243, 244, 247, 369
Orion, South Africa, 291
outsourcing, 333-334
overseas installation, 2-3, 91-93
Owen, David, 201-202
ownership of LEO systems, 81-82, 331

paging, 198
paper tape input/output, 11, 27, 29, 31-32, 78, 170, 248, 250, 321, 324, 340-342, **340**, 372
paperless office concept, xvi
Pareto principle, 177, 330
parity checking, 198
Parnall company, 120
patents, LEO I, 45
PAYE (*see* payroll applications)
Payman, Arthur, 55, 71, 95, 144, 163, 195, 206, 208-209, 293, 300
payroll applications, 1, 2, 8, 20, 26, 29, 36-39, 40, 52-55, 62-64, 73, 75, 77, 79-81, 103, 106, 127, 162-164, 179, 189, 208-209, 226-227, 229-242, 275-285, 296-297, 305, 329, 348, 370, 372
PCC computers, 274-275
Peat Marwick, 104
Pegasus computer, 327, 329
Peled, Moshe, 311
Pennsylvania, University of, 18, 348, 349-350
Pentagon, 17, 53
Pentium chip, 203
Perseus computer, 52, 291
Phoenix Assurance, 126
Pierce, Bernard, 143, 241
Pinkeron, John, xxii, 2, 11, 23-24, 27, 29, 39, 43, 48, 52, 60, 65, 72, 74, 82, 86, 89, 95-96, 98, 99, 101, 113, 119–120, 134, 144-145, 158, 199, 218, 254, 259, 367-368
Pirow, Peter, 297
pivotal selection operations, 192
planning for programming, 322
Plessey, 133
point-of-sale terminals, 76, 126
Poland (*see also* Soviet Union/Eastern Europe), 317-319
Polley, Dennis, 166
Pollock, Neil, 62-63, 105, 136-137, 163, 166, 244-248
Popham, E.W., 210, 211-215

Post Office (*see* General Post Office)
Powers Accounting Machine Co., 83
Powers Machine Co., 16
Powers Samas, 52, 62, 82-83, 240, 260, 274
Powers, James, 83
Premium Bonds, 124, 250, 252, 254
Princeton Institute for Advanced Studies, 1, 18, 348
Princeton University, 342, 348
printers and printing technology, 2, 28, 29, 30, 61, 62, 91, 119, 120, 131, 132, 197, 239, 240, 250, 255, 277-278, 321, 324, 328-329
processing speed and techniques, 11, 26, 44, 77, 82, 87, 100, 110-112, 128, 136, 172, 203, 230-240, 252, 328-329, 333, 339, 344-345, 352-353
production control applications, 57, 81, 327
programming personnel recruitment efforts, 66-68
Prudential Assurance Co., 83
Prudential Insurance, 19, 21, 350, 351-352
punch card systems, 46-47, 52-53, 74, 78, 82-83, 111, 170, 175, 179, 198, 207-208, 210, 219, 226-227, 248, 265, 274-275, 321, 324, 329, 333, 338, 340-342, 365, 371-372
Pye, Geof, 71, 90, 163, 164, 246

RACE magnetic card file, 329
radix arithmetic, 87, 200
Radley, Sir Gordon, 3, 97
railway distancing application, 2, 73, 194-196
Railway Laboratories, 3
Rajchman, 350-351
RAMAC 650 computer, 74
RAMAC computer, 75
Rampton, Anthony, 124
Rand Mines, 2, 91-93, 166, 289-305
random access storage, 178, 321, 326
Rank Xerox, 329
rationing, WW II, 10-11
RCA, 75, 101, 114, 127-128, 329, 350-351
RCA 501 computer, 75, 101, 114-115
RCA Spectra, 3
RCA Spectra 70 computer, 127-128
reconciliations, accounting, 166, 192-193, 207, 237-238, 324
Recordak invoicing system, 49, 361-362
recovery routines, 51
reengineering business processes, 330-331
Reeves, Colin, 186, 201
reliability, 112-113, 115-116
Remington Rand Co., 23, 83, 275
Renold Chains, 108, 126, 216
research and development efforts, 89-90, 107, 121-122, 258-259
restart control, 198, 207, 238, 324, 326
Richards Shops, 138, 307

Riley, Don, 314
RISC technology, 199
Roberts, Ernest, xxiv, 50, 71, 87-88, 159, 161, 162, 191, 200, 202
Robey, A.K., 131
Robinson, Cliff, 98, 134
Romania (*see also* Soviet Union/Eastern Europe), 317-319
rounding errors, 189, 190, 195, 203
Rowley, Ted, 51
Rowntrees, 196
Royal Air Force (*see* Army/Air Force Officers payroll)
Royal Army Pay Corps. 79-80, 104, 110
Royal Bank of Scotland, 126
Royal Dockyards, 3, 127, 130, 274-285, 328
Royal Warrant for J. Lyons & Co., 13
Royle, Derek, 98, 115
Rudnev, 313
Runge-Kutta techniques, 161, 191, 203
Ryan, 176
Rymell, Adrian, 88

sales force, LEO Computers Ltd., 48-49
Salmon and Gluckstein, 13
Salmon, Anthony, 1, 3, 14, 48, 49, 61, 65, 78, 90, 97, 107, 121, 205, 241
Salmon, Felix, 14, 47, 225
Salmon, Geoffrey, 13, 30-31, 32
Salmon, Harry, 13, 23, 367
Salmon, Julian, 14, 47
Samstronic printer, 62, 213, 239, 240
Samuelson, 191
SANLAM, South Africa, 291
SASOL, South Africa, 290
Scattergood, Jim, 242
Schartau, Derek, 106
Schweppes, 102
Science Museum, xxiii-xxiv, 21
scientific applications, 33-35, 44, 103, 190, 191-192, 364-365
Scott, W.E., 3, 98, 101, 113-115
Sears Roebuck Co., 17
Sebek, 125-126, 309
Selectron, 343
selling the LEO systems, 70-72, 94-95, 102, 178, 181, 194-197, 215-216
semiconductor technology, 76, 86
Shaw, Raymond, 24, 60
Shell Australia, 116, 130
Shell Mex and BP (SMBP), 3, 103-104, 109, 116, 123, 124, 142, 327-328, 329
shells, 203
Shill, Louis, 304
short-term memory, 343
Simmons, John R. M., xix-xxiii, 1, 14, 15, 16-17, 21, 23, 25, 29, 30, 39, 41, 44-45, 48, 54, 56-57, 59, 61, 62, 64-66, 96, 101, 104, 105, 131, 137,

158, 167, 173, 181, 205, 212, 218, 224, 330-331, 334, 360-374
simulation applications, 103, 161-162
size of LEO computer, 11
sizing the computer (*see* configuration)
Smith and Nephew, 103
Smith, C.R. (Nick), 108-109, 119, 138, 251, 253, 254, 255, 256, 258
Smith, Jim, 50, 63, 88, 159, 161, 218
Smith, John, 108
Smith, Peter, 262, 268, 270
Smythson, John, 69
social life at LEO, 205-206
Social Service Ministry, Prague, 130
software development, 87, 88, 111, 114-115, 142, 185-206, 239, 299
  CLEO language, 200-201, 326
  LEO I, 197-198
  LEO II, 197-198
  LEO III, 198-199
  master routines, 202
  memory-sharing control, 201
  merge operations, 200
  microprogramming, 199-200
  multiprogramming, 201
  radix arithmetic, 200
  system software, 197-202
  test programs, 201-202
  utilities, 197-202, 202
sort operations, 87, 198, 234, 325, 326
soundtrack recording, 343
South Africa, 2, 91-93, 131, 166, 289-305
South West Gas Board, 126
Soviet Union/Eastern Europe, 117, 125-126, 130, 139, 173, 306-320
  Bulgaria, 317-319
  Czechoslovakia, 309-312
  Hungary, 317-319
  Poland, 317-319
  Romania, 317-319
  Soviet Union, 312-317
  Yugoslavia, 317-319
specifications, 322, 323, 325, 330, 331-332
Spectra 70 series computers, 114-115, 127
sports activities at J.Lyons, 72
SPREAD project (IBM), 111
stack concept, 100
Stammers, H.V., 83
standard deviation calculations, 210
Standard Motors, 2, 81
Standard Telephones (STC), 28-29, 30
standards at J. Lyons & Co., 15
Standingford, Oliver (*see also* U.S. visit, 1947), xvi, xxiii, 1, 16-18, 20, 23, 26, 57-58, 337-359, 363-364, 366, 368
Stanford Research Institute, 52
statistical analysis applications, 103-104, 190, 196, 214
Steel, Bob, 224

Stewarts and Lloyds, 2, 62-64, 70, 74, 76-77, 79, 105, 108, 136, 163, 166, 229, 243-248, 290
stock control (*see* inventory applications)
Stock Exchange, London, 80, 131
storage and memory, 185, 197, 198, 207, 239, 240-241, 250, 252, 257-258, 321, 338, 339, 342-343, 352, 355-359, 371-372
stored-program computers, 22-23
Strachey, Christopher, 205
Sylvester, John, 199
syntax, 165
System 4, 3, 128, 129, 130, 131, 133, 135-136, 139, 250, 255, 311, 314-316, 318, 319, 321
system software, 185-206
Systems Research Office (*see also* Organization & Methods), 25, 31, 82, 158-161, 169, 170, 171

Tate & Lyle, 64, 163-164, 216, 229
tax table calculations, 80-81, 160, 173-174, 189, 236
Taylor, Jack, 293
tea blending application, 58, 174-175
team sports at Lyons, 205
Teashop Computer Manufacturer: J. Lyons, The, xxiii, 29, 140
Teashops Distribution application, 45-47, 51, 171, 223-228, 370, 375-383
telephone billing application, 4, 108, 118-119, 123, 251-254, 258-259
teleprinters, 11, 28, 30
test programs, 29-30, 159, 172, 197, 201-202, 253, 325
testing of first LEO computer, 28
Thatcher, Margaret (Roberts), 12
Thompson, Mrs., 268
Thompson, T.R (*see also* U.S. visit, 1947), xvi, xxiii, 1, 12, 16-17, 18, 20, 23, 25-26, 28, 49, 52-53, 54, 59, 65, 69, 87, 92, 96, 98, 99, 101, 104, 134, 136, 142, 145, 158, 167, 171, 187, 195, 190, 203, 205, 216, 218, 248, 249, 259, 306, 307, 308, 337-359, 363-364, 366, 368, 375
thrashing, 198
time (*see* processing time)
time-sharing (*see* multiprogramming)
Tocher, K.D., 205
Tower Hamlets consortium, 131
training programs, 68-69, 96, 210-211, 244, 374
Transport Commission, 81
Trapeznikov, 313
Tubemakers Steel Co., Sydney, 95, 105-106
Tully, Colin, 47, 142
Turing, Alan, 100, 355

U.S. Steel, 52, 74
U.S. visit, 1947, 16-17, 337-359, 363-364
U.S. visit 1955, 51-54
U.S. visit, 1958, 73-76
Union Corporation, South Africa, 295
UNIVAC, 310
UNIVAC computer, 23, 52, 53, 74, 309

UNIVAC II computer, 74
University (*see* name of state/province)
user-driven innovation concepts, xx-xxi
Users' Guide to LEO, 158
utility company applications, 126, 176, 216
utility programs, 197

Vajda, Steven, 205
validity checking, 203-204, 207
valuation applications (*see* accounting applications)
van Rooyen, Faith, 291, 292, 297, 301, 302
virtual machines, 87, 136
virtual office concept, xvi
von Neumann architecture, 20
von Neumann, John, 19-20, 22
Vypocatni Laborati Dopravy (VLD), 3, 125-126, 309
VZKG steelworks, 311

W.D. & H.O. Wills (*see* Imperial Tobacco Co. ITC)
Walker, Frank, 242
Walker, Sandy, 319
Warner, 158
Warriner, Jack, 143, 242
Watermeyer, Chris, 290
Waters, Sam, 68, 71, 142
Watson, Dick, 84
Watson, Thomas J., 16, 40, 83
Waymouth, Liza, 291, 297, 301, 302
Wayne Kerr laboratories, 11
weather forecasting applications, 34, 160
Wedd, Durlacher, 131
  stock jobbers and, 280
Westminster Bank, 74
Wheeler, David, 22, 25, 191, 203
White, Len, 292
Wilkes, Maurice, xxiii, 7-8, 18, 19-20, 22, 23, 24, 187, 191, 199, 259, 353-354, 367-369
Wilkinson, Jim, 193
Williams, Fred, 23
Wills (*see* Imperial Tobacco Co. (ITC))
Wilson, Harold, 89, 121, 255
Wood, Peter, 38, 90
Woods, Stan, 175
word processing applications, 20, 347-348
word size, 44, 239, 326
World Trade Corp., 83
Wormersley, 355
Wright, A.G., 62, 212, 215
Wrigleys Co., 75

Xerox/Xeronic printer, 119, 120, 131, 132, 255, 329

Yellow Book, 158
Yugoslavia (*see also* Soviet Union/Eastern Europe), 317-319

Zuse computers, 309
Zworykin, 350-351